The Politics of
Development in
Botswana

The Politics of
Development in
Botswana
A Model for Success?

Louis A. Picard

Lynne Rienner Publishers • Boulder & London

Published in the United States of America in 1987 by
Lynne Rienner Publishers, Inc.
948 North Street, Boulder, Colorado 80302

Library of Congress Cataloging-in-Publication Data

Picard, Louis A.
  The politics of development in Botswana

  Bibliography: p.
  Includes index.
  1. Botswana—Politics and government—To 1966–
2. Botswana—Politics and government—1966–
3. Botswana—Economic conditions.   4. Botswana—
Economic conditions—1966– .   I.   Title.
JQ2760.A2P53 1987   968.1'1   86–31331
ISBN 0–931477–95–6 (lib. bdg.)

Printed and bound in the United States of America

The paper used in this publication meets the
requirements of the American National Standard
for Permanence of Paper for Printed Library
Materials Z39.48–1984. ⊗

Contents

Tables and Figures

A Note on the Usage of Terms

It should be noted that in this book, following the Sotho-Tswana practice, the people of Botswana are called Batswana. One person is a Motswana; the language is Setswana. The root word, Tswana, is used to describe attributes such as "Tswana culture." Ethnic subdivisions subdivide in the same way, for example, Ngwato, Mongwato, and Bamangwato.

Currency use in Southern Africa can be confusing. Until 1961, the South African pound (£) was used throughout the High Commission Territories. In 1961, the South African government divided the pound in half and renamed it the Rand. From 1961 until 1976, the Rand was used in Botswana. In that year the Government of Botswana introduced a national currency, the Pula, which was initially at a par with the Rand.

It has been necessary for historical accuracy to use a number of terms that today have negative or inaccurate connotations. The use of such words has been limited as much as possible. At various points, however, terms such as "native authority," "tribal," and "tribal administration" appear in the text. Rather than clutter the book with quotation marks, the terms are simply used in the context which they would historically or legally appear. The term "tribal administration" in particular continues to be used in an informal and non-disparaging sense in Botswana and it is in that sense that I use the term here.

Preface

I trace the origins of this book to July of 1980 and my arrival in Botswana for an eighteen-month assignment at the Institute of Development Management, just a few days before the death of the country's first president, Sir Seretse Khama. As I witnessed the events surrounding President Khama's funeral and the orderly transition to the presidency of Quett Masire, I felt that this might be an opportune time to examine the nature of the post-colonial state in this unique African country and to relate post-independence developments to the some eighty years of colonial rule that preceded the establishment of the Republic of Botswana. I did not think then that this task would occupy my time off and on for the better part of six years.

In 1975 I spent nine months in Botswana on a Fulbright fellowship conducting dissertation research on role changes among field administrators. As is the case with many dissertations, mine had several different, somewhat contradictory, focuses and a methodology (role analysis) with which I had become increasingly uncomfortable while in the field. Rather than shucking the theory and finding a new analytical framework, I plodded on and completed a dissertation that was overly long and more than somewhat disjointed. Although it was an adequate dissertation, it was not, and never would be, a book.

Had I not returned to Botswana in 1980, I would have published a number of academic articles out of the dissertation and then gone on to other research. The return to Botswana gave me a second chance. This book is the result.

The research for the book took place in three phases. In spite of the imperfections of the dissertation, the research conducted in 1975 provided a great deal of the documentary material. Two sojourns at the University of Wisconsin in 1976 and 1978 (the latter year at the superb Land Tenure Center) provided me with much of the primary and secondary documentation on rural development and land tenure.

The third phase of the research was carried out between 1980 and 1984 after I had finally defined a topic for the book. Eighteen months of residence in Botswana and extended visits to the country during 1982 and 1984 were essential both to complete my collection of documentary materials and to keep up-to-date on political changes and policy shifts.

Critics of Botswana's policy process point to the country's reputation as a "paper mill." Shelf after shelf in the Botswana National Archives are filled with policy documents, many written by expatriates, that gather dust. As one who has contributed to that "paper mill," I would acknowledge the validity of the criticism. And yet, the "paper mill" process has also created a richness of documentation on development strategies and experiments that is unrivaled even among larger and more important African states. In this time of a fundamental evaluation of African development strategies, the Botswana experience (and its record of significant success) provides important evidence for scholars and practitioners. This book tries to make that Botswana experience accessible to those who may not have had a direct involvement in Botswana or in the southern African region.

Any reseach effort of this size, no matter how imperfect in its completion, ultimately is dependent upon the assistance of others. Because of the ambitious nature of this project, ranging over a period of twelve years, I cannot possibly name all of those who helped me. However, I would like to acknowledge at least some programs and individuals.

The field research for my dissertation was financed by a 1975 fellowship under the Fulbright-Hays program for Doctoral Dissertation Research Abroad. I would like to thank the government of Botswana for granting me permission to do research under the terms of the Anthropological Research Act of 1967. In 1980-1982 my work at the Institute of Development Management, Botswana, Lesotho, and Swaziland was funded by the U.S. Agency for International Development (USAID) under its Southern Africa Manpower and Development Program. The USAID offices in Gaborone and Harare provided the financial support for my 1982 and 1984 visits. Since 1985 I have been Director of the USAID-funded Technical Cooperation Project of the National Association of Schools of Public Affairs and Administration (NASPAA), and my research has been supported under USAID's Cooperative Agreement with NASPAA. The Cooperative Agreement is funded by the Rural Development Division of USAID's Bureau for Science and Technology as part of its Performance Management Project.

Additional research support was provided by the University of Wisconsin's Research Committee and Political Science Department. In 1978 the World Development Program of Gustavus Adolphus College granted me a summer fellowship to work on the rural development component of this book. I also received three summer fellowships from the Research Council of the University of Nebraska. Finally, I am particularly grateful to the

Institute of Development Management, Botswana's Ministry of Local Government and Lands and the Swedish International Development Agency for their research support during my 1980-1982 visits to Botswana.

More than anyone else in Botswana, I would like to thank Brian Egner and Chris Sharp for their continual support and criticism of my reseach over the last twelve years. Late night discussions with them (sipping Scotland's most famous export) provided me with more insights into Botswana's rural development policy than all of the material I perused at the Botswana National Archives. Chris Sharp was the senior planning officer in the Ministry of Local Government and Lands between 1980 and 1984 and had worked for that ministry in one form or another since 1970. His support and confidence in my work were indispensible. Brian Egner, who has worked in Botswana since 1957, was assistant secretary in the Ministry of Local Government and Lands between 1973 and 1975 and has continued to be a major force in the evolution of Botswana's rural development policy. His invaluable advice and the long hours that he spent with me in 1975 and after significantly contributed to the insights that I gained into Botswana's administrative process.

I am also particularly grateful to Jon Gant, human resource and training officer, USAID, Gaborone, 1980-1983; and Lou Cohen, director of the USAID mission in Botswana during that period. Jon Gant's support of my activities was particularly important. I would also like to thank Sam Mpuchane, permanent secretary of the Ministry of Local Government and Lands, 1981-1982, and Fred Schindler, then director of the Institute of Development Management, for their support.

The resources of the Public Records Office in London and the Botswana National Archives in Gaborone contributed significantly to the documentation used in this manuscript. I would like to acknowledge the support of the staff in both institutions. I would like to take particular note of the insights provided by E. B. Gwabini, assistant archivist of the Botswana National Archives in 1975, who more than anyone else was able to sort out the complexities of the Mafeking Secretariat's filing system.

At the University of Wisconsin, I would like to thank the members of my dissertation committee—Dennis Dresang, Crawford Young, and Charles Anderson—who did so much to shape my original dissertation, and John Armstrong, Henry Hart, Mel Croan, and Don Emmerson, who did so much to shape my thinking about the study of politics. Crawford Young's criticism led me to recognize the defects in my original manuscript, and his own magnificant research and writing style provided a model that continued to push me toward the completion of this book long after I had left Madison. Ed Keller of the University of California at Santa Barbara read the manuscripts critically and his comments were essential to the completion of a publishable work. Mike Schatzberg's research, skepticism, and companionship and Steve Morrison's insights and good humor also contributed to the completion of this book. The editorial talents of Tamara Bender contributed to the final manuscript.

I would like to thank the more than four hundred people I interviewed in England, southern Africa, and Botswana between 1975 and 1982. Their interviews provided a richness of insight that is not available in written texts. The several hundred participants in local government and management courses whom I taught at the Institute of Development Management in Gaborone read through and criticized much of the material that is presented here.

More than two dozen people at the University of Wisconsin, the University of Nebraska, and Botswana's Institute of Development Management assisted in the preparation of the manuscript at various stages. Space does not permit me to mention them all. I am most appreciative of Jan Sallinger-McBride, whose critical insight (and a willingness to articulate it) forced me finally to shape my research into a book, and most especially of Lorraine Gardner, whose sharp eye caught most of the peccadilloes that continued to plague this manuscript in 1986. My thanks as well to Lynne Rienner and her editorial staff who worked to bring this manuscript to print.

Apologies are in order to my wife, Lene Gaemelke, who suffered through the moves and other disruptions in our life that were linked to the preparation of this manuscript. It is to her and to my parents, Vincent and Katherine Picard, that this book is dedicated.

1

The State and Society

Early morning listeners to the radio on 13 July, 1980 were warned to stay tuned for a special announcement. At precisely 7 A.M. the Vice-President, Quett Masire, made the announcement, first in Setswana, then in English, that the country's first President, Sir Seretse Khama was dead. All other events, including the crucial independence of neighbouring Zimbabwe, were overshadowed by Sir Seretse's death.

. . . Sir Seretse's funeral at the National Stadium in Gaborone and his burial at the Royal Cemetery in Serowe climaxed a month of national mourning. The funeral was an international tribute to one of the founding members of the Front-line States of Southern Africa and delegations included six Heads of State and Government (King Moshoeshoe of Lesotho, President Machel of Mozambique, President Banda of Malawi, President Banana and Prime Minister Mugabe of Zimbabwe, President Kaunda of Zambia and President Nyerere of Tanzania). Other delegates included the Duke of Kent representing the Queen, Donald McHenry from the U.S. and the S.A. mining magnate, Harry Oppenheimer (who was the only private individual allowed to lay a wreath at the funeral).[1]

The death of President Khama in 1980 brought to a close a chapter in Botswana's history and provides a convenient focal point to this discussion of the evolution of state authority and power in Botswana. The crisis of succession is a major stumbling block in the institutionalization of political structures in much of Africa, Asia, and Latin America. The constitutional transfer of power to Vice President Quett Masire suggests that Botswana's political institutions may be more permanent than those in other less-developed countries (LDCs).

1

Botswana's Significance

An understanding of the nature of politics in Botswana is important for a number of reasons. First, Botswana is one of the few states in Africa that still has a multiparty electoral system, and it is the only state on the continent that has maintained this system continually for more than two decades.[2] Electoral politics have been free and open since independence. Botswana has a parliamentary system with genuinely competitive elections, protections for individual rights, and an independent judiciary. Furthermore, the state and its political institutions have taken a major role in defining and managing the rapid economic development that has characterized this landlocked country since its independence in 1966.

Although Botswana's politics share characteristics with many of the nation's neighbors, fundamentally "the Botswana State is different."[3] Examining what is unique about Botswana and how Botswana fits into the broader pattern of politics and state formation common in other African and Third World states will contribute to our understanding of the political processes in newly independent countries.

Botswana also plays an important role because of its geographical position. The country is strategically located in the center of the conflict-ridden southern African region; Botswana is hemmed in by South Africa and South African–occupied Namibia in the south and west and shares common borders with Zimbabwe and (briefly) with Zambia in the north. Botswana's location in southern Africa is of special significance because "the Southern Central Africa quadrant . . . holds possibilities of great power confrontations and because more than any place else in the world it is torn by that most explosive of all issues: black and white conflict for power."[4] A general military conflict, if and when it does occur in southern Africa, almost certainly will be fought across the fields and grasslands of Botswana.

Finally, the country is important because of its dramatic economic success. In 1965 Botswana's economic difficulties were labeled "chronic" by one observer.[5] Its population barely subsisted on poor-grade cattle and on an agricultural system that, due to extreme drought, only could produce a crop every third year. A mere 5 percent of the land was under cultivation in 1965 and much of the country's grassland was deteriorating rapidly from overgrazing. Education and health services were woefully inadequate. Yet even with this minimal level of services, "Bechuanaland [could] not balance its budget, and [was] heavily dependent on financial aid from Britain and on cooperation from South Africa."[6]

In 1980, by contrast, the World Bank pointed to Botswana as the best economic performer in Africa during the decade of the 1970s. There was a 16.1 percent growth rate during the period, and the per capita Gross National Product (GNP) was estimated at $900 in 1982. The country had a strong balance-of-payments surplus, and the debt service ratio stood at 2 percent, one of the lowest in Africa. Road construction, educational development, water reticulation, and increased health delivery services contributed to raising the standard of living in the countryside. Although problems in agriculture remained, the cattle industry was one of the most active in Africa. In 1982, after a severe downturn in the diamond and copper industry, the International Monetary Fund noted that shrewd and timely fiscal action to decrease government spending had neutralized much of the damage. Botswana's economic success must be seen within the context of a continent where many countries have experienced severe, absolute declines in the standard of living since 1960.

The nature of Botswana's multiparty political system, its strategic geographical position within southern Africa, and the rapid economic changes occurring in the country suggest that we have much to learn from an examination of the formation and evolution of Botswana's state structures. In the next several chapters, I will be examining colonial and post-colonial public policy in Botswana and its relationship to political and bureaucratic structures. Primary focus will be on four areas of policy making.

1. colonial and post-colonial human resource policy and the evolution of the bureaucratic system which acts as a bulwark of the Botswana state;
2. center-periphery relationships and patterns of local administration and government;
3. economic policy and strategies of rural development before and after independence; and
4. the evolution of state institutions and mechanisms of political control.

Since the state is not neutral, coalitions of interests that influence the policy process and its beneficiaries are of primary concern.

Before turning to the evolution of Botswana's state structures, I will present an overview of contemporary Botswana and its people. Following this I will place Botswana's political system within a broader analytical framework by examining the overall nature of Botswana's state structures.

Population and Environment

The Population

Although Botswana is approximately the size of Texas or France, it is one of the least densely populated countries in the world, with only 1.6 people per square kilometer.[7] Current estimates suggest that the total population of the country (including noncitizen residents and absentees abroad) is between 1 and 1.2 million people. (See Table 1.1.)

Table 1.1 De Jure and De Facto Population 1971–1985 (all figures in '000)

	1971	1978	1981	1985 (est.)
De jure Population[1]	647	805	936	1,181
Less Absentees Abroad	63	60	41	35
Plus Noncitizen Residents	11	18	25	25
Gives De facto Population[2]	595	763	920	1,171
Total Population[3]	658	823	961	1,206

Source: Central Statistics Office as reproduced in National Development Plan, 1979–1985 (Gaborone: Government Printer, 1980), p. 6; and 1981 Census as reported in the Botswana Daily News, November 4, 1981.

[1]De jure population: The number of Botswana citizens, whether resident in Botswana or not.

[2]De facto population: The number of Botswana residents, whether citizens or not.

[3]Total population: De jure population of nonresident residents.

Botswana's relatively small population is somewhat misleading for two reasons. First, the country's population growth is quite rapid, between 3 and 4 percent a year. Over 45 percent of the population is under twelve years of age. If current growth projections (based on a 1981 census) are accurate, the population will double by 1995 and will triple just after the turn of the century. Second, Botswana's population distribution is extremely skewed. An eighty-mile-wide eastern strip, the best-endowed and most-developed region of the country, contains over 80 percent of the total population. The line of rail traverses the more densely populated eastern part of the country.

Although Botswana is still very much a rural society, urban migration is increasingly a factor of concern for the government. Currently over 19 percent of Botswana's population live in urban areas and by 1988–89 the urban population will have grown to 25 percent. The growth of the major urban centers is striking, and projections by the Ministry of Local Government and Lands indicate that the capital, Gaborone, will increase from a current population of 70,000 to over 170,000 in 1990. Francistown will grow to 60,000 people, Lobatse and Selebi-Phikwe to 35,000 each, and the new mining towns of Jwaneng and Orapa will have 12,000 and 8,000 people, respectively. Several of the so-called major villages (traditional towns without city services) are likely to have populations of more than 50,000 people.[8]

The people of Botswana are intimately linked to, and affected by, the Republic of South Africa and events that occur there. Although a substantial number of migrant laborers continue to work in South Africa, the number decreased from a peak of 50,000 per year in the early 1970s to just under

20,000 in 1981. This drop, which reflects South African government policy, will have a major impact on Botswana. Projections suggest a decline of 3,000 to 4,000 jobs per year in South Africa through 1987.

As has been the case in most parts of Africa, colonial borders have partitioned people with a common language into separate states. Although there are over 700,000 Setswana-speaking people in Botswana, there are 2.7 million Setswana speakers in South Africa, with small numbers in Zimbabwe and Namibia as well. Similarly, the northern border with Zimbabwe partitioned 120,000 Kalanga-speaking people in Botswana from some 190,000 Kalanga-speaking people on the other side of the border.

Although Botswana is much more ethnically homogeneous than most other African states, ethnic divisions are not unimportant. Linguistic information is not readily available, but it is estimated that approximately 80 percent of the population are Setswana speaking, and Setswana is one of the country's national languages.[9] The Setswana-speaking majority, however, is split into a number of subgroups, which has social and political implications for society. The eight major subgroups are Kwena, Ngwato, Ngwaketse, Tawana, Tlokwa, Kgatla, Rolong, and Malete.[10]

A precise breakdown of Botswana's subgroups is difficult to obtain due to the government's commitment to a nonethnic and nonracial society. Assuming a Setswana-speaking population of about 700,000, however, the eight principal subgroups account for 620,000 people. The largest subgroup is the Ngwato (living in Central District) with a population of 280,000, or about one-fourth of the total population of the country. Central District accounts for one-fifth of all the land. The next two largest subgroups are the Ngwaketse (in Southern District) and the Kwena (Kweneng District). Each has a population of about 98,000. These subgroups are followed by the Tawana (in Ngwaketse District), with a population of about 59,000. Among the smaller subgroups, the Kgatla (Kgatleng District) number approximately 44,000, the Malete (Southeast District) about 20,000, the Rolong (Southern District) about 16,000, and the Tlokwa (Southeast District) about 5,600.[11] A map of the ten districts of Botswana is produced as Figure 1.1.

These eight major subgroups do not constitute the entire population of the country. Forming the largest non-Setswana language group are the 120,000 Kalanga speakers who account for 13 percent of the total population. About 30,000 San, or Sarwa (usually referred to as "bushmen") live in the western part of the country, as do 14,000 Kgalagadi, who constitute a separate branch of the Sotho-Tswana–speaking peoples. Smaller groups of several thousand each include the Kaa, who are Setswana speaking; the Tswapong, who are northern Sotho in origin; and the Yei, Koba, Mbukushu, and Subiya, who have their roots in central Africa. The several thousand Damara, or Herero, who live in Botswana fled from what is now Namibia when it was under German rule in 1905.

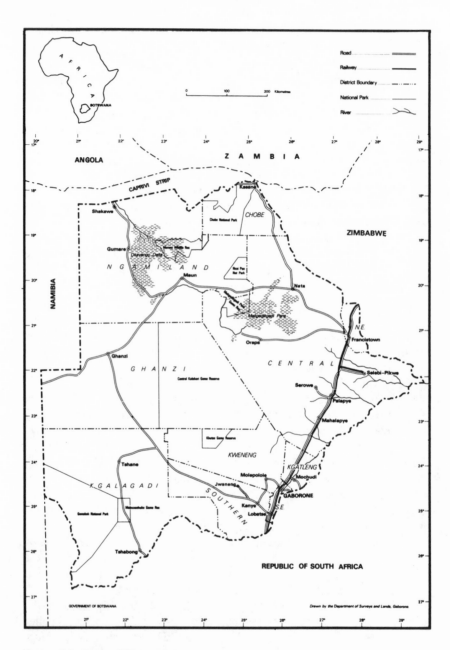

Figure 1.1   Map of Botswana

Approximately 14,000 Europeans of different nationalities live in Botswana (including noncitizen residents); less than one-half (6,000) are permanent residents. About 5,000 people of mixed race live in Botswana, including a number of Nama and Basters along the Molopo River and in the Bokspits area of western Botswana. In addition, there are about 11,000 Asians living in the country.

The Physical Environment

For a visitor the most striking aspects of Botswana's physical environment are the dryness and the dust, particularly in the winter months. Desert and near-desert conditions exist in most of the country, and the shortage of water, sometimes severe, is a major impediment to development in almost all areas of economic activity. Rainfall ranges from an annual high of 27 inches in the east to an annual low of 8 inches in the west. The Kalahari Desert is the major ecological influence on the country.

Botswana's climate is generally subtropical and desertlike, although the northern part of the country lies within the tropics. The hottest months of the year are December, January, and February, and rain is most likely to occur between November and April. The winters are very dry, and frost conditions are possible at night. August is generally very windy with a high potential for sandstorms in the desert.

Botswana is approximately 220,000 square miles in area and is located in the downward-sloping Kalahari basin of the great southern African plateau. Most of the country is a vast tableland with a mean altitude of about 3,300 feet. The eastern section is hilly, with dry riverbeds, and is somewhat more rugged than the rest of the country. The hills of the east give way to the Kalahari sands of the west, which are overlaid in parts with grass, thornbush, and scrub brush. In the southwest true desert conditions exist, with open sand dunes in evidence. The vastness of the desert, broken only by gentle shifts in elevation, covers Archean rocks and mineral wealth whose value is as yet undetermined.

The eastern part of the country is the most fertile, and the majority of agricultural activities occur there. This area has just sufficient rainfall for the growing of some food crops, and its vast grasslands provide grazing for Botswana's ample cattle herds. In the west the only available water is underground; in some places, however, such as in the Ghanzi area, water is near the surface.

The vast delta of the Okavango River intrudes upon the desert in the northwest, forming a landscape of rich and varied vegetation and bird and animal life. The seasonal flow of the river into a number of lakes, including Lake Ngami and Lake Xau and into the Makgadikgadi salt pans means that much of the water disappears or evaporates. Apart from several of the rivers that form the country's borders, the Okavango is the only source of permanent surface water for Botswana. Scientists have tried unsuccessfully for over forty years to devise a scheme to tap the Okavango's water resources for economic development.

In the far northeast there is forest and dense bush, some of which cover land suitable for agriculture and grazing. A number of large game reserves in the west and northwest provide the country with several of the few remaining vast animal herds in Africa. Botswana is bounded by Zimbabwe and Zambia in the north (the latter at the confluence of the Zambezi and Chobe rivers). In the west and northwest Botswana shares a border with Namibia and its Caprivi Strip. A long southern boundary with South Africa completes the circle of countries surrounding landlocked Botswana. Rivers provide the borders for much of the country: the Molopo in the south, the Limpopo and Marico rivers in the east and southeast, the Chobe in the northwest and the Nossop in the southwest. A series of smaller rivers defines most of the northeastern border with Zimbabwe. The border with Namibia was created by the standard colonial straightedge ruler in the late nineteenth century along a line from longitude 21, as far south as latitude 22, and from there southward along longitude 20. The northern part of the Zimbabwe-Botswana border along the Pandamatenga (or "Hunter's Road"), was drawn by a series of commissions during the colonial period.

The area under the soil has evoked the most interest in Botswana in recent years. Copper and nickel are being mined at Selebi-Phikwe in the east and coal at Morupule near Serowe. Botswana also has considerable untapped coal deposits in Central District as well as sizable deposits of manganese, asbestos, and salt. Diamonds, however, have had the major impact on the country. Mines at Orapa, Letlhakane, and Jwaneng have made Botswana the third largest producer of diamonds in the world, and the new (1982) Jwaneng mine alone doubled the country's diamond production.

The Importance of the State

Until recent years, there had been a decline in interest in the structure and processes of the state. Both behavioral social science and Marxist-influenced dependency theory have tended to relegate state structures to the status of a dependent variable. For David Easton, "the word [state] should be abandoned entirely: no severe hardship would result; in fact clarity of expression demands this abstinence."[12]   This antistatist bias also is inherent in the structural-functional approaches that have dominated much of the study of Third World politics since the 1960s.[13]

Dependency theory also downplayed the importance of the study of political structures and processes. For many dependency theorists, state structures are simply tools in the hands of a ruling elite that can be used to structure economic relationships of inequality. Shivji, a representative of this approach, argued that "the post-independence state [has become] the instrument for making the hitherto embryonic class a *ruling class* (also helping it to carve out an economic base) and thereby initiating the establishment of certain specific social relations within the domestic society."[14]

The movement away from the study of state structures and processes may have gone too far. The problem is that "the behavioral circularities of modernization theory . . . were as difficult to *use* as have been . . . market determinisms of underdevelopment theory."[15] While recognizing the mechanistic nature of much of the earlier institutional approaches, I suggest that the state and its role in society can be indicators of the dynamics of the political process. The nature of public life and "the collective forms through which groups become aware of political goals and work to attain them arise, not from societies alone, but at the meeting points of states and societies."[16] An understanding of evolving state structures and processes is crucial to the study of African politics, and the activities of the state within society can act as a litmus test of social and economic relationships. Lonsdale correctly suggested that in the study of Africa

> there seems . . . no good reason why one should not employ both Marx and Weber, particularly at different levels of explanation. . . . It seems. . . profitable to work with a set of what might be called axiomatic uncertainties, each dependent upon the initial premise that for any reasonably significant historical development, mono-causal explanation is ipso facto wrong.[17]

Focus on state structures and processes can allow an eclectic use of various theoretical contributions. The complex nature of the state as a concept "makes impossible its reduction to a single dimension, or its definition in a parsimonious phrase."[18] Carnoy noted the importance of context in our understanding of state formation. The function of the state varies "according to the historical conditions in which it is situated."[19] Thus, a number of theorists and theories contribute to our understanding of the policy process in a developing country within the specific historical analysis of that society.

A focus on state structures and institutional processes assists us in understanding Botswana's relative uniqueness within the context of African politics. Morrison noted the irony in the timing of the decline in the state's role among political analysts in the 1950s and 1960s; while at the same time among students of development, this was a period of great faith in the role of the Third World state as a catalyst for economic growth. Likewise, the later resurgence of interest in state structures occurred in tandom with a decline in this developmental optimism.[20] Rather than stimulating economic growth, through the development of a precapitalist, parasitic bourgeoisie states may contribute to economic decline.[21] The new (or, more accurately, the resurgent) interest in privatization and nongovernmental organizations reflects skepticism about state-managed development.

An important set of essays on class and state formation includes chapters on Uganda, Zaire, and Nigeria, states that are vitally important to the understanding of African politics but may not be representative of the entire continent.[22] The focus of many analyses of the African state has been on state failure. The state was "soft" and could not deal with the precapitalist "economy of affection,"[23] or it was "prebendal"[24] or "patrimonialized" and "personalist."[25]

The focus on states in decline or in varying stages of collapse may have diverted our attention from another pattern of institutional development in Africa. At the very least, one should be sensitive to degrees of state "softness" on the African continent. There are a number of "harder" states (at least in comparison to countries such as Chad and Uganda), such as the Ivory Coast, Tanzania, Senegal, Kenya, Swaziland, Botswana, and (perhaps) Zimbabwe. These "harder" states have developed a degree of institutionalization of bureaucratic and political procedures or have gone through that critical crisis of succession, with the death or retirement of the first head of state, without a collapse of political structures. Botswana's degree of institutionalization is critical. To a greater extent than any other African state, Botswana has a relatively developed state system "where probity, relative autonomy and competence have been nurtured and sustained."[26]

An examination of the historical evolution of the Botswana state should provide us with at least a partial picture of the forces that account for Botswana's two decade movement toward state autonomy and the relative success of its state managed private sector economy. A number of historical and social influences on state-societal relationships in Botswana contribute to the framework for this study of the country's politics.

Pre-Colonial Influences

The colonial administrator did not find a tabula rasa after the partition of the continent. The traditional or pre-colonial political system is an often-neglected aspect of continuity in African state formation. Joseph pointed to the adaptability of kinship ties as groups struggle for public goods in Nigeria.[27] Patterns of elite recruitment and political control often transcend the colonial period and remain an important influence on the nature of the post-colonial state.

The literature on southern Africa has emphasized the syncretic blend of pre-colonial, colonial, and post-colonial mechanisms of political control and quiescence at the local level. Schapera, for example, indicated ways in which traditional authorities were able to adapt to the changes that came about as a result of colonial intervention. Throughout the colonial period, chiefs continued to be an important source of top-down social change.[28] Whitaker took note of the possibility of dysrythmic social and political change,[29] and Vengroff, in his study of Kweneng District, suggested a "syncretistic model" of local politics. Traditional leaders in Botswana have been able to selectively adapt aspects of Weberian and other European bureaucratic and political norms without undermining the existing value structures of their societies. Traditional authorities, according to Vengroff, "continue to represent the most direct communications link with the populace." Among the so-called modern political leaders, such as district councilors, "local-leadership positions . . . are characterized by a syncretistic blending of traditional and rational bureaucratic values."[30]

The traditional political system in Botswana continues to influence policy making and political control in a number of ways. First, a clear continuity exists between the present generation of political and administrative elites and pre-colonial traditional rulers. With access to education limited, only the sons of the chiefs had access to such South African schools as Tiger Kloof and Fort Hare during the colonial period.

In many African countries, post-colonial administrative and political elites were recruited from high-ranking traditional families. This was certainly true in Botswana where traditional elites, such as cattle owners, saw themselves as the natural inheritors of power in the decolonization process. They and their families had access to education, material resources, positions in the state and, in many cases, could command the loyalty of significant sections of rural society.[31]

Pre-colonial traditional patterns of authority have influenced contemporary politics in another way. Tlou, in his study of Batswana pre-colonial state structures, pointed out that "the Batswana political system had a tendency towards segmentation, a characteristic shared by other Batswana groups."[32] This tendency toward fragmentation influenced post-colonial elites' fear of segmentation occurring within the artificial boundaries of the colonial state, a fear the leadership of contemporary Botswana shares with African leaders in other countries.

The nature of pre-colonial dynasty creation and legitimation is also a factor in the evolution of contemporary political institutions and processes in Botswana. Comaroff rejected long-standing anthropological assumptions that political change in pre-colonial Botswana proceeded "*as if* stated rules did determine the course of the political process."[33] He argued that the traditional political system was inherently flexible, using rules and prescriptions in an ex post facto manner in order to justify the actions of the politically successful. Before the imposition of the Protectorate, Batswana states were characterized by intradynastic rivalries. One faction of the royal family would challenge the political position of another for control of the political system. Both winners and losers were legitimized afterward by dynastic history. One line of historical rulers might be demoted geneologically while another line would be promoted in order to provide legitimacy for a victorious faction. Thus, changes in dynastic history served to build legitimacy for a faction in power. Comaroff's theory suggests a political flexibility that is absent from more traditional analyses of dynastic succession during the pre-colonial period. Traditional politics embodied "the ideational and organizational framework within which the processes of competition for power occurs. In this sense, it is the fulcrum of a dynamic political system."[34]

Similar patterns of dynastic quarrel and geneological dispute occurred during the colonial period. Although it is too soon to say how post-colonial regimes deal with the issue of succession and whether or not mythological manipulation of the kind described by Comaroff will play a role, we should not assume that post-colonial elites will be lacking in flexibility as regards mechanisms of political legitimacy and quiescence.[35] If Comaroff's reinterpretation of the flexibility of traditional institutions is correct, it will contribute to our understanding of contemporary state structures at both the national and local levels.

Miller, in his study of Tanzania, noted the ability of traditional leaders to maintain political influence in a socialist political system.[36] Markovitz pointed out that "some modern political leaders still rule as direct descendants of ancient aristocratic families. They may continue to rule for the same interests for whom they always ruled, even though they may have changed their manner."[37] Seretse Khama, far from trying to abolish the chieftainship, came to power with its support. The Khama administration, as did the colonial administration that preceded it, made a number of attempts to control the chiefs' power, and Sir Seretse engineered "the tranformation of governance from a patrimonial system to a liberal democratic, statist one."[38] Nonetheless, the regime's legitimacy remained tied to Sir Seretse's position as head of one of Botswana's most prestigious aristocratic families.

Weisfelder and Potholm noted the adaptations made in the nature of traditional authority in the monarchies of Lesotho and Swaziland.[39] President Khama's political success in moving away from traditionalism and Chief Bathoen's transformation into an opposition party leader indicate that elements of the traditional political leadership in Botswana were able to adapt to a new set of political circumstances as independence approached. Extrapolating from Comaroff, Khama came to power as an elected monarch through the electoral process, rather than by the traditional means of selection that had been used to legitimize a chief's position; subsequently, he began a process of transforming institutional arrangements within Botswana.

The Comaroff thesis may have implications for political succession in Botswana and could bode ill for the long term rule of President Masire. The Khama family remains influential in Botswana; there continues to be discussion of the political future of the president's son, who is both traditional authority of the Ngwato and (in a demonstration of political adroitness and adaptability) is second in command in the military. Although

President Masire succeeded to the presidency through constitutional mechanisms at Sir Seretse's death, many in Botswana, at least at first, considered the new president a caretaker who lacked his predecessor's traditional mantle of legitimacy. Masire's success in the 1984 elections suggests, to this point at least, that Botswana's political structures continue to be an adaptive and syncretic blend of traditionalism and liberalism.

Colonialism and the Bureaucratic State

Administrative structures and bureaucratic processes that have their origins in colonial Bechuanaland play an important role in contemporary state-societal relationships. Gunderson labeled the Botswana political system an "administrative state." In this administrative state, the social order is indistinguishable from the administrative order:

> Resources are allocated by commands issued by administrative elites, and there is no control by any other social group over decision-making. Authority in the administrative state flows downward from the rulers to the ruled; the administrative elites have complete control over the decision-making process.[40]

The political party and its leadership act as a vehicle to organize mass support at the polls for government policy and to blunt opposition to the state. The similarity to the Kenya "no-party" system is striking, however, in that the political organization has little influence over the policy-making process.

The nature of colonial rule in Bechuanaland between 1885 and 1966 sustained a nonpolitical social order in the country, a legacy passed on to post-colonial political leaders. The growth of state power in Botswana began during the colonial period when the imperial administration needed an apparatus to control both traditional elites and new social forces within the territory. Ashton noted that as early as the 1940s relations between the elites and the masses had changed as a result of colonial rule. As a result of British intervention, traditional authority became less democratic and more powerful, yet much more subservient to imperial interests.[41] Prior to European involvement in the Batswana states, traditional authority had been subjected to a number of checks and balances designed to keep the chiefs from becoming too authoritarian. Under colonial rule, the "resources of social energy . . . move[d] in a downward authoritarian flow from the top."[42]

After independence the state's power and pattern of intervention expanded as the independent government maintained the colonial monopoly of control over the economy in the absence of a strong, indigenous capitalist class. The nature of inherited institutions was such that by the time political independence occurred, "strong institutions of governance [were] already in place at the center."[43] These institutions of government were bureaucratic in nature, and they were more rooted in African states than were the

Westminster parliaments and ministerial systems hastily constructed prior to decolonization.

In this study I will be examining patterns of bureaucratic government as they evolved in colonial Bechuanaland. These patterns provided a unity of administrative routines and institutionalized structures that transcended the colonial period to influence the policy process in the post-colonial state.

Strategies of Rural Development

Strategies of rural development in Botswana and other African states must be seen within the context of the struggle for autonomy by domestic political elites. The failure of most local-level development efforts has delineated the weakness of local elites in this very unequal struggle for domination of the political economy. A number of factors at different levels of state structures and processes account for rural development failures.

Economic development in Botswana today has been influenced and constrained by colonial patterns of underdevelopment. Both what Halpern calls the "total neglect"[44] by the British colonial administration and the more fundamental elements of structural dependency limited choice and determined the direction of rural development efforts during the colonial period. This structural dependency[45] continues to limit Botswana's options in its relationships with both the regional and the international economic systems.

What can be called the local-central gap acts as a second constraint upon strategies of development and economic progress in rural Botswana. Binder and his colleagues pointed to the difficulty of extending state authority throughout a country.[46] Botswana's political structures have been unable to penetrate into or influence activity in the rural areas. The organs of party and government have not proved effective in bridging the gap between the center and the periphery in Botswana, nor have they been able to coordinate development activities in the countryside. The state is overdeveloped at the center and underdeveloped in the periphery, and "in spite of the loss of much formal authority, traditional leaders still control the local judiciary, and the flow of information to the people."[47] The failure of local-level institutions has meant that traditional leaders maintain considerable strength in the rural areas.

A third constraint on the promotion of development schemes in Botswana must be linked to patterns of bureaucratic routine and role expectations that were formed during the colonial period.[48] These routines have not been conducive to the kind of entrepreneurial effort needed to promote development activity. Inadequate role expectations and underdevelopment in addition to the country's more general human resource problems continue to plague Botswana today.

Close to twenty years after independence, neglect by the colonial and post-colonial state has led to a shortage of crucial skills and areas of expertise within both the national civil service and the local government administration. Botswana's salaried employees in the public sector are more consumers than producers of scarce resources.[49] It has been argued elsewhere that in many African states "there are fundamental administrative, institutional and political barriers to the effective use of a domestic strategy of dependency reversal."[50]

At the same time, in one sector of rural development policy, the cattle industry, Botswana elites have been able to create a degree of autonomy. For most Batswana, politics are the politics of cattle. By examining a century of colonial and post-colonial policy making in the rural areas, we see how critical the relative success of the cattle industry is to an understanding of the stability of Botswana's state system.

The Bureaucratic Elite and State Autonomy: The Search for Residuals

There is general agreement that the only major groups with high economic status in many African countries are the administrative officials and technical specialists of the civil service. The state and party bureaucracies have accumulated, and conspicuously consume, the scarce resources in many post-colonial African states.[51] Markovitz pointed to the "organizational bourgeoisie" as the "combined ruling group consisting of the top political leaders and bureaucrats, the traditional rulers and their descendents, and the leading members of the liberal professions and the rising business bourgeoisie."[52]

What is less clear is the extent to which these organizational elites operate autonomously to influence public policy. A number of dependency theorists emphasized the lack of autonomy among elites at the national level in LDCs.[53] Leys, for example, downplayed the autonomous role of the bureaucracy.[54] Key decisions are not made by the LDC, but by metropolitan bourgeoisie located in developed states. As von Freyhold stated, "The actual dynamics of economic and social development . . . are determined by the metropolitan bourgeoisie . . . rather than indigenous elites."[55] Parson argued that in Botswana the position of the governing "petite bourgeoisie" depends upon its connections with external, capitalist states.[56] Other theorists suggested that this view of local elites might be too simplistic.

Richard Sklar transferred "the dynamic of class formation out of the economic and into the political realm."[57] According to Sklar, class relations are determined on the basis of power rather than production.[58] Likewise, Samoff and Samoff suggested a complex dynamic in the relationships between national and international political and economic development.

> It is melodramatic and misleading to regard them [bureaucratic and political elites] as simply the local agents of international capital. Even zealous guardians of the national patrimony can persuade

themselves and their fellow citizens that their own prosperity reflects that of their country.[59]

Sklar's thesis, supported by Samoff and Samoff, opened the way for dialogue between scholars primarily concerned with class analysis and scholars concerned with an understanding of the role of the state.[60]

In an important study of Kenya, Swainson suggested that although Africa was integrated into the international economic system through the force of colonial capitalism, important areas of autonomy remained for national political elites. She pointed to the "hegemony of the indigenous bourgeoisie" in Kenya that is interdependent with the international capitalist system but not totally subordinate to it. In Kenya "it is still the case that value formation is *nationally* based and the state is able to support the interests of the internal bourgeoisie."[61]

The approach here assumes that certain sectors of the policy process will provide a greater degree of policy-making autonomy than do others. For example, livestock production and agricultural development may allow Botswana's local elites more room for maneuver than do patterns of trade and mineral exploitation. Dependency theorists have pointed correctly to dependency links between LDC elites and the metropolitan bourgeoisie that manages the international system. The degree of dependency as well as autonomy is an empirical question, however. In the next few chapters a search will be made for both degrees of dependency and degrees of autonomy at the national level. The search is for residuals (after the statistical technique), or areas of autonomy in which Botswana's elites can use the state's power to manipulate public policy. An example of residuals is found in the economic sectors that are not primarily under international control.

Social and political relationships exist at a number of levels. There is the internal relationship between national political elites and the domestic bureaucracy. Conflict and consensus can occur between the combined organizational bourgeoisie and the metropolitan managers of the international economic system. Elements at each level can create temporary coalitions that transcend the boundary of the state. My discussion of residuals has benefited from Schatzberg's study on the contextual analysis of class.

> Social classes are constantly changing in response to differing sociopolitical contexts. . . . The individual actor can, and does, belong to differing class alliances at the same time. . . . The degree of class identity will vary depending upon the geographic, social, political, and economic junctures of the moment in question.[62]

Following from Schatzberg, if certain sectors of the policy process can provide a greater degree of autonomy than others, domestic elites can, in various policy areas, be both coopted by the international system and engaged in a struggle with it to preserve areas of their autonomy.

In assuming an instrumentalist view of the state, I view power "in its visible exercise rather than as a many-sided social relation."[63] I have focused on the empirical state, rather than on the juridical state as defined by the rules of the international order.[64] The state can be understood as a mechanism by which dominant elites achieve certain predetermined or bargained public policy goals. In most of Africa the dominant element has been a bureaucratic elite that strives to better its position both internally and vis-à-vis the managers of the international economic system. Thus, "ready access to state institutions is therefore literally what makes classes dominant; it economizes their class effort. . . . Institution-building is therefore more correctly construed as class-formation than political development."[65]

The bureaucracy is a major factor in the policy-making process of Botswana. A pattern of role relationships and bureaucratic routines, developed during the colonial period, continues to influence political choice and bureaucratic behavior. The bureaucrats also form a major portion of Botswana's dominant political and economic elites. As Lonsdale pointed out, class formation in Africa has occurred within the institutions of the state. Civil service salaries have provided the basis for the surplus accumulation that allows "straddling." As Lonsdale explained, "successful careers [are straddled] between a variety of occupations . . . government employment . . . [is linked to the private sector] by the use of public wages as private investment funds."[66]

Class formation in Africa involved "a profound change, a silent cataclysm in the deepening of state power over the lives and choices of Africans."[67] Bureaucratic strength has often meant a weakening of political institutions. Parson stated that the bureaucracy, which he viewed as the dominant force in the petite bourgeoisie, "dominates policy making through control of institutions of parliamentary democracy and through apparently generalized acquiescence of the dominated class between elections."[68]

Corporatism and the Statist Paradigm

An understanding of the evolving role of state institutions in Botswana and other African countries is enhanced through the insights provided by theories of corporatism (systems of interest representation based on noncompeting groups that are sanctioned and subsidized by the state). Martin Carnoy stated that

> Social Corporatism is a logical countertheory to pluralism for those who think that liberal democracy cannot survive in modern society but who are fearful of authoritarian alternatives. For them, a progressive, humane but powerful state decision-making mechanism, separated from mass participation, is necessary in a complex, modern world.[69]

Although corporatism may be questioned as a normative goal, it can shed light on an empirical reality of elite interaction. Because of the personalism of African politics and the seeming lack of organized interest groups, corporatist theory has been used more often in studies of European and Latin American politics than in studies of African politics. In the former studies organized corporate entities are understood to be limited in number, singular and non-competitive in their function, and hierarchically ordered and recognized by the state.[70] A number of analysts have called for more attention to be placed on the relationship between state structures and group influence. Zolberg, in his pathfinding study, defined the "new institutional order," which had evolved in West African states as early as the mid-1960s, as

> a system of government with a monocephalic and nearly sovereign executive; a national assembly which is consultative rather than legislative and which is based on functional and corporate representation rather than geographical and individual . . . and a governmental bureaucracy in which the criterion of political loyalty is given overwhelming weight.[71]

Shaw called our attention to the utility of corporatist theory in the study of African politics, suggesting that the concept complements, rather than conflicts with, dependency theory. According to Shaw, "distinctive forms of state structure are emerging [in Africa] within a 'corporatist' mold."[72]

Shaw made a number of points that are important for this study. He suggested the existence of a conflict of interest between African domestic elites and metropolitan elites. African domestic elites are concerned with manipulating the domestic economy in their own interest rather than integrating it within the international economic system. African elites seek areas of relative autonomy in which they can exert their influence. "African states [and the elites which dominate them] are not robots that merely react to 'external' inputs and instructions."[73] Instead, periphery elites in periphery states have developed state structures that can "broaden the economic base of the new 'bureaucratic' bourgeoisie."[74] A hierarchy of social groupings overlaps with, and is dominated by, the bureaucratic segment of the national elite. National elites are neither autonomous nor dependent, instead there is "a semi-autonomous state in the context of a semi-autonomous local bourgeoisie in the post- and neo-colonial situation."[75] Thus, corporatism describes the post-colonial system in most of Africa.

Although it seems somewhat dubious to try to force the square pegs of all African regimes into the round hole of corporatism, the concept is of some utility in distinguishing between "soft" and "hard" states. An understanding of politics in Botswana and, by implication, in other institutionalized African states, benefits from an analysis of elite social groupings and their use of state structures to preserve areas of autonomy from encroachment by the dictates of the international economic system.

A number of analysts have pointed to the relationship between interest group action and state policy in Botswana. In his classic analysis of traditional government and politics, based largely on his study of Tswana states, Schapera painted a picture of traditional African politics resembling that of many later corporatist theorists. In a system without competitive groups or separation of powers, chiefs and their advisors initiated legislation, promulgated decisions, and administered justice. The elders provided the checks and balances for a political system that was consensual, rather than authoritarian.[76] Kuper stressed the consensual nature of what he called the corporate agnatic connection. Agnatic corporations "are the lowest-level dispute-settling body in the village. Such a moot can only arbitrate."[77]

Holm called attention to the importance of a statist paradigm in the post-colonial period.[78] Increasingly, interests are articulated through informal networks and organized groups that are linked with, but subordinate to, state structures that have taken a central role in capitalist development. Morrison, in a crucial study of the evolution of Botswana's cattle industry, described the

> stable and relatively autonomous form of statist authority involved in the complex and dynamic interplay of three dimensions of Botswana's political economy: the phasing of state action, the trajectory of elite politics, the character of foreign capital.[79]

Critical to an understanding of the state system in Botswana are "the ties which bound together diverse actors, domestic and international . . . [and the] corporatist-style, inclusionary impulse [that] sought to minimize confrontation and rejection."[80]

Conclusion

To what extent are areas of autonomy and dependency, at the national level or in relation to the international system, related to the needs of Botswana's dominant socio-economic groups? I believe that by exploring the answers to this question in the Botswana case, we will be led to a concept of state formation in southern Africa that links pre-colonial procedures and processes with the administrative practices and structures introduced during the colonial and post-colonial periods.

In this study I take a broad view of state formation. Lonsdale warned us to be sensitive to the inability of a single mode or level of analysis to "explain all the myriads of different textures of human life."[81] Rather than search for a single paradigm, I will be focusing on patterns of state evolution over time. Four areas of policy making—mechanisms of political control, economic and rural development policy, center-periphery relationships, and human resource development policy—will be analyzed in colonial Bechuanaland and post-colonial Botswana in an attempt to link patterns of elite formation to the instrumentalist state structures evolving under their control.

Notes

1. "Botswana," *Africa Contemporary Record, 1980-1981,* Colin Legum, ed. (New York: Africana Publishing Co., 1981), p. B659. This chapter was written by the present author.

2. Other multiparty states (in 1983) included Nigeria, Zimbabwe, Uganda, Egypt, and Senegal. Except for Zimbabwe, which has been independent for only four years, each of these states has returned to a multiparty system after a period as a one-party state or a military regime, or both.

3. J. Stephen Morrison, "Development Optimism and African State Failure: The Dynamics of Successful State Action in Botswana" (Ph.D. diss., University of Wisconsin, 1987), chapter 3, p. 1 (in draft).

4. Gwendolen M. Carter and Patrick O'Meara, "Introduction," in *Southern Africa: The Continuing Crisis,* 2nd ed., Carter and O'Meara, eds. (Bloomington, In.: Indiana University Press, 1982), p. ix.

5. Jack Halpern, *South Africa's Hostages: Basutoland, Bechuanaland and Swaziland* (Harmondsworth: Penguin, 1965), p. 297.

6. *Ibid.*

7. Much of the following is based in part upon Louis A. Picard, "From Bechuanaland to Botswana: An Overview," in *Politics and Rural Development in Southern Africa, The Evolution of Modern Botswana.* Louis A. Picard, ed. (London: Rex Collings, 1985).

8. Louis A. Picard with Klaus Endresen, *A Study of the Manpower and Training Needs of the Unified Local Government Service, 1982–1992 ,* vol. 2 (Gaborone: Government Printer, 1981).

9. Language, Setswana; one person, Motswana; two or more people, Batswana; the country, Botswana. English is the official language of the country.

10. The Malete are actually Ndebele, but they have completely assimilated the Setswana language and culture.

11. Figures should be seen as approximate. They are taken from Richard P. Stevens, *Historical Dictionary of the Republic of Botswana* (Metuchen, N.J.: The Scarecrow Press, 1975), p. 13. Stevens' figures were adjusted for estimated population growth between 1971 and 1981.

12. Quoted in René Lemarchand, "The State and Society in Africa: Ethnic Stratification and Restratification in Historical and Comparative Perspective," in *State Versus Ethnic Claims: African Policy Dilemmas,* Donald Rothchild and Victor A. Olorunsola, eds. (Boulder, Co.: Westview Press, 1983), p. 44.

13. *Ibid.,* pp. 44-45.

14. Issa G. Shivji, *Class Struggles in Tanzania* (New York: Monthly Review Press, 1976), p. 33.

15. John Lonsdale, "States and Social Processes in Africa: A Historiographical Survey," *African Studies Review,* vol. 24, nos. 2/3 (June/ September 1981), p. 140.

16. Theda Skocpol, "Bringing the State Back In: Strategies of Analysis in Current Research," *Bringing the State Back In,* Peter B. Evans, Dietrick Rueschmeyer, and Theda Skocpol, eds. (Cambridge: Cambridge University Press, 1985), p. 27.

17. Lonsdale, "States and Social Processes," p. 140.

18. Crawford Young and Thomas Turner, *The Rise and Decline of the Zairian State*, (Madison: University of Wisconsin Press, 1985), p. 12.

19. Martin Carnoy, *The State and Political Theory* , (Princeton: Princeton University Press, 1984), p. 255.

20. Morrison, "Developmental Optimism and African State Failure," chapter 1, *passim*.

21. See for example, Richard A. Joseph, "Class, State and Prebendal Politics in Nigeria," *State and Class in Africa*, Nelson Kasfir, ed. (London: Frank Cass, 1984), pp. 23-24.

22. *Ibid.*, articles by Joseph on Nigeria, Thomas M. Callaghy on Zaire, and Nelson Kasfir on Uganda.

23. Goran Hyden, *Beyond Ujamaa: Underdevelopment and an Uncaptured Peasantry* (London: Heineman, 1980).

24. Joseph, "Class, State and Prebendal Politics," *State and Class in Africa*, p. 30.

25. See Young and Turner, *The Rise and Decline of the Zairian State*, p. 30; and Robert H. Jackson and Carl G. Rosberg, *Personal Rule in Black Africa* (Berkeley: University of California Press, 1982).

26. Morrison, "Developmental Optimism," Preface, pp. iv-v.

27. Joseph, "Class, State, and Prebendal Politics," *State and Class in Africa, passim*.

28. Isaac Schapera, *Tribal Innovators: Tswana Chiefs and Social Change, 1795-1940*, (London: The Athlone Press, 1970), p. 238.

29. C.S. Whitaker, Jr., *The Politics of Tradition, Continuity and Change in Northern Nigeria, 1946-1966* (Princeton, N.J.: Princeton University Press, 1970).

30. Richard Vengroff, *Botswana: Rural Development in the Shadow of Apartheid* (Rutherford, N.J.: Fairleigh Dickinson University Press, 1977), pp. 69-72 and pp. 134-135 (quote).

31. Jack D. Parson, "Cattle, Class and the State in Rural Botswana," *Journal of Southern African Studies*, vol. 7, no. 2 (April 1981), pp. 239-240.

32. Thomas Tlou, "The Nature of Batswana States: Towards a Theory of Batswana Traditional Government—The Batawana Case," *Botswana Notes and Records*, vol. 6 (1974), p. 67.

33. John C. Comaroff, "Rules and Rulers: Political Processes in a Tswana Chiefdom," *Man*, vol. 13, no. 1 (March 1978), p. 1.

34. *Ibid.*, pp. 12-18, p. 12 for quote.

35. One cannot fail to take note of the transformation of governmental media after a military coup as, at least, a superficial example.

36. Norman H. Miller, "The Political Survival of Traditional Leadership," *Journal of Modern African Studies*, vol. 6, no. 2 (August 1968), pp. 183-201; idem., "The Rural African Party: Political Participation in Tanzania," *American Political Science Review*, vol. 64, no. 2 (June 1970), pp. 548-571.

37. Irving Leonard Markovitz, *Power and Class in Africa* (Englewood Cliffs, N.J.: Prentice-Hall, 1977), p. 159.

38. Morrison, "Developmental Optimism," chapter 3, p. 14.

39. Richard F. Weisfelder, "The Basuto Monarchy: A Spent Force or a

Dynamic Political Factor?" *Papers in International Studies*, paper no. 16 (Athens: Ohio University Center for International Studies, 1972) and Christian P. Potholm, *Swaziland: The Dynamics of Political Modernization* (Berkeley: University of California Press, 1972), *passim*. For a continental approach, see René Lemarchand, ed., *African Kingships in Perspective: Political Change and Modernization in Monarchical Settings* (London: Frank Cass & Co., 1977), *passim*.

40. Gilfred L. Gunderson, "Nation Building and the Administrative State: The Case of Botswana" (Ph.D. diss., University of California, Berkeley, 1971), p. 7.

41. E. H. Ashton, "Democracy and Indirect Rule," *Africa*, vol. 17, no. 4 (October 1947), pp. 242-246. See also Paul Maylam, *Rhodes, the Tswana, and the British: Colonialism, Collaboration and Conflict in the Bechuanaland Protectorate, 1885-1899* (Westport, Conn.: Greenwood Press, 1980), p. 20.

42. Leonard Barnes, *Soviet Light on the Colonies* (Middlesex: Penguin, 1944), p. 108.

43. Donald Rothchild and Victor A. Olorunsola, "Managing Competing State and Ethnic Claims," in *idem., African Policy Dilemmas*, Rothchild and Olorunsola, eds., p. 5.

44. Halpern, *South Africa's Hostages*, p. 108.

45. See Heraldo Munoz, ed., *From Dependency to Development: Strategies to Overcome Underdevelopment and Inequality* (Boulder, Co.: Westview Press, 1981).

46. Leonard Binder et al., *Crises and Sequences in Political Development* (Princeton, N.J.: Princeton University Press, 1971).

47. Vengroff, *Botswana*, p. 72 (quote) and pp. 123-143.

48. See Louis A. Picard, "Role Changes Among Field Administrators in Botswana: Administrative Attitudes and Social Change" (Ph.D. diss., University of Wisconsin, Madison, 1977) for an analysis of bureaucratic routines in Bechuanaland and Botswana.

49. Louis A. Picard, "Bureaucrats, Cattle, and Public Policy: Land Tenure Changes in Botswana," *Comparative Political Studies*, vol. 13, no. 3 (October 1980), pp. 313-356.

50. Louis A. Picard, "Self-Sufficiency and Delinkage in Agricultural and Rural Development" (Paper presented at the Twenty-fourth International Studies Convention, Mexico City, April 5-9, 1983), p. 28.

51. P. Raikes, "Rural Differentiations and Class Formation in Tanzania," *Journal of Peasant Studies*, vol. 5, no. 2 (April 1978), pp. 285-325; I. Shivji, *Class Struggles in Tanzania*; G. Arrighi and J. S. Saul, *Essays on the Political Economy of Africa* (Nairobi: East African Publishing House, 1973).

52. Markowitz, *Power and Class*, p. 208.

53. For example, Samir Amin, *Neo-Colonialism in West Africa* (New York: Monthly Review Press, 1973); J. Saul, "The Unsteady State: Uganda, Obote and General Amin," *Review of African Political Economy* , no. 5 (April 1976), pp. 12-38; Hamza Alavi, "The Post-Colonial State: Pakistan and Bangladesh," *New Left Review*, no. 74 (1972), pp. 59-81; Shivji, *Class Struggles in Tanzania*; and Colin Leys, "The Overdeveloped Post-Colonial

State: A Re-Evaluation," *Review of African Political Economy*, no. 5 (April 1976), pp. 39-48.

54. *Ibid.*, pp. 43-48.

55. M. von Freyhold, "The Post-Colonial State and Its Tanzania Version," *Review of African Political Economy*, no. 8 (January–April 1977), p. 81.

56. Jack D. Parson, "The Political Economy of Botswana: A Case in the Study of Politics and Social Change in Post-Colonial Societies" (Ph.D. diss., University of Sussex, 1979), pp. 19-21.

57. Crawford Young, "Class, Ethnicity, and Nationalism" (Unpublished paper, n.d.), p. 67.

58. Richard Sklar, "The Basis of Class Domination of Africa," *Journal of Modern African Studies*, vol. 17, no. 4 (1979), p. 537.

59. Joel Samoff and Rachel Samoff, "The Local Politics of Underdevelopment," *Politics and Society*, vol. 6, no. 4 (December 1976), p. 398. See also Joel Samoff, "Class, Class Conflict, and the State in Africa," *Political Science Quarterly*, vol. 97, no. 1 (Spring 1982) pp. 105-127 and *idem.*, "The Bureaucracy and the Bourgeoisie: Decentralization and Class Structure in Tanzania," *Comparative Studies in Society and History*, vol. 21, no. 1 (January 1979), pp. 30-62.

60. Young, "Class, Ethnicity, and Nationalism," p. 68.

61. Nicola Swainson, *The Development of Corporate Capitalism in Kenya, 1918–77* (London: Heineman, 1980), p. 290.

62. Michael G. Schatzberg, *Politics and Class in Zaire: Bureaucracy, Business and Beer in Lisala* (New York: Africana Publishing Co., 1980), p. 31.

63. Lonsdale, "States and Social Process," p. 151.

64. Robert H. Jackson and Carl G. Rosberg make this distinction. See "Why Africa's Weak States Persist: The Empirical and Juridical in Statehood," *World Politics*, vol. 35, no. 1 (October 1982), pp. 1-24.

65. Lonsdale, "States and Social Processes," p. 162.

66. *Ibid.*, p. 195.

67. *Ibid.*, p. 194.

68. Parson, "Political Economy of Botswana," p. 350.

69. Carnoy, *The State and Political Theory*, p. 249.

70. Louis A. Picard, "Decentralization, 'Recentralization,' and 'Steering Mechanisms,' Paradoxes of Local Government in Denmark," *Polity*, vol. 15, no. 4, (Summer 1983), pp. 536-554.

71. Aristide R. Zolberg, *Creating Political Order: The Party-States of West Africa* (Chicago: Rand McNally & Co., 1966), p. 108.

72. Timothy M. Shaw, "Beyond Neo-Colonialism: Varieties of Corporatism in Africa," *Journal of Modern African Studies*, vol. 20, no. 2 (June 1982), p. 240.

73. *Ibid.*, p. 241.

74. *Ibid.*, p. 241.

75. Hamza Alavi, "The State in Post-Colonial Societies: Pakistan and Bangladesh," *Politics and the State in the Third World* , Harry Goulbourne, ed.

(London: MacMillan, 1979), pp. 41-42, cited in Shaw, "Beyond Neo-Colonialism," p. 250.

76. Isaac Schapera, *Government and Politics in Tribal Societies* (New York: Schocken Books, 1967), pp. 92-93.

77. Adam Kuper, *Kalahari Village Politics* (Cambridge: Cambridge University Press, 1970), pp. 134-135.

78. John Holm, "The State and Rural Development in Botswana and Lesotho," (Unpublished paper, August 1979).

79. Morrison, "Development Optimism," chapter 3, p. 18.

80. *Ibid.*, p. 26.

81. Lonsdale, "States and Social Processes," p. 140.

2

The Tswana Polities and British Colonialism in Southern Africa

The Kwena now living in the Kweneng District of Botswana are generally acknowledged to be senior in rank to all the other "tribes." . . . They themselves claim to have . . . been a part of the tribe known as Bakwenabaga Mogopa of Rustenburg District (Transvaal). . . . There was a very serious famine and people scattered in all directions in search of food.[1]

The Pre-Colonial Period

Before 1800

It has been customary to talk of the arrival of migrants to southern Africa from other parts of the continent as a relatively recent event. Increasingly it is clear that such an approach does not present an accurate picture of the evolution of society in southern Africa. Parsons has stated succinctly:

> Once it was the fashion, especially in Southern Africa, to attribute all historical change to personalities or to "invasions," "migrations," "treks," "conquests," and "explosions" of populations. All of this was tied up with the idea that "tribes" that can now be identified have identities which can be projected back indefinitely into the past. As a result numerous "tribal histories" that taper off into myth have been produced. . . . [Emphasis should be on] gradual patterns of indigenous continuity and development, rather than on sudden alien additions and innovations."[2]

The history of the people now living in the Sotho-Tswana areas of southern Africa begins in the fifth to the sixth centuries A.D. and "there do not appear to be any abrupt cultural discontinuities from that time through to the development of Bantu-speaking iron-working societies."[3]

The presence of a Khoisian population in the region certainly predates this, going back well before the beginning of the first millenium. What

25

appears most accurate is to envision this region as continually populated for at least the past two thousand years, with gradual changes in culture, language, physical type, and economy occurring independently of one another. A "pre-culture" to the Sotho-Tswana emerged in the Sotho-Tswana core area of the western Transvaal some time before A.D. 1000 with the emergence of Sotho-Tswana polities occurring in approximately A.D. 1500.[4]

Sotho-Tswana groups entered the Botswana region in a number of movements sometime after A.D. 500. The first to arrive were the Kgalagadi. They met the San, or Sarwa, people who already inhabited the eastern part of what is now Botswana. Following the Kgalagadi was a second movement that brought the Rolong and the Tlhaping into the region of Botswana and the northern part of the Cape Colony. The third and last movement brought the ancestors of all the other Tswana groups from the core area into the southwestern Transvaal and later into Botswana.

As Tswana society evolved and absorbed the existing inhabitants of earlier societies, the new groups divided and subdivided. There was "a process of intermingling and presumably acculturation between the members of the newly arrived lineage-cluster and the earlier inhabitants" of the region. As a corollary to this, Tswana society was characterized by "the fragmentation of a number of lineage-clusters which dispersed themselves widely" throughout southern Africa.[5] It was a continually reoccurring feature of Tswana history "for part of a tribe to secede under a discontented member of the ruling family and move away to a new locality."[6]

In Botswana, the three parent clusters were the Rolong, the Kgatla, and the Kwena. In about 1720 a group of Kwena broke off and settled in what is now southeastern Botswana under a leader named Kgabo. Shortly thereafter the Ngwato and the Ngwaketse broke off from the Kwena and moved north and south, respectively. In 1795 the Tswana broke off from the Ngwato and moved to the northwest section of what is now Botswana.

European Influence

The last group of migrants to arrive in the region were the Europeans. The first Tswana-speaking people to come into contact with Europeans were the Tlhaping in 1801, although indirect contact probably preceded this by a considerable period. Trade between European settlers and the Tswana peoples is likely to have occurred as early as the eighteenth century if not earlier. Certainly by the beginning of the nineteenth century, trade links were well established.

Between 1800 and 1850, numbers of missionaries and traders made contact with the peoples of Botswana. As early as 1826, Ngwaketse leaders sought the assistance of two European travelers (and their firearms) in a fight with the Kololo. After the arrival of missionaries from the London Missionary Society (LMS) under the leadership of David Livingstone in

1844, contact between Tswana leaders and Europeans was almost continuous. By the end of the 1850s, karosses (skin garments), ivory, ostrich feathers, and other products were reaching European markets by way of traders and merchants in Cape Colony. At the same time, European consumer items were appearing in Tswana towns and villages.

Labor migration to South Africa began about this time. As early as 1844, labor migrants were going to the Cape Colony and the South African Republic. By mid-century, "David Livingstone . . . reported that, as a result of drought from 1848 to 1851, great hunger forced many Bakwena into the Kgalagadi in search of wild foods, while 66 went to the 'Cape Colony' to find work."[7] The first labor recruiter appeared among the Ngwato in 1877, and 105 men had been sent to the diamond mines by the end of that year.

With the arrival of missionaries, traders, and labor recruiters, colonial rivalry and regional conflict were soon to follow. Religious rivalries between the LMS and the German Lutheran missionaries and clashes with the Boer Republics greatly affected the people in the area. By the last half of the nineteenth century, Tswana polities were embroiled in rivalries between the British, the Germans, and the Boer settlers. Conflicts of values and strategies took a number of Tswana societies to the verge of civil war during this period.

Regional conflict escalated after 1850. The first clash with the Boers occurred in 1852 when Transvaal farmers attacked the Kwena capital, Dimawe. Tensions increased as the strategic position of Botswana, the "road to the north," became appreciated by various European factions. The discovery of gold in the Tati district in 1867 exacerbated the process. By 1880 the missionary and trader presence in the major towns of Botswana had become permanent. Boer invasions of Tswana territory were increasing, and British influence over the chiefs became the dominant factor in Tswana-European relations.

An informal protectorate relationship developed by 1880 between the British government in Cape Town and the Tswana chiefs. A rebellion of southern Tswana chiefs in 1878 had resulted in a military expedition, led by Sir Charles Warren, to restore British control. Boer and German activities in the early 1880s stirred the British to declare a formal protectorate over the southern part of Tswana territory (British Bechuanaland) in 1884. British Bechuanaland became a crown colony in September 1885 when a protectorate was declared over the northern territories (the Bechuanaland Protectorate, or Botswana today). The 1889 charter provided for the eventual cession of the Bechuanaland Protectorate to Cecil Rhodes's British South Africa Company (BSCA).

The southern part of Tswana territory, as British Bechuanaland, was transferred to Rhodes's Cape Colony in 1895. The Bechuanaland Protectorate, however, as a result of the visit of Chiefs Bathoen, Sebele, and Khama to Britain and the discrediting of the BSAC after the Jameson Raid, remained under direct British imperial control. The ultimate fate of the Bechuanaland Protectorate, promised to both South Africa and the BSAC's Rhodesia at various times before 1910, remained uncertain until well into the 1950s.

Origins of Colonial Rule

British rule in Bechuanaland is part of the complex and confusing history of Southern Africa in the late nineteenth and early twentieth centuries. The question was not whether external rule would be established over the Tswana polities of the area, but what form that rule would take. Early patterns of colonial rule in both British Bechuanaland and the Bechuanaland Protectorate were to have a crucial impact on decisions taken much later.

British Bechuanaland

The new British crown colony, declared in what is now the northern Cape, consisted of five districts and had an area of 51,000 square miles. The colony was located south of the Molopo River down to a latitude of 28°20' S. It has a 1983 population of around 600,000 people and parts of British Bechuanaland made up the core of the South African homeland of Bophuthatswana. British Bechuanaland was incorporated into the Cape Colony in 1895.

British Bechuanaland is important to the political and administrative history of Botswana. The early administration of the Bechuanaland Protectorate was established in British Bechuanaland, and the educational and health services of the southern area served the Protectorate through most of the colonial period. The Protectorate's administrative capital was established in British Bechuanaland, first at Vryburg and, after 1895, at Mafeking, where it remained until 1965. Thus the Bechuanaland Protectorate had the curious distinction of having its capital located outside its borders, sixteen miles south (in Mafeking).

After 1885 British administration and influence gradually moved north of the Molopo into the Protectorate. There was only one resident administrator in the Protectorate prior to 1891, however, an assistant commissioner was stationed at Gaberones (now Gaborone). British Bechuanaland was governed by the governor of the Cape Colony who was also the British high commissioner for South Africa. British Bechuanaland's administrative structure, however, was kept separate from that of the Cape, which had attained internal self-government in 1872.

The high commissioner was assisted by a deputy commissioner residing in British Bechuanaland, who was also formally responsible for British interests in the Bechuanaland Protectorate. Aside from the deputy commissioner, later called the resident commissioner, the civil establishment of British Bechuanaland consisted of three resident magistrates. These resident magistrates, the forerunners of the district administration in the Bechuanaland Protectorate, had both judicial and administrative responsibilities. There were government stations at Vryburg, Taung, and Mafeking. Each resident magistrate had some European clerical assistance and a few African messengers and translators. The entire civil establishment, prior to 1895, including the Bechuanaland Protectorate administration, cost £5,800 a year.

The Bechuanaland Protectorate

As the British became involved with the Tswana polities in the northern territories in the late nineteenth century, they followed the line of least resistance in establishing political control. Although the three High Commission Territories came under British rule in a somewhat haphazard way, it was not without purpose. Three factors influenced British expansion prior to the outbreak of the Boer War: cultural-religious, strategic, and economic. The cultural-religious factor is linked to the nineteenth century value system of pseudoscientific racism. British missionaries, traders, and administrators assumed a cultural and racial superiority over the indigenous peoples of southern Africa. Trusteeship and "humanitarianism" were based on Christian ideals and paternalism. The missionary purpose was to convert subject peoples to Christianity and thereby expose their converts to a higher form of "civilization."

Missionary activity in the Bechuanaland Protectorate occurred within a political context in southern Africa that was slightly different from other parts of the continent and was directed toward a number of limited goals. The threats from the Boers and from Germany were real in the 1880s, and a basic goal of much of the missionary activity was to put pressure on Britain to prevent Boer or German rule over the Tswana polities. The expansive movement of the missionaries "was political as well as humanitarian."[8] The trustee concept, based on the idea that there was a need to bring about the transition of a subject people to a higher state of improvement, was constructed specifically on British values. In the southern African context, this concept was competing with another set of European values that were based on Boer exclusiveness.

The Boer and German threats illustrate the second factor influencing British colonial activity in the late nineteenth century: Bechuanaland's strategic importance within the region. Some form of protection was necessary for Bechuanaland because the "protracted conflict between Boer and Briton beyond the borders of [the Protectorate] made it a necessary, if not particularly attractive move on the South African chess-board."[9] By 1895 the choice was clear—a separate relationship with Britain or eventual incorporation into one of the white-ruled states.

Incorporation into one of the Boer Republics was unacceptable to British imperialists. The critical importance of Bechuanaland was "in its being what Cecil John Rhodes called 'the Suez Canal of the North.'"[10] In the last quarter of the nineteenth century, what came to be known as the Missionaries' Road was carved out of the fertile areas of eastern Bechuanaland, from Mafeking in British Bechuanaland to Bulawayo and on northward. For Rhodes and for the British imperialist, Bechuanaland was a steppingstone to central Africa and "it was a vital strategic point for the [British South Africa] company's operations north of the Limpopo, serving as both a base and a rear guard."[11]

Beyond the religious and strategic influences, economic factors also were involved in Britain's expansion north in the late nineteenth century. During the decade after the declaration of the Protectorate (in 1885) concession hunters crisscrossed the country seeking access to Tswana territories. The prospect of trading stations, mineral exploitation, and the possibilities of European settlement motivated the concessionaires. Rhodes and the British South Africa Company were by far the most influential. Although the Jameson Raid thwarted Rhodes's political ambition to rule the territory, his BSAC continued to influence events well into the twentieth century.

Rhodes had three goals for Bechuanaland. His first goal was to use the territory as a basis for communications with Rhodesia. In the broadest sense the building of the railway was at the heart of the region's economic development. Second, Rhodes had visions, only partly realized, of large scale European settlement in the Protectorate. Settler communities established by Rhodes in Ghanzi District in the west and along the east in the Tuli, Gaberones, and Lobatse blocks had a major impact on Bechuanaland politics throughout the colonial period. Rhodes also hoped to discover rich mineral resources in the territory. Most of the BSAC's activity in the 1880s and 1890s was directed at obtaining mineral concessions from the Tswana chiefs. The mineral promise of the nineteenth century petered out, however (partly from a lack of effort), and Bechuanaland's vast mineral resources were left for the post-colonial government to exploit.

Ultimately, labor determined the nature of Bechuanaland's economic relations within the region. By the 1840s, men from the southern Tswana polities had taken employment on the Boer farms in the Transvaal. By the 1880s and 1890s Batswana were migrating to the diamond mines in Kimberly and later to Southern Rhodesia. In addition, the construction of the railway demanded considerable indigenous labor. By the end of the nineteenth century, migration to South Africa, and especially to the Witwatersrand, became "more systematic and pervasive, its cause now not emanating from factors internal to the social formation but from externally imposed tax and land arrangements."[12] Bechuanaland officials came to play a prominent role in labor recruitment and in the supervision of Tswana laborers in South

Africa. This colonial policy had the effect of creating a rural labor reserve in the territory to be tapped by South African industry whenever needed.

The Bechuanaland Administration

British rule over Bechuanaland was assumed at the outset to be one of short duration, expected to last only until political relationships within South Africa were defined clearly. Thus, it seemed to make sense to import both administrators and administrative patterns directly from the south rather than linking Bechuanaland to patterns of recruitment and administration emanating from the Colonial Office in London.

The pattern of administration used in the Cape Colony at that time was repeated first in British Bechuanaland, then in the Bechuanaland Protectorate. Often the administrators involved were transferred from the Cape and, after 1895, from British Bechuanaland. Thus, the South African pattern of administration had a major influence upon patterns of control in Bechuanaland prior to the mid-1930s.[13] South Africa's ad hoc policy of segregation and "tribal reserves" was transferred to Bechuanaland as well.

Recruitment Patterns

In addition to their role as an imperial interest group, a number of missionaries worked formally or informally in the Bechuanaland administration prior to 1891. John MacKenzie, perhaps the most important of the missionaries active in Bechuanaland, had served for a time as deputy commissioner and resident commissioner for British Bechuanaland. John Moffat, the first assistant commissioner appointed north of the Molopo, had spent much of his adult life in missionary work in southern Africa.

The normal career pattern of a Bechuanaland civil servant changed after 1891. The missionaries in the administration were replaced by English-speaking South Africans with police or clerical experience. These early administrations at the district level were headed by resident magistrates.

A career in the Bechuanaland administration must be seen in the Southern African context of the late nineteenth century. Bechuanaland was a frontier in a frontier society. As the British Empire expanded into the Tswana polities, a variety of traders, adventurers, and rogues roamed the countryside. Thus, the early years of colonial rule in Bechuanaland are linked to the special role played by Bechuanaland's Border Police.

The Border Police were formed in 1885 with the declaration of the Protectorate. During the first ten years of British rule, the police force consumed 60 percent of the combined budget of the colony and the Bechuanaland Protectorate. "In approving the creation of a small standing army of European horsemen the British Government with all of their desire for economy, had in fact chosen the most expensive of all forms of administration."[14]

Although the Border Police was disbanded in 1895, the Protectorate Police that replaced it still consumed 51 percent of Bechuanaland's budget by 1899. The economic impact of the police force, however, was secondary compared to its psychological impact on the evolution of political control in Bechuanaland. Many of the early administrators in Bechuanaland had police experience in their background. Indeed, during the first thirty years of the colonial period, "the colonial administration . . . was largely a police force. . . . Drawn for the most part from the police service, they rejoice, as a group, in the mental habits and range of outlook customary in that walk of life."[15]

Bechuanaland's resident magistrate at this time carried the title of captain. All administrators held a commission in the Bechuanaland police, a semi-military status that, although largely honorary, was part of the imagery of the early Protectorate government.[16] A set of attitudes developed about the kind of rule necessary to keep the peace and preserve order. "The British," Leonard Barnes laconically commented, "came into the Bechuana country to keep the Boers out, and they have ever since been inclined to suppose that in safeguarding the Bechuana peoples from outside aggression . . . their duty has been done."[17]

By 1920 the influence of the police on the administration had somewhat diminished, although Bechuanaland's police image continued. By the end of World War I, the more normal pattern of recruitment was directly into the administration. Men in their early twenties from South Africa were brought into the district administration as clerks. They were given a number of clerical and accounting tasks and had an apprentice-master relationship with the resident magistrates.

Although the senior staff recruited mainly before 1920 had police experience, it was usually not more than a couple of years. Any "police mentality"[18] that the younger district officers might have had in the 1930s was received secondhand from the senior administrators. It would probably be more accurate to classify the mentality of the younger staff as "clerical." (See Table 2.1.)

Because of the (presumed) temporary nature of the British administration in Bechuanaland, all recruitment was local. The cost of a South African recruit was much lower than that of a recruit from Britain. Locally recruited officers also had the advantage of previous knowledge of the South African environment. An informal network developed in the High Commission Territories and in South Africa among British South Africans working in government, and available positions were communicated throughout the region. It was common practice for one to assist one's friends and relatives in finding a position in Southern Africa;[19] this was certainly true in Bechuanaland. The paternal connection, for example, was an important

Table 2.1 Police Force Background of Bechuanaland District
Officers, 1935

(n = 17)

	Recruitment through Police Force[1]	Recruitment Directly into the Clerical Establishment
Resident Magistrates	5	0
Assistant Magistrates and Grade-II Clerks	2	10
Total District Officers in 1935	7	10

Source: Bechuanaland Protectorate Blue Books and Staff Lists, National
Archives, Gaborone, Botswana.
[1]Without exception all Bechuanaland district officers recruited from the police
forces had subsequent clerical experience.

element in the selection process of these officers. (See Table 2.2.) The
potential candidate belonged to a very small segment of a very small society.
People tended to know each other well, and informal connections were an
important criterion for entry into the system.

Because of the localized pattern of recruitment, the administrative officer
in the High Commission Territories before the mid-1930s generally was
unacquainted with the policies or procedures of British rule elsewhere in
Africa. Critics of Britain's southern African policy argued that administrators
were often frustrated and made clumsy by the complex communication
procedures in the region. Lord Hailey, although clearly sympathetic to the
colonial system in general, observed that "for all the earlier period of British
rule very little guidance was given to them in regard to the policy to be
followed in the matter of Native Administration."[20] Policy was generally ad
hoc, day-to-day, and limited to law and order and tax collection. Given the
colonial ideal, administrators should have been learning to understand and
assist, and on occasion to guide, the people among whom they worked, and
chiefs should have been drawn into discussions at the very inception of all
far-reaching measures. Many administrators were not able to accept this
colonial ideal and felt uncomfortable with even the mildly reformist nature of
colonial policies after World War I. Their racial attitudes, formed in South
Africa, often were unacceptable to the Colonial Office and the Dominions
Office, both of which articulated colonial racial policy as a liberal alternative
to South African separatism.

Table 2.2 Familial Connections of Bechuanaland District Officers: Pre-1937 Recruitment Pattern

Serving Officer/Date of Recruitment/First Position	Paternal Connection to Bechuanaland for South African Administration
1. V. F. Ellenberger/1915/ Subinspector of Police	Father, Jules Ellenberger, Administrative Officer and Resident Commissioner at Bechuanaland
2. G. E. Nettleton/1914/ Subinspector of Police	Father, Captain Nettleton, Bechuanaland Police (Son born in Protectorate)
3. Alastair J. T. MacRae/1928/ Grade II Clerk	Father, Medical Doctor, Bechuanaland Protectorate Service
4. A. N. W. Mathews/1935/ Grade II Clerk	Father, Land Surveyor, Transvaal Government
5. S. V. Lawrenson/1928/ Subinspector of Police	Father, Bechuanaland Police
6. P. G. Batho/1932/ Grade II Clerk in Swaziland	Father, Assistant Director of Prisons, Pretoria
7. J. D. A. Germond/1925/ Grade II Clerk	Father, Missionary, Basutoland
8. E. H. Midgley/1926/ Grade II Clerk	Father, P. R. Midgley, Labor Agent, Basutoland, later service in Bechuanaland (Son born in Basutoland)
9. C. C. McLaren/1927/ Subinspector of Police	Father, Clerk, Municipal Government, Johannesburg
10. W. H. Cairns/1926/ Grade II Clerk	Father, Medical Practitioner, South Africa, later British High Commissioner in South Africa (close friend of J. P. R. Maud)

Source: Personnel files, Bechuanaland Protectorate; Public Records Office, London; Botswana National Archives, Gaborone.

Early Colonial Structures

Prior to 1925 the three High Commission Territories were administered from the Dominions Department of the Colonial Office, which also governed relations with Canada, Australia, South Africa, and the other self-governing dominions. In 1926 when the cabinet level Dominions Office became responsible for South African affairs, responsibility for the High Commission Territories was transferred as well.

Within southern Africa the official in charge of the High Commission Territories was the high commissioner, who additionally served as the British representative to South Africa. Prior to 1910, the high commissioner of Basutoland, Bechuanaland, and Swaziland was also the high commissioner of the Cape Colony, then, after the formation of the Union of South Africa, the governor general of South Africa. In 1931, after the Statute of Westminster, the high commissioner position was paired with that of British high commissioner (and, after 1961, ambassador) to South Africa.

Internally, Bechauanaland was governed by a resident commissioner based in Mafeking. The Government Secretariat and several of the colony's departments were headquartered in what came to be known as the Imperial Reserve. At the district level, the administration was headed by a resident magistrate with both judicial and administrative responsibilities.

In 1896, Proclamation No. 2 of the High Commissioner formalized the organization of the judicial and administrative system. The proclamation, based on earlier legislation in British Bechuanaland, defined the judicial responsibility of the assistant commissioners and resident magistrates as extending to all criminal and civil cases, except murder, and excluding cases in which only Africans were involved. Significantly, the model used for the office of resident magistrate was South African. The courts of the resident magistrate in Bechuanaland were to have the same powers as the courts of the resident magistrates in Cape Colony.

The legal system imposed upon Bechuanaland was South African as well. According to the Order in Council prevailing in the Bechuanaland Protectorate on December 22, 1909, "the laws in force in the Colony of the Cape of Good Hope on June 10th, 1891, shall *mutatis mutandis* . . . so far as are not inapplicable be the laws in force and [will] be observed in the Protectorate."[21] Not only were certain statutory enactments (including patterns of segregation) transferred from Cape Colony to Bechuanaland, but the Roman-Dutch law of the Cape Colony also became the common law of Bechuanaland (as a result of the 1896 proclamation) and remains common law in Botswana today. All of this had an important effect on a host of questions from recruitment patterns to areas of administrative responsibility.

It was not until 1899 that the final steps were taken to systematize the administration of Bechuanaland. In that year a boundary commission delineated the boundaries of five of the major ethnic groups and established reserves for them. The boundaries defined in 1899 are the basis of Botswana's districts today. In the same year a tax system was begun with the establishment of a ten-shilling hut tax to be collected by the chiefs. By 1913 the imperial government's grants-in-aid had been phased out.

Gradually, after the turn of the century, the authority of resident magistrates became defined in a number of areas. Because their authority was based initially on the regulation of Europeans in the tribal reserves and on direct administration in scheduled areas (areas or blocks of land alienated by Europeans), two colonial administrative structures and policies evolved, one for Africans and one for Europeans. In the European areas, the resident magistrate had direct responsibility for the district's population, both European and African. In the reserves the magistrate heard cases involving Europeans and heard serious cases and appeals from the chief's *kgotla* (traditional open meeting). Magistrates conveyed government instructions and communications to the chiefs, disbursed government monies, and in general were supposed to be in close touch with the life of the Africans in the reserve and with the activities and needs of their chiefs. An early minute by H. F. Neale, resident magistrate in the Bamangwato reserve in 1926, provides a glimpse of the magistrates' perceptions of their responsibilities and their attitudes toward their job.

> Most of my mornings are taken up with interviews with the chief, and sundry Europeans. There are Civil and Criminal cases which at the present moment are accumulating, and it is seldom that I can attend to correspondence and Revenue work for any length of time. . . .
> There is also the gaol. . . . The gaol and the prisoners require attention as do also the local police Messengers.
> I have now seven Criminal Cases for trial on the roll. Three of these are cases of alleged Murder and none of them have been worked up ready for trial as they should be by the police. . . . The position is entirely unsatisfactory. . . .
> . . . Monthly Returns, Store Returns, [and] Grain and Forage Returns have to be rendered monthly to the C.O. Police, Palapye Road by the [Serowe] police. . . . The Police Store has also to be kept and checked regularly and the Station Ledger and Diary kept. . . .
> Crime in this Reserve appears to be on the increase. Probably the fact that kaffir beer drinking is now universal may account for it. . . .
> This Station is the Headquarters of a large District, with the second largest number of Europeans and three times the number of natives of other districts.[22]

Parallel Rule and the Resident Magistrate

The unwilling, step-by-step nature of British intervention in Bechuanaland had a decisive impact on the set of relationships established between the resident magistrate and the chief in the reserve areas. In 1885 the high commissioner defined the role of the British government as follows:

> We have no interest in the country to the north of the Molopo, except as a road to the interior; we might therefore confine ourselves for the present to preventing that part of the Protectorate being occupied by either filibusters or foreign powers doing as little in the way of administration or settlement as possible.[23]

This external protectorate assumption led to a set of policies (perhaps nonpolicies would be a more appropriate term) that developed around the terms "parallel rule" (also known as "dual rule"). Tswana societies, it was assumed, were being protected from outside forces; thus, the establishment of the Bechuanaland Protectorate should have no impact upon internal relations between chiefs and their subjects.

Under parallel rule the British colonial government and "native" authorities were "two parallel and mutually exclusive administrations."[24] The European administration would regulate the affairs of traders, labor recruiters, missionaries, and other Europeans in the district, and the magistrates would mediate relations between the chiefs and the outside world. This would give the chiefs a great deal of latitude in the management of tribal affairs, and the European administration would be content to collect taxes from the chiefs and, if necessary, help to maintain order. As long as order was maintained and taxes collected, the resident magistrates were not concerned with how the chiefs ruled or how their subjects fared.

During the first decade of British rule, administrative pronouncements did little to dissuade the chiefs from believing that the Protectorate meant anything other than simply protection. Speeches and correspondence with chiefs throughout the 1880s and into the 1890s promised noninterference in the internal affairs of the Tswana polities, and stated policy was to leave the settlement of disputes between chiefs to the contending parties. Policy directives from Colonial Secretary Joseph Chamberlain encouraged the chiefs' sense of autonomy.[25]

Autonomy of the chiefs was unsatisfactory and unworkable from the beginning, however. Resident magistrates began to interfere in the affairs of the chiefs as soon as they arrived in the reserves. The seeds of intervention were contained in the Order in Council of 1891 that authorized the high commissioner to provide "for the administration of justice, the raising of revenue, and generally for the order and good government of all persons."[26] Under the 1891 Order in Council, the British government made the high commissioner the legislative authority in the High Commission Territories by giving him the power to issue proclamations.

After 1895 intervention was an ever-present possibility. Early attempts by the resident magistrates to intervene with the chiefs were couched as requests to amend or modify traditional law. In such instances the administration "did not itself impose the laws it wanted, but preferred to have them made for the Tswana by their own chiefs."[27] This policy was a reflection, in part, of the directives laid down by the Order in Council of 1891. It may also have been a reflection of the lack of personnel at the district level.

Under government by proclamation the chiefs' powers were gradually eroded. Furthermore, the high commissioner had the overall power to depose or banish a chief. Tlou, in his discussion of the history of northwestern

Botswana, provided a case study of the changed relationship between the chiefs and the administration. In 1892 the high commissioner sent a magistrate and small police detachment to Maun, Ngamiland to control the sale of arms and enforce British laws. In his letter to Sekgoma, chief of the Batawana people, the high commissioner wrote of his "friendship" and assured him that the magistrate was appointed

> to deal with white men and to regulate the sale of ammunition under a law which is now in force in the country. . . . You are still chief and you will recommend the men who are to get permits.[28]

By 1906 the administration had deposed Sekgoma on the pretext that he was unpopular among his people. In fact, almost from the establishment of British administration in Maun in 1894, friction had developed between Sekgoma and the various magistrates. The source of the friction "was what Sekgoma saw as interference in Tswana affairs. He regarded the magistrates merely as advisors, rather than policy makers. The magistrates . . . , on their part, asserted their superiority over the king."[29] The deposition of Sekgoma pointed the way to the future. From that time on, the administration would intervene in the internal disputes within the Tswana reserves "and impose solutions favorable to imperial interests regardless of the people's feelings or traditional procedures."[30]

During the first three decades of British rule, as the colonial administration moved to entrench its authority in Bechuanaland, instances of interference in the affairs of the chiefs were numerous. That interference ultimately affected the entire fabric of the social, political, and economic life of the Tswana polities. The role of the chief as the traditional authority, for example, was gradually transformed into a financially and politically dependent, bureaucratic extension of the colonial administration.

In their search for stability, the British tended to support the chiefs unquestioningly against their critics and rivals. Colonial rule destroyed the traditional balance of power between the chiefs, their advisors, and the *kgotla*, and the chiefs became increasingly authoritarian. Befeathered and dressed in a parody of the colonial military uniform, the chiefs were now far removed from the nineteenth century monarchs who had ruled the Tswana polities prior to British intervention.

By the late 1920s and early 1930s, British officials and their critics had become more dissatisfied with the parallel rule concept. Leonard Barnes, a frequent critic, wrote a scathing attack on the effects of British administration. Barnes argued, in a book that was fairly widely read at the time, that the chief "had (been) materially strengthened but morally weakened by the Government which stands between him and the consequences of failure or neglect."[31] The colonial administration had weakened the tribal system as a whole by its unqualified support of the authority of the chiefs at the expense of other institutions, especially the *kgotla*. Because their authority was supported in almost all cases by the resident magistrates, the chiefs, unless they challenged colonial rule, could do more or less as they wished. The tribal council had become "mere couriers and flatterers, selected by himself [the chief] as being easy tools to work with."[32] Traditional rule had become harsher and more capricious, and there had been a loss of personal freedom among the Batswana since the beginning of the Protectorate.

Lord Hailey articulated the viewpoint of the colonial administration toward parallel rule and its weakness.

> [Parallel Rule was] a system in which the Government denied itself the power to intervene in the administration of a wide range of matters intimately affecting the welfare of the majority of the population, while a relatively small ruling class, highly tenacious of its position *vis-à-vis* the Government, could combine to render ineffective any measure projected by the latter for the betterment of the people at large.[33]

At least formally, the government was, in effect, denying itself the power to intervene in the administration of a wide range of matters. This passive approach to colonial administration in the High Commission Territories was in contrast to the prevailing colonial values in the rest of British Africa after World War I, where trusteeship and indirect rule were the order of the day.

Despite the weakness of parallel rule as a theory and its nonapplicability in practice, little was done before the mid-1930s to implement reforms in Bechuanaland's administrative system. The overriding assumption was that British rule in Bechuanaland was temporary, and the transfer of all three of the High Commission Territories to the Union of South Africa was imminent. Only after 1930 did dissatisfaction with the condition of the High Commission Territories become apparent, and it would take another decade for reforms to be introduced.

The Question of Transfer

Colonial rule in Bechuanaland was influenced from the beginning by the question of its possible transfer, with the other two High Commission Territories, to the Union of South Africa. The question of transfer became an issue that generated a complex set of relationships between the high commission administration and Britain on the one hand and the various regimes in South Africa on the other. It was an issue that continued to plague colonial administrators and Batswana traditional leaders until almost the eve of independence.

The 1910 Act of Union creating the Union of South Africa exacerbated the uncertainty over Bechuanaland's future. The Preamble of the Act of Union said, "It is expedient to provide for the eventual admission into the Union, as Provinces or Territories, of such parts of South Africa as are not originally included therein." This sentence referred to the High Commission

Territories and Rhodesia and provided the legal basis for a South African claim of eventual incorporation.

In 1910 officials both in the Cape and in London felt that the pains from the Boer War were still too fresh and missionary pressures too strong for immediate incorporation. In London "the official view was that the passage of time was clearly in favour of the transfer and it saw no reason to doubt that this would take place in due course." [34] Transfer was to take place after consultation with the chiefs and approval by the British Parliament.

After Union in 1910, demands for incorporation began almost immediately, with vehement protests against incorporation from the paramount chiefs in each of the three High Commission Territories beginning around the same time. The question of transfer was raised for the first time by General Botha in 1911, and periodically the South African government would reintroduce the question to various British administrations. Although refusal was never absolute, transfer was always delayed on the grounds that the time was not right for a final decision.

Attitudes toward the transfer issue gradually changed. Two factors influenced British attitudes. The British had anticipated that with the consummation of the Union, traditional attitudes on the questions of race in the former Boer states would be influenced progressively by the more liberal views of the Cape. African opinion in Bechuanaland, which opposed transfer in any form, would undergo a favorable change as the Cape's more moderate politicians established control over the Union. Neither of these conditions came to pass, however.

The turning point occurred in 1927 when Secretary of State for Dominions L. S. Amery (who was also the colonial secretary) visited Swaziland. Dominions Office interest in the High Commission Territories dates from that trip. In a letter that same year to General Hertzog, then prime minister of South Africa, Amery stated that there could be no question of the High Commission Territories' transfer to the Union for many years because thus far the imperial government had made no attempt to provide anything close to an adequate or "progressive" government for the three territories. "We have simply treated them as sort of [a] game reserve . . . with little done for them. They have been 'little stagnant pools,' the same people staying on the same jobs for 20 years on end." [35] Administrators in London, led by Amery, found transfer an increasingly unacceptable option after 1927 and directed their attention toward a long-term postponement of the question, with the result that "the discussions over transfer never seemed quite to have the air of reality which they possessed until the mid-twenties." [36]

Opposition to transfer was solidified by the Statute of Westminster in 1931 and the Status of the Union Act in 1934. With the Statute of Westminster:

> South Africa [had] thus to her own satisfaction established her independence as a sovereign independent state. The implications of

her constitutional status were far reaching in relation to the High Commission Territories. . . . If a clear transfer had taken place . . . South Africa . . . could legislate as it deemed fit in regard to the High Commission Territories and neither the British Government nor the Westminster Parliament would be in a constitutional position to express any opinion.[37]

After passage of the Status of the Union Act, South Africa almost immediately began the dismantling of the limited, non-European civil rights and franchise legislation in the Cape. This action pointedly illustrated the vulnerability of the High Commission Territories were transfer to occur. By the early 1930s,

it was becoming increasingly clear to the authorities in Great Britain that the application of the policy of segregation on which Gerneral Hertzog's Government was now entering, and which was to culminate in the enactment of the Representation of Natives Act of 1936, was likely to make it increasingly difficult for any British Minister to sponsor in Parliament a proposal for the transfer of the Territories to the Union.[38]

Uncertainties over the future of Bechuanaland were bound to affect the administration in the Protectorate. The key to the history of all three High Commission Territories was that "for forty years of this century the British Government worked on the underlying assumption that they would be incorporated into South Africa."[39] As a result of the uncertainty over the future of the territories, the administration took a wait-and-see attitude toward policy issues. The question of transfer was often used as an excuse, however. British government files are replete with examples of administrators using the question in connection with the postponement of political or economic change. Annual payments of British grants-in-aid to Bechuanaland were less than £175,000 between 1946 and 1960, extremely low in comparison with payments to other British colonies. Substantial British assistance to the country did not begin until after 1962 when Bechuanaland's path toward independence was assured.

The more immediate effect of the impending transfer, however, was its psychological impact on the administrative officers. Within Bechuanaland, administrative officers were always sensitive to the transfer issue in terms of both administrative policy and their careers. Any administrative question or any request "from either European or African interests within the Protectorate, was always considered in light of any possible impact on the Union of South Africa."[40]

The individual administrative officers in the High Commission Territories were personally concerned with discussions of transfer. These administrators were almost always of British, or British South African, descent and were not likely to feel comfortable with the thought of transfer to the Union. According to Hugh Ashton, a former district commissioner in Bechuanaland, "most officials would [have disliked] being transferred to the

Union service, which insisted on bilingualism [English and Afrikaans], is reputed to favour Afrikaans and to be governed by political favouritism."[41] It seems likely that administrators in the field supported continued British control either by preventing any political "rocking of the boat" over the whole gamut of interests that South Africa saw as sensitive, or by keeping Tswana traditional authorities sensitive to threats of transfer and generally "sharpen[ing] Tswana awareness of their position and . . . [allowing] public opinion to form."[42]

The transfer issue was to be raised periodically by the South African government throughout the colonial period. Every time the issue was raised, it was firmly opposed by the Tswana chiefs. The uncertainty over the issue of transfer is a partial explanation (as well as an excuse) for the lack of a British commitment to developing educational, social, and physical infrastructures in Bechuanaland, whose administration was parsimonious even in comparison with other British colonial territories. Colonial officials were affected by the transfer issue and, as a result, administrative activity remained in a state of limbo during most of the colonial period.

Conclusion

Britain's intervention in the affairs of the Tswana polities, during the last half of the nineteenth century, froze traditional political institutions in the form that existed during the 1880s. Colonial rule interrupted a pattern of segmentation and regrouping that went back at least a thousand years. Although hierarchical state structures existed long before colonial intervention, the Tswana polities were transformed significantly by eighty years of British administration. Independent kingdoms became bureaucratic extensions of British imperial rule.

Patterns of political and administrative control were established very early in the Bechuanaland Protectorate and were related to the origins of the protectorate status. A combination of forces led to British involvement in the Tswana polities: concern over regional competition with the Boers and the Germans, anticipation of mineral exploitation and European settlement in the area, and the need to use Bechuanaland as an access point for Britain's central African conquests.

Relations between colonial administrators and chiefs remained vague during the first years of Bechuanaland's administration. The murky concepts of the external protectorate and parallel rule were contradicted from the beginning as colonial administrators involved themselves in the affairs of Africans and in the disputes among traditional elites. The pre-colonial balance of power within the traditional administration was weakened by colonial intervention, and little else was established in its place.

The administrative model of political control in Bechuanaland evolved from the British government's assumption of an impending transfer of the High Commission Territories to South Africa. Because of this assumption, patterns of recruitment and procedure were adopted almost unchanged from the Cape Colony. Four decades of economic neglect were also a result of the transfer question. British tax monies would not be used in a territory soon to be given over to a foreign power.

Administrators in Bechuanaland saw themselves, and were seen by others, as working in a backwater administration in an economic as well as a literal desert. The police force and clerical origins of the administrators and their close ties to a small circle of English-speaking South Africans meant that, even from the standpoint of observers in Britain, the colonial administration was hopelessly stagnant, parochial, and outside the grander vision of imperial policy. The administrative officer's magisterial responsibility, based on Roman-Dutch law, was directed toward more limited goals of control in Bechuanaland than in the more northern British African colonies where, after the Nigerian and Tanganyikan pattern, the field administration's political role was stressed. Prior to 1933 administrative behavior as well as patterns of recruitment were an extension of those in the Union of South Africa.

The hardening of political lines and the developing racial policy in the Union meant that transfer became increasingly unlikely after 1927, and both officials and public opinion leaders in England began to take a second look at the High Commission Territories. Old school imperialists, such as L. S. Amery, who was then Colonial Secretary, came to the conclusion that if Bechuanaland and the other two High Commission Territories were not going to be transferred to South Africa, then they should be brought more fully into the imperial pattern of governance. By the early 1930s, policy makers in the Dominions Office were ready to introduce a number of changes in order to pull Bechuanaland into the imperial administrative orbit. It is to these proposed changes and their impact on the evolving administrative state that we now turn.

Notes

1. Isaac Schapera, "Notes on the Early History of the Kwena," *Botswana Notes and Records*, vol. 12 (1980), p. 83.

2. Both quotes in Q. N. Parsons, "On the Origins of the bamaNgwato," *Botswana Notes and Records*, vol. 5 (1973), p. 82.

3. Martin Legassick, "The Sotho-Tswana Peoples Before 1800," *African Societies in Southern Africa*, Leonard Thompson, ed. (London: Heinemann, 1969), p. 87.

4. Parsons, "On the Origins of the bamaNgwato," p. 91.

5. Both quotes in Legassick, "The Sotho-Tswana Peoples," p. 102 and p. 106, respectively.

6. Isaac Schapera, *The Tswana: Ethnographic Survey of Africa, South Africa, Part III* (London: London School of Economics Monographs, 1952), p. 15.

7. William Duggan, "The Kweneng in the Colonial Era: A Brief Economic History," *Botswana Notes and Records*, vol. 9 (1977), p. 42.

8. Anthony J. Dachs, "Missionary Imperialism—The Case of Bechuanaland," *Journal of African History*, vol. 13, no. 4 (December 1972), p. 657.

9. Anthony Sillery, *Founding a Protectorate: History of Bechuanaland, 1885–1895* (The Hague: Moulton & Co., 1965), p. 20.

10. Jack Halpern, *South Africa's Hostages: Basutoland, Bechuanaland and Swaziland* (Harmondsworth: Penguin, 1965), p. 81. See also Anthony Dachs, "The Road to the North, the Origin and Force of a Slogan," Occasional paper no. 23, Central African Historical Association, Salisbury, Rhodesia, 1969, pp. 1–13.

11. Paul Maylam, *Rhodes, the Tswana, and the British: Colonialism, Collaboration and Conflict in the Bechuanaland Protectorate, 1885–1899* (Westport, Conn.: Greenwood Press, 1980), p. 126.

12. Jack D. Parson, "The Political Economy of Botswana: A Case in the Study of Politics and Social Change in Post-Colonial Societies," (Ph.D. diss., University of Sussex, 1979), p. 57.

13. For a discussion of administrative roles in Botswana see Louis A. Picard, "Role Changes Among Field Administrators in Botswana: Administrative Attitudes and Social Change" (Ph.D. diss., University of Wisconsin, Madison, 1977).

14. See Sillery, *Founding a Protectorate*, p. 57.

15. Leonard Barnes, *The New Boer War* (London: Hogarth Press, 1932), p. 193.

16. Notes on the Ranking of Resident Magistrates, 6 March 1923, C.O. 692/5354/11667 Establishments. Public Records Office, London. In all references to government files, the first reference will include, where appropriate, the file's title, date, and number; the author, if known, of minutes and memoranda; and the collection, depository, and location of depository, if possible.

17. Barnes, *New Boer War*, p. 191.

18. Margaret L. Hodgson and William G. Ballinger, *Britain in Southern Africa*, no. 2, *Bechuanaland Protectorate* (Alice, South Africa: Lovedale Press, 1933), p. 66.

19. See Leo Marquard, *The Peoples and Policies of South Africa* (Boston: Little, Brown and Co., 1966), p. 115.

20. Lord (William M.) Hailey, *An African Survey*, revised ed. (London: Oxford University Press, 1956), p. 271.

21. Akinola Aguda, "Legal Development in Botswana from 1885 to 1966," *Botswana Notes and Records* vol. 5 (1973), p. 56.

22. Botswana National Archives, file no. p.f. 17.

23. Bechuanaland Protectorate, *Blue Book* C 4588, p. 106, Botswana National Archives.

24. Hailey, *An African Survey*, 1956, p. 272.

25. Hodgson and Ballinger, *Britain in Southern Africa*, p. 114.

26. Lord (William M.) Hailey, *Native Administration in the British African Territories*, part V, *The High Commission Territories: Basutoland, the Bechuanaland Protectorate, and Swaziland* (London: Her Majesty's Stationery Office, 1953), p. 324.

27. Isaac Schapera, *Tribal Innovators: Tswana Chiefs and Social Change, 1795–1940* (London: The Athlone Press, 1970), pp. 53-54.

28. Thomas Tlou, "A Political History of Northwest Botswana to 1906" (Ph.D. diss., University of Wisconsin, Madison, 1972), p. 260.

29. *Ibid.*, pp. 286-287.

30. *Ibid.*, p. 293.

31. Barnes, *New Boer War*, p. 168.

32. *Ibid.*, p. 169.

33. Hailey, *Native Administration*, part V, p. 134.

34. Hailey, *An African Survey*, 1956, p. 177.

35. Amery to Hertzog, n.d., D.O. 9/8/v.4/D.10918. *Future of High Commission Territories.*

36. Ronald Hyam, *The Failure of South African Expansion, 1908–1948* (London: MacMillan, 1972), p. 124.

37. Isobel Edwards, *Protectorates or Native Reserves?* (London: Africa Bureau, 1956), pp. 10-11.

38. Hailey, *An African Survey*, 1956, p. 179.

39. Halpern, *South Africa's Hostages*, p. 51.

40. Gilfred L. Gunderson, "Nation Building and the Administrative State: The Case of Botswana" (Ph.D. diss., University of California, Berkeley, 1971), p. 167.

41. In Sir Charles Dundas and Hugh Ashton, *Problem Territories of Southern Africa* (Johannesburg: South African Institute for International Affairs, 1952), p. 41.

42. Gunderson, "Nation Building," p. 170.

3

Bureaucrats and Chiefs:
Contradictions of Indirect Rule

In 1927 Colonial Secretary L. S. Amery toured the High Commission Territories. During the course of his trip, he wrote to London about his reactions to those neglected territories. "I had no idea what a backwater they were until I saw them myself. All the new stir and life in the Colonial Empire has hardly touched them at all."[1] The new stir and life that Amery referred to were the ideas of indirect rule that moved throughout Britain's African possessions after the first World War. Following Amery's 1927 visit, events were set in motion to introduce indirect rule in Bechuanaland and the two other High Commission Territories.

The Indirect Rule Concept

The British policy of indirect rule demonstrates clearly the dilemmas and contradictions inherent in the bureaucratic policy process that was the colonial system. When the British introduced indirect rule, they used bureaucratic means to modify political structures. The form of traditional administration that followed was supposed to be autonomous while also controlled by the district administration. Bureaucratic structures would give birth to political structures. The improbability of this pattern of political change becomes apparent when we examine indirect rule as a form of local government and administration.

Lord Lugard's experiments in northern Nigeria and Sir Donald Cameron's policy in Tanganyika set the stage for indirect rule experiments elsewhere. Lugard published *The Dual Mandate in Tropical Africa* in 1922.[2] Ultimately, in one form or another, commissions throughout east, west, and southern Africa recommended the adaptation of the indirect rule model until by the 1930s, the policy had arrived in the High Commission Territories in southern Africa.

As Lugard envisioned the policy, it was essential that, wherever possible, British administrators govern their subjects through the subjects' own institutions. Although in theory, African political institutions were not conterminous with traditional authority, "in practice, indirect rule laid heavy emphasis on the role of the chief in the government of African peoples, even for those peoples who traditionally did not have political as distinct from religious leaders."[3]

Indirect rule, as it was to be introduced in Bechuanaland, was "interventionist" in that its origins were in the dissatisfaction with the more passive ideas of parallel rule. Under indirect rule, the administrative officer would not only be an advisor to the chief but also an agent of reform for the structures and processes of local administration.

As a policy of local administration, the specific model chosen for contrast with Bechuanaland was Tanganyika.[4] Tanganyika, whose administration had been entirely reconstructed after World War I, represented an approach that approximated an experiment in colonial planning and the controlled introduction of the indirect rule. By contrast, Bechuanaland had no system of local administration. The Tswana chiefs acted *imperia in imperio* and functioned with a minimum of supervision from a district administration with an almost nonexistent budget.

The Dominions Office proposed the establishment in Bechuanaland of a system of "native [administration] incorporated into a single system of government and subjected to the continuous guidance, supervision and stimulous of European Officers."[5] The Tanganyika model suggested five major areas of reform in the system of traditional administration:

1. Legislation would regulate the powers and jurisdiction, administrative and judicial, of chiefs, subchiefs, and headmen.
2. Administrative officers who had been specifically selected to train traditional authorities would be appointed to the district administration.
3. Tribal councils would be introduced to provide an element of participation at the local level.
4. Tribal treasuries would be created under the supervision of the district officer.
5. A trained, salaried, clerical administration would administer the affairs of the tribe.

The latter concept, bureaucratic in nature, would transform patterns of local-level control throughout Bechuanaland.

Indirect rule in tropical Africa was "aimed at eventually providing a democratic system of local government based on some form of representation."[6] Proponents argued that traditional forms of government in many parts of Africa had democratic features. With the encouragement of colonial officials, these features could be modernized and would flourish at the local level. Indirect rule in Bechuanaland was more ambiguous, however. In southern Africa, prior to World War II, no such democratic theory existed. It was not until the 1950s that "democratization" of traditional structures became official government policy.

The indirect rule system contained contradictions from the beginning. In an important, critical analysis of the Tanganyika model of indirect rule, Ralph Austen argued that the "conscious expressions of dedication to Indirect Rule were consistently accompanied by the strengthening of a bureaucratic apparatus which denies the possibility of autonomous local development." The position of the chiefs deteriorated during the colonial period when they were neither completely government agents nor fully autonomous.[7]

> In theory, [the colonial administrator was] committed to encouraging the growth of miniature African governments functioning spontaneously and semi-autonomously upon a traditional base. In terms of administrative practice, however, their aim had to be the creation of local subunits which could be conveniently manipulated to produce modernization.[8]

As a result indirect rule came to be seen throughout Africa as a contradiction to, rather than an expansion of, participatory local government. After World War II administrators throughout British Africa abandoned indirect rule. With the approach of independence, European administrators and African politicians would look outside the traditional framework for a local administration.

Impetus for Reform

Officials in the Dominions Office began to discuss political reforms for the High Commission Territories in 1930. At the same time a series of incidents occurred in Bechuanaland, including the deposition of a Kwena chief and an attempted assassination of the Ngwato regent, Tshekedi Khama. Mafeking officials professed concern about a number of issues in the territory, including the perennial problem of Tswana treatment of the Basarwa ("Bushmen").[9] In addition, Bechuanaland administrators expressed dismay about the amount of tribal money handled by chiefs and about the chiefs' use of unpaid labor.

In March 1930, Sir Eric Machtig, an assistant secretary in the Dominions Office, proposed that reforms should be made in Bechuanaland along the lines of the "Tanganyika Reforms" of Sir Donald Cameron.[10] Later that year, the resident commissioner ordered district officers throughout Bechuanaland to raise the issue of "the future of the tribal administration" at the *kgotla*.[11]

The colonial administration officially committed itself to administrative reforms in 1931. In a memorandum to resident commissioners, the high commissioner in Pretoria stated that the imperial government intended to apply the principles of "Imperial Administration" to the High Commission Territories. Bechuanaland's resident commissioner made this clear to the Native Advisory Council in 1931. The new proposals for administrative reform were discussed by the chiefs without conclusion.

Two critical studies of Bechuanaland appeared in print in London in 1932: *The New Boer War*, by Leonard Barnes, and *Britain in Southern Africa, No. 2: Bechuanaland Protectorate*, by Margaret Hodgson and William Ballinger. They were followed in 1933 by the official and highly critical Pim Report.[12] The public criticism made an attentive British public aware of the situation in the High Commission Territories and provided an impetus for colonial officials to introduce reforms.

Both Barnes and Hodgson and Ballinger made scathing attacks on the economic and administrative neglect in Bechuanaland and the other High Commission territories. Barnes pointed to "stagnation" in Bechuanaland and commented, "the regime as a whole has resulted not only in incoherence of policy but in a general laxity of administration."[13] Hodgson and Ballinger pointed to "the rising tide of criticism which the failures of the last half century in Bechuanaland have induced."[14] Describing the chiefs as tyrannous and absolute monarchs, both books called for a reform of traditional authority and an introduction of indirect rule in southern Africa.

Sir Alan Pim's report went far beyond either the Barnes or the Hodgson and Ballinger studies in its investigation of both the administrative and the economic and financial situations in Bechuanaland. Pim argued that colonial authorities had failed to bring traditional institutions in Bechuanaland into conformity "with the essential requirements of a modern civilized Administration."[15] There had been no definition of the powers and responsibilities of the chiefs, nor had there been any attempt to train "the Native Authority [in] executive or judicial responsibilities or in sound principles of government." Pim called for the development of a single "government machine" at the district level, with the tribal administration as an integral part of this machine. The powers of the chiefs should be carefully defined by the imperial government, and safeguards for handling income introduced. Funds should no longer be "paid to and handled by the Chief alone. . . . It is clearly desirable that some satisfactory arrangement for controlling tribal expenditure should be devised." To Pim, the problems of traditional administration and financial arrangements were centered on the "unscrupulous or extravagant chief," a situation which could be controlled, if not avoided, under strict indirect rule.[16]

The publication of the Pim Report in 1933 coincided with the formal announcement of the indirect rule reforms in Bechuanaland. At the 1933 session of the Native Advisory Council, the resident commissioner, Charles F. Rey, announced that the indirect rule proposals would be implemented in a high commissioner's proclamation the following year. Opposition to the new proposals was immediate and would continue for the better part of the next decade.

The 1934 Reforms

The two 1934 proclamations (the Native Administration Proclamation of 1934 and the Native Tribunals Proclamation of 1934) represented a tentative first step toward the application of indirect rule in Bechuanaland. The new policies followed directly from the earlier ideas of parallel rule. Both assumed that Europeans and Africans were culturally distinct and that the European colonial power, representing the superior civilization, should govern its African subjects through the Africans' own political institutions. Indirect rule differed from the earlier concept, however, in the assumption that indigenous institutions would be modified significantly by the colonial government. The district officer was to function as an agent of political change that would fundamentally transform the responsibilities of chiefs, subchiefs, and headmen throughout Bechuanaland. The purpose of indirect rule was to impose greater levels of control by the colonial administration over recalcitrant chiefs. Chiefs had to be "more or less fully subordinated" and the administrative system changed "from a [formal] two tier system of European and African rule to a single hierarchy system in which the African 'layer' [would be] completely subordinated to the European 'layer.'"[17]

The immediate reason for the shift to indirect rule was a deepening dissatisfaction with the majority of Bechuanaland's chiefs. With two exceptions, Bathoen II of the Ngwaketse and Tshekedi Khama of the Ngwato, colonial officials saw chiefs as backward, lazy, incompetent, and, in several cases, drunkards. Colonel Charles Rey, the resident commissioner, minuted in 1934, "At the moment officers of the administration, though without statutory authority, are guiding and holding up a system which as presently constituted appears perfectly hopeless."[18]

In December 1934 Sir Herbert Stanley, the British high commissioner, signed the two proclamations, concerning the duties and powers of the chiefs and tribal courts, that brought the traditional administration directly under government control. As an attempt at indirect rule, the 1934 proclamations were cautious. The Native Administration Proclamation laid down procedures for the designation and recognition of chiefs, and provided the means for dealing with those chiefs who did not or could not perform their duties as the government expected. It also provided for the nomination of councilors with whom the chiefs were required to consult in the exercise of their functions, defined their other duties in detail, and made conspiracy against the chiefs or subversion of their authority statutory offenses.[19]

The Native Tribunals Proclamation regulated the composition and procedure of traditional courts, defined their area of jurisdiction, and curtailed several types of punishments which previously had been imposed. The

Native Tribunals Proclamation further required the traditional courts to keep records of their cases and provided for a mechanism by which decisions could be appealed to the district commissioner.

The effect of the 1934 Proclamations was to make the chiefs a link between the administration and the Africans and ensured that the chiefs were under the control of the district commissioner. In effect the chiefs became subordinate government officers responsible for the maintenance of law and order in the district. They were required to obey all instructions and orders from the resident commissioner and to give any assistance requested to the district administration.

Two of the chiefs, Bathoen II and Tshekedi Khama, challenged the 1934 Proclamations. Their challenge illustrates the breakdown in communications between the chiefs and the government and the lack of influence that colonial authorities had over traditional administration at the time. Both chiefs reacted sharply to what they saw as a break with Tswana tradition and a unilateral decision to change the relationship between the chiefs and the British. The two chiefs filed suit in December 1935, and the court had to deal with two substantive issues. First, did the government have the right to interfere with traditional laws and customs? In this respect three aspects of the 1934 proclamations were objectionable: (1) the creation of tribal councils changed the chiefs' relationship with the *kgotla*; (2) restrictions were placed on the judicial authority of the chiefs; and (3) provision was made for government intervention in and regulation of the selection and deposition of chiefs. The second issue in the suit followed from the first: were the two proclamations in violation of the rights of the Ngwato and Ngwaketse peoples as defined by the original treaties of protection?

The attitudes of the two chiefs were clear. As Tshekedi perceived the situation, it was the authority of the district commissioner and the administration which was limited, not the authority of the chiefs. Each chief had a direct relationship with the high commissioner and any lesser authority, whether the resident commissioner in Mafeking or the district commissioner in Serowe, could deal with local and nonsubstantive matters only.[20] Parallels were drawn between the roles of an ambassador (the district commissioner) and head of state (the chief). The argument ultimately went back to the original negotiations between the Tswana chiefs and the imperial government. The external protectorate idea was never far from the chiefs' minds during this period.[21] As Bathoen II stated in his case challenging the 1934 proclamations, the district commissioner should have a quasi-diplomatic relationship with the chief. All authority in the reserves should be with the traditional authority, not the other way around.[22]

There was, of course, no possibility that the High Court would overrule the 1934 proclamations. Ignoring possible violations of the original nineteenth century treaties, the High Court argued that the Bechuanaland administration had "unfettered and unlimited power to legislate for the government and administration of justice among the tribes of the Bechuanaland Protectorate and that this power was not limited by Treaty or Agreement."[23] Ultimate authority lay with the High Commissioner and the colonial administration. The court concluded this to mean that the colonial administration could modify traditional authority in any manner deemed necessary by the imperial government.

What were the motivations of the chiefs? In a 1975 interview, Bathoen said that he and Tshekedi had expected to win the case inasmuch as the customary rights argument was hard to avoid. The original Order in Council establishing a protectorate clearly protected the chiefs from infringement of their rights. He went on to say that he felt the chiefs had won because their realistic goal was to gain a modification of the two proclamations, rather than a return to the *status quo ante*. Bathoen also made it clear that their opposition to the proclamations was based on a concern for the constitutional integrity of the tribe since, as he pointed out, in the event of Bechuanaland's transfer to South Africa, the tribe's only defense would be the residual rights of traditional authority.[24]

The failure to give effect to the provision for tribal councils and other such provisions of the 1934 proclamations and the decision in 1943 to revise the 1934 proclamations were, according to Lord Hailey, a vindication of the chiefs since the provisions "constituted so wide a departure from previous custom that they were difficult to operate in practice."[25]

Thus, while the Bechuanaland government won the legal skirmish with the chiefs, in a sense it lost the major battle. In his farewell report to the High Commissioner, Rey admitted as much. He blamed much of the failure to implement the reforms on the district administration, however, particularly on their lack of training and ability that left the entire responsibility for implementing indirect rule to the resident commissioner and the government secretary.[26]

Tribal Treasuries and the 1943 Reforms

In spite of the inauspicious start of indirect rule, the next stage, the introduction of tribal treasuries (the Native Treasuries Proclamation of 1938), went fairly smoothly. This was so partially because of Rey's replacement by Charles Arden-Clarke in 1936. There had been a personal animosity between Rey and Tshekedi Khama, which neither tried to hide. Arden-Clarke, on the other hand, "after observing that Tshekedi was the key to the country's advancement . . . thereafter sought Tshekedi's advice and criticism."[27] Both Bathoen and Tshekedi had attempted to establish tribal treasuries earlier but had been rebuffed by the administration. In 1937, after long consultations with Bathoen and Tshekedi, Arden-Clarke announced to the Native Advisory

Council that measures were being taken to introduce tribal treasuries. Proclamations to that effect were issued in 1938.

The predecessor to the tribal treasury was the tribal fund. These funds, under the personal control of the chiefs, were abolished by the tribal treasury proclamations in order to prevent the "misuse of funds" by the chiefs. A treasury would require an institutionalized administration, and the monies would be used for tribal purposes as opposed to the chiefs' inclinations. Revenue would come from a fixed percentage (35 percent at first) of the total tax collected in the district served by the tribal treasury. Supervision of the treasuries was left to the district commissioner, who would ensure that all chiefs and their councilors fully understood the new treasury system.[28]

In 1942, a progress report on changes in Bechuanaland since the Pim Report took note of the new system of tribal administration and the establishment of the tribal treasuries. While praising the achievements of the past ten years, the report indicated the need to reevaluate certain aspects of the tribal administration system, pointing to elements of the 1934 proclamations that had not been implemented. Among other things, the failure to create tribal councils meant that there was no representative body in the district to influence the behavior of the chiefs.[29]

Lord Harlech (Ormsby-Gore) became the high commissioner in southern Africa in 1941 and was shocked to see how little of the policy of indirect rule had been implemented. A strong advocate of indirect rule, Harlech initiated a new series of discussions with the chiefs to modify the tribal administration system again.[30] The chiefs accepted Harlech's 1943 proclamations partially because of the success of the treasury system. The Harlech proclamations modified the 1934 proclamations in a number of ways. In order to make tribal councils more palatable to traditional authorities, Harlech's proclamations stripped them of so many of their responsibilities that the councils "practically dropped out of the picture."[31] The proclamations also restored more responsibility for the selection of chiefs to the people, while retaining the government's right to intervene.

It might be argued that the policy shifts between 1934 and 1943 were little more than window dressing inasmuch as ultimate authority over the people of Bechuanaland remained in the hands of the administration. The struggle over the issue of authority, however, does illustrate the amount of influence, although largely negative, that a capable chief could have on the colonial administration. This continuity of traditional influence would affect politics after independence in 1966.

Ultimately, the introduction of the indirect rule reforms had a major impact on the administrative and political authority of district-level colonial administrators. Patterns of political control developed at the district level after 1934 would continue to be used after independence.

Indirect Rule in the Districts

The indirect rule reforms defined patterns of political control and change in Bechuanaland prior to independence. Between 1937 and 1949, when the Seretse Affair effectively put an end to the indirect rule experiment, district colonial officials were responsible for the establishment of the new system of traditional administration in the larger reserves of eastern and northern Bechuanaland. The first major attempt to alter traditional structures came with the introduction of tribal treasuries after 1937. Chiefs traditionally controlled certain amounts of tribal wealth, usually in the form of cattle and agricultural produce. By the early 1930s, an increasing percentage of this wealth was in the form of money derived from such sources as the rents paid for traders' stands, or fines imposed in the course of trials. The chiefs also imposed special levies for specific purposes such as the maintenance of schools or the construction and maintenance of roads.

Tribal Finances and Institutional Authority

Before 1937 little attempt was made to distinguish between the personal resources of the chief and the corporate finances of the tribe. All income went to the chiefs and was controlled by them alone. The first attempt to establish a separate tribal fund occurred in Kweneng in 1902 when the Bechuanaland government insisted that certain royalties paid to the tribe be set aside for social purposes. Before 1920 other chiefs began to keep some income apart for expenditures on education and other similar projects deemed necessary by the *kgotla*.

Government dissatisfaction with tribal finances increased in the 1920s. There were several cases of alleged mishandling or misuse of funds. Between 1930 and 1937 several district commissioners, with the concurrence of the Mafeking Secretariat, took control of all tribal funds except the two largest, those of the Ngwaketse and Ngwato.[32]

Interventions were first thought to be temporary. It was assumed that the district officers would instruct the chiefs in accounting and, after a short period, would be able to withdraw to an indirect supervisory role. This did not happen. The district administration became a permanent fixture in the financial affairs of the reserves in most of the eastern districts. Moreover, district officers often simply did the books themselves on a regular basis, rather than trying to train the chiefs.

The shift to tribal treasuries in 1938 occurred as a result of a congruence of several factors:

1. The two most capable chiefs, Bathoen and Tshekedi, in their concern to avoid the kind of direct intervention by their district commissioners that had occurred in other areas, began to press for an institutionalized

financial arrangement similar to that which existed in Nigeria and other British colonies.

2. District-level officials, both individually and at the annual administrative conferences, concluded that an effective tribal administration would need a salaried staff that could be trained in administrative and financial routines.

3. The Resident Commissioner Arden-Clarke concluded that many district officers would continue to administer the books themselves unless a system for training traditional authorities were institutionalized.[33]

4. The indirect rule model itself called for the introduction of a treasury system as the culmination of local administration reform.

At the time of the proclamation on tribal treasuries (1938), district officials received detailed guidelines from the Secretariat on the structure and authority of the treasuries.[34] The district administration in seven of the districts (a number of the smaller districts were excluded) began discussions with the chiefs on the institutionalization of the treasury system. Tribal funds, where they existed, were abolished, and their assets were transferred to the new treasuries.

District administrators proceeded in a number of directions on the basis of the Secretariat guidelines. District commissioners sought potential tribal treasurers (and other staff) who could be hired and trained by the colonial administration. Funds were transferred from the chiefs' control, or in some cases from the district commissioners' accounts, to the treasuries. Whereas the 1934 reforms had caused considerable controversy, the introduction of treasuries met little resistance. Although political events soon bypassed the indirect rule system, the formation of treasuries was significant. For the first time an indigenous bureaucratic structure had been introduced at the local level. Patterns of administrative behavior had been developed that would affect the administrative capacity of the country for many years after independence.

The Limits of Indirect Rule

In addition to the establishment of tribal treasuries, district officials, by the beginning of World War II, had started to introduce a variety of other political and administrative changes into the tribal administrations. Tribal councils had been selected and had begun to meet, albeit on an irregular basis, in a number of districts. Judicial limits were defined and procedures institutionalized. Throughout the territory colonial officials began to take a more active role in the inspection and regulation of tribal courts. Administratively, district officials became more involved in the establishment of crucial bureaucratic procedures and mechanisms of communication, some of which continue to be used in independent Botswana.

Some chiefs responded favorably to colonial initiatives at the district level after 1943. Capable chiefs, such as Bathoen and Tshekedi, often moved more quickly than their district officers. More resistance came from colonial officials in the district, many of whom felt uncomfortable in the role of innovator. Their resistance became most apparent during World War II. Several district officers, certainly short-handed and overworked, suggested that because of wartime needs and manpower shortages, new patterns of finance and administration should be postponed until peacetime.

District files and the minutes of district commissioners' conferences indicate that the human resource shortages were only part of the cause of administrative resistance. Lord Harlech complained that "district commissioners regard their job as sitting in their offices doing clerical or court work and are reluctant to stand up to the chiefs or establish real contacts with the common people."[35] Many officials were insecure in their responsibilities and did not understand the importance of the reforms.

By the end of the war, however, a system of mutual understanding had evolved in some districts between the colonial officials and the chiefs. New roles evolved on both sides. In many districts chiefs had "taken off the backs of the Administrative Officers much of the grinding routine of police, court and magisterial duty."[36] Traditional authorities had developed a vested, if dependent, interest in the colonial system and held a privileged position in a very poor society.

Problems remained, however. The indirect rule system did not work as it was intended throughout the colonial period. Archival evidence suggests that the passage of time influenced Dominions Office perceptions of the success of indirect rule. Once the new policy had been in effect for a certain amount of time, administrators simply assumed that indirect rule was being implemented. As late as 1944, Lord Harlech had pointed to problems in the implementation of the reforms.[37] At some time in the policy implementation process, however, a subtle change of emphasis began to occur, and administrators began to assume that a previous policy had been implemented. For example, in 1945, Sir Evelyn Baring, the new high commissioner, made note of what he saw as the keenness among all officers for the development of indirect rule as a policy, and he stated that the "Native Authority system" was "well established."[38]

Archival evidence does not confirm Baring's optimistic view. There is no evidence of any change either in the abilities of the chiefs and headmen or in their acceptance of indirect rule reforms. Many colonial officials continued to ignore the policy. Although active resistance to indirect rule had receded in the postwar period, there was little enthusiasm for the reforms.

Between 1945 and 1950 in London and Pretoria, dissatisfaction with the evolution of tribal administration or with the role played by colonial officials in the promotion of indirect rule is not apparent, in contrast to the regularly expressed concerns during the war years. It had come to be accepted that the shift to the indirect rule system was complete. In 1946 Sir Evelyn Baring concluded that

> the British "Native Authority" works well. . . . The integration of indigenous institutions into the system of Government works well. Tribal sense is strong. Most chiefs are better educated than their people. They are influencial but checked by the rough democracy of the tribal meetings where all business is discussed and speech is very free.[39]

Yet the tribal administrations were not "working" in 1950 any more than they had worked prior to 1943. By the time the Bechuanaland Protectorate entered the last full decade prior to the nationalist period, indirect rule had failed as a mechanism of participation and administrative control. The evidence suggests that the system was fundamentally flawed and would be abandoned in the aftermath of political controversy.

The Chiefs vs. Colonial Authority

Lord Hailey, in his study of Bechuanaland's administration, made a detailed examination of district-level administration. He came to the conclusion that most tribal administrations were not working. Only two of the seven districts examined functioned properly, there were mixed reports on two others, and three were outright failures.[40] Anthony Sillery, then resident commissioner, concurred. Colonial officials had difficulty in developing a financial system, even for the larger ethnic groups. In discussing the exercise of drawing up tribal treasury estimates, Sillery complained that

> In the course of this work . . . many irregularities in the conduct of the tribal finances have been discovered. Nothing dishonest of course, but consistent overspending of votes and unauthorized expenditure, sometimes deliberate and sometimes based on ignorance of financial procedures.[41]

Hailey, while not an opponent of colonial administration, complained of the low level of budgetary support for tribal authorities. (See Table 3.1.) Absurdly low district budgets as late as 1950 clearly indicated the limited ability of the tribal administration system to effect even minimal social support in the districts.

Tribal administrations as a whole were not working effectively or independently in 1950. The Malete and the Tlokwa chieftanships, went through long periods of weak regency. The government used its authority to suspend recalcitrant chiefs in Kgatleng and Ngamiland from power. Tribal authorities complained about severe shortages of staff with clerical and accounting skills, and district officials made frequent, detailed audits because of the irregularity of accounts. In a number of districts, the district

Table 3.1   Reserve Administration Budgets, 1950

	Revenue £	Expenditure £	Surplus/ Deficit, £	Revenue % of Total
Tlokweng	1,094	1,514	- 420	01.47
Malete	2,340	2,257	+ 83	3.15
Kgatleng	8,557	8,367	+ 190	11.51
Kweneng	10,803	10,297	+ 506	14.53
Tawana	8,018	7,807	+ 211	10.78
Ngwaketse	14,407	14,128	+ 279	19.37
Ngwato	29,140	27,830	+ 1,310[1]	39.19
Total	£74,359	£72,200	£+2,159	100.00

Source: Lord (William M.) Hailey, Native Administration in the British African Territories, Part V: Basutoland, The Bechuanaland Protectorate, and Swaziland (London: Her Majesty's Stationery Office, 1953), pp. 229–281.
[1]The excessive Ngwato surplus reflects the breakdown of Ngwato's administrative capacity after the clash between Tshekedi and Seretse Khama in 1949.
(£ = U.S. $5.00)

commissioners maintained two sets of treasury books and tax registers, one in tribal headquarters and one in the district government camp. Routine accounting matters continued to take a great deal of colonial officials' time, "to the exclusion of all other duties."[42] Finally, no attempt was made to introduce the indirect rule system in the western part of the country outside of the reserve areas, which meant that reforms were almost nonexistent in three of Bechuanaland's ten districts.

The colonial system was hierarchical, and from the beginning entrants into the system were socialized in hierarchical patterns. The indirect rule reforms represented an attempt to introduce bureaucratic principles to traditional authority systems. According to Max Weber, societies are freed from the status quo of tradition when authority is based on clear and impersonal rules.[43] The clash between Weberian principles and traditional administration is illustrated by the attempts to explain to chiefs the fine distinctions between their personal responsibility as chiefs and their bureaucratic responsibility for the functioning of tribal administration. The question of tax collection illustrates the hybridization of this issue.

In 1946 the legal advisor to the high commissioner chastized Bechuanaland officials for misunderstandings over "native taxes." These taxes were collected by the chiefs or their representatives then paid directly to the government. None of this money went into the tribal treasuries. District officials argued that they were unable to convince most chiefs that in effect they were expected to wear two hats. One hat carried personal responsibility for such functions as tax collection, and the other (bureaucratic) hat carried administrative responsibilities for supervisors of a staff of people who performed administrative tasks, such as the operation of tribal treasuries. The chiefs often confused the two roles and would try to make up for tax deficiencies by using funds from the treasuries. Many chiefs could not understand why, as head of the tribal administration, they could delegate responsibility for tribal accounts to the treasuries, but could not delegate responsibility for tax collection to subordinates. Nor could they understand why tax money and tribal treasury money could not be combined. Matters were further complicated by the Bechuanaland government itself which regarded the chiefs as both its agents and its local authorities, the latter charged with providing services for the people. The distinctions being made were complex, and records from this period do not indicate whether colonial officers were significantly better able to make these distinctions than the chiefs were.[44]

The nature of the documentation on the colonial period is such that the researcher dependent upon written archives is presented with events only from the point of view of the colonial official. Thus, the motives of the chiefs are unclear. To what extent were the chiefs unable to understand financial and administrative arrangements? A chief's "ignorance" could be a kind of sham, a form of subtle resistance to excessive colonial interference in what the chiefs perceived to be their internal affairs. Common sense suggests that a combination of both explanations is likely.

Local Administration Prior to Independence

The broader political implications of the Seretse Affair will be examined in Chapter 6. Suffice it to say at this point that the political crisis involving Seretse Khama, his uncle Tshekedi Khama, and the Bamangwato (later Central) district administration effectively terminated the indirect rule experiment in Bechuanaland. The conflict over the implications of Seretse's marriage to a British woman, Ruth Williams, resulted in the collapse of the tribal administration in Serowe and the appointment of the district commissioner as the tribal authority. By the time the political controversy ended (in 1956), colonial officials clearly had abandoned the principles of indirect rule. It was less clear, however, what form local administration would take.

In 1947 Arthur Creech Jones, secretary of state for colonies, issued a circular memorandum calling for the rapid development of local government throughout Africa. In this dispatch he emphasized the need for an efficient and democratic system of local councils.

> I wish to emphasize the words efficient, democratic, and   local. . . . I
> use these words because they seem to me to contain the kernel of the
> whole matter; local because the system of government must be close

> to the common people and their problems, efficient because it must
> be capable of managing local services in a way which will help to
> raise the standard of living, and democratic because it must not only
> find a place for the growing class of educated men, but at the same
> time command the respect and support of the mass of the people.[45]

His memorandum caused the concept of indirect rule to fall out of fashion throughout much of British Africa, and colonial administrators scrambled to establish some form of elected council at the district level.

The effect of the 1947 memorandum was much less immediate in the three High Commission Territories, however. Because the question of their transfer to the Union of South Africa had not been resolved, neither London nor Pretoria interpreted the memorandum as being applicable to the High Commission Territories. As a result the *kgotla* was the only recognized, district-level voice for the Africans in Bechuanaland until the mid-1950s. Similarly, trial by *kgotla* replaced the system of tribunals that had been proposed in the 1934 proclamations. Furthermore, attempts to reintroduce the concept of a tribal council were not made until after 1957.

Nonetheless, after 1950 administrators grew increasingly dissatisfied with the system of tribal administration in Bechuanaland. Lord Hailey toured the High Commission Territories in late 1950 and early 1951 in preparation for his book on "native administration" in southern Africa and concluded that the tribal administration had failed to provide a mechanism for local level participation. He questioned the extent to which

> the present system of Native Administration provides a sufficient
> opportunity for the people at large to voice their own views or makes
> an adequate contribution to the process of educating them in the
> responsibility for handling their own affairs.[46]

Hailey speculated about the possibility of establishing local councils at the village and subdistrict level but described as "fantastic" any proposal to establish councils that would be separate from or outside the tribal administration. The population of Bechuanaland "[is] far removed from the stage in which any form of election to such councils is possible or desirable."[47]

Throughout the 1950s, colonial authorities continued to see local government reform within the context of tribal administration. Administrators broadened the base of the chiefs' representatives within the district and allowed them to control expenditures on certain minor local projects.[48] This action would not threaten the chiefs as long as no attempt was made to increase council authority at the tribal level. Colonial timidity was partially caused by the fear of a replication of the events that had followed the 1934 proclamations, that is the vigorous resistance to government policy by Bechuanaland's senior chiefs.

In June 1954 a circular memorandum was sent to all district commissioners by the government secretary, indicating that Government should initiate and encourage development towards a more representative form of government in tribal areas, taking care to avoid measures that might maim the chieftainship. . . . [Councils will not be introduced at the native authority level since] it will be remembered that the 1934 Native Administration Proclamation foundered because it imposed on the chief an obligation to designate a council and not to act independently of it.[49]

The Secretariat envisioned that councils should first develop at a subordinate native authority level. In order words, subdistrict councils would be created in two stages. The first stage would be a meeting of administrative officers to gain general agreement on major objectives. The second stage would be "to persuade a committee composed largely of Africans to adopt those views themselves insofar as they are acceptable to them."

The district administrators were invited to comment upon the government's proposals in writing. Their commentaries not only provide a colonial perspective on the issue of local government nearly ten years before independence but also demonstrate the low esteem in which the tribal administration was held in 1954, some twenty years after indirect rule was introduced in Bechuanaland.

A memorandum prepared by one administrator, entitled "Constitutional Reform—The Bechuanaland Protectorate" gave vent to administrative frustration with tribal authorities and reflected the attitudes of at least some colonial administrators about the nature of the society within which they worked. Describing the tribal administration as both isolated and hostile to British rule, the administrator argued that

the native administrations as at present extent do not work. They are regarded as an imposition of the central government and are not regarded as belonging to the people. They are inefficient and barely function. As local governments they are incompatible with the traditional system of tribal administration which the backwardness and hostility preserve.

[Nevertheless] I can see no point in setting up any sort of District or Tribal Councils so long as it is possible for any assemblage [referring to the *kgotla*] of recalcitrant, aged and hateful savages . . . to veto every wise decision that the younger and even more reasonable elders may make.[50]

Another colonial official described what he felt was the fundamentally "deteriorating . . . [and] unsound state of Chieftainship" in Bechuanaland.[51]

By the mid-1950s British administrators had come to the conclusion that indirect rule had been an abject failure. Yet, "the institution of the Chieftainship should be upheld."[52] In 1954 colonial officials limited initiatives at the district level to a request that the chiefs appoint a more formal council from the *kgotla* membership and make the *kgotla* purely advisory.

Instead of local councils, one administrator suggested the creation of "Development or Finance Committees" that would allocate a certain amount of money within specific areas under the overall authority of the Native Authority. Such a committee would not be a threat to the chiefs, and they would be less likely to oppose the proposal.

An element of local government reform after 1955 broadened the tribal administration by increasing the authority of the existing tribal councils at the district level. Time and again, however, the administrative correspondence from this period refers to the 1934 reforms which had floundered on the issue of tribal councils because of their implied loss of power for the chiefs. Tribal councils had almost dropped out of the picture completely after the 1943 proclamations. With this precedent in mind, all talk of strengthening the tribal councils rested on the principle that "the Chief and Subordinate Native Authority . . . still and always will be the main inspiration on the executive side, they will see that schemes are carried out by the tribes, and will keep interest alive."[53] It was believed necessary to avoid any whittling down of the chiefs' position because of the office's symbolic significance among the bulk of the population and the generally stabilizing effect of the chiefs' rule on the administration of the district. According to M. R. B. Williams, later the architect of Botswana's system of local government, "up until the late 1950s, as a result of the legacy of Indirect Rule, the District Administration continued to see government policy administration through the chief and the chief's views were seen as reflective of the needs of the area."[54]

In 1955, the government formed a committee of African Advisory Council (AAC) members to study the question of subdistrict councils, with the hope that these councils would evolve "naturally" from the chiefs' deliberations with the AAC. In a major concession to the chiefs' autonomy, officials assured the AAC that subdistrict councils would vary in membership and function from district to district. Mafeking asked district officials to draw up plans on the basis of conditions in each area that would then be presented to the chiefs for approval. By 1957, at least on paper, subcouncils were established in most districts.

The Local Councils Proclamation of 1957 embodied attempts at evolutionary reform. The proclamation mandated the institutionalization of tribal councils at the district level, with an elected executive committee to assist the chief. The executive committee membership included individuals elected indirectly through the *kgotla* and a number of the chief's nominees. The major effect of the proclamation was to shift the emphasis of tribal administration "from Chief as 'sole Native Authority' to Chief-in Council."[55] Movement toward representative government at the district level was rather slow considering the fact that in 1957 Ghana was already an independent state.

Even the 1957 proclamation's limited changes met with resistance from some of the senior chiefs. Prior to 1957 tensions had been high between the tribal administration on the one hand and both Mafeking and the Commonwealth Relations Office on the other. A number of chiefs had resisted the 1954 Secretariat initiatives, limited though they were. London's instructions on local government reform were "followed in only a half hearted way, [and] the chiefs opposed any change, fearing that their powers might be whittled down."[56] A number of chiefs agitated for the establishment of a legislative council during that period and opposed local government reform as an unsatisfactory substitute for broader territorial change.

A limited breakthrough occurred in 1956 as a result of the resolution of the Seretse affair. The agreement announcing the settlement also provided that "a Tribal Council of an advisory nature [would] be established for the Bamangwato."[57] When, as a result of the agreement, Tshekedi Khama was again empowered to play a part in the affairs of the Bamangwato (Central) District, he changed his approach to the question of tribal government. Forbidden from the chieftainship as a result of the settlement, he took on the position of tribal secretary of the Bamangwato tribal council (after some initial British resistance). From that point on, Tshekedi was eager to strengthen the administrative and political capability of the tribal council, which he may have viewed as a base from which to assume territorial political office as constitutional developments occurred. Although Tshekedi's death in 1959 prevented his emergence as a territorial politician, his change of position on the issue of councils ended effective resistance to local government reform and paved the way for more substantive reforms during the 1960s.

Administrative thinking on local government changed very little, very late. The 1957 Local Councils Proclamation was only an enabling act that was to be put into force gradually by the district commissioners after negotiation with the chiefs in each of the eight tribal reserves. In Bechuanaland,

> reform of the old tribal system was slow and gradual—indeed until the early sixties there was little real change. Tribal Administration remained as the personal rule by the chief who . . . made his own decisions in matters of administration. He was closely associated in this attitude with the central government which acted to a great extent through the District Commissioner.[58]

The decision to shift from a tribal administration to an elective council system in the early 1960s came about because the tribal administration was "overtaken by Constitutional changes at [the] national level."[59] The sequence of events was thus the reverse of the normal pattern in most of British colonial Africa.

It was not until 1963 that a local government committee of the Legislative Council was set up to make recommendations on improving the structure of local government. The committee met with the assumption that the modernization of local government would necessitate the development of a system that did not depend upon the personality and office of the chief. The committee recommended, therefore, that a system of district councils with a majority of elected members be established to provide services that would be financed from local revenue.[60]

After 1962 British officials concluded that independence was near, and colonial administrators wrote to Kenya and Tanganyika for documentation on their programs of local government reform. Those reports formed the basis of Legislative Council discussions in 1963 and 1964. Most of the tribal administrators continued to oppose elected local government as late as 1964. One colonial observer, very close to the scene, commented, "politically many of the chiefs were far to the right of the Europeans. They hated any new developments. They had old attitudes, craved despotic powers and harkened back to the Chamberlain agreements as a justification for their position."[61]

Government proposals on district councils were given preliminary approval in 1964 by the Legislative Council, and, after somewhat grudging, nonbinding consideration by the newly established House of Chiefs, were finally approved with the passage of the Local Government Act in 1965. As one of the architects of the 1965 law put it, "operating in a newly centralized administrative system [the Ministry of Local Government and Lands] we were given 15 months to change the whole system of local government." The rapidity of events came close to overwhelming colonial officials in the final few years of British rule.

The Local Government Law established a system of nine British-style district councils (The Northeast District Council represented both Ngamiland and Chobe districts) which were to replace tribal councils as the basic unit of local government. Chiefs were left with only their judicial and some of their ceremonial functions along with mainly symbolic representation in a body separate from the national assembly. Elections for district councils were held at the same time as Parliamentary elections, in March of 1965, and the new councils officially came into existence on July 1, 1966, only three months before independence. The new councils were thus clearly a phenomenon of the post-colonial period.

Conclusion

The colonial administration in Bechuanaland had a number of stated goals after 1933, both administrative and political. The primary political goal was to introduce a system of indirect rule in Bechuanaland comparable to the system being established in other parts of British Africa. Indirect rule would fundamentally transform the traditional political leadership in Bechuanaland, binding it to colonial authorities for its future existence. Administratively the colonial authorities hoped to synthesize traditional authority with Weberian patterns of hierarchical administration imported by the colonial government.

The impact of indirect rule on Bechuanaland's evolution was not inconsiderable. The policy increased the capability of colonial authorities to control events in the districts and changed the traditional administration into a salaried bureaucracy. Under indirect rule the chief was replaced by the district commissioner as the supreme political authority in the district and a solidified administrative structure linked the various parts of the territory to the administrative center in Mafeking. Although the effects of indirect rule were to linger well into the post-colonial period, as a policy it began to be discarded almost as quickly as it was introduced.

By the early 1950s colonial leaders had become disenchanted with indirect rule as a pattern for local government. It was in the area of political change that results were most disappointing for officials in Mafeking and Pretoria. The postwar period started out with great optimism for indirect rule as an innovative alternative to the previous policy of parallel rule. There was some feeling that the tribal administration could be "modernized" and made more responsive to the popular will. Within five years, however, the policy had collapsed in the context of a major political crisis (the Seretse affair) that paralyzed the administration for almost seven years. It was not only the Seretse Affair that was to blame for the ultimate abandonment of indirect rule as a policy, however. From the beginning a number of district officers were suspicious of indirect rule and uncomfortable with their role in its implementation. The contradiction between the formal commitment of administrators to strengthen traditional political institutions and an inevitable tendency of administrators to intervene increasingly in the affairs of the district resulted in the undermining of pre-colonial political structures. No other political arrangements were available as alternatives to the hierarchial authority of the district commissioner.

Although by 1950 colonial administrators had become sceptical of the entire policy of indirect rule, the shift to a new political strategy in the district and the formation of district councils was to wait another twelve years. Both the traditional authorities' resistance to change and the continuing uncertainties about Bechuanaland's ultimate future caused this delay. It was only during the last decade of British colonial rule that administrative policy, as a result of changing political realities in southern Africa and in the rest of the continent, began to prepare for a Bechuanaland without Britain. Economic as well as political developments began to mirror developments in Britain's larger colonies in east and west Africa. The British local government system, the Westminster model, and the Colonial Development and Welfare programs were the three devices most commonly used to prepare a patchwork of political and economic structures which would tide a territory through to independence, and it was this patchwork which propelled Bechuanaland toward independence in 1966.

Undoubtedly the collapse of the indirect rule system of local government should be seen in conjunction with the policy's more general abandonment in the wake of African nationalist pressures. The impact of indirect rule and the manner of its abandonment over a relatively long period of time, however, are important to an understanding of both the colonial political process and the pattern of political control which exists in Botswana today.

The contradiction between the bureaucratic initiative of such a major public policy as indirect rule and the absence of a political process to generate policy alternatives continues to reflect the nature of the state in Botswana today. At the heart of indirect rule was the idea of "guided autonomy," which is a contradiction in terms. The failure of indirect rule after 1950 would force the administration in Mafeking to resort to direct political control over the districts. The district administration, as we shall see in Chapter 4, was much more conducive to the political control function of government than it was to the introduction of social or political change. The improbability of bureaucratic structures giving birth to political institutions and social and economic policy was not limited to the colonial period. Patterns of decision making and the role of administrative elites in the decision-making process are part of the package of political characteristics inherited by the successor state after 1966.

Notes

1. L. S. Amery to "Billy" (W. A. Edgecume, Amery's private secretary), 24 September 1927, D.O. 9/7/v.3/D.10443. Public Records Office, London.

2. Lord (Frederick D.) Lugard, *The Dual Mandate in Tropical Africa* (London: Oxford University Press, 1922) and Lord (William M.) Hailey, *Native Administration in the British African Territories*, part V, *The High Commission Territories: Basutoland, the Bechuanaland Protectorate and Swaziland* (London: Her Majesty's Stationery Office, 1953).

3. Michael Crowder, *West Africa Under Colonial Rule* (Evanston, Ill.: Northwestern University Press, 1968), p. 169.

4. The decision to make use of Tanganyika as a model was made explicit in a 1931 memorandum, High Commission Territories Secretariat Files, S. 458/1—Dominions Office, London.

5. *Ibid.*

6. Clyde R. Ingle, *From Village to State In Tanzania: The Politics of Rural Development* (Ithaca, N.Y.: Cornell University Press, 1972), p. 112.

7. Ralph A. Austen, *Northwest Tanzania Under German and British Rule* (New Haven: Yale University Press, 1968), pp. 254, 255.

8. *Ibid.*, p. 179.

9. E. S. B. Tagart, *Report on the Conditions Existing Among the Bamangwato Reserve of the Bechuanaland Protectorate and Certain Other*

Matters Appertaining to the Natives Living Therein (Pretoria: Government Printer, 1933).

10. Minute, Sir E. Machtig, 7 March 1930, in D.O. 35/365/1053/2.

11. Isaac Schapera, *Tribal Innovators: Tswana Chiefs and Social Change, 1795-1940* (London: The Athlone Press, 1970), p. 60.

12. Sir Alan Pim, *Financial and Economic Position of the Bechuanaland Protectorate, Report of the Commission Appointed by the Secretary of State for Dominion Affairs, March, 1932*, Parliamentary Report, Cmd. 4368 (London: His Majesty's Stationery Office, 1933).

13. Leonard Barnes, *The New Boer War* (London: Hogarth Press, 1932), p. 198.

14. Margaret L. Hodgson and William G. Ballinger, *Britain in Southern Africa*, no. 2, *Bechuanaland Protectorate* (Alice, South Africa: Lovedale Press, 1933), pp. 73 and 78.

15. Pim, *Bechuanaland*, p. 28.

16. Pim, *Bechuanaland*, pp. 104, 107, and 103, respectively.

17. Jack D. Parson, "The Political Economy of Botswana: A Case Study of Politics and Social Change in Post-Colonial Societies" (Ph.D. diss., University of Sussex, 1979), pp. 77-78.

18. Charles Rey, Memorandum, 25 October 1934. S.397/4.

19. Isaac Schapera, *Tribal Innovators*, Botswana National Archives, Gabonne, Botswana, pp. 61-62.

20. Interview with Tshekedi Khama by Charles Rey, 6 April 1935, S.423/23 and S.422/7—Native Proclamations of 1934 Botswana National Archives, Gabonne, Botswana.

21. Oral interviews with Bathoen Gaseitsiwe (Bathoen II), Gaborone, 2 September 1975 and 17 July 1980.

22. S.448/1-10—Tshekedi Khama and Bathoen II. Court Case Botswana National Archives, Gabonne, Botswana.

23. *Bechuanaland Protectorate Report, 1959* (London: Her Majesty's Stationery Office, 1959), p. 83.

24. Oral interview with Bathoen Gaseitsiwe, 2 September 1975.

25. Hailey, *Native Administration*, part V, p. 222.

26. D.O.35/906/y26/3. Public Records Office, London.

27. Richard P. Stevens, *Lesotho, Botswana and Swaziland: The Former High Commission Territories of Southern Africa* (New York: Praeger, 1967), p. 132.

28. Circular Memorandum on Native Treasuries, No. 6146/3 of 13 February 1937.

29. Lord Harlech to Arden-Clarke, 19 December 1942. D.O.25/1172/y708/1—Progress Report: Bechuanaland Protectorate. Public Records Office, London.

30. Harlech to Clement Attlee, Secretary of State for Dominions, 16 April 1942, D.O.35/905/y8/68—Administration, Basutoland, Bechuanaland, and Swaziland.

31. Lord Hailey, *Native Administration*, part V, p.225.

32. S.313/13—Control of Tribal Funds. Botswana National Archives, Gabonne, Botswana.

33. Minute, Charles N. Arden-Clarke, Resident Commissioner, 15 November 1937, S.313/13. Botswana National Archives, Gaborne, Botswana.

34. Circular Memorandum No. 8499, 25 October 1937—Native Treasuries.

35. Lord Harlech to Sir Eric Machtig, 16 June 1941, in D.O.35/900/y1/65—District Administration.

36. In D.O. 35/1172/y701/1/4.

37. Lord Harlech to Sir Eric Machtig, 5 August 1944, in D.O. 35/174/y756/20—Staff: General Matters.

38. Sir Evelyn Baring, Report on a visit to the Bechuanaland Protectorate, 1945, in D.O.35/1172/y701/12.

39. Sir Evelyn Baring to Eric Machtig, 18 September 1946, D.O.35/1425/y706/8—Transfer of the Territories to the Union.

40. See Hailey, *Native Administration*, part V, pp. 229-281.

41. Anthony Sillery, Resident Commissioner, Minute, 11 February 1948, in S.477/3.

42. *Ibid.*

43. See H. H. Gerth and C. W. Mills, eds., *From Max Weber* (New York: Oxford University Press, 1972).

44. Based on material in S.331/5—District Commissioner's Conferences.

45. Dispatch from the Secretary of State for the Colonies to the Governors of the African territories, 25 February 1947.

46. Hailey, Native Administration, part V, p. 328.

47. Ibid., pp. 332 and 329, respectively.

48. Circular Memorandum No. 58, 25 June 1954, private archives, London. This document and others referred to below that do not have an archival number were made available to the author by a number of former Bechuanaland administrative officers, from their personal archives, during the course of research carried out in London in June and August of 1979.

49. Circular Memorandum No. 58, 1954.

50. Both quotes from "Constitutional Reform—The Bechuanaland Protectorate," n.d., prepared for 1954 Administrative Conference, private archives, London.

51. "Development of Local Government," n.d., written in the mid–1950s, private archives, London.

52. "Development of Local Government—Part II," n.d., private archives, London.

53. John F. Millard, Divisional Commissioner, Northern Protectorate, "A Plan for the Development of African Local Government in Bechuanaland," prepared for the 1954 Administrative Conference, private archives, London.

54. M. R. B. Williams, Oral interview, London, 10 August 1979.

55. William Tordoff, "Local Administration in Botswana Part I," *Journal of Administration Overseas*, vol. 12, no. 4 (October 1973), p. 174.

56. Oral interview with Sir Peter Fawcus, 18 August 1979.

57. Mary Benson, *Tshekedi Khama* (London: Faber and Faber, 1960), p. 272.

58. J. E. S. Griffiths, "A Note on the History and Functions of Local Government in Botswana," *Journal of Administration Overseas*, vol. 10, no. 2 (April 1971), pp. 130-131.

59. Simon Gillett, "The Survival of Chieftaincy in Botswana," *African Affairs*, vol. 72, no. 287 (April 1973), p. 181.

60. S.596/7—Administrative Conference, 1963. The administration's major concern was the relationship between the new councils and the traditional administration, and for this reason it was decided that the relationship between the two had to be strictly defined by law. See also Griffiths, "Local Government in Botswana," pp. 131-132.

61. Oral interview (name withheld by author), 18 August 1979.

4

Recruitment in the Civil Service: The Oxbridge Model, Localization, and the Protectorate

In a speech to senior officials of the High Commission Territories (Basutoland, Bechuanaland, and Swaziland) in October 1941, Lord Harlech, then the high commissioner for South Africa, stated,

> We are bureaucratic governments in both form and structure, and in the absence of the clash and counter-clash of active public opinion among the masses we need constant self-criticism and reminder of our obligations to progress and the government.[1]

Lord Harlech's statement touches on the dilemma of the bureaucratic formulation of policy that was characteristic of colonial rule, a dilemma to which at least some colonial officials were not insensitive.

The indirect rule reforms discussed in Chapter 3 were coupled with administrative changes in southern Africa. Colonial policy makers in the 1930s viewed changes in the recruitment of colonial officers as related directly to their policy goal of moving Bechuanaland and the two other High Commission Territories closer to the mainstream of British colonial administration.

Prior to 1935 Bechuanaland's administrative structure and patterns of civil service recruitment were part of a southern African administrative pattern that had evolved in the late nineteenth century. There were no direct ties with the political entity in Britain. The Dominions Office relationship with the Southern Africa High Commission and the high commissioner's relationship with the resident commissioners were largely undefined. Patterns of recruitment were informal and based on personal contacts and friendships. For the most part, administrators were not university educated but rather developed an apprenticeship relationship with more experienced district officials.

Officials in London saw patterns of administration in British southern

Africa as both alien to those in the rest of the empire and inferior to the Colonial Administrative Service (CAS) ideal developed by Sir Ralph Furse, the officer in charge of recruitment at the Colonial Office. After 1935 attempts were made to restructure the Bechuanaland administration in order to bring it in line with the "Imperial Model" that had developed north of the Zambezi River. Ideally, administrators sent to southern Africa would be recruited from Oxford and Cambridge, where they could be inculcated with the values of British imperialism and the principles of indirect rule.

Changes in recruitment began to affect the colonial administration in southern Africa after World War II, but within a few years the African Civil Service Association had begun to make demands for greater localization. Although some systematic attempt was made to address the question of localization after 1961, a national civil service system was not developed in Bechuanaland prior to independence in 1966. The primary effects of colonial personnel policy prior to independence were to solidify Bechuanaland's link to the British colonial system as transfer to South Africa became less likely. Beyond this, changes in recruitment patterns after 1935 and 1961 contributed significantly to the high socio-economic status of civil servants and other public sector employees in independent Botswana.

The Dominions Office and Bechuanaland Protectorate

Prior to 1925 the Colonial Office had exhibited little interest in Bechuanaland and the other High Commission Territories. At the beginning of 1926, responsibility for Britain's relations with its self-governing territories (Canada, Australia, New Zealand, Ireland, and South Africa) was transferred from the Colonial Office to the newly created Dominions Office and those five territories came to be known as dominions. Due to the close links between South Africa and the High Commission Territories (and the special status of Southern Rhodesia) the southern African territories were also made the responsibility of the Dominions Office. Critics argued that this transfer to the Dominions Office was linked to the relative lack of development in Bechuanaland and the other territories.[2] Somehow, the quality of administrators in the Dominions Office was thought to be inferior. These accusations do some injustice to the Dominions Office in that no major policy changes occurred during the forty years that the Colonial Office ruled Bechuanaland, and within five years of Dominions Office control, officials had debated and implemented a series of reforms that prevented the transfer of the High Commission Territories to South Africa. Figure 4.1 illustrates official lines of communication between the Dominions Office and Bechuanaland.

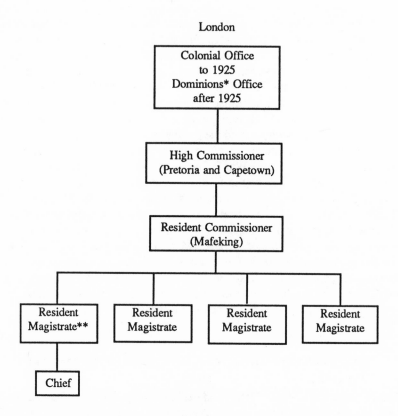

London

Colonial Office
to 1925
Dominions* Office
after 1925

High Commissioner
(Pretoria and Capetown)

Resident Commissioner
(Mafeking)

Resident Magistrate** | Resident Magistrate | Resident Magistrate | Resident Magistrate

Chief

*Commonwealth Relations after 1947
**District Commissioner after 1936

Figure 4.1 Official Lines of Communication in Bechuanaland.

Dominions Office Policy Makers

The effect of the shift from the Colonial Office to the Dominions Office should not be exaggerated. Dominions Office policies toward Bechuanaland generally followed lines set by the Colonial Office. Throughout the colonial period, the Dominions Office and the Colonial Office continued to maintain a common staff establishment. After the Dominions Office was created, it set up a specific department to deal with colonial matters. A handful of civil servants made decisions on major policy questions referred to them by the High Commission in Pretoria.

Seven individuals held primary responsibility for the Bechuanaland Protectorate during the 1930s and 1940s. (See Table 4.1.) There is little

Table 4.1 Dominions Office Officials with Primary Responsibility for Bechuanaland Protectorate

Name and Date of Entry to Service	Rank in 1938	Year Became Primarily Responsible for Dominions Office Responsibilities over Bechuanaland	Prior Experience in the Colonial Office
Sir E. J. Harding 1903	Permanent Undersecretary	1920	Clerk, General Department; Board of Trade; Distressed Colonial Seaman; Private Secretary to Secretary of State; Secretary to Royal Commissions; Resettlement of ex-servicemen
Sir Harry F. Batterbee 1915	Asst. Under- secretary of State	1925	Private Secretary to Secretary of State; First Class Clerk, East African Division
Sr. E. G. S. Machtig 1915	Asst. Under- secretary of State	1930	First Class Clerk, East Africa Department; Principal, General Division; Principal, Tanganyika and Somaliland Division
C. W. Dixon 1911	Asst. Secretary of State	1916	Clerk, General Department; Clerk, Crown Colonies, East Asia Division; Private Secretary to Undersecretary of State
H. N. Tait 1911	Asst. Secretary of State	1912	Clerk, Chief Secretary's Office, Ireland; Secretary to Rhodesian Commission
R. A. Wiseman 1916	Asst. Secretary of State	1925	Clerk, Ministry of Shipping; Private Secretary to Under- secretary of State
P. Liesching 1920	Principal	1927	Joint Secretary of Colonial Survey Commission; Secretary to Committee on Private Enter- prise in Tropical Africa; Asst. Principal Tanganyika and Somaliland Division; Private Secretary to Parliamentary Undersecretary of State; Asst. to High Commissioner for Great Britain in Canada

Sources: *Colonial Office Lists, 1900–1925* (London: Waterlow & Sons, Annual); *Colonial and Dominions Office Lists, 1926–1949* (London: Waterlow & Sons, Annual).

indication that the assignment of these officials to the Dominions Department of the Colonial Office, and later to the Dominions Office, was based on any special characteristics that distinguished them from their counterparts in the other departments of the pre-1925 Colonial Office. All seven had prior experience in other Colonial Office departments and four of the seven had at least ten years of experience in colonial affairs prior to their transfer to the Dominions Office.

Throughout the colonial period, two issues were kept out of Dominions Office hands. By the mid-1930s responsibility for recruitment and training of administrative officers for the High Commission Territories had been given to the Colonial Office recruitment section and the faculties in charge of tropical Africa courses at major British universities. In addition, treasury officials who dealt with tropical African territories approved all financial expenditures. Patterns of dependency and underdevelopment in the High Commission Territories had more to do with the parsimony of the British treasury and with the evolving three-sided relationship between Britain, South Africa, and the High Commission Territories, than with intragovernmental organizational responsibilities of British ministries.

A New Resident Commissioner

After 1927 the likelihood of early transfer to South Africa diminished. If the Dominions Office were to administer Bechuanaland and the other High Commission Territories for some time to come, a modicum of long-range planning would be needed. The Dominions Office secretary, L. S. Amery, argued for an "effective black or dual policy." From the perspective of the colonial administrator, the High Commission Territories should be treated as a part of the colonial empire for all intents and purposes. In order to prevent further "stagnation," Amery decided to fill the three resident commissioner positions from outside the territories.[3]

The resident commissioner in Bechuanaland, Jules Ellenberger, retired in 1927. A search began for an administrator from outside the territory and with prior Colonial Office experience. The Dominions Office found a suitable candidate in one Charles Fernand Rey. Rey had previous African experience in Ethiopia and was employed by the Ministry of Labor. Mary Benson described Rey as

> a small brisk man with a bristling moustache and a reputation for being a hustler. [Rey] was shocked by the stagnation into which Bechuanaland had sunk both through its meager resources and the Administration's lack of vision.[4]

With the appointment of Rey as resident commissioner, British policy in Bechuanaland was about to undergo some dramatic changes. Rey, the High Commission, and the Dominions Office interacted closely, and the main lines of policy were determined prior to Rey's departure for southern

Africa.[5] The appointment of Herbert Stanley as high commissioner in 1931 and the separation of that office from the governor-generalship of South Africa provided new impetus for reform.

A number of critical commentaries on the administration of Bechuanaland appeared in print in 1932.[6] The source of the political and economic stagnation of the territory was seen to be linked with the need to reform its administrative structure. Observers blamed patterns of administrative recruitment for the weaknesses of the district level administration. To one observer, "It seems highly desirable that the High Commission should draw its administrative staff directly from the Appointments Department of the colonial office."[7]

Resident Magistrates

Administration in the Protectorate in the 1930s had changed very little since the beginning of British rule. The district administrator was called a "resident magistrate" (the resident commissioner was the territory's administrator) and he was assisted by a European clerical staff. The judicial functions of the resident magistrate in the reserve areas were limited to cases involving Europeans or when it was necessary to maintain order or prevent violence.[8] In the European areas, the resident magistrate had more direct, districtwide judicial responsibility and was the court of origin for all cases involving non-Africans and cases involving Africans from different "sub-groups." The legal system in the Bechuanaland Protectorate was based on Roman-Dutch law rather than on English law, although in cases involving Africans, the magistrate—as was the case in the Cape—relied upon custom.[9] The Resident Magistrate's training was all on the job. The Grade II clerk, as a prerequisite for promotion to assistant resident magistrate, was required to pass a two-part Setswana exam and a three-part law exam; the law examination was held outside southern Africa.

The day-to-day judicial responsibilities of the resident magistrates included the adjudication of criminal and civil cases, interviews with Europeans and Africans, routine correspondence with administration headquarters and the other districts, attendence to his duties as a sub-accountant and responsibility for the care of the jail and its prisoners. Aside from judicial functions, the resident magistrate's major responsibility was to ensure the collection of taxes, especially the "native hut tax." In addition, resident magistrates in the African reserve areas frequently spent hours in the *kgotla* (sometimes camping where it was held) dealing with administrative matters that concerned the chief's authority.

With the functions of the magistrate limited, the administration of society on the reserves remained largely in the hands of the chiefs. The magistrates' sphere of entry into indigenous decision making lay in their tact, ability to persuade, and personal relationship and influence with the local chief. Critics argued, however, that the background and experience of most Bechuanaland officials was such that they lacked the skills to establish meaningful relationships with the chiefs.

Resident Commissioner Rey, in a 1933 memorandum, suggested that the future of district administration lay in an increasing involvement in the affairs of African society. The most important duties of a magistrate should be the "multifarious work coming under the general definition of native affairs, including all aspects of the Resident Magistrate's connection with the various tribes lying outside the court and office. Very large areas are under the Resident Magistrate and he needs to keep in touch with the people."[10]

Initiative for Reform

As early as 1931, the Dominions Office began moving to change the procedures for recruitment and training of Bechuanaland administrators. In 1929 the reforms in Colonial Office recruitment, initiated by Sir Ralph Furse, were institutionalized by the Fisher Committee.[11] The Dominions Office initiated discussions on administrative reform in 1931 by suggesting that Bechuanaland needed the appointment of administrative officers who had been specially trained in the methods of "native administration" if proposed moves in the direction of indirect rule were to have any chance of success.[12]

On 22 July 1932, a meeting was held at the Colonial Office; those present included Sir George Tomlinson, head of the Colonial Office personnel division; Sir Charles Jeffries, head of the Colonial Services Department; Sir Edward Machtig, assistant undersecretary of state in charge of the High Commission Territories; Colonel Rey, resident commissioner of Bechuanaland; and Sir Ralph Furse, Colonial Office recruitment director. The primary concern at the meeting was the issue of recruitment. The consensus was that the type of person who had been entering Bechuanaland was well below the standard required for the efficient conduct of administration. Several officials at the meeting expressed concern that the majority of administrative officers were "clerical types" without university education or "traditions." Rey argued that Bechuanaland and the other territories should recruit their administrative staff from the Colonial Administrative Service and that all recruitment from South Africa should cease. Colonial Office representatives agreed in principle to this with the proviso that the movement be into the high commission territories only. They wanted to ensure that "unqualified" officers from southern Africa were not brought into the Colonial Administrative Service cadre.

The recruitment problem was addressed on an experimental basis. The committee agreed to the appointment of one candidate from the United Kingdom who would be assigned to Bechuanaland at an assistant magistrate level. This appointment would allow time to evaluate the situation in

Bechuanaland and give Rey the opportunity to handle the local resentment that was bound to result from such a policy change.

In London Furse addressed himself to the problem of finding a suitable candidate for the Bechuanaland post. Because of the experimental nature of the situation and the fact that there were more demands for cadets than the Colonial Office was able to fill, it was decided that the candidate selected for Bechuanaland would have failed to qualify for the Colonial Administrative Service by only a small margin. A formal request was solicited from Sir Herbert Stanley, high commissioner in South Africa at the time. Furse takes up the story:

> The possibilities latent in this experiment were exciting. Swaziland and Bechuanaland lay on the borders of the much criticized and highly critical Union. Basutoland was surrounded by it. The importance of giving them administrations comparable to those of Nigeria or Tanganyika stood out a mile. Fortune favoured me. In 1932 the C.A.S. Board placed a certain E.P. Arrowsmith, of Trinity, Oxford, one place outside the number of those selected for the Colonial Administrative Service. I thought they had made a mistake in doing so, swooped on Arrowsmith and packed him off to Bechuanaland.[13]

E. P. Arrowsmith was appointed to the Colonial Administrative Service on 3 October 1932, and he became the assistant resident magistrate for Serowe in early 1933. A careful, hesitant step was made toward administrative reform.

In his 1933 report on Bechuanaland, Sir Alan Pim reiterated the arguments for linking the administration of the High Commission Territories to the Colonial Administrative Service. He believed that direct recruitment from Britain was crucial. He also pushed for modifications in the role of district level administrators. In his report Pim made three major proposals:

1. The magistrates' role should involve more "development" activities, both political and economic.
2. Clerical and administrative duties should be separated.
3. The relationship between the administrative officer on the one hand, and the chief and the department heads on the other, should be clarified.[14]

Rey pressed for reorganization of Bechuanaland's district administration throughout 1934. His enthusiasm for reform was fed by his satisfaction (and his personal friendship) with Assistant Resident Magistrate Arrowsmith, whom he treated as a favorite son. According to Rey, Arrowsmith was "the type of young officer whom we want to encourage and develop."[15]

It was as much Arrowsmith's background and education as his performance that impressed Pretoria and Mafeking officials. As a candidate for the Colonial Administrative Service, Arrowsmith had a background similar to Furse's recruits in other African dependencies. The informal committee in London, as well as imperial representatives in southern Africa, had been concerned that the district administrators in Bechuanaland were not "a ruling group," and the Dominions Office was convinced that only officers of exceptional caliber could exert a personal influence on the chiefs.[16]

The attitudes of the colonial officials were central to the Colonial Administrative Service model articulated in London and exhibited by officials in the field. An example of the more desired attitudes was expressed in the 1978 recollections of an early recruit to Bechuanaland under the post-1933 reforms.

> In the Colonial Service (about which I learnt when I was at Oxford) there were the inducements of foreign travel, adventure, responsibility at an earlier age, in addition to the ideal of service to the community. Probably the same ideals as inspired the American Peace Corps volunteers, but on a more solid and lasting basis. I was proud to be selected to assist in bringing the benefits of civilization to under-developed parts of the world.[17]

Arrowsmith put it succinctly. "What they were looking for was someone with a university training, an open mind and a sense of adventure—someone who enjoyed the open life, the hunting, and the isolation of life."[18]

The Colonial Administrative Service was an elitist corps made up of men with certain qualities of character and personality who lived by a code of paternalism. A look at Arrowsmith's background confirms this. He came from a well-to-do family (his father's occupation was listed as "independent means"); he was educated in a public school; then Trinity College, Oxford, and received an Honors Degree in Modern History; and he was active in sports such as rugby and cricket. In short, this man had the "qualities to rule . . . over areas which might even be as large as Palestine; winning the trust and loyalty of their charges by their integrity, fairness, and likeableness."[19] Arrowsmith stood in contrast to most of his colleagues in the Bechuanaland Protectorate.

What Arrowsmith and those like him who came after represented, in contradistinction to local South African administrators, was the capacity to maintain "distinct differences between rulers and ruled." Furse's recruits could command a respect and a status in the African colonies because they appeared to be "born rulers from a superior civilization." Locally recruited South Africans, representatives of an "outback" society, simply could not command such deference.[20]

By 1935 the Dominions Office faced increasing pressure from Rey for a new recruitment policy. He had a critical shortage of staff, and the new indirect rule proclamations were being implemented with an establishment of administrative officers that was at the same level as in 1922.[21] Several administrative positions were vacant, and a number of officers were on the verge of retirement. In a letter to the Dominions Office, Rey complained, "I have repeatedly asked for two additional European Officers for district administrative purposes and I have in addition submitted on more than one occasion plans for reorganization. To the latter I have received no reply."[22] In October 1935 Furse toured the three High Commission Territories and concluded that the administration in British southern Africa was archaic. The scope of the district officer, he later reported, was limited and parochial because of the low standards for initial entry into the service.

> I felt sometimes as if I was back in the Days of Queen Victoria. Administration, by comparison with what I saw later in Central and East Africa, was archaic. Maps were often poor: staff lists for the most part non-existent. Money . . . had always been short . . . [and the members of] the service had been recruited locally by the "office boy" method of entry. Most officers had apparently joined before they were twenty, so hardly anyone had had a university education. Pay was low, promotion slow, prospects terribly restricted. The period of probation was too long and the examinations to be passed before confirmation unnecessarily difficult.[23]

His tour of the territories reinforced Furse's conviction that under the existing circumstances officials in the High Commission could neither be transferred nor promoted into the administrative services of other colonies. Movement would be one way. By reforming recruitment for the services in southern Africa so that officers there would have training, educational background, and general standards similar to those in the Unified Colonial Service, the Dominions Office would be providing the territories ultimately with quality administrators comparable to administrators in other parts of the empire. Only at that point could the officers in southern African territories be interchanged with officers in the other African colonies.

At a meeting of the high commissioner and the three resident commissioners in Pretoria, Furse presented his findings and recommendations. All agreed that improvement of service conditions would be necessary to attract men of the type recruited by the Colonial Administrative Service. Although improved conditions would be expensive to effect, they were considered imperative for the introduction of new patterns of administrative recruitment in southern Africa. The resources of the Colonial Office, especially Furse and his appointment selection procedure, would be required for the recruitment of high quality personnel for the High Commission Territories.[24] On 7 July 1936 Furse met with representatives of both the Dominions Office and the Colonial Office (the informal coordinating committee) and supported the changes in recruitment. The Colonial Office, he argued, should be given a free hand in selecting the best candidates available for the High Commission Territories and should control the salary scale and promotion patterns of scheduled officers in southern Africa. Dominions officials agreed, and little more than ten years after the Dominions Office had assumed control of the High Commission Territories, it returned a significant portion of its policy-making authority to the Colonial Office. Application was made to the treasury in September of 1936 to implement the financial aspects of the reforms, including the introduction of a new pay scale designed to provide conditions of service sufficiently favorable to attract men of Colonial Administrative Service stature. District administrators, restyled as district commissioners in the imperial pattern, henceforth would be recruited from an Oxbridge socialization environment.[25]

Locally Recruited Officers and the Colonial Administrative Service

With the introduction of a new system of district administration in Bechuanaland, the Secretariat in Mafeking faced a major problem.[26] In effect, two sets of conditions and two sets of standards were being created within the administrative cadre. Locally recruited personnel who entered the service prior to 1936 continued to receive remuneration and benefits under the southern African schedule. Newer recruits, brought from England, came under Colonial Administrative Service (CAS) conditions that were much more favorable.

In addition, certain pay, overseas leave, and travel arrangements were applicable only to CAS scheduled officers. The Mafeking Secretariat was confronted with a delicate situation. The Secretariat was concerned that the older members of the administrative cadre not feel inferior to the new members, even though this was precisely the judgment made by the Dominions Office and why the reforms had been introduced.[27] The Dominions Office looked forward to the day when all locally recruited officers, through the passage of time, would be replaced with CAS officers. Until that day, however, CAS personnel and locally recruited administrators would have to work together.

Indeed, there was a great deal of resentment among locally recruited administrators who felt they were being passed over. One of them, E.H. Midgley, complained, "Cadets were brought in from the U.K. and with no legal or local language qualifications, placed over us with bench powers. . . [and] unqualified local recruits were also promoted over me."[28]

By 1936 three designated officers (i.e., originally recruited by the secretary of state in London) had been recruited, W. H. J. Cairns and E. H. Ashton in addition to E. P. Arrowsmith. At this point the Mafeking Secretariat, which had heartily supported the reforms, had to decide what to do with the men recruited under the pre-1935 conditions. Little could be done for those who had already entered the administrative cadre. Retirement would gradually see them replaced by CAS recruits. There were eight grade-II clerks in the administration, however, who would be eligible for promotion to the administrative service. The Secretariat suggested that the grade-II clerks be absorbed gradually into the administrative cadre under a transitional arrangement. Rey proposed a two-year period of probation at the assistant district commissioner level.

Furse, responding for the Colonial Office, viewed Rey's proposal as perpetuating the same clerical-police type of administrator in the High

Commission Territories that the colonial administration was trying to eliminate. The problem with the compromise, according to Furse, was that those clerks who were too good to revert to the clerical rating would not be good enough to be absorbed into the CAS. To accept the clerical staff into the administrative cadre would be to perpetuate the old system. Locally recruited officers would block the promotion of younger, more qualified CAS officers for many years.

The question of what to do with the Grade II clerks was never answered satisfactorily. The compromise was accepted by the Colonial and Dominions Offices in spite of Furse's objections, and the resultant strategy combined existing staff with the new type of recruit and the quick promotion of the latter when proven superior. Ultimately, all of the Grade II clerks but one (who retired) were promoted into the district administrative cadre. Furse and the Dominions Office had fought actively against three or four of them, and the Mafeking Secretariat had tried to dismiss two of them.[29] The staff shortages during World War II, however, ultimately overruled all objections. By 1949 the ratio of CAS officers to locally recruited officers was somewhat better than in 1937. (See Table 4.2.) Nevertheless, locally recruited officers still dominated the top administrative posts including the government secretary, the two top Secretariat administrators, and four of the five senior district officers.

Although locally recruited officers continued to play an important role in the administration of Bechuanaland almost until independence, after 1935 the only new recruitment of administrative officers took place through CAS channels. Except during the war, an annual average of two to three recruits was sent to the Bechuanaland Protectorate. After 1937 all new recruits attended the Colonial Administrative Service course at Oxford or Cambridge

Table 4.2 **Proportion of Locally Recruited Officers & CAS Officers, 1937 and 1949**

Administrative Cadre	1937 (n = 27)		1949 (n = 25)	
	%	(#)	%	(#)
Locally Recruited Officers	63	(17)[1]	52	(13)
CAS Officers	37	(10)[2]	48	(12)[3]

Source: Archival Files. Botswana National Archives.

[1]Includes three officers, recruited locally by Rey, with university education and CAS-type backgrounds. One of the three officers had been rejected by the CAS.

[2]Includes Resident Commissioner Charles Rey, Acting Resident Commissioner Charles Arden-Clarke, and Government Secretary A. D. Forsyth-Thompson.

[3]Includes Resident Commissioner Anthony Sillery.

prior to their departure, and many of the new officers in the Protectorate attended the follow-up courses two years later.

It was not until the mid-1950s that CAS officers began to dominate the Bechuanaland administrative service. Outside the administrative service, moreover, the majority of middle-level administrators continued to be recruited from South Africa through the end of the colonial period. By the end of 1957, of the 302 European officers employed by the colonial administration in Bechuanaland, almost two-thirds (196) were South African citizens while many more (58) held dual British-South African citizenship. As late as 1964, only 177 out of a total of 531 European officials in Bechuanaland were designated officers. The rest had been recruited from South Africa. By that time, however, although tensions remained between these two groups, their competition was secondary to the increasingly sensitive question of localization.

Localization

In sharp contrast to the measured debate and firm commitment that went into the change to Colonial Administrative Service recruitment, very little serious discussion of localization occurred in Bechuanaland until the eve of independence. Colonel Rey's attitude toward Africans illustrates why such neglect was inevitable. "African traditional leaders are practically all degenerate, ignorant of their own native law and custom, with a veneer of the wrong sort of education, which fits them for little of practical value, and which renders them of comparatively little use in the roles which they are supposed to fill."[30]

Early Views on Localization

Developments in other British African territories after World War II forced policy makers to begin to pay at least minimal attention to the issue of localization. Prior to the war Africans had been excluded from all but the most menial clerical positions and the lowest levels of the police force. Even such low-level positions as typist, registry clerk, and postal clerk were filled by Europeans.[31] Many Europeans were recruited locally in Mafeking, the administrative headquarters.

There was some pressure for African advancement within the African Civil Service during the early postwar period. In 1948 the Fitzgerald Commission, established to investigate postwar colonial service conditions in the High Commission Territories, conceded, "The time will come when the African will possess all the qualifications necessary to enter the higher grades of the services. . . . [The process, however,] is bound to be a slow one."[32]

Following upon the Fitzgerald Commission, the first African assistant district officer, K. G. Kgopo, was appointed in 1951. Although the precedent had been set, no further appointments of Africans were made until 1959, seven years before independence.[33] Throughout the 1950s officials assumed that European recruits, from South Africa as well as from overseas, would continue to be needed. In order to continue to entice European recruits from South Africa, two separate pay scales were maintained, and even at the highest levels an African administrator would be restricted to a salary that was three-quarters of what was paid to a European.[34]

By the early 1950s, African civil servants began to demand some access to the higher levels of government service. During a 1953 administrative conference, it was noted that "representations have been made by the African Civil Service Association . . . for the creation of a number of [Africanized] clerical posts."[35] Bechuanaland Resident Commissioner M.O. Wray's view is striking, given that it was stated in late 1954. "I would prefer not to effect a replacement of European by African clerks at the present time. [That replacement would] result in the lowering of the efficiency of the service. Time is not yet appropriate."[36]

The African Advisory Council, debating the appointment of a development secretary in 1955, argued,

As his [the development secretary] activities will primarily be in connection with areas inhabited by African people, we not only hope but request that Africans of suitable qualifications be appointed to assist him in some of his responsible duties with a view to acquiring experience which will qualify them for appointment to similar and other responsible posts.[37]

The stress on gradualism in localization was set by the Fitzgerald Commission in 1948, and this gradualist approach continued virtually to the end of the colonial period. The argument for gradualism emphasized qualifications for meeting standards of service. The government's response to the African Advisory Council request included the judgment that

the whole crux of the matter lies in . . . "Africans of suitable qualifications." Such Africans are rare and probably in the BP [Bechuanaland Protectorate] at any rate, almost non-existent. There can be no question at this early stage of a deliberate policy of replacing white with black.[38]

In 1959 Sir Rex Surridge, investigating the salary structure and conditions of service in the High Commission Territories, rejected any idea of either equal salaries for equal work or a policy of localization in the administrative service. At this time there were only two administrative-level African civil servants and two professional-level African officials. Surridge believed that the pace of African recruitment in Bechuanaland would remain gradual because a sufficient number of African replacements at the senior level would "not be found for a very long time." Equal pay and a common establishment would "make the gap still wider between the African peasant and the African bureaucrat and would tend to create a mandarin caste, divorced in income and interests from their fellows." In his report Surridge concluded that the equalization process that had occurred in west Africa was wrong (Ghana was independent by then) and that "most Africans employed in the three Territories have some distinct advantages over their European counterparts—they have rights to cultivate land and to graze their cattle on tribal grazing land, and they do not pay income tax."[39] The whole thrust of the Surridge report flies in the face of the "winds of change" that would be announced by Prime Minister Harold MacMillan a year later in Cape Town.

The Ramage Commission Report

Political events finally caught up with colonial administrators in Bechuanaland. By 1961 the decision had been made to move the territory toward internal self-government, if not independence. A Legislative Council was established at that time and an Executive Council would soon follow (see Chapter 6). South Africa's withdrawal from the Commonwealth finally sealed the coffin on the transfer issue. Bechuanaland's civil service remained almost completely European, however, and a new commission, headed by Sir Richard Ramage, was established to review the civil service in each of the three High Commission Territories.

In his 1961 report, Ramage noted that the "racial operation" of the civil service was "causing serious and increasing ill-feeling amongst African staff generally and . . . leading to political difficulties." Although he concluded that a civil service must be developed that would "not have a racial basis," he also noted in passing that such a change would be a long time in coming.[40]

The Ramage Commission created the basic structure of the civil service in Botswana, and a pattern of administration was set that would not be changed until 1978. Ramage abolished the racially based staff divisions and created four main classes in the public service: administrative and professional, technical and executive, clerical, and a subordinate industrial class.

Although the commission's report contained some fundamental changes essential for an evolution toward independence, the assumption of gradualism remained. Ramage expected that the majority of the higher-level staff in the civil service would remain expatriate, and that most of the expatriates would be South Africans. Thus, the Ramage Commission recommended that civil service salaries be increased dramatically, between 20 and 30 percent at the senior level.

By the early 1960s, Bechuanaland had "gained a bit of a reputation as a dumping ground for colonial civil servants who had lost their jobs elsewhere." Many of them considered southern Africa as their home. Even by colonial standards there was "an unusually strong stand by Europeans against too rapid a localization of the civil service."[41] They argued, as do expatriates today in Botswana, against a decline in standards of service and quality of work. A pattern of gradualism in localization evolved that was more pronounced in Bechuanaland than in most other African states.

The Transition to Independence

By 1963 Britain was committed to the internal self-government and eventual independence of Bechuanaland. A constitutional conference held at Lobatse in July of that year set Bechuanaland on the path toward majority rule. After elections the government would be headed by a chief minister selected from the membership of an elected legislative assembly. The new constitutional arrangement was ratified in London in June 1964. Elections were to be held in March of 1965.

As the political process accelerated, it became clear that political independence would occur more quickly than would the development of an indigenous civil service. The extreme social and economic neglect of the Bechuanaland Protectorate caused a paucity of educated Africans for staffing the upper levels of the bureaucracy. The severe neglect in education had left Bechuanaland with only eight known university students in 1960, five at Pius XII University College in Basutoland and three in Britain. Government figures projected merely eight to ten graduates per year by 1970. At the secondary school level, there were no graduates in 1960, although the government hoped to matriculate between forty and fifty at the Cambridge school-certificate level by the mid-1960s. The number of Cambridge school-certificate recipients would peak out at 165 per year by 1970.[42] In 1961, according to the member of Parliament for local government, social services and commerce,

> The gap between supply and demand within the next five years or so will probably be proportionately greater [in Bechuanaland] than in almost any other African territory, and the importance to us of one or two trained men is, correspondingly, greater than that of dozens in a more advanced country.[43]

Within the civil service in 1962 there were only four Batswana (out of a total of 155) in the administrative and professional grades, fifteen (out of 260) at the technical grade, and only twenty-two (out of 182) at the middle-level executive grade. Even at the clerical level the government continued the widespread use of European stenographers and typists, especially at headquarters in Mafeking.

After 1961 the colonial government made some attempt, although a cautious and conservative one, to develop a localization policy. In October 1961 colonial authorities appointed a standing advisory commission to examine the potential for localization during the decade of 1962-1972. The Commission presented a white paper to the Legislative Council in March

1962. In it the Commission warned of "increasing distrust to the prejudice of sound administration" if localization did not occur and went on to define a "local officer" as an officer who was born in Bechuanaland or had permanent residence there.[44] Rejecting the more radical "Africanization" demands of the African Civil Service Association, the government applied the term "local" to Bechuanaland administrators, whether they were Asian, European, or African.

The 1962 white paper continued the gradualism that characterized government policy until independence. Local officers were warned that they would have to work alongside of expatriates for at least the next decade. The white paper reflected an almost defeatest approach to localization in its assumption that localization policy would have little, if any, effect until the middle or late 1970s. Viewing the education cycle in twelve-year increments, the commission assumed that the educational system would have to start from scratch in 1962 if the government were to have staff available by 1975. "In these circumstances, continued expatriate recruitment will be needed to make good the shortfall of local candidates."[45]

In addition to the issue of localization, the commission was mandated to draw up a training plan to meet the government needs over the 1962-1972 decade. The commission's projections were very conservative and underestimated dramatically the staffing needs of a post-colonial administration. It estimated that the government would need only 87 administrative-class officials, 259 technicians, 182 executive-class officials, and 80 clerks. Government sowed the seeds of a localization problem that Botswana officials would continue to grapple with well into the 1980s.

The situation in 1972 demonstrates graphically the consequences of this conservatism for Botswana. The 1962 projections suggested that a total of 608 positions would have to be filled by 1972. Ironically, 682 citizens were in senior- and middle-level positions by that year. Out of a total establishment of 1,620 at the executive level and above, however, 578 were expatriates and 400 were vacancies.[46] Botswana would have to expand its training capacities rapidly in order to fill its expanding civil service with citizens. That it was not able to do so, at least during the first twenty years of independence, was partially the result of crucial decisions made during the early 1960s.

With the publication of the 1962 white paper, the government decided that no additional expatriate officers would be recruited for Bechuanaland on a pensionable and permanent basis. The British government also agreed to begin "topping off" U.K. officers on contract in Bechuanaland. Most important, beginning in 1963 the government committed itself, at least nominally, to a policy of complete localization. In May of that year the Protectorate government announced the appointment of a localization and training committee to provide a vehicle for the localization process to proceed.

The committee presented its first report to the government in November 1963. The committee recommended the localization of all clerical positions as soon as possible. In order to provide in-service training, the committee suggested the establishment of a government training center. It also recommended the creation of a system to monitor localization and suggested that closer links be developed between secondary and postsecondary institutions and the government departments in order to publicize career opportunities in the civil service. "Both the 1962 White Paper and the 1963 Report of the Localization and Training Committee place much emphasis on improving and strengthening the educational system to ensure a steady stream of candidates for the Public Service."[47] The proposals in the 1963 committee report were very modest, considering that not only was independence just a few years away but a constitutional framework also had already been developed.

In February 1964 the government established the Botswana Training Center with colonial development and welfare monies. In June of that year, an advisory public service commission was established. Not surprisingly, at the end of 1964 the government published yet another white paper on localization.

The 1964 white paper addressed the increasingly controversial issue of standards. As the African Civil Service Association grew more militant on the subject of localization, European administrators responded by demanding that there be no decline in standards. The white paper supported the European civil servant's position and emphasized,

> It is, and must always be, the paramount concern of Government that an efficient and just administration is maintained in the interests of the community at large. There is no intention of abandoning either the normal standards of efficiency or the criteria for promotion within the civil service.[48]

Debate over the 1964 white paper reinforced the idea of gradualism. Although the government secretary, Arthur Douglas, did stress the need to accelerate the localization process, he also pointed out that a local candidate must have "the necessary qualifications and experience. I personally hope," Douglas went on, "there will not be a deterioration in our standards."[49] The theme of the debate suggested an underlying fear that expatriate officials might leave before enough qualified local staff were trained. Prime Minister designate Seretse Khama reflected this fear,

> We do not have any men sitting around at either Victoria or Euston Station waiting for the first train to take them to the coast so that they can come and do some work here in Bechuanaland. . . . On my last trip to the United States of America I talked to the Peace Corps people and . . . they could not promise that we would be considered after independence because even Americans are not anxious to leave the States and come and work in the Territory.[50]

A 1964 report on civil service wages reinforced the gradualist assumptions of the Protectorate government. Although allowing for the possibility that in the forseeable future the civil service would be staffed entirely by citizens, the author of the report assumed that in the immediate future widespread dependence on expatriate administrators would continue. At that point approximately 43 percent of the expatriates were from South Africa. In order to ensure a continued supply of South Africans, a significant increase in civil service salaries was recommended. The Skinner Commission supported the existing practice of determining salary scales by following explicitly the racially based South African salary scheme.[51] As a result, "Botswana inherited a civil service salary structure at independence which at that time was amongst the most unequal in Africa."[52]

Critique of Localization Policy

Throughout the period preceding independence in 1966, European administrators continued to stress gradualism and the need to maintain standards. Spokesmen for the European civil service association argued against rapid localization of the civil service and "demanded retention of their services . . . under the guise that it would be inefficient and ineffective to lower administrative standards."[53]

Until the eve of independence gradualism remained official colonial policy, and the maintenance of standards became a code for the continued expatriate presence in the civil service. By the end of 1964, expatriates filled 27 percent of the total civil service establishment of 2,575 positions, occupying 82 percent of the executive-level positions and above. The situation at the senior level was particularly dramatic with 88 percent of the 182 positions at the superscale, professional, and administrative grades filled by expatriates.

Much of the criticism of localization policy came from African civil servants. Not surprisingly, they were less concerned about standards than about previous patterns of racial discrimination in employment. Many argued for Africanization rather than localization, which would have excluded white citizens from civil service employment after independence. In 1966 the Bechuanaland Civil Service Association (formerly the African Civil Service Association) accused the colonial administration of "blatant discrimination against the African in favour of the white man . . . the local man is simply not given a chance to prove his worth, being perpetually kept in a lowly job."[54] According to the Association, posts which could be filled by Africans were given to whites or kept vacant, and government had failed to implement the recommendations on training and localization that had been proposed by its own commissions.

By the end of the colonial period some of the political leaders were expressing concern over the slow pace of localization. In November 1964, during a Legislative Council debate, Leetile Raditladi, then a member of the Council, argued that the Medical Department discriminated against African nurses. During the same debate, the strongest criticism of localization policy came from Quett Masire, who was deputy leader of the Democratic party at the time. Masire, the current president of Botswana, argued,

> We must also recognize that self-government means nothing if the locals are not able to take up the running of the country. We cannot rely on the expatriate forever. . . . We should do all we can do to localise.[55]

Masire called for an end to "the slave mentality" that assumed only Europeans could perform the technical and professional tasks of a modern government, and he suggested that after independence civil servants should be politically loyal to the governing party.

T. C. Luke, a Ghanaian commissioned by the government to survey localization in Bechuanaland, produced a scathing commentary on the localization policy.[56] He was particularly critical, in his report, of the paucity of resources committed to educational development as compared to most other former British colonies. Although recognizing the financial constraints on Bechuanaland, he faulted the administration for not taking steps toward localization until 1961.

Luke recommended urgent commitment to the improvement of the educational system in Bechuanaland. He argued that the territory had to have an aggressive policy toward localization and that in the beginning the government had to expect some lowering of standards in noncrucial areas. No harm would be done if standards were kept at a level that provided satisfactory governmental activity and services. Of prime importance was Luke's emphasizing that "localization calls for and entails extraordinary and often unorthodox measures to achieve its goals."[57]

Luke recognized the tremendous difficulties that localization presented: the lack of educated candidates for civil service employment, the financial and budgetary constraints faced by the government, and the likelihood of a rapidly increasing need for expatriate expertise as the post-colonial government embarked upon development projects. He acknowledged that expatriate recruitment would be necessary in some circumstances but stressed it should occur only if an acceptable local candidate were not available. Unless localization were given the "highest priority" and a "sense of urgency, of emergency," the hard issues of developing a national civil service would be ignored.

Luke emphasized the symbolic importance of localization in a newly independent state.

> [Localization] is necessary for national pride and national aspiration and fulfilment. . . . [A]t first at least some of the higher policy-making posts as well as . . . posts of lesser rank and importance should be filled by Batswana.[58]

He went on to say that localization entails the "transformation of the colonial civil service into a national civil service over a short period of time."[59]

Luke's report was not well received by many in the colonial administration, who believed that the number of African candidates qualified to staff all civil service cadres would be insufficient for years to come. They also repeated the argument that localization would result in a lower standard of government services. Since the report was released only six months before independence, nothing was done about localization in the waning days of the colonial period. Thus, Botswana became an independent state without a systematic localization policy or a governmental commitment to localization. The demand for a rapid expansion of the government's activities after independence would take precedence over the need for human resource development.

Conclusion

Between 1933 and the eve of independence, Bechuanaland's system underwent a number of changes as policy makers in London and Pretoria tried at first to bring it in line with the British colonial model, then attempted to transform a colonial administration into a national civil service. Uncertainties about the future of the territory meant that alternative recruitment patterns would lag behind the political priorities of both colonial authorities and national elites.

Bechuanaland's problems were much more than organizational, however, and administrative changes did not have the impact on the territory that colonial officials had anticipated. Dissatisfaction with administrative patterns would continue to plague the political leadership after independence. The new government would inherit many of the problems of the former government: a small population spread over a large area, an uneven distribution of land, extreme differences in the sizes of districts, and difficult communication between the districts and the center. Questions of administrative recruitment and human resource development would become the order of the day after 1966. Commitment to economic development would lead to an increase, rather than a decrease, in the number of European expatriates in the country during the 1960s and 1970s.

Personnel changes after 1933 left many administrative practices in Bechuanaland that originated within South Africa. The district-level administrator, in spite of the change of name to district commissioner in 1936, continued to spend a great deal of time as a magistrate until well after independence. Bechuanaland's legal system, based largely on the Roman-Dutch system of the Cape Colony, became Botswana's legal system. As a result, the courts in Botswana "had, and still have, to consult South Africa writers, whose opinions are based on that law as subsequently developed by their courts."[60] Furthermore, until 1959, "the close proximity of the seat of the High Commissioner to the seat of the Government of the Union [of South Africa] led to a large number of Proclamations designed to create segregated communities within the same state on the pattern of what obtained—and still obtains—in the Republic of South Africa."[61]

Proximity to South Africa had other implications as well. Economic patterns, as we shall see later in this study, were established very early in Bechuanaland and placed the territory in an extremely disadvantageous position. Budgetary and financial constraints limited policy options vis-à-vis administrative recruitment and human resource management throughout the colonial period. In addition, the specter of political transfer to South Africa continued to hang over the High Commission Territories at least until the 1948 nationalists' rise to power in South Africa.

By bringing Bechuanaland closer to the Colonial Administrative Service model in the 1930s, policy makers influenced the organizational processes of what was to become Botswana. The elitist status of the imperial civil servant contrasted sharply with the informality and familiarity of Bechuanaland's earlier administrative service, and influenced class formation in Botswana. The status of Botswana's administrators and their position as a socio-economic and political force in the country in many respects originated in the post-1933 administrative reforms. Yet those reforms were necessary within the context of Bechuanaland's position at the time. It was vitally necessary, as a number of the liberal critics of Britain's southern Africa policy pointed out, to bring Bechuanaland (and the other southern African territories) more closely into the imperial embrace. After all, the only alternative in the 1930s would have been the gradual absorption of the territory into the Union of South Africa.

Unlike the extensive and sustained efforts in the 1930s to change administrative recruitment patterns, efforts at localization in the 1960s were too little, too late, and too gradual overall. In the last years of colonial rule, gradualism created a backlog of staff and training needs that would plague Botswana for years to come.

In addition to insufficient localization, salary decisions and, in particular, the tying of conditions of service to those in South Africa contributed to the development of a civil service system that was extremely unequal even by African standards. The elitist status of the colonial administrative service combined with the high socio-economic status accorded bureaucrats sowed the seeds of Botswana's "bureaucratic state." After independence, civil servants were the most important, and perhaps the only significant domestic interest group in the country, and they influenced policy decisions far out of proportion to their numbers. The development of a bureaucratic elite, combined with a colonial policy of budgetary neglect and economic underdevelopment, severely limited policy alternatives after independence.

Notes

1. D.O. 35/900/Y8/57. Conversations between the High Commissioner and the Resident Commissioners, October 15 and 16, 1941.

2. For a discussion of this relationship see Anthony Sillery, *Botswana: A Short Political History* (London : Methuen & Co.,1974), pp. 142-143.

3. Personal letter, L. S. Amery to William Woly, Colonial Office, 1927, D.O.9/7/v.3/D.10443—Appointment of Resident Commissioner; and Minute, 25 October 1927, D.O.9/7/v.3/D.10249—Future of the High Commission Territories.

4. Mary Benson, *Tshekedi Khama* (London: Faber and Faber, 1960), p. 70.

5. Minute, 27 February 1930, D.O.35/365/10503/2—High Commissioner for South Africa, Future Arrangements.

6. Margaret L. Hodgson and William G. Ballinger, *Britain in Southern Africa*, no. 2, *Bechuanaland Protectorate* (Alice, South Africa: Lovedale Press, 1933); Leonard Barnes, *The New Boer War* (London: Hogarth Press, 1932); and Sir Alan Pim, *Financial and Economic Position of the Bechuanaland Protectorate: Report of the Commission Appointed by the Secretary of State for Dominion Affairs*, Parliamentary Report, Cmd. 2929 (London: His Majesty's Stationery Office, 1933).

7. Barnes, *New Boer War*, p. 194.

8. Lord (William M.) *Hailey, Native Administration in the British African Territories*, part V, *The High Commission Territories: Basutoland, The Bechuanaland Protectorate and Swaziland* (London: Her Majesty's Stationery Office, 1953), p. 211.

9. Lord (William M.) Hailey, *An African Survey*, revised ed. (London: Oxford University Press, 1956), p. 594.

10. S.353/3, C. F. Rey, Minute, Memorandum on Sir Alan Pim's Report on Bechuanaland Protectorate, 3 November 1933.

11. See Robert Heussler, *Yesterday's Rulers: The Making of the British Colonial Service* (Syracuse, N.Y.: Syracuse University Press, 1963), pp. 58-68.

12. S.458/1—Native Administration in Bechuanaland.

13. Sir Ralph Furse, *Aucuparius, Recollection of a Recruiting Officer* (London: Oxford University Press, 1962), p. 247. The following is also based on an oral interview with Sir Edwin Arrowsmith, London, England, 1 June 1979.

14. Pim, *Bechuanaland*, pp. 58-60.

15. Rey to Furse, 18 December 1935, S.437/6—District Administration Reorganization.

16. Minute, 13 January 1936, D.O. 35/486/ 21319/2—South African High Commission Territories.

17. Personal communication, 25 June 1978. Anonymity requested.

18. Oral interview with Sir Edwin Arrowsmith, London, England, 1 June 1979.

19. Furse, *Aucuparius*, p. 263.

20. D.O.35/4689/21319/9—District Administration Reorganization.

21. Rey, Memorandum on District Administration, 16 October 1935, D.O.35/379/6512—District Administration Reorganization.

22. *Ibid.*

23. Furse, *Aucuparius*, pp. 248-249.

24. D.O.35/468/21319/2 and S.440/14.

25. Minute, 31 July 1935, D.O.35/468/21319/10—Dominions Office, Treasury.

26. The administrator in the district was redesignated District Commis - sioner and Assistant District Commissioner in 1936.

27. D.O.35/4689/21319/9.   Arrowsmith credits Rey with a skillful handling of the two groups. He says, "I think he must have been pretty skillful in the way he handled things, because there was never any "needle" between me and the clerks with whom I worked and played games. I suppose the resentment built up as the numbers coming out from England increased." Personal communication with the author, 21 January 1977.

28. E. H. Midgley, letter to the author, 17 March 1976.

29. E. H. Midgley, one of those so targeted, describes this effort. "I got this peculiar letter. I was told that we [the clerks] had no future. We must leave the service, resign. They then spent over ten years trying to get rid of us, though they were never able to do it." Oral interview, E.H. Midgley, Durban, South Africa, 31 October 1981. The extent to which preference or rejection of a clerical officer was based on the officer's capability as opposed to his attitudes is an interesting one. The case of Midgley is illustrative. The Committee and Mafeking spent twenty years trying to get rid of Midgley, ostensibly because of his incompetence. According to Mafeking, Midgley was not good at the routine administrative tasks of a Grade-II clerk—typing, accounting, and correspondence. However, Midgley also was perceived to have had radical, left-of-center political views. Midgley in a letter to this writer denied any left-of-center views and held he was disliked in part because of his Quaker religion. Letter to the author, 25 January 1977. Once in office he proved to be "unusually well-informed and he is still remembered . . . as an outstanding District Commissioner." Adam Kuper, *Kalahari Village Politics* (Cambridge: Cambridge University Press, 1970), p. 64. According to H. P. Jankie, until his death M.P. for the Ghanzi District, Midgley built, with no support from Mafeking, the road between Eastern Botswana and Ghanzi, across the Kalahari Desert. According to Jankie, Midgley is still widely remembered by people in Ghanzi for his energy and interest in developing the district. Oral interview with H. P. Jankie, Ghanzi, Botswana, 8 August 1975.

30. C. F. Rey, Notes by Resident Commissioner of Bechuanaland Protectorate on Questions under Consideration by High Commission Territories Committee, No. 7136, 25 October 1934 S.397/4.

31. J. C. N. Mentz, "Localization and Training in the Botswana Public Service, 1966–1976" (Ph.D. diss., University of South Africa, 1981), p. 48.

32. T. Fitzgerald, *Report on the Salaries and Conditions of Service in the Public Services of the South African High Commission Territories, 1947–1948* (Maseru, Basutoland: Government Printer, 1948), p. 16.

33. Oral interview with M. L. Kgopo, Gaborone, Botswana, 5 June 1975.

34. Christopher Colclough and Stephen McCarthy, *The Political Economy of Botswana: A Study of Growth and Distribution* (London: Oxford University Press, 1980), p. 183.

35. Administrative Conference Minutes, 13 July 1953, S.547/7. Clerks, African: Creation of a General Clerical Service.

36. Letter, Resident Commissioner to Deputy High Commissioner, Pretoria, 20 December 1954 in S.548/1. Clerks, European: Establishment and Salary Scales and Creation of General Clerical Services.

37. African Advisory Council's Reply to H.H.'s Opening Address, 35th Session of the African Advisory Council, 20–27 October 1955, S.405/9, Development in the Bechuanaland Protectorate.

38. Minute, 13 December 1955, S.408/9.

39. Sir Rex (E. R. E.) Surridge, *Report of the Commission Appointed to Examine the Salary Structure and Conditions of Service of the Civil Service of Basutoland, Bechuanaland and Swaziland, 1958–1959* (Capetown: Cape Times Ltd., 1959), pp. 17, 18, and 19, respectively.

40. Sir Richard Ramage, *Report on the Structure of the Public Services in Basutoland, Bechuanaland and Swaziland, 1961* (Capetown: Cape Times, Ltd , 1962), p. 12.

41. Gilfred Gunderson, "Nation Building and the Administrative State: The Case of Botswana" (Ph.D. diss., University of California, Berkeley, 1971), p. 239.

42. Education in Relation to Government's plans for the Localization of the Public Sector, Report made on behalf of the Advisory Committee on Social Services, S.104/5. Localization Policy.

43. Savingram, Member of Local Government, Social Services and Commerce to Director of Education, 24 October 1961, S.104/4, Education–African Policy: Post Matriculation, University.

44. Standing Advisory Committee, *The Localization of the Bechuanaland Public Service*, White Paper (Mafeking: mimeographed, 1962), SM 96(2), Botswana National Archives, p. 1.

45. *Ibid.*, p. 10.

46. *Report of the Presidential Commission on Localization and Training in the Botswana Civil Service and the Government Statement on the Report of the Commission* (Gaborone: Government Printer, 1972), p. 23.

47. Mentz, *Localization*, pp. 5-6.

48. *The Development of the Public Service*, Legislative Colonial Paper No. a20 of 1964–65 (Gaberones: Government Printer, 1964), p. 7.

49. Records of the debates in the Bechuanaland Legislative Council, 19 November 1964, *Extract: Bechuanaland Protectorate Motion: That this House supports the Views and Proposals set out in the Government White Paper entitled "The Development of the Public Service"* (Gaberones: Government Printer, 1964), p. 24.

50. Ibid., p. 12.

51. T. F. Skinner, *Review of Emoluments of the Public Service of the Bechuanaland Protectorate*, (Gaberones: Government Printer, 1964).

52. Colclough and McCarthy, *Botswana*, p. 184.

53. Gunderson, "Nation-Building," p. 239.

54. Quoted in *Ibid.*, p. 240.

55. Records of the debates..., *Extract: Motion..."The Development of the Public Service,"* p. 9.

56. T. C. Luke, *Report on Localization and Training* (Gaberones: Government Printer, 1966).

57. *Ibid.*, p. 20.

58. *Ibid.*, p. 25.

59. *Ibid.*, p. 20.

60. Akinola Aguda, "Legal Development in Botswana from 1885 to 1966," *Botswana Notes and Records*, vol. 5 (1973), p. 57.

61. *Ibid.*, p. 54.

5

Colonial Economic Policy: Benign Neglect or Structural Underdevelopment?

The pre-World War II colonial period in Bechuanaland was once described most aptly as "the locust years."

> Having reluctantly assumed responsibility for the High Commission Territories, Britain proceeded to neglect them totally for fifty years. Such development as has taken place, whether political, economic or social is, in all three, effectively a post Second World War phenomenon.[1]

To what extent was British economic policy in Bechuanaland one of "benign" neglect? The economic effect of British colonial rule can be interpreted in two ways. On the one hand, British colonial policy, if it did little to develop the territory, economically was at least neutral, keeping the territory out of South African hands and leaving the people of Bechuanaland with their socio-economic system largely intact. This interpretation suggests that colonial economic policy was part of the more general external protectorate concept. The British protected the territory from German, Transvaal and South African invasion and left an independent Botswana in a position where it could cross "the development threshold" after independence.[2]

An alternate view suggests that British colonial rule had a decisive impact on Botswana and its economic status within the region. It has been proposed that as a result of British colonial rule what had been a vigorous pre-colonial African economy was subordinated to a minor role at the periphery of the southern African region.[3] Rather than being neutral economically, British colonial rule resulted in the "structural underdevelopment" of the Botswana economy.[4]

In order to understand Britain's impact upon the Bechuanaland economy, we should disaggregate the question. Britain's fiscal pattern vis-à-vis the Bechuanaland Protectorate clearly reflects a pattern of neglect and was parsimonious even by comparison with other colonial territories. Throughout the colonial period, budgets were kept to a bare minimum or below. Even when officials increased the level of expenditures slightly after the second World War, the primary effect was an increased level of confusion about the responsibilities of administrators and technical specialists.

An examination of Britain's regulatory policy suggests broader patterns of change as Bechuanaland's economy became wedded to that of South Africa. The resulting increased dependency of Bechuanaland's economy would be a legacy to the Botswana government after independence. Thus, in terms of its regulatory policy, British colonial decision making more closely approximated structural underdevelopment than the more neutral benign neglect.

The Protectorate and Fiscal Allocations: A Policy of Neglect

That the British colonial administration was parsimonious in its fiscal policy towards Bechuanaland is beyond question. When Britain established the Bechuanaland Protectorate in 1885, colonial administrators were preoccupied with two concerns: (1) that the imperial government limit its activities in the territory to the maintenance of law and order, and (2) that the territory's population absorb the costs of the colonial administration as quickly as possible. These concerns were resolved with an efficiency unrivaled even in the generally tightfisted economic policy that Britain followed throughout its colonial empire.

Revenue and Expenditure

There are a number of reasons for the failure to develop Bechuanaland's economy. The historical and political conditions were such that when Britain reluctantly assumed responsibility for Bechuanaland, its role was largely defensive, designed to keep someone else out. Furthermore, given that era's prevailing ideologies governing the relationship between the colonial power and dependent state, it was not in Britain's interest to develop the territory. Beyond the ideological factor, however, was the reality of Bechuanaland's position in southern Africa and the fact that its prospective future was seen then as one and the same with South Africa's. British administration was seen as a holding action until transfer could take place.

British administrators in Bechuanaland thus suffered from absurdly low levels of revenue and lacked a consistent policy of internal development for territory. Throughout the colonial period (with the exception of the few years before independence),

> disbursements from the recurrent budgets on central and district administration, police, prisons, and the administration of justice

averaged between sixty percent and eighty percent of total annual expenditures.[5]

Almost nothing was spent on the development of an infrastructure, and health, welfare, and education were left almost entirely to the local missionary communities.[6]

The major expenditure undertaken by the Mafeking administration was for the police. Already by 1899 the Bechuanaland Protectorate police was consuming 51 percent of the territory's budget, and during the first ten years of colonial rule the combined police force budget for both British Bechuanaland (later transferred to Cape Colony) and the Bechuanaland Protectorate was 60 percent of the total budget.[7]

After the turn of the century, expenditures continued to provide graphic evidence of a policy of parsimony and neglect. Nor had patterns of spending changed significantly. In 1908 in the Bamangwato district,

> the two largest items of the £75,801 government expenditure were "police" (£39,584) and "railway subsidy" (£8,333): "district administration" was a poor fifth (£3,584) and African social services totaled £500 subsidy to trades education. There was minimal government spending even indirectly on the African population of a Native Territory.[8]

Although the expenditure for the Bechuanaland police had dropped to 30 percent of the budget by 1912, no attempt had been made to use this savings to generate any kind of internal development. Instead, in 1901 a hut tax was imposed on the population, and this and the poll tax which replaced it in 1903-04 were used to reduce the amount of grants-in-aid money received from Britain so that the territory would become self-sufficient economically. In 1912 all grants from Britain ceased and the costs of administration were carried by the tribal administration and the Tswana taxpayer.

From that point until the mid-1930s, the Mafeking administration had to limit its expenditures to an amount equal to its domestic revenues. The period prior to World War II was one of fiscal stagnation, with no significant expansion of Bechuanaland's public services. Expenditures for the police force and the central and district administrations comprised approximately eighty percent of the annual outlays throughout the period.

The situation in the Bamangwato (later Central) district was not atypical of the other districts in the territory. The tax on Africans grew steadily, approximately 10 percent per year during the first ten years the tax was in operation. (The figure for 1902 was £5,300; by 1909 it had grown to £13,225.) This pattern of taxation continued throughout the colonial period. By 1908

> direct taxation of Africans accounted for 61% of all government revenues [in Bamangwato] and from 1911-12 until late colonial times the Bechuanaland Protectorate (tax) revenue matched or exceeded expenditure.[9]

Bechuanaland showed few signs of economic development until World War II. As late as 1948, government expenditures for health and education remained under £5 million per year. What development that did occur, such as the railway line through the eastern part of the territory, was financed by private investment through a royal charter to the British South Africa Company. Although in the case of the railway African taxpayers paid an annual subsidy of approximately £20,000 between 1899 and 1909, which softened the risks for the British South Africa Company.

External Criticism

By 1933 both the critics of Bechuanaland's administration and the senior administrators themselves were aware of the gravity of the territory's fiscal and economic situation. Two analyses of British colonial policy in Bechuanaland, published in 1933, contained scathing critiques of the territory's economic stagnation.[10]

Leonard Barnes pointed out that "The Bechuanaland Protectorate reproduces the general economic features of the other High Commission Territories. The population appears to be stationary in number; economic advancement is almost entirely arrested; standards of living are falling."[11] To Hodgson and Ballinger, the only solution to the Protectorate's problems was "a great deal of money to develop it."[12]

Sir Alan Pim provided the first sectoral analysis of Bechuanaland's economic situation. Although more restrained than the unofficial critics, he was equally damning.

> The economic life of the Protectorate is at a very low ebb, and this is particularly marked in the southern Districts. . . . The general position can only be described as one of severe depression, and it is felt all the more hardly as the natives are no longer content to live on the old standards, and have learnt to regard many European products not as luxuries but as necessities.[13]

Along with the general downturn of economic activity because of the worldwide depression, the cattle industry was hit in 1931 with hoof and mouth disease. This resulted in a total embargo of Bechuanaland cattle in the Union of South Africa—a situation which Pim described as a disaster of the greatest magnitude for Bechuanaland.

Pim was realistic enough not to recommend the input of large sums of money to the territory; he most certainly knew that this would not occur. He saw Bechuanaland's economic future in its cattle industry, and his first priority for development in the often drought-stricken territory was to search for sources of water. He proposed an investment of £24,500 to survey for possible bore holes and clear the river channels in the Okavango delta (in addition to a number of other, cattle related projects).

Little action was taken prior to World War II despite Pim's recommendations. To a large extent the economy remained stagnant, and the largest sources of income continued to be the export of labor to South Africa and the export of cattle, the latter only when not prohibited by hoof and mouth disease. Not until the late 1950s did any significant investment in Bechuanaland occur.[14] It is difficult to find any evidence during the interwar years of a genuine concern on Britain's part for African prosperity and advancement.

Imperial Aid

The first hesitant steps toward aid to Bechuanaland from the imperial government came out of the Colonial Development Act of 1929. Under the new law Britain provided three modest grants designed to meet territorial deficits on a case-by-case basis. In addition, a few loans were approved for special works projects. By 1937-38 the total grant to Bechuanaland had risen to £70,000. In 1940 the British Parliament passed the Colonial Development and Welfare Act, which established a regularized system of financial aid to Britain's colonies during the postwar period.

World War II cut short any plans for further grants-in-aid during the war years. A policy of extreme fiscal stringency became the order of the day, and all staff replacements were postponed. The administration in Mafeking was required to maintain in reserve a surplus balance equal to six months' ordinary expenditures throughout the war years. By the end of the war the reserves stood at £346,000.

After the war ended, a revised 1945 Colonial Development and Welfare Act granted some development funds to Bechuanaland. By 1950 the expenditure of British funds had increased to £105,000. Until the mid-1950s, however, limits placed on the recurrent budget prevented significant development expenditures. In 1954 a commission assigned to investigate the needs of the territory concluded that there was little scope for increasing local expenditure; surpluses were "only achieved by the curtailment of practically every activity of Government. Social and administrative services were maintained at a dangerously low level and the construction and maintenance of public works was drastically restricted."[15] The commission recommended a renewal of British budgetary support for Bechuanaland and an expansion of capital assistance.

The period between 1955 and 1965 was a transitional one economically as the colonial government began to direct its economic activity toward the type of intervention that would be characteristic of the post-colonial government. "The period from 1955 until the granting of internal self-government ten years later stands out in strong contrast to the earlier periods of colonial rule. During this time Bechuanaland at last began to make political and economic progress."[16] After 1955 the annual payments of

British grants-in-aid gradually increased so that by independence in 1966 they had reached what might be called a more reasonable level, accounting for one-third of the Botswana budget. (See Table 5.1.)

At the same time, but slowly at first, the government began to toy with the idea of using economic planning as a development tool. In 1955, with the first long range commitment of British government grants-in-aid, the colonial administration began to think in terms of sectorwide multiple-year planning. Major goals discussed included improved telecommunications and major village infrastructure development. At the district level, priority would be given to the preparation of water development schemes through the participation of the new rural councils. Before 1962, however, any planning which occurred was ad hoc and came largely out of the annual administrative conferences.

In 1959 the British government commissioned an economic survey of the territory, the first full-scale survey since the 1933 Pim Report. The survey's priorities were water development, improvement of communications, and improvement of cattle production. Note was also taken of regional possibilities for crop improvement and mineral exploitation.[17] In 1962, after several years of experience in the preparation of annual and semi-annual development plans, the colonial government published the first five-year Bechuanaland development plan, intended as a comprehensive effort at listing the government's goals and how they would be met.[18]

At the end of the 1950s, the seeds were sown for two rural development strategies that would influence post-colonial thinking. In 1959 the "Moffat Report on Community Development" was presented to the administration. Moffat suggested the creation of a community development officer separate from the district administration, whose function would be to promote the development of the community from within.[19] The administrative cadre was divided on the question of community development, with a number of officers skeptical of "dreamy-eyed academics." All agreed on the need for a method of community development, without clearly stating what that method should be, but they were divided on the utility of having a separate community development cadre. Typical of one set of responses to the Moffat Report was "that sort of thing is already being done here," and one department official even suggested that "it was clear from the Moffat Report that the author wished to eliminate the Agricultural Department and the District Administration!"[20] Nonetheless, the seeds of the concept had been planted and the idea accepted that at some point it might prove useful to recruit separate district administration staff specifically for community development. Moffat concluded,

> Officers must continue to bear in mind the importance of self-help among the peoples of the territory and to encourage it in every sort of activity. The District Administration must spend more and more time on pasture and water control.[21]

Table 5.1   Annual Payments of British Grants-in-Aid, 1956 to 1968.   (British Pound = U.S. $5)

Fiscal Year	Amount (in £ Sterling)[1]
1956/57	140,000
1957/58	480,000
1958/59	560,000
1959/60	650,000
1960/61	750,000
1961/62	1,000,000
1962/63	1,680,000
1963/64	1,300,000
1964/65	6,000,000[1]
1965/66	3,378,000
1966/67	8,564,000

Sources: Chandler Morse, et al., *Basutoland, Bechuanaland and Swaziland: Report of an Economic Survey Mission* (London: Her Majesty's Stationery Office, 1960), p. 41; Edwin S. Munger, *Bechuanaland: Pan-African Outpost or Bantu Homeland?* (London: Oxford University Press, 1965), p. 115; Gilfred L. Gunderson, "Nation Building and the Administrative State: The Case of Botswana" (Ph.D. dissertation, University of California, Berkeley, 1971), p. 353; and B. A. Young, *Bechuanaland* (London: Her Majesty's Stationery Office, 1966), p. 11.

[1]Includes grants for construction of new capital at Gaborone.

The report of the 1959 economic survey included a similar set of suggestions regarding the possible expansion of district-level planning and developmental activities. In that report's discussion of improving the cattle industry, it was suggested that nontechnical aspects of the development process were a matter for the district administration.

> . . . There is no satisfactory substitute for the Administrative Officer in this sphere and . . . the administrative staff have so many routine preoccuptions of court or office that they cannot undertake the necessary detailed field work, which must be virtually continuous if it is to be effective.[22]

It was also suggested in the economic survey report that the district administration be strengthened with a limited number of members of the administrative service recruited specifically to explain and implement government development policy in the field and to maintain close contact with the rural population. Those officers, who would be relieved of all routine responsibility, would be called assistant district officers (develop - ment). Both the Moffat Report and the economic survey report promoted the idea of a development-oriented officer cadre working within the district administration. This idea would be picked up by administrators after independence, and the position of district officer (development) would become a focal point for rural development planning in Botswana.

British economic policy in Bechuanaland throughout most of the period under discussion can only be described in terms of extreme neglect. Until the late 1950s little was done to modernize the economy and even less was done to provide basic social services. Government contributions to education and public health were nonexistent. The colonial administration faced a continual shortage of administrative personnel, especially in the technical departments, and almost no training of African staff took place prior to independence.

The Growth of Technical Departments

Prior to 1934 the Public Works Department in Bechuanaland consisted of one man, the government engineer. He was assisted by a European clerk of works and a coloured (of mixed race) foreman. In a 1934 government engineer's report to the resident commissioner, it was noted that "nothing had been done to endeavor to meet the incessant cry for assistance in a territory so neglected and yet so dependent upon development of its water supply."[23]

Since the Protectorate was established, its main economic activity had been the livestock industry. In 1905 a single veterinary officer was appointed to Bechuanaland. The first stock inspector was recruited in 1908. They were joined by a second veterinary officer in 1914. By 1935 there were five veterinarians and a number of stock inspectors and livestock officers in the territory.[24] Sixty-six African cattle guards were appointed in 1936. The Veterinary Department remained largely unchanged until the mid-1950s and suffered from severe shortages of staff, transport, and equipment throughout the colonial period, a shortage that was especially acute during and after the second World War. Until 1935 a department for agriculture did not exist.

A sector-by-sector analysis of the technical departments in Bechuanaland would indicate a similar picture of staff shortages and neglect. At the end of 1936, the senior technical establishment for the entire Texas-size territory consisted of:

11 Medical Officers	4 Agricultural Officers
6 Veterinary Officers	1 Director of Education
6 Government Engineers	1 Forestry Officer
(Public Works Department)	1 Resident of the Special Court

The number of technical officers in Bechuanaland grew slowly during the 1930s, and the outbreak of World War II ended all recruitment overseas, creating severe staff shortages throughout the territory. The technical departments continued to grow only after the war, although the size of the administrative cadre was almost the same by 1949, the technical cadre had more than doubled to almost eighty officers. Growth in the numbers of administrative cadre and senior positions, the "superscale" posts, occurred during the 1950s and 1960s but not as dramatically as the increase in numbers of specialists. By 1966 there were over 1,000 specialists in Bechuanaland. (See Table 5.2.)

Although the total amount of grants-in-aid to Bechuanaland was pitifully small until the late 1950s, the influx of funds was felt very quickly within the small Protectorate administration. As early as 1937, "the general increase in the activities of all branches of the administration," according to Resident Commissioner Rey, "has imposed a very much heavier burden on the district administration, especially with regard to the technical departments."[25]

After World War II, district officers became increasingly involved in the financial and economic affairs of their districts. They began to interact with builders and engineers over proposed additions to their districts' physical infrastructures. By the end of the decade, the rudiments of a system of district level planning would be in place.

Technical officials began to demand increased access to the chiefs in order to assess needs and determine the location of local projects. In water development, for example, some of the costs of digging bore holes had to be met by the tribal administration. What had been a two-way relationship between the district officer and the chief became three-way, as technicians, because of their increased responsibility, began to interact with traditional authorities at the district and subdistrict level. This became an increasingly tense situation prior to independence and attempts to resolve it were largely unsuccessful. The colonial administration's inability to integrate the technical specialist into the administrative system as part of a district team was left for the newly independent government in Botswana to resolve.[26]

Because of the paucity of development funds, administrative activity during the postwar period was characterized primarily by competition between

Table 5.2 Distribution and Number of Administrative Positions in Bechuanaland

Year	Senior Superscale	Administrative	Professional Specialist
1937	7	19	36
1949	10	21	79
1964	29	42	247
1966	40	41	1,038

Sources: Bechuanaland Staff Lists, 1937 and 1949 (Mafeking: Government Mimeograph); and Gilfred L. Gunderson, "Nation Building and the Administrative State: The Case of Botswana" (Ph.D. dissertation, University of California, Berkeley, 1971), pp. 230 and 249.

the newly expanding technical departments and the long established administrative cadre over almost nonexistent funds. Several attempts to clarify relationships met with little success, and attempts to reorganize the district administration did not have any lasting effects.

Administrative reorganization schemes in the 1950s, such as the creation of divisional commissioners, may well have been used to deal with a situation of uncertainty. An inordinate amount of energy was put into efforts at organizational change during the last fifteen years of British colonial rule.[27] It appeared that reorganization was, in effect, a partial substitute for the lack of available resources with which to confront the political challenges (see Chapter 6) and the financial stagnation that characterized much of the postwar period. Fiscally, British policy was characterized by an extreme parsimony until the 1950s. Administrative reform was inexpensive and could also be introduced on the spot without the approval of either London or Pretoria. As a method of solving a problem, its weakness seems clear, but as a pattern of administrative behavior, it did have the advantage of providing at least the illusion of movement.

Colonial Economic Policy: Origins of a Dependency Relationship

In the nineteenth century Tswana peoples were subjected to political partition as a result of regional developments in southern Africa. Today two-thirds of the approximately 3.5 million Setswana-speaking peoples live in the Republic of South Africa.

From the beginning Bechuanaland, in spite of its vast size, was a rump state, with marginal agricultural possibilities, with much of its land area desert or semi-desert, and with a small population whose primary function was that of a cheap labor reserve for South Africa.

To examine Botswana's fiscal policy without an analysis of the origins of its economy and of the impact that Britain had upon the economic development of the entire southern African region is to risk a misinterpretation. For example, one economist could write in all seriousness that "Botswana had no real colonial history" in terms of its economic development.[28] Quill Hermans, in spite of a much closer relationship to Botswana's economic development, could come to a similar conclusion.

> It was quite clear that nothing occurred between 1885 and 1955 which contributed significantly to Botswana's economic and financial development. Bechuanaland's economy and the domestic fiscal resources available to its Administration were inadequate for the purposes of achieving social and economic advancement. . . . It was a passive period, devoted to the avoidance of involvement, to the maintenance of a *status quo.*[29]

Hermans' description is accurate in terms of the impact of British fiscal policy on the Bechuanaland Protectorate. It does not, however, give us a true picture of how British colonial rule influenced the Southern African region's economy. As early as 1933, Sir Alan Pim pinpointed the major economic impact of colonialism on Bechuanaland.

> . . . The main factor in destroying the old subsistence economy has
> . . . been the introduction of a money economy, and more especially
> of taxation levied in money. . . . To pay taxes the Native has to raise
> money and he could do this only by selling his possessions to
> European traders or by going outside his reserve to earn money in
> European service.[30]

By 1966 the people in what is now Botswana had been interacting economically with the mercentile capitalists at the Cape for the better part of a century and a half. During that period, and particularly during the eighty-one years of British colonial rule, the economy of Bechuanaland had changed dramatically.[31] Britain's fiscal parsimony should be viewed as only one aspect of a broader policy of economic regulation, taxation, and regional integration, the effect of which was to leave the post-colonial economy in a dependency relationship with the larger states of the southern Africa region and the international system as a whole.

The importance of Britain's regulation and manipulation of the Bechuanaland economy becomes clearer by examining four major areas of economic activity: regional and domestic patterns of trade, the evolution of labor migration to South Africa, livestock and agriculture, and mineral development.

Regional Patterns of Trade

Under British colonialism Bechuanaland's regional trading patterns were bound firmly to those of South Africa. The economic integration of southern Africa operated at a number of different levels during the colonial period.

1. Bechuanaland and the two other High Commission Territories were linked to South Africa through the customs union and common market established in 1910.
2. The High Commission Territories' use of South African currency, banking, and other financial arrangements created a kind of de facto currency union.
3. Bechuanaland's communication and transportation systems were tied to those of South Africa.

The ties between Bechuanaland and South Africa strengthened throughout the colonial period, and by 1966 South Africa had a firm grip on the territory's export and import markets, controlled its transportation and communications, marketed its agricultural products and employed most of its labor force.

The major cause of this dependency relationship was the customs union itself, set up in 1910 as a prelude to transferring the territories to the Union of South Africa. Britain and South Africa agreed that the three High Commission Territories and the Union would have no internal customs barriers. Instead, South Africa would pay 1.31097 percent of its own total customs and excise revenue to the High Commission in Pretoria. The High Commission, in turn, would pass on a fixed proportion to the administration in each of the three territories. In Bechuanaland's case the administration received 0.276 percent of the total customs and excise revenue.

The customs union permitted South Africa to develop the markets of Bechuanaland and the other two territories as integral parts of the Union's economy.[32] The most obvious negative effect of the 1910 customs union agreement was the division of revenue among the four territories, calculated from a derivative formula established during a period of recession in southern Africa which did not change for sixty years.

A less obvious impact of the customs union was its effect on manufacturing within the region. There is little reason to doubt that throughout the colonial period the operation of the customs union was detrimental to the interests of the three High Commission Territories. The Union of South Africa was able to encourage its secondary industries by instituting a protective tariff and quantitative import restrictions. The protection which was afforded to South African products in the three territories allowed South African commercial firms to assume a dominant position in the markets of those territories. The excess between the cost of the South African products and what such imports would have cost overseas fell on the three territories.

The customs union, throughout the colonial period, only exacerbated the "polarization effect" that the Union of South Africa had upon Bechuanaland as well as the other territories in southern Africa. A polarization effect ensures that industry is attracted to the most developed sector of a regional economy. The existence of the customs union ensured that Bechuanaland could produce very little at costs that were lower than those prevailing in South Africa.

The natural consequences of the polarization effect were increased by South African trade restrictions on the High Commission Territories. At the apex of any customs union is the principle of the free exchange of goods. As Peter Robson charitably noted, however, in the southern African context "the term 'free interchange' is ambiguous."[33] Although the goods moving into South Africa from the High Commission Territories were duty-free, those goods only had a limited access to South Africa's vast markets. South Africa could and did impose quantitative restrictions upon goods from the three territories.

Nowhere are these restrictions clearer than in the case of Bechuanaland's cattle exports to South Africa. Beginning in 1923 the Union government, bending to pressure from South African ranchers because of the postwar decline in beef prices, imposed restrictions on Bechuanaland's cattle. Two techniques were used. Beginning in 1923, severe weight restrictions (ultimately 1100 pounds for oxen and 840 pounds for cows) were placed on cattle originating in the High Commission Territories. With the outbreak of hoof and mouth disease in 1932, the South African government imposed additional restrictions on imports that "were applied more stringently than necessary for veterinary reasons."[34]

Ettinger placed the blame for allowing such discriminatory restrictions squarely on the shoulders of the British High Commission. In spite of vigorous protests from the Secretariat in Mafeking, according to Ettinger, "it appears . . . that the High Commissioner's Office did not really put a great deal of pressure on South Africa to lift the Embargo." Even in the Mafeking administration, he notes, "it appears that some officials . . . may have been more concerned with the welfare of European farmers (who could meet the weight restrictions) than of the African ones." The problem was that

> British officials in the B.P. seem to have had the interest of Bechuanaland at heart, but they did not receive very much support from the High Commission. . . . In the case of the cattle embargoes, [the High Commission] seems to have been more concerned with maintaining good British-South African relations than with looking after the economic interests of the [High Commission Territories].[35]

The import restrictions placed on Bechuanaland cattle clearly demonstrate the ambiguity of intergovernmental relations between the Protectorate administration in Mafeking and the High Commission in Pretoria. The nature of the High Commission was such that the high commissioner performed a dual role as the official in charge of the High Commission Territories and the British government's representative in South Africa. The informal understandings and agreements between the South African government and the high commissioner allowed restrictions on cattle imports to reach major proportions during the interwar period. South Africa's ability to limit Bechuanaland's production of beef and beef products for export was undermining the territory's economy.

Domestic Patterns of Trade

In Mafeking and in the various districts throughout Bechuanaland, British colonial administrators placed their stamp on patterns of domestic trade within the first few years of colonial rule. Having acquiesced to South African domination of the region, British officials, during much of the colonial period, placed overt restrictions on African participation in the system of domestic trade that was evolving throughout the territory.

Colonial policy at the district level can be documented as early as 1891 in the Kweneng District. The Kweneng district administration intervened directly in the economic affairs of the Bakwena with a decree stating that all traders, whether European or non-European, would have to obtain licenses from the district colonial authorities. This decree was challenged forcefully by the Bakwena tribal administration to the point of an armed confrontation in 1892. According to Duggan, although the Bakwena authorities ultimately submitted to this interference in what they saw as internal Bakwena affairs, the question of the control of trading in the districts remained in dispute throughout most of the colonial period.[36]

It is in the history of the Bamangwato reserve that the most evidence exists to suggest that district colonial authorities and the colonial government in Mafeking actively intervened to discourage Batswana participation in the trading sector. The experiences of Chief Khama (Khama the Great) and his participation in the firm of Garrett, Smith and Co. between 1910 and 1916 are documented fully by Parsons.[37]

In 1909, when a trading firm in central Bechuanaland came close to collapse, Chief Khama of the Bamangwato decided to implement an experiment in economic planning for his area. He bought the assets of the dying firm and named the new company after its European managers. By adding additional capital, Khama had built the worth of Garrett, Smith and Co. to £20,000 by 1916.

With Chief Khama's sponsorship, the trading firm became financially successful. Consequently, by 1912 it was raising the ire of a number of the other trading companies, including the Bechuanaland Trading Association, a large-scale enterprise with interests primarily in Northern and Southern Rhodesia. By 1916, through a series of maneuvers, both fair and foul, the Bechuanaland Trading Association had succeeded in discrediting Khama's trading firm and convincing the British authorities that a firm sponsored by an African chief was a threat to European trade interests. The British authorities, fearing that Khama's example might be emulated by other chiefs because of his success, forced Khama to disengage himself from Garrett, Smith and Co.

> If "Khama and Co." had been allowed to succeed, there is every indication that its success would have been copied to bolster the economies of other Tswana states under the Protectorate. Chief Seepapitso . . . of the Ngwaketse was apparently ready to follow Khama's example before he was assassinated in 1916. And as late as 1928 a Chief's brother tried to set up a trading store among the Rolong. He was refused permission by government, using the 1923 Credit Sales to Natives Proclamation as [its] basis.[38]

What happened in Bamangwato district was not an isolated case. During the 1930s the Batswana faced considerable European opposition throughout Bechuanaland to any bid to enter the trading arena. European traders were routinely backed by the colonial administrators who would reject applications from Africans for trading licenses on the grounds that the territory was sufficiently served by existing European shops and that Africans did not have enough capital to open a general store.

During World War II, European-African entanglements over the trade issue continued and Africans continued to be discouraged from entering into retail trade. Although in the late 1940s the administration gradually began to accept the need for African traders, it continued to oppose either grocers' licenses or general licenses for Africans because of the dangers of "undercapitalization, overly aggressive European competition, and lack of experience."[39]

After the war Chief Kgari Sechele of the Bakwena applied for a reduced license fee for grocers in order to allow Bakwena traders to enter villages that did not have general dealerships. The colonial administration put the matter to the Northern Chamber of Commerce. The chamber's reply was that such action would result in

> a lot of poor traders, both European and Native, which will reduce the Government's income considerably. This Chamber considers that the building up and care of the native's cattle industry, which is the life blood of the country, would be a much better prospect than fostering trade.[40]

At that point, the matter was dropped. Resident European traders profited from the cattle trade, and competition of any type was not welcomed.

As late as 1949 there were only ten stores owned by Africans in the Bechuanaland Protectorate, all of them either in or close to the major villages. All ten traders operated under restricted dealers' licenses that permitted Africans to trade solely in the reserves, limited their sales turnovers, and prevented their trading stands from being closer than five miles to a European general dealer. Not until the 1950s did Africans make any significant gains in the trading area; by 1959 Batswana had fifty-three trading licenses in Bechuanaland. Until the eve of independence, however, few Africans attempted to compete with either Indians or Europeans in reserve headquarters or major railheads such as Francistown, Palapye, or Gaberones. British colonial economic regulation of retail trade left the bulk of the retail economy in the hands of foreigners at independence.

Labor Migration to South Africa

Nowhere was the Bechuanaland Protectorate altered more as a result of colonialism than in the area of adult male work patterns. During the century of contact with South Africa, seasonal migration to work in the mines and the farms of South Africa became a way of life for Batswana males, and as the colonial period progressed Bechuanaland's economy became increasingly dependent upon monies returned to the Protectorate by the labor migrants.

The movement south to find work was not a new phenomenon. There were labor migrants going to the Cape Colony and the South African Republic to work on European farms as early as 1844.[41] In spite of the long history of labor movement to the south, the impact of labor migration on Bechuanaland seems to have been limited prior to the turn of the century. After 1899, "migration for employment became more systematic and pervasive, its cause now not emanating from factors internal to the social formation but from the externally imposed tax and land arrangements."[42] In 1902, 357 Batswana were recruited for the mines, and by 1905 the number had increased to 2,352. During the period from 1905 to 1925, the number of labor migrants fluctuated from a low of 2,400 to a high of almost 9,000.

The first hut tax was introduced in Bechuanaland in 1899. The imposition of taxes and the provision that 10 percent of the tax collected would be turned over to the chiefs, created a need for a cash income among Batswana and acted as a direct stimulant to employment. After the introduction of taxation, "labour migration became an obvious means of enabling poor men to earn money for the payment of their taxes; and the chiefs, perhaps partly because of the 'commission' they themselves received, often urged their subjects to go." Alliances developed between the labor recruiters and the chiefs and in several cases chiefs "made men who could not pay a tax seek work from labour recruiters."[43] Seepapitso, chief of the Ngwaketse, declared in 1911 that any member of the tribe who could not pay the tax "would be sent abroad to work for his tax money."[44] A standard procedure in many instances was to deduct the tax that laborers owed from the advance given to them by the labor recruiter, and often, as was the case in Kgatleng under Chief Isang (1920-1929), chiefs actually drafted tax defaulters to work in the mines.

The Protectorate government became, as the colonial period wore on, increasingly dependent upon monies returned to the Protectorate by labor migrants. According to Duggan, "Native Tax, which usually accounted for more than three-fourths of district administration revenue, rose to more than £5,000 annually by 1938, and then to more than £10,000 annually during the Second World War."[45] If these figures are correct, taxation was taking from one-fourth to one-third of the cash income from South Africa.

The fact that labor migration increasingly was seen as being directly linked to the administrative survival of the Protectorate government led officials in the territoy and in South Africa to establish administrative support for the migration process. In 1939 one district commissioner, cognizant of this link, commented, "the wages earned by these [migrant] workers form the main source of income in the district and without them trade and tax collection would be almost at a standstill."[46]

Thus, the Bechuanaland Protectorate administration encouraged labor migration, and the imposition of taxes introduced an element of compulsion to the process. One of the functions of the district commissioner was to act as district labor officer.

> District Officers themselves have at times actively encouraged recruitment. This has usually taken the form of instituting a special drive against tax defaulters, the men being warned that they will be prosecuted unless they pay their arrears immediately, if necessary by taking an advance from a labour agent.[47]

The Bechuanaland administration established permanent arrangements for the control process instituted by the Native Recruiting Corporation (NRC) and the Witwatersrand Native Labor Organization (WNLA) as the two agencies searched for recruits in the territory. Labor recruitment was also supported by an Agency on the Rand, an organization responsible for looking after the affairs of mine workers from the High Commission Territories. The Agency on the Rand was started as an office to collect taxes from migrant workers and later went on to incorporate many functions of a welfare nature. The three offices of the Rand High Commission Labor Agency were staffed by district officers seconded to the High Commission. The main office in Johannesburg functioned under a representative of the Basutoland government, a branch office in Randfontein was directed by an officer from Bechuanaland, and a second branch in Springs was under the charge of a Swaziland administrator.

The annual number of labor migrants from Bechuanaland to South Africa approached twenty thousand in the late 1940s, slightly less than the twenty-three thousand estimated in the prewar period. By independence the annual number of Bechuanaland's labor migrants to South Africa had reached forty-five thousand. Only a small amount of the money earned by the labor migrants was returned to the High Commission Territories. Writing of Basutoland, Lord Hailey pointed out that although Basuto laborers earned more than £3.5 million by working in the Union of South Africa in 1950, only £0.6 million was returned to the territory in cash, including deferred wages, family remittances, and taxes collected from absentees. The rest of the money stayed or flowed back into the South African economy.[48]

British colonial policy on labor migration in southern Africa was deliberate, consistent, and directly linked to the overall administrative and economic policy for Bechuanaland and the two other High Commission Territories.

> Sufficient monies were spent to ensure the simple reproduction of the minimum infrastructure necessary for the system of migrant labour to continue and other expenditures were kept as low as possible to ensure that there would not be opportunities within the Protectorate which would attract labour away from migration.[49]

The pattern of labor migration to South Africa would force the new Botswana government into a series of dilemmas vis-à-vis its economic development strategy in the years after independence.

Livestock and Agriculture Policy

It was in the area of rural development that British colonial economic policy was closest to the categorization of total neglect. In 1965 Halpern drew a bleak picure of Bechuanaland's rural areas.

> In an area of 225,000 square miles, most of the . . . people subsist on ranching some 1 1/2 million poor-grade cattle. There is a chronic shortage of water, and when the rains fail, which happens frequently, finding work in neighbouring territories is for many Batswana the only alternative to starvation.[50]

Beyond this neglect there was a clear economic policy that held firm for much of the colonial period. Britain's priorities in Bechuanaland were to stimulate the cattle industry and encourage labor migration at the expense of an expanded role for Batswana in the trading sector or in agriculture. Britain's interest in Bechuanaland's agricultural production was limited to the small European community resident in the eastern part of the territory. The colonial administration's limited interest in African agriculture was linked to the vested interests in the preservation of the European traders' role as agents for food imports, part of their larger monopoly of the entire import trade.

The destructive impact of British policy on rural development went even further, however. The systematic encouragement of healthy men to leave the rural areas for the South African mines "left the tasks of agriculture and animal husbandry . . . to the very old and the very young, and to women, in other words to those least physically equipped to perform them."[51] Employed on short-term contracts, the healthy men were returning to rural life with changed values and work patterns. Thus, the process of labor migration created a "proletarianized" peasantry, that is, a working class dependent upon urban conditions but residing and subsisting in the rural areas.

In spite of the lack of priority given to the rural economy during the colonial period, it remained a major contributor to the overall economy of Bechuanaland. William Duggan graphically documented the impact that rural production had on the economy of the Kweneng District immediately after World War II. The total exports from that district during 1947 were valued at £20,000. "This can be assumed to have been derived entirely from the traditional economy: skins, hides, karosses, cattle, sorghum and beans." During the same year, food imports amounted to approximately £22,000. Since the annual income from labor migration was also about £22,000, the Bakwena "were almost able to meet the total cost of their food exports with production from the traditional economy."[52]

What little resources the colonial administration had prior to World War II were expended in the area of animal husbandry. Administrative efforts at the district level focused on improved breeding and herding. The priorities of the Veterinary Department were in the control and eradication of stock diseases. Later, after the tribal fund was inaugurated, part of the money was used to provide new water supplies and better bulls. During the period from 1934 to 1943, the Department of Veterinary Services initiated a number of programs for livestock improvement throughout the territory. The goal was for each district to have a livestock improvement center that demonstrated improved animal husbandry techniques and provided bulls and rams to local stock owners.[53]

During the 1940s and 1950s the government concentrated on the problem of hoof and mouth disease. Periodic outbreaks of the disease were devastating to Bechuanaland's economy. The cattle trade was an export trade and the outbreaks brought about immediate restrictions on exports to South Africa. Since the bulk of the cattle went to South Africa (smaller amounts went to the Rhodesias and the Belgian Congo), the South African government could effectively control the Bechuanaland cattle trade.

Throughout the colonial period, the cattle industry remained the lifeblood of the territory. During the period from 1947 to 1955, cattle accounted for between 70 and 90 percent of Bechuanaland's total commodity exports and constituted 80 percent of agriculture's contribution to the territory's income. Prior to 1954, export of cattle was on-the-hoof through hundreds of miles of parched scrub country in the Kalahari Desert. A new export abattoir was built by the Colonial Development Corporation in Lobatsi in 1954, after which cattle could be slaughtered and processed first, then carcasses exported to South Africa and overseas. During the latter years of colonial rule, 5 percent of all African cattle were exported, as compared to 15 percent of all European cattle. Ownership of the abattoir is a good indication of the pattern of economic control during those later years. Fifty percent of the abattoir and meat processing plant was owned externally by the Colonial Development Corporation, and 25 percent was owned locally by the cattle producers, mainly European. The final 25 percent was owned by the Bechuanaland government.

For most of the colonial period, the Bechuanaland authorities did not see the value in any undue emphasis on crop production (as was previously mentioned, there was not even a separate Department of Agriculture until 1935). Agriculture remained, in any event, uncertain due to the perpetual drought conditions that exist in the country. Rainfall is extremely uncertain and badly distributed.

The colonial administration viewed the land as infertile and traditional agricultural methods simply as aggravating bad soil. The little effort expended on agricultural development was in an abbreviated training of African agricultural demonstrators who would show farmers new techniques. After 1930, the administration introduced better varieties of seeds and organized annual agricultural shows. The impact was minimal. As Schapera pointed out, "the agricultural practices of the Tswana had not changed fundamentally by 1940. In the main, people still grew the same kinds of crops as before, chiefly kaffircorn [sorghum], supplemented by maize, millet, sweet cane, beans, earthnuts and melons."[54] As late as 1953 there were only seventeen agricultural demonstrators in the whole territory. Considerable control over the agricultural production process was exercised by the chiefs who tended to favor the planting of traditional crops and the use of traditional methods, and it was often the case that ploughing and harvesting could not begin until the chief gave the word.

During the 1945 to 1950 period, Colonial Welfare and Development funds began to enter the territory and become available for agricultural and livestock development. Of the total amount allocated for rural development, 32 percent was earmarked for water projects, 23 percent was given to veterinary projects, and 14 percent was allocated to the geological survey. The Department of Agriculture used the remaining funds to support the small number of European farmers in the eastern part of the territory who supplied foodstuffs to the urban areas.

Throughout the colonial period most of the nontraditional foods were imported, and during the droughts, Bechuanaland was dependent upon imports even for basic foodstuffs. In general, little was done to try to stimulate agricultural development or the search for water until 1957, when the Maud-Fawcus administration committed Bechuanaland to self-government. When asked what role Bechuanaland's administration played in the rural development process, a former colonial official who had stayed on after independence responded, "There were so few contributions made during the colonial period. We had so few strengths. So little development was done. Somehow we managed to maintain a reasonable relationship with the Batswana. That was about it."[55] At independence, "the agricultural system was so underdeveloped that even in relatively good years, maize, which is the country's staple food, had to be imported."[56] The vacuum in the area of agricultural development would be very difficult to fill after independence.

Mineral Development

Nowhere in the colonial economy was there so little awareness of Bechuanaland's potential than in the area of mineral development. As late as 1956, Lord Hailey could say, for example, that "Bechuanaland has a considerable variety of mineral occurrences but for the most part on a scale that does not permit economic working."[57]

It was not for the want of trying. The search for minerals began in the late nineteenth century when gold was discovered at the Tati area in what is now the Northeast District of Botswana. The Tati Company operated the Monarch gold mine from 1890 to 1964. The mine did not prove to be the rich source of gold that early predictions had foretold, however, and it did not become a major revenue earner for Bechuanaland.

The search for other mineral deposits met with little success during the colonial period, and there was no further interest in mining prior to the establishment of the Geological Survey Department in 1948-49. Part of the lack of interest in mineral development may have been caused by the suspicions of the chiefs about its benefits. There were four possible causes for the chiefs' suspicions.

1. They had seen the effect of mining in South Africa and feared the increased European presence that would result from extensive mineral exploitation.
2. They feared that the discovery of minerals might lead to new and stronger demands for transferring the Protectorate to South Africa.
3. They were concerned about a repetition of the unsavory example of the Tati Company. The Tati District was run by the Company along Rhodesian lines. (Non-Europeans were not allowed to own farms in the Tati District and it had become a location of tense racial relationships as a result of the overt racial discrimination.)
4. They recalled the autocratic attempts by the colonial administration to push the chiefs into making mining concessions to the British South Africa Company during the 1920s.

In the mid-1950s interest in mining and mineral exploration grew, and a number of mining and surveying companies prospected for minerals. In the Northeast District in 1959, the Roan (formerly Rhodesian) Selection Trust (RST), through Bamangwato Concessions Company, began prospecting after negotiating successfully the mining exploration terms with the Bechuanaland administration and the Bamangwato tribal administration. Tshekedi Khama, who had developed a close relationship with Sir Ronald Prain of the Roan Selection Trust, acted as the Batswanas' principal spokesman in the negotiations.[58] In 1958, following a roundtable conference between the Bechuanaland administration, the Bamangwato Tribal Administration, and the mining companies, the concession was agreed upon and signed. The Bamangwato tribal administration was given token representation on the Bamangwato Concessions company board and the terms of the agreement granted exploration rights to Bamangwato Concessions. Eighty-five percent of the Bamangwato Concessions Company was owned by the Bechuanaland subsidiary of RST while 15 percent was to be owned by the Bechunanaland government. (Roan Selection Trust was, and is, owned by American Metals Climax [Amax] and Anglo-American.)

Although the basic agreement on exploration and on the eventual profits from the Northeast District's mines was established prior to 1966, on the eve of independence knowledge of the actual resources underground was scanty not only in that district but throughout Bechuanaland. Asbestos had been discovered in the 1920s, and manganese and coal deposits had been found as well. During the colonial period, mining activity was limited to two small manganese mines, one small asbestos mine, and small amounts of gold and silver. Asbestos and manganese mines were located in Ngwaketse (Southern) district, and a manganese mine was located in Bamalete (Southeast district). The total production of manganese between 1957 and 1963 was 45,787 short tons, valued at £341,093; the total production of asbestos between 1951 and 1964 was only 14,500 short tons, with a value of £1.5 million. Mining values in 1965 stood at just under two million South African rand for the territory as a whole.

Aside from the manganese and asbestos, there was a vague idea just prior to independence that there might be a use for soda ash and high-grade salt from the sodium carbonate-bearing brines of the Makgadikgadi pans. There were only hints about any major copper deposits, and the possibility of diamond reserves was being investigated by the De Beers/Anglo-American group. Although the basic pattern of relationships between the mining companies and the Botswana government was determined during the colonial period, the exploitation of mineral reserves would wait until after independence.

Conclusion

That the economic development of the Bechuanaland Protectorate was severely neglected during the colonial period is beyond question. An examination of British fiscal policy toward Bechuanaland reveals a parsimony that was unparalleled in the British empire. Even when Colonial Development and Welfare funds began to enter Bechuanaland in the 1930s and 1940s, the amounts were still so paltry that the major effect was to stimulate rivalries between the administration and the technical departments over authority in the districts. Only in the last decade of British colonial rule did economic assistance reach levels that began to have an impact on Bechuanaland's economic development.

As stated earlier, examining colonial fiscal policy in isolation provides a distorted view of the effect of British colonialism on Bechuanaland. Britain's regulatory policy was the decisive factor in that territory's underdevelopment. Rather than characterizing Britain's economic policy toward Bechuanaland as one of benign neglect, we must look to the clear pattern of impact in the regulatory policy that ultimately determined the nature of the political economy of post-colonial Botswana.

British regulatory policy locked Bechuanaland into a dependency relationship with South Africa. Both the customs union and the trade limitations imposed on the territory allowed the South African economic community to gain a dominant position within Bechuanaland and within the region. The situation vis-à-vis South Africa was exacerbated by the ambiguous role played by the High Commissioner who was both the final governing authority for the three High Commission Territories and Britain's diplomatic representative to the Union of South Africa.

Domestically, British regulatory policy committed Bechuanaland to cattle production at the expense of developing arable agricultural or trade activities. Agriculturally, the territory changed very little under British colonialism, and the limited support that was made available went to Bechuanaland's small European community. Throughout the colonial period trade patterns were structured so as to exclude an active African participation in the commercial sector, and South Africa was given carte blanche to exploit the territory's mineral deposits.

Thus, Botswana inherited a badly neglected and underdeveloped economy. But it did not inherit an economy with a clean slate. Much of the post-colonial period would be dominated by economic relationships and trade links that had been forged prior to 1966. Although the fiscal neglect would be altered easily by mineral development and international technical assistance, the effects of British regulatory policy in the areas of regional and domestic trade, labor migration, and agricultural and mineral development went much deeper and, to a great extent, would determine the nature of Botswana's political system.

Notes

1. Jack Halpern, *South Africa's Hostages: Basutoland, Bechuanaland and Swaziland* (Harmondsworth: Penguin, 1965), p. 108.

2. David B. Knight, "Botswana at the Development Threshold," *Focus*, vol. 26, no. 2 (November–December 1975), p. 9. Knight, for example, labels British economic policy as indecisive.

3. Q. N. Parsons, "The Economic History of Khama's Country in Southern Africa," *African Social Research* , no. 18 (December 1974), pp. 643-644 and 672-673.

4. See Samir Amin, "Underdevelopment and Dependence in Black Africa—Origins and Contemporary Forms, *Journal of Modern African Studies*, vol. 10, no. 4 (December 1972), esp. pp. 520-521.

5. Quill Hermans, "Towards Budgetary Independence: A Review of Botswana's Financial History, 1900 to 1973," *Botswana Notes and Records*, vol. 6 (1974), pp. 101-102.

6. Jack Parson, "Political Culture in Botswana: A Survey Result," *Journal of Modern African Studies*, vol. 15, no. 4 (December, 1977), p. 640.

7. Anthony Sillery, *Founding A Protectorate: History of Bechuanaland, 1885–1895* (The Hague: Moulton & Co., 1965), p. 57.

8. Parsons, "Economic History of Khama's Country," p. 666.

9. *Ibid.*

10. Leonard Barnes, *The New Boer War* (London: Hogarth Press, 1932), pp. 128-151 and Margaret L. Hodgson and William G. Ballinger, *Britain in Southern Africa*, no. 2, *Bechuanaland Protectorate* (Alice, South Africa: Lovedale Press, 1933), pp. 32-63 and *passim*.

11. Barnes, p. 118.

12. Hodgson and Ballinger, *Britain in Southern Africa*, p. 57.

13. Sir Alan Pim, *Financial and Economic Position of the Bechuanaland Protectorate: Report of the Commission Appointed by the Secretary of State for Dominion Affairs, March, 1932*, Parliamentary Report, Cmd. 4368 (London: His Majesty's Stationery Office, 1933), p. 33.

14. Direct grants-in-aid on a regular basis only began in 1956.

15. Symon Mission Report, *Economic and Financial Report on the High Commission Territories*, Unpublished, CRS No. 24, 1954, cited in Hermans, "Towards Budgetary Independence," p. 93.

16. Hermans, "Towards Budgetary Independence," p. 94.

17. Great Britain, *Basutoland, Bechuanaland and Swaziland: Report of an Economic Survey Mission* (London: Her Majesty's Stationery Office, 1960).

18. Bechuanaland Government, "Transitional Development Plan, 1963" (mimeographed, Mafeking, 1963).

19. Moffat, "Report on Community Development" (mimeographed, Bechuanaland, 1959), S. 574/11.

20. Both quotes from Minutes of Administrative Conference, 1959, S. 574/11.

21. Moffat, "Report on Community Development."

22. Great Britain, *Economic Survey Mission*, p. 60.

23. Rey Report on the Development of the Protectorate, D.O. 35/936/570/1. PRO, London.

24. J. Falconer, "History of the Botswana Veterinary Services, 1905–1966," *Botswana Notes and Records*, vol. 3 (1971), p. 75.

25. Rey Report on the Development of the Protectorate, D.O. 35/936/57011. PRO, London.

26. See Lord (William M.) Hailey, *An African Survey* (London: Oxford University Press, 1938), pp. 413-416 *passim*.

27. For a further discussion of the reorganization and its impact on local level administration in Botswana see Louis A. Picard, "Administrative Reorganization—A Substitute for Policy? The District Administration and Local Government in the Bechuanaland Protectorate, 1949–1966," *Botswana Notes and Records*, vol. 12 (1984).

28. Penelope Hartland-Thunberg, *Botswana: An African Growth Economy* (Boulder, Co.: Westview Press, 1978), p. 2.

29. Hermans, "Towards Budgetary Independence," p. 108.

30. Pim, *Bechuanaland*, pp. 23-24.

31. For a discussion of early European contacts with Botswana see Neil Parsons, "The Economic History of Khama's Country in Botswana, 1844–1930," in *The Roots of Rural Poverty in Central and Southern Africa*, Robin Palmer and Neil Parsons, eds. (Berkeley: University of California Press, 1977), pp. 116-119.

32. Biff Turner, "A Fresh Start for the Southern African Customs Union," *African Affairs*, vol. 70, no. 280 (July 1971), p. 479.

33. Peter Robson, "Economic Integration in Southern Africa," *Journal of Modern African Studies*, vol. 5, no. 4 (December 1967), pp. 469-490.

34. Stephen Ettinger, "South Africa's Weight Restrictions on Cattle Exports from Bechuanaland, 1924–1941," *Botswana Notes and Records*, vol. 4 (1972), p. 25.

35. All quotes, *Ibid.*, pp. 22, 25, and 28 respectively.

36. William Duggan, "The Kweneng in the Colonial Era: A Brief Economic History," *Botswana Notes and Records*, vol. 9 (1977), pp. 11-12.

37. Q. N. Parsons, "'Khama & Co.' and the Jousse Trouble, 1910–1916," *Journal of African History*, vol. 16, no. 3 (1975), pp. 383-408.

38. *Ibid.*, p. 407.

39. Alan G. Best, "General Trading in Botswana, 1890–1968," *Economic Geography*, vol. 46, no. 4 (October 1970), p. 603.

40. Duggan, "The Kweneng in the Colonial Era," p. 45.

41. *Ibid.* p. 42.

42. Jack Parson, "The Political Economy of Botswana: A Case in the Study of Politics and Social Change in Post-Colonial Societies" (Ph.D. diss., University of Sussex, 1979), p. 60.

43. Both quotations from Isaac Schapera, *Tribal Innovators: Tswana Chiefs and Social Change, 1795–1940* (London: The Athlone Press, 1970), p. 117.

44. Isaac Schapera, *Migrant Labour and Tribal Life: A Study of Conditions in the Bechuanaland Protectorate* (London: Oxford University Press, 1947), p. 153.

45. Duggan, "The Kweneng in the Colonial Era," p. 43.

46. *Ibid.*, pp. 42, 47; Schapera, *Migrant Labour*, p. 151.

47. Schapera, *Migrant Labour*, p. 151.

48. See Lord (William M.) Hailey, *An African Survey*, revised ed. (London: Oxford University Press, 1956), p. 1286.

49. Parson, "The Political Economy of Botswana," p. 62.

50. Jack Halpern, *South Africa's Hostages: Basutoland, Bechuanaland and Swaziland* (Harmondsworth: Penguin, 1965), p. 297.

51. Parson, "The Political Economy of Botswana," p. 57.

52. Duggan, "The Kweneng and the Colonial Era," p. 44, for both quotes.

53. Falconer, "History of the Botswana Veterinary Services," pp. 75-76.

54. Schapera, *Tribal Innovators*, p. 101.

55. Oral interview, P. L. Steenkamp, 20 August 1975.

56. Halpern, *South Africa's Hostages*, p. 303.

57. Hailey, *African Survey*, 1956, p. 1496.

58. For a discussion of these negotiations see Mary Benson, *Tshekedi Khama* (London: Faber and Faber, 1960), pp. 63-66 and 281-283.

6

Crisis and Containment: The Limits of Nationalism in the Bureaucratic State

According to Evelyn Baring's biographer, the South African high commissioner gave the following reason for his decision not to recognize Seretse Khama as chief of the Bamangwato in 1949:

> As regards the Union the situation is the gravest which has faced us since I first came to this country. . . .[T]he political consequences in the Union of recognition would be far more serious than I had recognized. . . . The more extreme Nationalists will . . . say that South Africans should not and cannot remain associated with a country which recognizes officially an African chief married to a white woman and they will make Seretse's recognition the occasion of an appeal to the country for the establishment of a republic but of a republic outside the Commonwealth. . . . and we should, I believe, do everything we can to avoid a collision on this issue with the Union.[1]

The crisis involving the marriage of Seretse Khama was not only the most important political event in colonial Bechuanaland but also one of the major events delineating relationship between Britain and southern Africa. Britain's handling of the crisis is representative of a pattern of political sensitivity to white South Africa that permeated the colonial period. It also illustrates the contradictions inherent in Britain's desire to contain political change on the one hand and to continue tight political control on the other. The nature of Botswana's bureaucratic state and the pragmatism of its elites have their origins in the patterns of political control that evolved during the crucial period of the last three decades of colonial rule.

Origins of Botswana Nationalism

It has been argued that Botswana did not have a nationalist movement comparable to those in other African countries.[2] This is not strictly true, although a mobilizing mass political party did not exist in Botswana, and party politics did begin rather late. Parsons traced the origins of modern nationalism in Botswana to the 1920s and pointed out essentially two branches of an intellectual nationalist movement. The first branch consisted of a "progressive chieftaincy" exemplified by Tshekedi Khama and Bathoen II in the 1920s and 1930s, as well as by Regent Isang Pilane of the Kgatla and Chief Seepapitso of the Ngwaketse prior to 1925. These chiefs

> . . . were themselves educated men . . . and held progressive ideas of economic development . . . and of bureaucratizing their administrative machinery. . . . They also believed in their own kind of nationalism by presenting a more or less united front with the colonial authorities, appealing to the precedent of their "fathers" who had gone in united delegation to the Colonial Office in London in 1895.[3]

In spite of their progressive ideas and their nationalism, however, the chiefs acted firmly in the defense of their authoritarian privileges.

The second branch of the nationalist movement, an intellectual democratic nationalism, was made up of men such as Simon Ratshosa and S. M. Molema. Their background and education were similar to those of the progressive chiefs. Ratshosa and Molema had aristocratic origins (as descendants of royal families) and had sound educations but, because they were not in positions of power and influence within the traditional system, they gravitated toward a type of bourgeois nationalism. Bechuanaland, Ratshosa had argued, must move toward a western-style, elected parlimentary state and curb the dictatorial and feudal tendencies of the chiefs. Simon Ratshosa

> . . . was undoubtedly a nationalist: he called for a united Botswana (though he used the English term, "Bechuanaland") nation, which should include the so-called "subject tribes" (non-Tswana), and should be led by the national intelligentsia. He cannot be dismissed merely as a "proto-nationalist" because he was quite self-conscious about the concept of nationalism per se, and perceived the indigenous roots of nationality.[4]

An idealist rather than a revolutionary, Ratshosa was representative of those who reacted against the authority of the chiefs and identified with a reformist, but nonsocialist, nationalism in the context of a wider movement of democratic ideals within southern Africa. Although Ratshosa never envisaged a complete break with Britain, he did advocate the formation of a "native progressive party" within a national council to govern Bechuanaland.

Ratshosa died in 1939 without leaving a political movement in the territory. He represented an intellectual national consciousness that provides depth to an understanding of the Botswana nationalism that surfaced in the post-World War II period. An intellectual link can be made between the democratic nationalism of Ratshosa and the nonsocialist, but nationalist, views of the "new men" of the dominant Botswana Democratic party.

The New Men

By the end of World War II, Bechuanaland's social fabric began to take on a form that would characterize it into the post-colonial period. Increasing numbers of Africans were employed as clerical-level civil servants by the colonial administration. The African Civil Service Association became a much more vocal critic of the government's education and employment policies. Small numbers of Batswana passed through the portals of South African educational institutions such as Tiger Kloof, Lovedale, and Fort Hare. Many, but not all, of these men had links with the ruling families of the traditional chieftainships. Increasingly, the presence of "new men" of Botswana nationalism began to be felt in Bechuanaland towns and villages. The "new men"

> were younger men than the leading village elders, generally more literate than their peers, and with longer experience of paid labor, often as skilled workers or clerks. Some had been court-scribes or cattle guards. . . . A few had started entrepreneurial ventures.[5]

What has puzzled many observers of Botswana politics is the absence of a nationalist political movement in Bechuanaland until after 1960. An explanation may in part be linked to Bechuanaland's proximity to South Africa. A number of those men who would become nationalist leaders in Botswana had attended school in South Africa and, in many cases, had worked in South Africa during much of the period prior to 1960. The backgrounds of the founders of the Botswana Peoples Party (BPP) illustrate this.

K. T. Motsetse, the first president of the BPP, was educated at Tiger Kloof and in London, then worked for several years in South Africa. During the 1950s, Motsetse had contacts with members of the African National Congress (ANC) and was sympathetic to the ideals of a pan-South African movement as part of a broader southern Africa. He returned to Bechuanaland in 1960 and became involved in nationalist politics there. Motsomai Mpho (later leader of the Botswana Independence Party) attended Tiger Kloof and joined the ANC in 1952. He was arrested in 1956 for nationalist activities, served time in South African jails, and was put on trial for high treason. He remained active in South African nationalist politics until he finally was deported to Bechuanaland at the time of the Sharpeville massacre in 1960. Philip Matante of the Botswanan Peoples Party grew up in Johannesburg and joined the ANC in the early 1950s. When the ANC split up in 1958, Matante's sympathies lay with the Pan-Africanist Congress (PAC).

Until the banning of the nationalist movements in South Africa, many Batswana, who otherwise might have become involved in Bechuanaland nationalist politics, had directed their attention to what they perceived as the more fundamental problem: the entrenched minority regime in Pretoria. As pan-Africanists they took a regional approach to the problem of decolonization, perhaps assuming that change in Bechuanaland was predicated upon change in South Africa. After 1960, when the prospects for early change in South Africa diminished, a number of these individuals returned to Bechuanaland and became active in politics there.

The Concern for Political Containment

Although partisan nationalism developed late in Botswana, colonial administrators began to react soon after the war to what they perceived as potential threats to the colonial system. During the war a number of administrators from each of the three High Commission Territories had served as officers with the Royal South African Auxiliary Pioneer Corps. In a 1943 memorandum concerning demobilization of African troops, a Basutoland district officer serving in the Middle East warned colonial authorities of the impending return of soldiers with more critical attitudes about the authority of their traditional leaders and authority in general and with a new impatience over delays and obstructions inherent in the colonial administration.[6] Taking note of the sit-down strikes and other incidents of passive resistance by African troops during their tour of duty, the officer believed that

> a number of the more intelligent and better educated men will probably return with more or less progressive political views . . . because of contacts and discussions with soldiers from the North [from other African territories].

The memo had an important impact on administrative thinking in the High Commission Territories. The colonial authorities did not believe that the views of these returning soldiers would be extreme, but did expect them to want progress and development. These men would require careful handling in order to suppress potentially subversive political action and a desire for "rapid political and social emancipation." It would be up to the colonial administration to deal with the attitudes altered by war time experience and to prevent that portion of the population who were susceptible to political education from being exposed to "political agitators."

In 1944 a pamphlet was prepared for each of the three High Commission Territories on discharge procedures and the demobilization process. In the pamphlet it was stressed that the district officer must be sensitive to the difficulties faced by the demobilized soldier and it warned of the potential problems that the colonial administration and the chiefs would have to face. Return procedures for the demobilized units (recruited on an ethnic basis) became a carefully staged event. Each time a unit returned to the major village of its home area, it was welcomed formally by the district officer, the chiefs, and relatives of the soldiers. Speeches were very upbeat and tended to stress the important new development plans which would be implemented after the war. Also mentioned were possibilities of government employment in the district and other future opportunities for the veterans.[7] The colonial administration also drew up plans (largely unsuccessful) for improving economic conditions in the rural areas so that men looking for work would find sufficient incentive to stay in the territory.

The Secretariat in Mafeking took seriously the warnings it received about the dangers which could follow postwar demobilization. The resident commissioner warned of the possibilities of political agitation and told district officers, "I would finally remind you that you must be watchful and I would like you to report to me anything you may hear [about agitators] which may be of sufficient interest to report."[8]

If it can be said that political resistance in Africa spread as a result of the experience of African troops during World War II, then the High Commission Territories' example would suggest that British concerns about political resistance spread from one colony to another in a like manner. Administrators from the High Commission Territories, who served with the Royal South African Auxiliary Pioneer Corps, had contact with their counterparts from other areas of Africa in the war zones of the Middle East and Italy, and it is likely that they discussed questions of political activity in their respective territories. The South African units were one of several tropical African armies participating in the war and actions which were taken with regard to the Royal South African Auxiliary Pioneer Corps were based largely on the experience of these other colonial units. Dominions Office files for the war years are filled with precedents set from east and west Africa for handling African nationalists.

Within Britain, concern increased during the postwar period, particularly (but not exclusively) within the ranks of the British Conservative party over "nationalist agitations" and potential "Communist infiltration into the African colonies." As these "hard core imperialists" saw it, "The policies of the government provided further cause for anxiety. Far from acting to suppress the extremists the Government appeared to be pandering to them, thereby aggravating the situation."[9] Such concerns were passed down to officials in Bechuanaland.

During the early postwar period, colonial administrators increasingly became sensitive to any hints of mutiny within the ranks of traditional authority. Concern with dissidence was nothing new, of course, but in the postwar period events from other parts of Africa and Asia magnified such threats in southern Africa. Potential schisms within ethnic groups, resulting from religious differences or dynastic quarrels, were particularly threatening. Both Tshekedi Khama and Bathoen II, Bechuanaland's two most powerful chiefs, had been plagued by opposing factions during the interwar period. After the war, the new political winds, although still external to Bechuanaland, exacerbated administrative concern for intra-group conflict and caused colonial officers to exaggerate both the seriousness and the potential threat of such conflicts.

Intervention by the colonial administration ran the risk of either angering the chief or inflaming their opponents. If administrators uncritically backed a chief when there were genuine problems within the reserve, they ran the risk of splitting the district. On the other hand, a colonial administrator had to be sensitive to the fact that "a district commissioner or even a resident commissioner attempting to discipline a chief would find that in retaliation he was fomenting opposition to some other official proposal for whose success, popular approval, and therefore the chief's encouragement, was crucial."[10]

Administrators were also concerned with increased dissatisfaction of the "new men" and the demobilized troops who were hostile to both the traditional authorities and to Bechuanaland government. Dossiers were kept of Batswana who were politically active in South Africa and Southern Rhodesia, and increasingly parallels were drawn between the "new men" in Bechuanaland and their counterparts in east and west Africa who were at the forefront of organized resistance to colonial rule.

District Administration and Political Control

As colonial officials became more concerned about external political influences on Bechuanaland's African population, they developed institutional procedures to deal with those influences. Although administrative intervention in traditional affairs was nothing new in Bechuanaland (such interference dates back to the origins of colonial rule in southern Africa), colonial perceptions on the nature of the threat to political stability did change after 1945. The Zionist movement and the sequence of events surrounding the "Seretse Affair," although quite different from each other, were viewed together as externally stimulated challenges to British imperialism. The Seretse affair illustrates the combination of elements most threatening to colonial officials: the threat of rebellion from traditional authority and the challenge from the nontraditional elites, the "new men" of the territory. The manner in which the administration dealt with the two challenges provides a picture of colonial techniques of political contol in the postwar period.

The Zionist Movement

The Zionists are a separatist group of evangelical Christians with members scattered over most of southern Africa. Syncretistic in nature, the Zionist movement combines fundamentalist, spiritualist Christianity with traditional African beliefs and practices. After World War II, Zionists became very influential in the southern Bechuanaland town of Mochudi (in the Kgatleng District), an influence the colonial administration considered threatening.

The origins of the Zionist movement in Kgatleng dated back to the 1935 suspension of Chief Molefi Pilane of the Kgatla and "the difficulties created within the tribe by his impetuous and unbalanced conduct. . . ."[11] Two years later, after Molefi had been ordered to leave the reserve, a group of his followers formed a religious sect, the Zion African Church, and moved out of the district. The religious group was designed, initially at least, as a cover for a secret society called the *Ipelegeng*, described by colonial officials as "a sort of Jacobite society designed to support the chief financially and secure his return to the chieftainship."[12] The religious elements in the new Zion African Church, who had broken off from the Dutch Reform Church, quickly became dominant, however.

When Molefi made his peace with the administration after serving with the armed forces, he returned to the chieftainship. A number of the members of the Ipelegeng, seeing their political goals achieved, followed Molefi back to the reserve and disowned the Zionist movement. Under the leadership of a Kgatla elder, Bakatla Pilane, the movement took on the character of a religious cult.[13] Molefi began to see the movement as a threat because of what he perceived to be the anarchistic flavor of some of the members' behavior, and he set out to suppress it.

Initially after the war, the district administration was not concerned with Zionism in Mochudi, viewing the movement as harmless when Molefi's return removed its major disruptive threat. Even in 1947, in spite of the district commissioner's concern about the Zionists' continued presence because of some of the objectionable practices of the group, officials continued to see it as primarily an internal Kgatla responsibility.

The situation changed when Molefi, after a series of overtly political trials of members of the Zionist movement, sentenced a number of Zionists to prison terms or exile because of their religious affiliation. At that point the district commissioner, Alister MacRae, decided to become involved. He initially concluded that as a magistrate he could not justify sustaining Molefi's court decisions on appeal, because the Zionists had made no direct provocation against the chief or the Kgatla. In a letter to Mafeking, he pointed to the incongruity of a magistrate's involvement in a "political judgement."[14] Politically he sympathized with Molefi for wanting to control the Zionists but could find no legal justification for supporting the chief.

By the end of 1947, MacRae's reasoning had shifted. The Zionists had to be suppressed or they would damage the structure of traditional authority. Even more important to MacRae was his belief that the Zionists had defied constitutional authority. Although initially MacRae had ordered Molefi to refrain from further action against the Zionists, with the support of Makeki, he now imprisoned a number of members of the sect for eighteen months to two years and banished the rest from the district. MacRae justified his actions in the following terms:

> I am bound to record that in the event of a setback to the authority of the Native Administration in this connection, the situation may well become fraught with dangerous possibilities of violence and dissension. In my opinion, the authority of the Chief is being challenged by the senior ex-regent in a backhanded manner and the tribe will not lightly suffer this. . . . The problem of Bazionism was a threat to the administration. They had objectionable practices and . . . were communistic.[15]

The phrase "violence and dissension" has a distinctly modern flavor in the context of what appeared to be a very traditional dispute.

By 1949 the Zionists had left the reserve and were once again described as harmless and without influence among the Kgatla.[16] In one sense the Zionist case was a throwback to an earlier period of dynastic quarrels. The district administration's perception of the movement as a threat to constituted authority and its identification of this largely pacifist movement as "frought with dangerous possibilities of violence and dissension," however, presaged a new relationship between the district administration and those whom the government perceived as potential threats to imperial authority.[17]

There were a number of elements at work to convert the Zionist movement from a localized factional split to a possible threat to the system of traditional administration. First, the colonial administration fueled the tribal authority's determination to destroy the movement. "The hostility with which the Administration viewed the Z.C.C. [Zionist Christian Church] encouraged [Chief Molefi] to try more direct methods of destroying what was seemingly a much more insidious threat to his authority."[18]

When the district administration concluded that the continuance of the Zionist movement "could be detrimental to the good order and government of the tribe," an external source had to be found that could be blamed for instigating it. Thus, officials concluded that the Zionists had "possible affiliations with undesirable elements in the Union." The fact that the Zionists were not a threat to the traditional authorities after 1949 seems to have had little effect on the attitudes of the colonial administration. For example, during the 1955 administrative conference,

> it was agreed that although the Zionists could not really be classified as disturbers of the peace their activities could cause disturbances. The Government Secretary said that there was no doubt that these sects were generally harmful and he thought it should be left to District Commissioners to make it as uncomfortable as possible for the Zionists without actually infringing the law.[19]

This was in clear contradiction to the comments of the resident commissioner in the same year that the Zionists "have lived on their farm . . . in the Tuli Block for the past two years and have had no apparent effect on their neighbors in the Ngwato Reserve." [20]

The Seretse Affair and the Serowe Crisis

Polarization between the traditionalist nationalism of the chiefs and the bourgeois democratic nationalism of the "new men" crystalized as a result of the Serowe crisis in 1948. If the system of traditional administration did not collapse as a result of the chain of events which has come to be called "the Seretse Affair," it certainly suffered irreparable damage.

Seretse Khama was the legitimate heir to the chieftainship of the Bamangwato for whom his uncle, Tshekedi Khama, was acting as regent. In 1948, while in Britain studying law, Seretse announced his imminent marriage to a British woman, Ruth Williams. His uncle opposed the marriage because Seretse had not consulted the Bamangwato beforehand, according to custom, and because his wife-to-be was not a Motswana but a European and therefore posed a threat to the integrity of the Bamangwato.

Following his marriage, Seretse returned to the Bamangwato capital of Serowe to attend a series of Kgotla meetings regarding his status. At first the Bamangwato opposed Seretse's marriage and supported the position of his uncle, Tshekedi. During later meetings they switched their allegiance to Seretse and in July 1949 produced a majority for Seretse's installation as chief and the acceptance of his European wife. At that point, Tshekedi resigned as regent and announced that he would leave the Bamangwato district, taking his followers with him.

Until Tshekedi's departure, the dispute had seemed to be a very localized affair, with the colonial administration only playing a mediating role. When it appeared that Seretse had won in a power struggle with his uncle, however, the nature of the incident changed drastically for the administration. Tshekedi's lobbying within Bechuanaland and his call for a judicial investigation put the administration in a position where it had to take a stand, and colonial officials began to perceive the quarrel in terms of the survival of the traditional system. An added complication was that among Seretse's followers were relatively well-educated Africans who were known to hold progressive views—the "new men."[21]

Seretse's marriage began to receive wide publicity in England and elsewhere in the late 1940s as an example of that greatest of all racial sins, miscegenation. From the United States *Life Magazine* sent famed photographer Margaret Bourke-White to Serowe to do a photo essay on Seretse and Ruth Khama, and her rather sympathetic treatment of the situation brought forth a number of hostile letters from disapproving readers.[22] In England an article by Elspeth Huxley, although not for general circulation (it appeared in the in-house colonial journal, *Corona*), typified the simplifications being made at the time. She stated that all African leaders came in two types, zealots and herodians, and she described Tshekedi as a zealot who resisted government policy with "fanatical rigour. . . . The rise of the Zealots is making itself felt also in the spontaneous appearance of many fanatical, half-crazy, quasi-religious cults, each under a crackpot leader who preaches a return to ancient ways."[23] Seretse, she concluded, was a Herodian with a need to imitate European manners and master western techniques in every way. Implying that Seretse's decision to marry a European was part of this pattern, she ridiculed the "apparently ridiculous insistence on following the English curriculum slavishly, as if it was a sort of magic." Thus, because of the nature of such publicity and the reaction of people like Huxley, Seretse's marriage was engulfed in a rather sordid atmosphere.

By mid-1949, the marriage had been blown up into a minor diplomatic incident between Britain and Bechuanaland's two neighbors, Southern Rhodesia and South Africa. The nationalists had been in power in South Africa for little more than a year. On 29 September 1949 the South African press ran a long account of a speech by South African Prime Minister Dr. D. F. Malan to a meeting of the Nationalist party. The prime minister strongly condemned the marriage and announced that he had sent a telegram to the British government in which he had stated South Africa's views.[24] Shortly thereafter, Seretse Khama and his wife were declared prohibited immigrants in South Africa.

At this point a shroud of secrecy was drawn over the whole matter. The report of the judicial inquiry requested by Tshekedi was never published, but it was announced that the tribunal had advised against the recognition of Seretse, "whose absence from the Bechuanaland Protectorate was essential to the peace and good order of the Bamangwato Reserve."[25] Seretse was lured to England under what can only be called false premises and was not allowed to return to Bechuanaland. Tshekedi was ordered to live outside the Bamangwato reserve and was forbidden to enter it without special permission. Anthony Sillery, who was the resident commissioner during the incident, made it clear that "no one doubted that the real reason why recognition was withheld [from Seretse] was reluctance to upset the South Africans, who, on the subject of miscegenation, are 'hardly sane'."[26] He indicated that the decision not to publish the results of the judicial inquiry was because of the references in it about South Africa.

Although the Seretse affair lasted about three years in its most intense form, a formal end to the Serowe crisis eluded the colonial administration until 1956 when, after a series of long, complicated negotiations, Seretse Khama was finally allowed to return to Serowe. Needless to say, the international publicity that had helped to inflame the crisis disappeared within a year after its beginning.

Upheaval in the Ngwato District Administration

The effect of the controversy on the Ngwato District administration was devastating. Within Serowe, the district capital, conditions deteriorated very rapidly following the announcement that the district commissioner had replaced the chief as the authority for the Bamangwato Reserve. Within the Bechuanaland administration most of those involved with the controversy became tainted by it. Anthony Sillery lost his job as resident commissioner in 1950 as a result of the incident. Many of the district officers involved in the events in Serowe continued to be identified with the failure to handle the incident for several years afterwards.

It must be kept in mind that the Ngwato District was the largest and most important in Bechuanaland, covering 18 percent of the land area and containing roughly a third of the population. The district collected 40 percent of the revenue channeled through the reserve treasuries. Moreover, for ten years prior to the Seretse affair, the Bamangwato traditional administration had been held up, to all three of the High Commission Territories, as an example of the successful application of indirect rule.

When the high commissioner and resident commissioner tried to address the Serowe *kgotla* on the government's decisions, the meeting was boycotted. Two months later the district commissioner was rudely shouted down during a *kgotla* meeting. Shortly thereafter, two riots occurred, and several local policemen were killed or injured during one of them. Following the second riot, police were airlifted in from Southern Rhodesia and Basutoland to put down the disturbances.

Immediate decisions were made in the wake of the breakdown of traditional authority in the Ngwato District. W. F. MacKenzie, deputy resident commissioner of Swaziland, was brought in to take personal charge of the district. With MacKenzie's arrival, the Secretariat in Mafeking began to look back at the shambles of the administrative policy and try to evaluate what had happened.

At the 1950 district commissioners' conference, a major topic of discussion, both formal and informal, was, as one district commissioner put it, "Whither Bechuanaland Protectorate?"[27] Colonial administrators concluded that the Seretse faction was a threat to the administration. V. F. Ellenberger, the government secretary, stated that Seretse's "ardent supporters were radicals unrepresentative of the territory as a whole." The riots in Serowe were symptomatic of the whole postwar process of challenge to traditional authority by extremists all over the continent. It was written in the minutes of the conference that

> the conference feels that in these days when the dignity, standing and
> authority of His Majesty's Government and institutions need every
> visible backing and sign of strength and permanence, among African
> peoples, who are being increasingly subjected to disruptive influence,
> consideration should be given to the flying of the flag at [the district
> commissioners'] residence   [and to promoting] the dignity and
> bearing of officers and [focusing] increased attention to formal
> occasions.[28]

The consensus at the conference was that the dissidence plaguing British rule in other parts of Africa was moving south, a conclusion that in the early 1950s seems to have been largely in the minds of Bechuanaland's administrators.

The Issue of Security

Replacing the traditional leadership of the Bamangwato Reserve with the district commissioner was a turning point in administrative thinking about the relationship between the colonial administration and its subject population. An image of African radicalism had been created and the Protectorate's political problems were blamed on internal zealots and external threats. Time and again district officers and department staff were warned of the dangers of African nationalism.

> It is the duty of the district administration to keep its fingers on the public pulse, where security is concerned the police have a duty, but other departmental officers can also help a lot if they will pass on to the D.C. [district commissioner] . . . information and impressions gleaned in the course of their duty. But it is as I have said, the D.C.'s job is to keep in close touch with his people.[29]

It is a difficult and perhaps risky task to determine the extent to which colonial attitudes in one territory are influenced by perceptions of events in other territories. With this caveat in mind, I suggest that postwar events in other areas of Britain's African empire had a significant impact on Britain's policy toward Bechuanaland. Colonial officials in Bechuanaland were aware of the political changes occurring in west Africa and the political demands being articulated by the ANC in South Africa. The state of emergency in Kenya, declared in October of 1952, dominated the discussions at administrative conferences.

The most crucial issue in Africa at the time was internal security. According to one high official in Bechuanaland, "Unrest and violence is rife in Africa and we cannot overlook or side-track the possibility of trouble within our boundaries within the next few years."[30] In 1953 it was decided that each district would have an internal security plan locked in the district commissioner's safe. A year later attention turned to riotous assemblies. "We have learned in the Bamangwato Reserve that in times of riot or unrest, Government is powerless to control the situation adequately."[31] By the mid-1950s administrators were being trained in Britain on security matters and dealing with the police and special branches in an emergency.[32] The training, based on experience in Kenya, was designed to prepare for civil unrest. Each district commissioner prepared monthly intelligence reports and the divisional administration [for the Northern part of the territory] would use the district commissioner to compile what were called "Tergos," reports on developments within the divisions. In addition, special confidential files were kept on potential political activists in each district.

The Return of Seretse

Between 1952 and 1956, the exile of Seretse Khama dominated Bechuanaland affairs. Seretse and Tshekedi Khama reconciled their differences in 1952, but Bechuanaland's colonial officers resisted an end to Seretse's exile. A new Bamangwato traditional authority, Rasebolai Kgamane, was appointed in 1953. Although the original decision to exile Seretse came from London and Pretoria, officials within Bechuanaland, viewing Seretse as a potential political threat, opposed his return. Tshekedi Khama was allowed to return to Serowe in 1952, but Seretse's banishment continued.

In 1955 the British Labor party tried to make a political issue of the situation and sought a way to end Seretse's exile. The Labor party's commonwealth officer, John Hatch, was sent to Bechuanaland to make a firsthand report of the situation and to provide recommendations for future policy. A number of confidential files on the Hatch visit make an interesting case study on the relationship between British domestic politics and colonial administration at the district level.[33]

Before leaving London, Hatch met with a Mr. Baxter at the Commonwealth Relations Office (formerly the Dominions Office). Hatch pointed out that the Labor party as a whole suffered from a very guilty conscience regarding the Seretse affair and felt that a surrender had been made on the racial issue. Baxter argued that a reversal of Seretse's banishment would have the gravest effect on Bechuanaland and on colonial administration in general. It would undermine the "prestige and authority of, and confidence in Her Majesty's Government and make them impossible to administer properly."[34] Because of the traditional attachment to the royal house, it would be necessary for Seretse to renounce the chieftainship and allow a period of time to elapse so that the authority of a new chief could be established.[35] Baxter tried to persuade Hatch and the Labor party not to do anything until they [the Labor party] returned to power.

By the time Hatch arrived in Bechuanaland in June 1955, the divisional commissioner, north, had already received a copy of the Commonwealth Relations Office memo on the meeting between Baxter and Hatch. The Secretariat and the divisional commissioner were particularly concerned about a compromise plan Hatch carried with him. It proposed that the chieftainship be placed in a tribal committee of which Tshekedi and Seretse would both be members.[36] The Secretariat opposed the compromise because the mere announcement of it would undermine the authority of existing tribal authority Rasebolai Kgamane, and would be detrimental to the ideal of a strong chieftainship. "Moreover, it would be regarded as a reversal of the previously declared policy of Her Majesty's Government to make Seretse's exclusion permanent. This would result in loss of prestige and authority for the Bechuanaland Government."[37] The high commissioner felt that Seretse's return would weaken Britain's authority in the High Commission Territories and in other colonies. Such weakness would also have a negative effect on the Union of South Africa, increasing its mistrust of British policy in the area and provoking further pressure for transfer.

> Our reinstatement in a position of authority, on the Union's doorstep, of an African with a white wife and half-breed family would unite and inflame against us all the white population of the Union, and enable Mr. Strijdom [then South African Prime Minister J. G. Strijdom] with general support to embark on measures detrimental to the territories.[38]

Officials in Serowe tried to control whom Hatch saw while he was in the Bamangwato Reserve. Since Hatch was "pro-Seretse," there was a danger that he might convince people, including Tshekedi Khama, of the advantages of the Labor party compromise. The attempt to control Hatch was successful. Although he met with representatives of all factions, including Tshekedi, he was unable to promote the compromise.

The Secretariat's attitude toward the affair was summed up by Resident Commissioner C. R. Wray in a speech to administrative officers in December 1955. The administration, he noted, had survived the year even though Hatch, with little success, "was busy plotting behind the scenes."[39] The ban on Seretse was not lifted until the middle of 1956, and on 10 October of that year he returned to Bechuanaland as a private citizen.

After Seretse's return, the district administration continued to monitor and control district political activity. The movements of Tshekedi Khama and of Seretse Khama and his wife were watched carefully by the district authorities and the police. Seretse Khama's followers were particularly suspect. One memorandum described them as a "small band of anti-Europeans."[40] One of Seretse's close supporters, who held a cabinet-level appointment for many years after independence, was described as "an anti-European Nationalist" who was probably a member of the ANC. Even in 1959, when Tshekedi Khama died, officials feared that Seretse would use the occasion of Tshekedi's funeral to make a bid for the chieftainship.

The Independence Option

Changes in colonial policy toward political development in Bechuanaland coincided with the 1959 appointments of Sir John Maud as high commissioner and Sir Peter Fawcus as Bechuanaland's resident commissioner. Maud was viewed as sensitive to the problems of the High Commission Territories, and Fawcus, a shirt-sleeve administrator with disdain for the pomp and circumstance of colonialism, was widely respected and trusted as "progressive, able and with an expert knowledge of the country and its needs."[41] Both came into office with a clear view of Bechuanaland's political and economic needs and had a major impact on the nature of Botswana's political development over the next twenty years.

The first issue facing Fawcus involved the constitutional status of the territory. In 1958 Seretse and Tshekedi, supported by the chairman of the European Advisory Council, Russell England, had initiated a motion in the Joint Advisory Council calling for the creation of a legislative council. The creation of a legislative council involved the whole question of the constitutional development of the country, since a legislative council was a prerequisite first step in the British colonies to any movement toward independence.

With Fawcus's approval, the Joint Advisory Council established a constitutional committee in 1959. The committee recommended the establishment of executive and legislative councils, and in 1961 indirect elections were held to select an African majority for a legislative council. The way was set for Bechuanaland to progress through the familiar constitutional stages toward internal self-government.

Although an African majority existed after 1961, a clear commitment to complete independence had not yet been made. According to Fawcus, "At this point [1961] we were still not able to look ahead. We went straight to an elected majority, but we could not see the next step—internal self government—because of South Africa, who officials feared would intervene to prevent the normal constitutional development of the territory. We thought of the West Indies model; we could sail along perhaps for many years without internal self government."[42]

The idea of political independence for Bechuanaland first developed in the mind of Sir John Maud in early 1962. As late as 1963-64 the Colonial Office (which had taken over control of the High Commission Territories after South Africa left the Commonwealth) continued to hesitate because Britain would still be required to maintain the Bechuanaland budget even after political independence. As late as 1965 Fawcus and other colonial officials continued to predict independence at five to ten years in the future.

Partisan Politics

With the end of the Seretse affair, both Seretse and Tshekedi Khama were removed from any claim on traditional office in Bechuanaland. Tshekedi himself began to gravitate toward nationalist ideas of a nontraditional nature, taking an active role in African Advisory Council and Joint Advisory Council affairs and pushing for the establishment of a legislative council. In 1957 he took on the position of Bamangwato tribal secretary in Serowe, a position which could have been a springboard for nationalist political activity. Tshekedi's death in 1959 precluded his participation in national political activity.

It was to Seretse Khama, rather that Tshekedi, that the "new men" gravitated in the late 1950s. By 1957 a core of nationalists had coalesced around Seretse, and British intelligence reports clearly identified Seretse and his colleagues as a potential challenge to the Bechuanaland administration. There are a number of possible explanations for the late development of partisan politics in Bechuanaland. If not for Tshekedi Khama's untimely death, a political movement (perhaps traditional-modernist in nature) might have developed around him. Another development which might have forestalled a partisan nationalist challenge was the Bechuanaland Protectorate administration's gradual cooptation of the intellectual nationalists so that by 1961 they had become a de facto government in embryo. In fact, it might be argued that the future ruling elites in Botswana had no reason to invest time and effort in the formation of a political party until they were challenged by other political movements that potentially threatened the hegemony of their embryonic political coalition.

The nature of British political control did not change as much as did the goals to which control mechanisms were directed. Prior to 1959 the district administration and the police forces were used to maintain British colonial rule in the territory. Decisions taken after 1959 marked the adoption of a more clearly defined policy toward Bechuanaland. Then the control mechanisms were used to ensure the compatibility to Britain and South Africa of the type of regime that would inherit power after independence.

The development of party politics in Bechuanaland is conterminous with the 1959-1966 period. The territory's first political party was the Bechuanaland Protectorate Federal Party (BPFP), formed in 1959 after publication of the draft proposals for a legislative council. The party was led by Leetile Disang Raditladi. The BPFP's role in the evolution of the territory's political parties has been somewhat neglected and should be viewed in the context of the evolution of nationalist thought beginning in the 1920s. Raditladi's background was very similar to that of Simon Ratshosa of a generation earlier. Raditladi was from an aristocratic faction of the Bamangwato royal family that had been excluded from the inner circle of power by the Khamas. He was well educated and had attended the University of Fort Hare in South Africa.

The BPFP was conservative and called for the enhancement of traditional authority. In its program the party tried to link the evolution of a parliamentary system with a strong but nonpartisan traditional administration. Raditladi called for a chamber of chiefs with the entrenchment of "traditional" authority as a part of a federal system of government. Although the BPFP was conservative and warned against an immediate African majority in the Legislative Council, many of the party's ideas resemble those of Ratshosa and the intellectual nationalists. Politically,

Raditladi's party was stillborn, and by 1962 it no longer existed as a party. Intellectually, however, the BPFP was a link with the earlier intellectual nationalists and provided a transition to its successor party, the Bechuanaland (Botswana) Democratic Party (BDP) that was formed in 1962.

The first successful attempt to organize politically occurred in December 1960 when the Bechuanaland People's Party (BPP) was formed, partially in response to the establishment of the Legislative Council and partially as an aftereffect of the banning of the African National Congress and the Pan-Africanist Congress in South Africa in the wake of the Sharpeville massacre. Several members of the BPP had links with the South African nationalist movement. The leadership of the BPP was well educated but lacked the traditional status of the BDP leadership. Support for the BPP was limited to the eastern towns and some villages along the line of rail. The party demanded early independence, an Africanization of the civil service, and some nationalization of the land.

The BPP had a major effect on political development in Bechuanaland and stimulated a rapid spread of political consciousness in the territory. The party had a "modernist" outlook, and it showed signs of political support very early with a number of open-air demonstrations in Bechuanaland's major towns. The BPP quickly broke up into factions, however, dissipating its support. One faction, under Philip Matante, retained pockets of influence in the northeast and east, while a second faction, calling itself the Botswana Independence party and led by Motsamai Mpho, maintained some strength in the northwest. The membership and ideology of the BPP and its offshoots were more closely akin to those of the South African pan-Africanist nationalist movement than to the bourgeois nationalist tradition in Botswana as it evolved from Ratshosa and Raditladi to Seretse Khama and the BDP.

The initial success of what many saw as an Nkrumah-style political movement alarmed a number of the members of the newly elected Legislative Council (as well as members of the colonial administration). In January 1962, therefore, several Legislative Council members, led by Seretse Khama, formed the Bechuanaland Democratic Party (BDP), which quickly became the major political force in the territory. The BDP leadership was composed of younger men with both professional (several were schoolteachers) and traditional status among the various ethnic groups. The BDP stood as the intellectual successor to the early nationalists of the 1920s and 1930s, and Seretse Khama, through the BDP, became a progressive spokesman for traditionalists in Bechuanaland.

With Seretse's prestige as a traditional leader, his membership in the Executive Council, and the BDP formed from ten of the twelve members of the Legislative Council,

the Democratic Party (BDP) . . . became at one stroke a major force, and although the Democratic Party as such had no mandate from the electorate, it . . . to the administration assumed almost the character of a party in power.[43]

The De Facto Government

With a commitment to internal self-government in 1963, the colonial administration and the BDP leadership in the Legislative Council joined in an informal coalition to shape the nature of Botswana politics for the 1960s and beyond. After 1962 the BDP had the encouragement and unofficial support of the colonial administration, the organizational support of the bureaucracy, and the financial support of much of the European ranching and commercial community. The colonial administration, through the Executive Council, brought members of the BDP into the administration. The Executive Council was composed of five official members and four unofficial members (two Europeans and two Africans) and met weekly with Sir Peter Fawcus as the chair.

A kind of "trainee-minister" system was put into operation between 1962 and 1964, with the four unofficial members of the Executive Council becoming associated with various government departments. Seretse Khama, given the most senior of these posts, was associated with the work of the government secretary, Arthur Douglas.[44]   According to Fawcus, the government's goal at the time was straightforward, "This was a conscious attempt to give . . . [the new leadership] government experience in paired ministries prior to responsible government."[45] In 1963 a new constitution was announced that provided for elections and internal self-government. General elections were to be held on 1 March 1965.

The BDP won Bechuanaland's first parliamentary elections in 1965 with twenty-eight of the thirty-one elected seats, and formed a government with Seretse Khama as the prime minister.   The political framework for independence on 30 September 1966 was in place. Four factors led to the overwhelming victory of Seretse Khama and the BDP at the polls.

1. As a traditional leader Seretse was a prestigious figure.
2. The BDP received unqualified support from the colonial government. The colonial administration had treated the BDP as a de facto government, and by controlling ten of the twelve seats in the outgoing Legislative Council, in effect, the BDP was the incumbent party during the elections.
3. The BDP represented an intellectual tradition that was linked historically with the intellectual nationalism of the 1930s—a view of society that was firmly entrenched in the minds of the middle class intelligentsia who formed the backbone of the BDP as a political organization.
4. The BDP received the financial and organizational support of the majority of the financially influential European and Asian

communities, who feared the consequences of the more "radical" BPP coming to power.

The 1965 election was a decisive victory for what has become the ruling coalition of Botswana. The BDP successfully appealed to the vast majority of the population, rural people with strong ties to their traditional leader. The basis of their support lay in both the tacit acceptance of the BDP by the traditional leaders and in Seretse Khama's traditional political appeal. The rural population's solid electoral support of the BDP has continued and it is from the rural sector that any challenge to the Khama government would have to be made. The nature of the BDP's support and the formal legitimacy of the elections must be understood prior to any discussion of administrative activity in favor of the BDP between 1963 and 1965.

The colonial administration's sympathy for the BDP was clearly a factor in its victory, however, and even more important, colonial officials set a pattern of political-administrative relationships that would be carried into the post-colonial period. Former members of the colonial administration interviewed in 1979 made no attempt to hide the extent to which the colonial administration sympathized with the BDP's leadership. The bureaucracy's organizational abilities, in a pattern of mobilization that would be repeated often in the next twenty years, were directed toward presenting the aims of the BDP in the best possible light prior to the 1965 elections.

Government policy during the period between 1963 and 1965 ensured that the electorate would be aware of the positive achievements of the BDP-dominated Legislative Council under Seretse Khama's leadership. In 1963 Fawcus wrote a memorandum to the high commissioner concerning British financial aid to Bechuanaland. In it he said,

> At this important stage in the political and constitutional development of the Territory when the Democratic Party [the BDP] offers so much hope for a peaceful and happy transition to self-government, but is so badly in need of a sign of real United Kingdom interest in the future of the Territory . . . this (lack of assistance) would be a dismal story to recount at the next meeting of our Legislative Council.[46]

In addition to this type of support for the BDP, a subtle but clear alliance between the BDP and the colonial administration evolved during the period that ensured the containment of the nationalism developing in Bechuanaland. As the territory moved closer to independence, the district administrations maintained a vigorous control over events. In late March 1964 the Legislative Council passed a penal code that gave the colonial administration comprehensive powers, including that of acting against "subversion." Fawcus, as Queen's Commissioner (the name changed after the High Commission was abolished in 1964), was given the "unprecedented authority to declare as unlawful any society dangerous to peace and order."[47]

The police were strengthened and control of assemblies was enforced rigorously in the urban areas.

The major responsibility of the district administrations was to maintain law and order in the areas under their authority. Although political parties were allowed to operate relatively freely prior to the 1965 elections, all of them but the BDP were monitored closely by the colonial government, and there were a number of instances of administrative intervention in the political process. For example, district administrators assumed that Kenneth Koma, leader of the newly formed Botswana National Front who had studied in the Soviet Union, was a Communist, although Koma himself disclaimed any Communist affiliations. The district commissioner's office and "the CID chief at Mahalapye, Koma's home village, proceeded on that assumption, and most foreign visitors to the doctor have been most carefully interrogated."[48]

It is likely that all of the opposition leaders were closely watched by the administration. According to Robert Edwards, an American working with the Bechuanaland administration at the time, the colonial government overemphasized the left-wing connections of Motsamai Mpho, leader of the Botswana Independence party, and Philip Matante of the Bechuanaland People's party (BPP). Both were viewed as having Ghanaian and pan-African connections. Mpho was considered to be a Chinese agent, and Matante, who was "mysteriously opulent" after a visit to the Soviet Union, was feared to have Soviet connections.[49]

The leadership of the opposition parties made a number of complaints about being subjected to government harassment. In 1963 tear gas was used against a crowd of 2,000 people in Francistown who were demonstrating against the trial and detention of seven people accused of "intimidation" by the government. In addition, the traditional administration in Bamangwato briefly banned the BDP from holding public meetings, although the ban soon was suspended by the colonial government. Matante complained that the rigid penal laws and the government's emergency powers were a direct threat to the election campaign.   At various times he protested to both the Commonwealth Relations Office and the United Nations about the activities of the Bechuanaland government.

Much of the colonial administration's electoral influence was through the chiefs. In certain areas the chiefs were advised by administrators to support the BDP. Thus "Chief Mosajane actually received instructions from a District Commissioner in Francistown not to allow the People's Party [the BPP] to address political meetings in his reserve . . . otherwise they would get no land. Similarly, a sub-chief at Mathethe told recruits that if they did not vote for the BDP, 'he would not give them jobs on the mines.'" In the Northeast District, the district commissioner was accused of informing the electorate, through the chief, that "if you vote for the People's Party you are not going to plow."[50] Many BDP candidates for both national and local offices were minor chiefs or came from royal families. Some evidence suggests that food-for-work money to assist in drought relief was funneled through the chiefs as "BDP help," and that opposition supporters may have been excluded from employment in the drought relief program.

Although the colonial administration's actions vis-à-vis the opposition really did not affect the outcome of the 1965 elections (whether or not some incidents described by the various opposition leaders were entirely factual), those actions were important in establishing a pattern of administrative control over the political processes that would develop. An interdependence between the European-controlled bureaucracy and the Batswana-controlled political leadership continued after independence. The bureaucracy provided the expertise and organizational talents, while the politicians mobilized support at the polls. Thus, the BDP served the function of perpetuating and legitimizing bureaucratic rule.

Conclusion

A continuity of patterns of political control in Bechuanaland began with the first few years of British occupation of the territory and continued into the post-colonial period. The administrative structures and particularly the district administration were the ultimate source of political acquiescence and regional loyalty to the center. A pattern of subtle but firm prefectorial administration was established over local affairs in Bechuanaland's ten districts.

The goals of political control changed over time. Before 1959 Britain was primarily concerned with maintaining control over the area. After the "winds of change" had begun to blow over the region, administrative concern turned to the question of the type of regime that would take over after the British administrators had left. As we shall see later, the dominant socio-economic coalition that controls the Botswana (formerly Bechuanaland) Democratic party activated the administrative apparatus after independence in 1966 to ensure the maintenance of its political power.

The Seretse affair was less significant in terms of its effect on the Khama family and its rule over the Bamangwato reserve (since Seretse Khama ultimately gained control not only over that area, but over the entire country) than it was as an example of administrative control which existed over Bechuanaland's districts during the colonial period and which continues to exist largely unchanged in Botswana today.

The continuity of political control patterns and the nature of early Botswana nationalism clarify the apparent contradiction in the phenomenon of an exiled chief rising to the corridors of power within six years of his return from exile. The creation of the Legislative Council and the founding of the BDP were responses to the internal and external challenges to Britain's rule in southern Africa. The BDP was formed not only as a vehicle of nationalism but also as a partial response to it. It was a contained nationalism that developed dependent upon an administrative apparatus and ultimately, an economic system that were subject to external influences.

From the moment it was founded in 1962, the BDP was a "government party" in the sense that it had a monopoly of the resources and apparatus of the state. The phenomenon of the disappearing opposition, with no resources to distribute or rewards for its leadership, is common in post-colonial African states. This process began in 1962 in Bechuanaland. Because they lacked a traditional base and access to state resources, the opposition parties never had a chance. By the time Botswana gained its independence on 30 September 1966, the country was already a *de facto* one-party state although elections since independence have been formally free and open, they function as a symbol of a style of political rule rather than as a mechanism for a change of government. The socio-economic elite dominating the BDP had an administrative support and a traditional loyalty that assured it unchallenged control of the state system and the limited financial resources to which the state had access. Continuity, rather than change, characterized the patterns of political activity in Botswana after 1966.

Notes

1. Charles Douglas-Home, *Evelyn Baring: The Last Proconsul* (London: William Collins, 1978), pp. 183, 185.

2. See for example Jack Halpern, *South Africa's Hostages: Basutoland, Bechuanaland, and Swaziland* (Harmondsworth: Penguin, 1965), p. 285; and Christopher Colcough and Stephen McCarthy, *The Political Economy of Botswana: A Study of Growth and Distribution* (London: Oxford University Press, 1981), p. 41.

3. Q. N. Parsons, "Shots for a Black Republic? Simon Ratshosa and Botswana Nationalism," *African Affairs*, vol. 73, no. 293 (October 1974), p. 454.

4. *Ibid.*, p. 453.

5. Adam Kuper, *Kalahari Village Politics* (Cambridge: Cambridge University Press, 1970), p. 54.

6. All quotes from: D.O. 35/1427/y1069/9/1—RSAAPC Rehabilitation on Demobilization of Men in the Forces.

7. Draft pamphlet on discharge procedures, in D.O. 35/1433/y1069/9/1—Demobilization and Rehabilitation of Men in the Forces and D.O. 35/1433/y1069/ 9/1.

8. A. D. Forsythe-Thompson, Resident Commissioner, Address, 8 May 1943, S.331/4—District Commissioner's Conference.

9. David Goldsworthy, *Colonial Issues in British Politics, 1945–1971* (Oxford: Clarendon Press, 1971), p. 180, both quotes.

10. Simon Gillett, "The Survival of Chieftaincy in Botswana," *African Affairs*, vol. 72, no. 287 (April 1973), p. 180.

11. Lord (William M.) Hailey, *Native Administration in the British African Territories*, part V: *The High Commission Territories: Basutoland, The Bechuanaland Protectorate, and Swaziland* (London: Her Majesty's Stationery Office, 1953), p. 148.

12. Anthony Sillery, *The Bechuanaland Protectorate* (London: Oxford University Press, 1952), p. 158.

13. This is based on Mochudi District Files, B.P. 21/z.19 and B.P.31/z.20, National Archives, Gaborone, Botswana.

14. Mochudi Administration, S.331/3, National Archives, Gaborone, Botswana.

15. MacRae to Mathews, Assistant Secretary, 19 July 1948, B.P.31/z.20.

16. Mochudi Administration, S.534/10—Zionist Movement, National Archives, Gaborone, Botswana.

17. Mochudi Administration, B.P.31/z.20, National Archives, Gaborone, Botswana.

18. Sandy Grant, "Church and Chief in the Colonial Era," *Botswana Notes and Records*, vol. 3 (1971), p. 60.

19. *Ibid.*, pp. 60, 61 respectively.

20. Quoted in *Ibid.*, pp. 61-62.

21. Kuper, *Kalahari Village Politics*, p. 54.

22. Margaret Bourke-White, "The White Queen," Photo essay, *Life*, vol. 28, no. 10 (March 1950), pp. 95-97.

23. See Elspeth Huxley, "The Rise of the African Zealot," *Corona*, vol. 2, no. 5 (May 1950), p. 164 for this quote and the following one.

24. *Rand Daily Mail*, 29 September 1949, in Benson, Tshekedi Khama, p. 193.

25. Great Britain, *Succession to the Chieftainship of the Bamangwato Tribe*, Cmd. 7913 (London: Her Majesty's Stationery Office, 1950).

26. Anthony Sillery, *Botswana: A Short Political History* (London: Methuen, 1974), p. 149.

27. Vivian Gillete, District Commissioner, Lobatsi, S.331/8—District Commissioner's Conference, 1950.

28. Minutes, D.C.'s Conference, 1950, S.331/8.

29. Millard to E. B. Beetham, Resident Commissioner, 8 November 1952, in C.1549/14 (original file number 39). W. F. MacKenzie, Resident Commissioner, Administrative Conference, 1953, 20 March 1953, S.541/19.

30. District Commissioner's and Administrative Conference Minutes, 1953, S.541/19.

31. P. G. Batho, Letter to Government Secretary, 3 August 1954, S.555/6.

32. Oral interview with E. B. Egner, former Colonial Administrative Officer, Gaborone, Botswana, 1 July 1975.

33. These documents were not on deposit at the National Archives in Gaborone at the time I was doing my research. I found the documents in a spare room in the District Commissioner's Office in Francistown. There were over one hundred files in cardboard boxes awaiting transfer to the archives. I

read through a number of them with the permission of the then District Commissioner of Francistown. Reference to these files will be to their original number only.

34. Divisional Commissioner, North, File No. N.P.N./11.

35. Divisional Commissioner, North, File No. N.P.N./11.

36. There was concern that Hatch would be another Hancock, "the man who did the turnaround on the Kabaka" (N.P.N./11). Sir Keith Hancock was at that time Director of the Institute of Commonwealth Studies in London and had acted as an intermediary between representatives of the Buganda government and the Protectorate administration during the Kabaka crisis.

37. Government Secretary S. V. Lawrenson to John Millard, Divisional Commissioner, North, 22 June 1955, N.P.N./11.

38. *Ibid.*

39. Resident   Commissioner's   Speech,   December   1955, S.559/2—Administrative Conference, 1955.

40. Divisional Commissioner, North, File No. N.P.S./3.1958. One of the more outrageous activities of the District Administration was its monitoring of the future president's drinking patterns in "line of rail" taverns that were ostensibly limited to Europeans.

41. Halpern, *South Africa's Hostages*, p. 452.

42. Oral interview with Sir Peter Fawcus, Edinburgh, Scotland, 18 August 1979.

43. Halpern, *South Africa's Hostages*, p. 293.

44. Much of this section has been aided by interviews with the main colonial participants in the transition to independence. Oral interviews were conducted with Sir Peter Fawcus, Queen's Commissioner from 1959 to 1965, 18 August 1979 in Edinburgh, Scotland; Arthur Douglas, Government Secretary from 1959 to 1965, 16 August 1979, London, England; M. R. B. Williams, first Permanent Secretary, Ministry of Local Government and Lands, London, England, 10 August 1979; R. A. R. Bent, 24 June 1979 and N.V. Redman, 14 August 1979. Bent and Redman were, in that order, Assistant Secretaries for Development for much of that period. Interviews conducted in London or Cambridge or environs.

45. Oral interview with Sir Peter Fawcus, 8 August 1979, Edinburgh, Scotland.

46. Bechuanaland Government, Ministry of Finance, "Memorandum on Bechuanaland's Financial Needs, 1966–71, p. 4. Quoted in Gunderson, "Nation Building," p. 276.

47. Richard P. Stevens, *Lesotho, Botswana and Swaziland: The Former High Commission Territories in Southern Africa* (New York: Praeger, 1967), p. 151.

48. *Ibid.*, p. 155.

49. Robert Edwards, "Political and Constitutional Change in the Bechuanaland Protectorate," *Boston University Papers on Africa: Transition in African Politics* (New York: Praeger, 1967), p. 150.

50. Donald K. Kowet, *Land, Labour Migration and Politics in Southern Africa: Botswana, Lesotho and Swaziland* (Uppsala, Sweden: Scandinavian Institute of African Studies, 1978), quotes on pp. 167, 166 respectively.

7

Independent Botswana:
Containment, Electoral Mobilization,
and the Multiparty System

> The government is perceived to be a body that proposes and promulgates changes, which most rural people find offensive or at least irrelevant. More seriously they see the agents of government as rude ignorant "big-stomachs"—people living the good life in town who have lost touch with rural life, rural people, and the values and culture of the Tswana.[1]

Hoyt Alverson provides us with a rare and all too brief view of the Botswana government from the bottom up. His study of values and self-identity among the Tswana is a clear warning of the limits of government penetration into the rural areas in a less-developed country (LDC). Nor, in most cases, do LDC governments want to commit such ingression. Social distance is a defense mechanism. Government in Botswana, since independence, has been an urban affair. Few decision makers, including the still-important expatriate community, venture out beyond the borders of Gaborone, Botswana's capital. The small political, bureaucratic, and land-owning elites have been the primary beneficiaries of state power.

Government activities nationally, and particularly in the rural areas, have been symbolic efforts primarily designed to create a veneer of activity. The political leadership of the ruling Botswana Democratic Party (BDP) has been concerned mainly with political quiescence and electoral mobilization and has been willing to use administrative structures as mechanisms of political containment when necessary. Most of the responsibility for political containment, as was the case during the colonial period, rests with the district-level bureaucracy.

Three factors have contributed to the BDP's success since 1965: (1) the traditional status of the BDP's first president, Sir Seretse Khama; (2) the symbolic importance of the multiparty political system both domestically and internationally; and (3) the capacity of the civil service in both political and economic terms. The strength of the ruling party was complemented by

145

the impotence of those who tried to challenge the de facto one-party system that has evolved in Botswana since independence.

The Political System

The Bechuanaland Protectorate gained its independence as the Republic of Botswana on 30 September 1966. At independence, Sir Seretse Khama, the prime minister, became Botswana's first president. Formally, the country is a multiparty parliamentary system with the president as head of state and head of the government. The constitution provides for a national assembly that consists of the speaker, the attorney general (who has no voting rights), thirty-two elected members, and four specially appointed members who receive their mandate from the president.

Executive power lies with the president, who is commander-in-chief of the armed forces and the head of the cabinet. The president is elected in conjunction with the general electoral process but is formally selected by the National Assembly. If there are two or more candidates for each National Assembly seat, the candidates must declare their support for one of the presidential candidates prior to the election. The candidate for president who has the support of more than half of the elected members of the National Assembly is appointed to office. When the office of president is declared vacant, as it was at Sir Seretse Khama's death in 1980, the National Assembly selects a president who holds office for the duration of that Parliament. Thus Quett K. J. Masire, then the vice-president, secretary-general of the BDP, and Sir Seretse's confidant, was elected by the National Assembly to succeed Sir Seretse. Since 1970 the president has been an ex officio member of the National Assembly.

The cabinet is appointed by the president and is responsible collectively to the National Assembly for government policies. There is an independent judiciary body and the constitution contains a code of human rights enforceable by the High Court. There is also a House of Chiefs that consists of the eight chiefs of Botswana's principal ethnic groups, four representatives of unaffiliated (from minor ethinc groups) subchiefs, and three members selected by the House of Chiefs.

Legislative authority is vested in Parliament, which consists of the National Assembly and the president and acts in consultation with the House of Chiefs in certain matters (including constitutional change). Four multiparty elections have occurred since 1965: in 1969, 1974, 1979, and 1984. All of them resulted in overwhelming victories for the BDP.

Botswana's political elites legitimately have indulged in self-congratulation over their multiparty political system and the rapid economic progress made since independence. It is not surprising, therefore, to find an occasional attack on central government policy by opposition leaders in the

government-owned *Botswana Daily News*. Botswana's political process, in
the formal sense at least, is based on the principles of a multiparty cabinet
government, and elections are competitive and held in an atmosphere of free
and open debate.

In addition to the dominant BDP, three opposition parties have been
active in the country: (1) the Botswana National Front, an uneasy coalition
of urban dwellers and traditional interests, one of whose leaders is the former
chief, Bathoen II; (2) the Botswana People's party, a small left-of-center
political movement with most of its support in the smaller, densely
populated Northeast District; and (3) the Botswana Independence party, a
splinter movement with limited backing in the northwest.[2]

A disconcerting feature of the electoral process since 1965 has been the
declining proportion of registered voters who actually turn out to vote, a
pattern that was only partially reversed in the 1979 elections. A notable
feature of the political system has been the declining importance of the
opposition parties as a significant political force. The National Assembly
operates more in the pattern of an African one-party state than a multiparty
system, with BDP backbenchers frequently criticizing government policy.
Political dynamics in Botswana suggest a continuity between present
political realities and the aristocratic origins of the nationalists. The political
system is dominated by (and policy is set in the interest of) a coalition of
wealthy, well-educated, cattle-owning political elites who are committed to
rapid economic growth in the framework of a largely free enterprise system.
This coalition of traditional leaders, teachers, junior state functionaries, and
wealthy farmers was joined by more senior administrators beginning in the
1970s. Altogether, the members of this coalition represent educational and
economic characteristics quite unlike the majority of the population.

Beyond the ruling political elite of the BDP is the bureaucratic state. The
total number in the political elite, including cabinet members, Parliament,
district councilors, and other specialized political actors, is probably under
250. There are fewer than seven thousand people with significant salaries in
the formal private sector. Close to eighteen thousand people are employed
by the central government service and the unified local government services,
however. Thus, no single group rivals the central and local government
bureaucratic apparatus in terms of size, economic status, and political
influence. Although salaried civil servants have widely different income
levels, they all have a major stake in the policy-making process of the
government. In addition, a high correlation exists between status within the
civil service and the ownership of cattle. It is characteristic of the small
political elite in Botswana that it is content to leave the day-to-day running
of the country to the administrative cadre of the civil service.

Two points must be made about politics in Botswana. First, electoral
politics have been free and open since 1965. The electoral process has
characteristics that are usually identified with "democratic" politics: a secret

ballot, multiparty participation, opposition access to the public media, civil liberties, and the rule of law. No attempt is made here to disclaim the common assumption that Botswana is a "liberal democracy" in the usual sense of that term. In order to understand the Botswana political system, however, we also must examine the political responsibilities that administrators in Botswana carry within the context of this multiparty, and parliamentary African state.

The second point to be made about politics in Botswana is that the district administrator's political mediation role is only a small part of the responsibilities of that office. The majority of the district officer's time is taken up with a variety of tedious routines such as weddings, court review procedures, and attendence at a myriad of inconclusive meetings.[3] The role of the district officer in political control activities is intermittent, at times more avuncular than authoritarian, but nonetheless an aspect of the evolving system of political administration in Botswana.

District Administration and Political Control

In spite of an almost total neglect of Botswana's rural crisis after independence, a rural-based political activism has not developed to challenge the power of the ruling BDP. Taken together the three opposition parties—the Botswana People's party, the Botswana National Front, and the Botswana Independence party—barely have been able to garner a quarter of the vote.

The opposition has not been able to derive much support from the rural areas. Opposition strength comes from government employees, urban residents, and a number of disaffected ethnic groups. In spite of the general lack of rural support for the opposition parties, the BDP political elites have been more concerned with rural, ethnically based challenges to their position than with an urban-based opposition. It is for this reason that the government has turned to the district administrative apparatus to monitor opposition activities in the rural areas.

A striking feature of post-colonial administrations in Africa is the continuing influence of the colonial past on administrative behavior and procedures and the general nature of administrative life. The Botswana case is no exception to this pattern. As was noted in Chapter 6, the British colonial administration, while being scrupulously fair in a formal sense to all of the political parties during the period leading up to the 1965 elections, was not averse to harnessing the power of the state at the national and district level to support the BDP, perceived as a moderate political movement.

The district bureaucracy in Botswana has not changed since independence. Political elites inherited a political system that has been based for the better part of the century on the principles of indirect rule and political mediation vis-à-vis traditional authorities, and they continue to see the district bureaucracy as having a residual responsibility for political control. Post-colonial elites remain concerned with political quiescence, particularly in the rural areas. Such political quiescence is deemed essential if Botswana's socio-economic elites are to pursue a strategy of economic growth that is based on mineral exploitation and commercial cattle production while making "rural development a low priority item in terms of budget allocations and . . . [giving] the populace a very minimal control over the resources allocated."[4]

A key to understanding the district commissioners' (DCs) political responsibility lies in their residual responsibility for magisterial functions, in their role as security officers responsible to the office of the president, and in their delicate relationship with and supervision of the traditional authorities. The Botswana government views the DCs as an arm of central government.

The relationship between the DCs and the office of the president is critical. The office of the president consults directly with the district commissioner on questions relating to refugees, a major political question in many districts. The DCs are responsible for keeping the office of the president informed on all matters connected with internal security (and in some cases security-related correspondence is not copied to the Ministry of Local Government and Lands). The district administration must ensure that district security plans are kept up-to-date, that they conform to the central security plan, and that the district security team is prepared to put emergency plans into operation.[5] In the event of a state of emergency, the district commissioners are responsible directly to the office of the president for the implementation of security plans and the restoration of order. Beyond their formal security role, the DCs also have responsibilities as political agents, and they can and have initiated prosecution proceedings against political leaders who have exceeded the bounds of custom in their campaign rhetoric or activity.

Since independence there have been three potential sources of political opposition: (1) the possibility of European resistance to the new BDP-dominated African government; (2) the threat of an urban, ideologically radical, opposition movement in the major population centers; and (3) the threat of a conservative, rural-based resistance to BDP rule. The European threat dissipated quickly after 1966, and despite the rapid growth of the major urban centers and a continued undercurrent of urban discontent, the political elites have continued to be concerned primarily with the rural population. The political elites see their greatest potential political threat in an alliance between disaffected elements of the non-Setswana-speaking minorities and discontented traditional authorities who could use their influence to create a rural resistance movement. Although rural resistance to the BDP has not been strong, the potential threat has dominated the electoral strategy of the governing party through four elections after 1965.

District Commissioners and Traditional Opposition

Long-range policy in Botswana is said to be directed toward relieving the district commissioner of all judicial responsibilities.[6] At a 1974 meeting of district commissioners, the consensus of opinion was that

> . . . the function of the District Administration was becoming more and more development biased. It was also confirmed that District Commissioners had many statutory responsibilities to discharge in addition. The role of District Commissioners as ex-officio magistrates imposed a strain unbearable on their efficiency to perform their administrative duties. . . . [Therefore] judicial responsibilities of District Commissioners (should) be withdrawn in the shortest possible time and a programme of phasing out their role as magistrates be determined now.[7]

Relieving District Commissioners of their judicial responsibilities has not been a major priority for the government, however. I would contend that this policy is seen as a long-term process partially because of the type of potential political opposition that most concerns the political elites.

As ex officio magistrates, the district commissioners sit in a subordinate court, and their work covers remands and criminal and civil cases. They also sign warrants and inspect prisons. Most of their judicial work, however, is related to the customary courts operated by the traditional administrations. The DCs review all customary court cases, hear complaints and appeals from customary courts, and hold the overall responsibility for traditional administration. They inspect tribal records, submit tribal budgets, and generally are expected to give advice and guidance to the chiefs and headmen.

The direct relationship between the district administration and the traditional administration is related to the perceived threat that the chiefs pose to the government. The complete phasing-out of the district commissioners' magisterial role would cut off the district administration from direct supervision of the chiefs and thereby sharply reduce the DCs' effectiveness as agents of political control. It is the district officers' judicial function that allows them to monitor the activities of the traditional authorities. Since the government greatly fears a link between political dissidents and the traditional authority structure, day-to-day scrutiny of the traditional administration is essential. Reviewing their court cases and the chiefs' magisterial activities is one way to ensure that scrutiny in a relatively unobtrusive way.

The BDP came to power partially through a coalition with traditional authorities. With the establishment of district councils and the relegation of traditional authorities to a powerless House of Chiefs, however, dissatisfaction set in, particularly among the more able chiefs. Basic to the BDP's stated policy toward chieftainship was the need to replace the concept of "tribe" with that of nation. This was the political raison d'être for an establishment of local authorities. The District Councils, however, have been less than successful as an alternative to the traditional administration in providing the link between the central government and the local allocation process.

With party branches and District Councils not yet viable as local organs of influence, the traditional authorities as a potential political opposition group remain a potent, if still muted, force to be reckoned with. It is easier to strip the chiefs of their power than it is to deprive them of their influence. Central control of traditional leaders is limited by the high regard in which chiefs are held, despite the loss of most of their formal power.

The primary source of formal authority that still remains in the hands of the traditional leaders is their control of the village *kgotla*. It is in the *kgotla* that chiefs and subchiefs hold court, and the *kgotla* remains the only legitimate means of government communication with the people. Its importance

> lies in the fact that it represents the point of intersection of the traditional political system and the organizations of the central government and district council. It acts as the means of offering traditional legitimacy to the introduction of new ideas, ways of doing things, and regulations issued by the new elites at the central and district level.[8]

The government would like to use the chiefs as its agents of political control in the rural areas, but the chiefs are not dependent upon the government for their position in the same way that civil servants are. The chiefs have a constituency and support that is independent of either local or central government institutions. Their control of the *kgotla* provides a link between the government and the populace that neither the government nor the party has been able to duplicate. Except for the traditional authorities "no direct, effective communications link between center and locale exists in Botswana."[9] Conflict between the traditional leadership and the national elite can occur whenever the chiefs conclude that their existence is threatened. The first round of that conflict took place during the 1969 elections when the coalition between the ruling BDP and traditional leaders (led by Bathoen II) broke down.

The 1969 Elections:
District Commissioners as Political Agents

The district commissioners' role in the 1969 elections differed little from what it was in 1965. While remaining formally and scrupulously neutral during the political process, the DCs were to monitor events, inform the office of the president should the situation get out of control, and intervene in any activity deemed politically excessive by the ruling BDP leadership.

The 1969 elections were the first during which a political party attempted to appeal not only to urban radical voters and disaffected minorities but also to the rural, conservative voters who identified with the traditional leadership. The Botswana National Front (BNF) had been formed after the 1965 elections to unite all opposition parties, but it was largely urban-based and generally appealed to a similar constituency and ideology as the Botswana People's Party (BPP). In 1969 Bathoen II of the Ngwaketse, dissatisfied with the treatment traditional authorities were receiving from the BDP government, resigned his chieftainship and announced his support for the BNF. In spite of the opposition of some of the party's urban elements, the BNF nominated Bathoen as its national presidential candidate, rather than Daniel Kwele, BNF president at the time. The party's goal was to appeal to the left in the cities and the right in the rural areas, in effect outflanking the BDP in both political directions.

Although the opposition parties won only seven of the thirty-two National Assembly seats (the remainder going to the ruling BDP), at the district level the election results for the opposition parties (and the BNF specifically) shook the confidence of the BDP leadership. The BDP's share of the popular vote in 1969 decreased by 12 percent from that of 1965. In addition, the BDP lost control of the Southern District Council to the BNF (until government-appointed councilors were added to the council), and the BNF polled more votes than the BDP did in urban council elections in Lobatse and Gaborone.

The three opposition parties (BNF, BPP, and BIP) were active in four areas of the country and met with varying degrees of success in each. Opposition strategy and the district bureaucracy's response before and during the 1969 elections illustrate the nature of the district commissioner's role in the political mediation process.

Northeast District

The Northeast District is a small, land-hungry, overpopulated area with a majority of non-Setswana-speaking peoples. The Kalanga-speaking people are related to the Matebele of Zimbabwe, and in the Northeast District they have traditionally perceived themselves as being caught between Setswana speakers on one side and European farmers on the other. Francistown has been one of the most politically sensitive areas of the country not only because of its significant European population with Rhodesian Unilateral Declaration of Independence (UDI) sympathies but also because it is the home area of the BPP, one of the most militant of the opposition parties.

The BDP considered the Northeast District to be one of the three centers of hard-core opposition to the government (the other two being the non-Setswana-speaking areas in the Northwest District, and the Ngwaketse areas in the Southern District). One of the major responsibilities of the district administration in Francistown has been to keep abreast of BPP activities and its leadership. Philip Matante, who led the BPP until his death in 1979, was one of two opposition members of Parliament from the Northeast, representing the city of Francistown from 1965 to 1979. In the 1966 District Council elections, the BPP had captured a majority of the elected seats, forcing the government to appoint additional councilors in order to maintain a government majority. Since independence, the BPP has appealed primarily to the minority Kalanga-speaking people of the Northeast.

Three incidents illustrate the nature of the DC's political responsibilities in the Northeast District during the 1969 elections. In one incident District Commissioner Simon Gillett received a letter dated 19 July 1969 from BPP leader Philip Matante in which Matante complained about "the ugly behavior of the Botswana police at Ramaquabane . . . [in] disturbing the Northeast District Sportsday at which the BPP was speaking."[10] According to Matante one Officer Nyepe had heckled and finally broken up the meeting. Matante followed up with a similar letter to the minister of state in the office of the president on 23 July, requesting immediate intervention because neither the DC in Francistown nor the local subchief had done anything.[11] After an investigation Gillett reported that the accusations were unwarranted since "Sergeant Nyepi was provoked into heckling after being described by the BPP speaker in public as 'an offwhite Mongwato.'"[12] The office of the president agreed with Gillett's conclusion.

A second incident involving Matante occurred in October 1969, just before the elections. Again writing to Gillett, Matante accused Subchief Ramokate, the Northeast District's representative in the House of Chiefs, of telling people in his area that they would be thrown off their lands if they voted for the BPP. The DC's response was to reprimand Ramokate for inappropriate behavior by a subchief during an elction year. This kind of breach of neutrality, even if it was in favor of the government party, was not considered to be acceptable political behavior.[14]

A third incident involved the new Botswana National Front. One of the unspoken issues that haunted the 1969 campaign was the "Kalanga question." In May 1969 an event in Gaborone caused the Kalanga to be accused of plotting to take over the government. Although there was little evidence to support the accusations, tensions grew and the matter was raised in Parliament in August. Then BNF president, Daniel Kwele, is a Kalanga, and the resentment against the Kalanga of many of the Setswana-speakers in the National Assembly was directed toward the BNF. One of the results of this episode was that the BNF leadership became afraid to nominate Kwele as the party's presidential candidate, ultimately opting for Bathoen II of the Ngwaketse.

Within the Northeast District, the BDP faced the possibility of a two-pronged threat, from the BPP and from the BNF. Kwele was partially neutralized by the anti-Kalanga attacks that caused him to be unacceptable as the BNF presidential candidate. He resigned from the party as a result of this slight but remained a potential mobilizing force behind which the Kalanga-speaking peoples of the Northeast might rally in the future.

The district administration and the Ministry of Local Government and Lands then took an unusual step to neutralize Kwele's influence by offering him the post of secretary to the Northeast District Council. Kwele was council secretary from 1969 to 1978, and although the position is nominally nonpolitical, Kwele (an able administrator) continued to be an important Kalanga spokesman in the Northeast. The council he administered often had an opposition electoral majority that was overturned only when the government nominated enough BDP councilors to give the government a majority. Throughout the 1960s both Kwele and the council were outspokenly critical of government activities. The Northeast District Commissioner spent much of his time defending government policy at council meetings and trying to keep Council Secretary Kwele from moving too far out of line. Despite Kwele's tremendous influence in the Northeast, as long as he continued to be the council secretary, he was neutralized because he could not participate openly in electoral politics.[15]

In spite of the government's strategy, the Northeast District's two National Assembly seats went to the BPP in 1969 (and again in 1974). District voters did not accept the BDP, which they believed to be dominated by their traditional rivals, the Bamangwato. Matante, although a Mongwato, was reelected to the National Assembly on the strength of his opposition to the BDP, as was the second BPP member, K. M. Nkhwa.

Ghanzi District

In Western Botswana, the BPP tried to challenge the BDP in the Ghanzi District by appealing to the district's non-Batswana elements. The Bakhalaghadi, Ghanzi's majority population, are seen to be distinct from the eastern Batswana even though they speak a dialect of Setswana. The Bakhalaghadi do not have a paramount chief of their own, and they are dominated by eastern Tswana traditional authorities throughout much of western Botswana. The BPP began its election drive in Ghanzi in April 1969 with a series of speeches aimed at the Basarwa ("bushmen") and Bakhalaghadi squatters living on the ranches of European settlers and wealthy Batswana.

Friction developed in Ghanzi between the BPP's Matante and the DC in much the same way as occurred in the Northeast District. In a letter to the minister of state in the office of the president, Matante accused the DC of condoning public interference during BPP speeches and threatened to go public with his accusations. The opposition leader criticized the police for arresting people for brewing khadi (a kind of gin) and beer.[16] Accusing the district administration of condoning strong-arm tactics by European farmers against farm laborers, Matante went on to say that some people complained [about being beaten by farm owners], reported to the DC but nothing has been done. When they [Africans] are beaten up by farmers and report to the police, no action is ever taken. People are still called babboons, kaffirs, etc., worse than South Africa. There is need for action to be taken about the situation in Ghanzi.[17]

On 6 June 1969 the permanent secretary, Ministry of Home Affairs, writing through the Ministry of Local Government and Lands, directed the DC in Ghanzi to handle the situation there with the utmost urgency, as the matter was likely to come up in Parliament.[18] On 1 July the DC responded, indicating that the government intended to take a more aggressive attitude toward the "obscenities, slanders, half-truths and downright lies [that] have so far been the perquisite of the BPP speakers themselves."[19] Calling Matante's complaints "nonsense," the DC argued that the whole of Ghanzi township was a brewing center "for a particularly vicious and unclean brand of Khadi, the constituents of which are undoubtedly poisonous." He contended that the police had no choice but to break up the illegal brewing of khadi and that there was no proof to support the allegation that the police had condoned brutality against Africans on the part of European farmers.

What action the district administration took about the BPP allegations and activities is not clear from the records. This level of information is, of necessity, fragmentary. Ultimately, district administration activity had little effect on the outcome of the 1969 election, which the BDP strong-man in western Botswana, Harry Jankie, won by a wide margin over the BPP candidate. Nonetheless, fragmentary evidence available from both the Northeast and Ghanzi Districts indicates that the district administrations would become involved in partisan political competition if the subjectively defined fine line between "legitimate" and "illegitimate" political activity were crossed during the course of an election campaign.

Kgatleng District

Chief Linchwe II of the Bakgatla acceded to the chieftainship in 1963 at the death of his father, Chief Molefi. Since independence, Linchwe has played a curious role in Botswana politics. A protégé of Naomi Mitcheson, an author, active in British socialist circles, Linchwe was the only chief not to support the BDP in the 1965 elections. He was young, British-educated, and convinced that a bridge could be built between socialism and traditionalism. (Pictures commemorating Angela Davis and Che Guevara hung in Bakgatla headquarters in Mochudi in 1975.) While remaining nominally neutral in 1965, Linchwe apparently gave some tacit support to the successful BPP candidate.

After the 1965 elections, Linchwe became involved in discussions with a number of opposition political leaders (including Kenneth Koma, Daniel

Kwele, and Ngwaketse Chief-designate, Seepapitso Gaseitsiwe, son of Chief Bathoen II) about joining all opposition parties into a united front strong enough to challenge the BDP in 1969. In October 1965 the Botswana National Front was launched in Linchwe's village of Mochudi.

Apparently Linchwe had begun to have second thoughts about his flirtation with the opposition after independence, although he continued to criticize the weakness of the House of Chiefs. In 1968, when Botswana's Ambassador to the United States, Z. K. Mathews, died, the government offered the position to Linchwe; undoubtedly, it would be convenient to have the young chief out of the country during the 1969 elections. To the surprise of many, Linchwe accepted the ambassadorial post and, leaving the chieftainship in the hands of a regent, spent the period of 1969-1972 in the United States. Despite Linchwe's absence, the BPP candidate from Mochudi was returned to the National Assembly for a second term, although the BPP's victory may have been an indication of the BDP's unwillingness to challenge Linchwe during his absence.

The government's strategy with regard to Linchwe has been a very carefully stated respect for his neutrality, taking him at his word that his primary interests are in local and "tribal" politics.[20] After Linchwe returned to Botswana and resumed the chieftainship, government officials continued to cultivate his neutrality and encouraged him to be active in local affairs. Throughout the 1970s Chief Linchwe chaired the District Council and the Land Board and continued to experiment with methods designed to "modernize" traditional culture and traditional rights.[21] Linchwe's relationship with a number of the European DCs in Kgatleng was uneasy, with Linchwe portraying them as intruders into Kgatleng society. When the position of DC was localized in 1972 the government selected an older, experienced administrator, J. Lebani, to fill it. District Commissioner Lebani and Chief Linchwe appeared to get on well; Lebani had an avuncular relationship with the chief that the government saw as conducive to Linchwe's continued neutrality.

Linchwe's early flirtation with opposition movements and the BPP's success in the 1965 and 1969 elections in the Kgatleng District were reminders to the BDP leadership that its hold on power depended on at least the passive approval of the chiefs. Chief Linchwe was young and able, capable of mobilizing his own area for or against the government, and he would have some appeal beyond the Kgatleng District, even in urban areas. For the foreseeable future one of the major functions of the Kgatleng district administration would be to keep Linchwe nonpartisan.

The three case studies discussed thus far of the DCs' role as political agents are based on somewhat fragmentary documentary evidence and are limited in scope. They do suggest, however, that although the DCs do not participate openly in the electoral process, they are available to the government and, indirectly, to the ruling party to act as monitors of political events and as agents of control when political actors are perceived to be exceeding the boundaries of acceptable behavior. By their action or nonaction the DCs can function as agents of political mediation, directing their attention to political excesses, whether committed by the opposition or by BDP supporters, or they can function as neutralizing agents and arbitrators. Most district officers, whether expatriate or Batswana, have been sympathetic to the BDP and have viewed opposition politicians as being obtrusive and obstructionist. While there are limits to the amount of irregular activity the district administration would tolerate from BDP sympathizers, clearly it would be much less sympathetic to the opposition's complaints of political irregularity than to similar complaints from the ruling party.

In the last case to be discussed, I go beyond this argument by demonstrating that in one major political incident a District Commissioner did intervene in a conflict between the traditional administration and the government, acting as an agent of political control in a manner very similar to his colonial predecessor's.

Ngwaketse District

Bathoen II, appointed Chief of the Ngwaketse in 1928, was one of the two most powerful chiefs in Bechuanaland during the colonial period. During the 1965 elections, despite his doubts about the BDP's commitment to traditional authority, Bathoen supported Seretse Khama and the BDP and encouraged other tribal leaders to do likewise. After independence Bathoen became much more uncomfortable with political developments in Botswana, concluding that the chiefs were being eliminated by the BDP government.

Neither the president nor the vice-president (Quett Masire, who was then vice-president, is from Ngwaketse) made any attempt to accommodate themselves to the increasingly alienated Bathoen during the first four years of independence. Instead, a decision was made to render it impossible for Bathoen to remain in Kanye as chief, with the hope of forcing him into some kind of retirement.[22]

Between 1965 and 1970 the DC in Kanye was Julian Tennant. Tennant saw his role as that of controlling an obdurate old chief who was trying to negate the District Council's democratic features. He concluded that in order to protect the council, he would have to lean on Bathoen. The government backed Tennant on this and told him to put the chief in his place, which is precisely what Tennant did. After his resignation Bathoen wrote in a letter to President Seretse Khama, "This attitude [of hostility] of Mr. Tennant is nothing new, he has for several years been hostile towards me and he has now found a chance to display his hatred."[23] According to Tennant, "We'd got on top of him administratively—then he resigned."[24]

Rather than simply retiring, however, Bathoen decided to become active politically. He accused the government of keeping District Commissioner Tennant in Kanye in order to work against opposition parties. Bathoen claimed that Tennant still held a bullying attitude after Bathoen's resignation and that citizens in Ngwaketse saw Tennant's actions in Kanye as stifling free participation in the 1969 elections.[25] Bathoen's son, Seepapitso, had had contact with the BNF in its early days and it was to the BNF that Bathoen now turned. After a series of negotiations with party officials, Bathoen announced publicly that he and two supporters would challenge the BDP in Southern District under the banner of the BNF. Bathoen himself would take on Vice-President Quett Masire. The chief's response to the district-level pressures placed on him between 1965 and 1970 probably were not what the BDP leadership had in mind.

The BNF nominated Bathoen as its presidential candidate, calculating that this might draw rural voters away from the BDP. The plan backfired, however, since the urban-oriented faction of the BNF found it difficult to support Bathoen. After Bathoen joined, the BNF became an uneasy coalition of two factions, rural conservatives and urban radicals, with very little in common other than their opposition to the ruling party. The BNF party platform contained remarkable social reforms combined with a set of proposals for a federal system in which an upper house of nationalities would be given the final say in legislation.

In the elections the BNF was not successful among its urban constituencies. Lobatse and Gaborone remained BDP and Francistown remained BPP. The BNF's rural constituencies, however, gave the BDP a shock. In voting shifts of between 55 and 66 percent, the BNF captured all three Ngwaketse seats, with Bathoen defeating the vice-president. The BNF also won a majority of the elected seats on the District Council. The BDP became painfully aware of the influence that traditional leaders still held over a major Setswana-speaking group. Although the party secured an easy majority nationally, and Seretse Khama was reelected president, the party leadership was now sensitive to its vulnerability in the rural areas.

Within Southern District, the district administration found that very little had changed. Bathoen's son, Seepapitso who had become the chief when Bathoen resigned, was, if anything, more cantankerous than his father. In addition, the district administration faced a large number of hostile BNF councilors who had been elected on Bathoen's coattails. A new district commissioner, R. Fitzherbert, was appointed to decrease the level of hostility between the government and traditional forces.

Seepapitso saw his position in Kanye as that of an executive in a federal-style relationship to the central government and saw the district administration as an intruder in the district. According to Fitzherbert, Seepapitso "wanted to run the district as his farm."[26] Relations between the new DC and the new chief deteriorated rapidly, and the DC finally wrote to the Ministry of Local Government and Lands and to the office of the president stating that either the chief would have to go or the council system would collapse. After a series of almost violent, verbal confrontations between Seepapitso and representatives of the district administration, the government decided to suspend the chief. According to the district officer (development) in Kanye at that time,

> The D.C. found him a very trying person. Racial slurs were used to respond to routine letters. The situation deteriorated. The chief called a series of *kgotla* meetings. He would abuse me publicly as the representative of the District Administration.[27]

Although the incidents chosen as the basis for the government's action were decided locally, the decision to suspend Seepapitso was made in Gaborone. The actual reasons for the suspension were an illegal flogging that the chief had ordered in *kgotla*, and a land allocation made by the chief without consulting the Land Board. This confrontation, between a traditional authority and a district administration, was not dissimilar to those which occurred so often during the colonial period. After a year and a half of suspension, the chief was reinstated in February of 1975.

The conflicts with Bathoen and Seepapitso illustrate the major political role of the district commissioners in Botswana. The DCs were there to ensure that the potential threat of the traditional leaders did not become a reality. The four case studies presented, however, raise a number of questions. Of these the most important is to what extent the DCs' political role was simply a holdover from the colonial period, a holdover that would disappear when the office became localized. It should be noted that in the three cases of confrontation described—in Ghanzi, Francistown, and Kanye—the DCs involved were Europeans and that the last two areas of the country to be localized, Francistown and Kanye, were also the areas most firmly entrenched in opposition camps. While the BDP government clearly used European district administrators in much the same way they were used during the colonial period, the government would be less likely to use Batswana DCs in a similar manner. The BDP preferred mediation to confrontation, but with the withdrawal of the last of the European district commissioners at the end of 1974, the government had no tested mechanism to deal with a recalcitrant traditional administration that opted for confrontational tactics.[28] Before the 1974 elections, policy makers sought an alternative mechanism for political control in their rural development policy.

The 1974 Elections: The Shift from Containment

The results of the 1969 elections had shaken the BDP leadership. Although control of the government was never in doubt, the BDP did suffer significant losses. Vice-President Masire lost his seat to former chief Bathoen. The number of parliamentary seats held by the opposition increased from three to seven. Support for the BDP dropped from 80.4 percent of the electorate to 68.3 percent. In addition, the opposition picked up fifty-two local council seats, twenty-three more than in 1965.

As the BDP leaders approached the 1974 elections, their campaign plans contained strands of continuity within a broader strategy of electoral mobilization. The goverment continued to rely upon administrative officials, particularly at the district level, to contain political competition. BDP party leaders concluded after the setbacks in 1969, however, that political control mechanisms were not enough to ensure electoral predominance. Attempts had to be made to strengthen the party apparatus at both the national and local levels, and to provide visible if symbolic evidence of government development activity throughout the country.

Continuity

The BDP remained concerned primarily with potential opposition mobilized by dissident traditional leaders in the rural areas. Political containment strategies continued to focus on the relationship between the district commissioner and the chief. No further defections of senior chiefs occurred after 1969, and Chief Linchwe of the Bakgatla, after returning from a stint in Washington, maintained a guarded neutrality.

In 1965 and 1969 Linchwe had thrown his support informally to the BPP, which won the Kgatleng District seat in each of these elections. After his return from Washington, a concerted effort was made to woo Linchwe away from the opposition. By 1974,

> the Chief [Linchwe] realised that he was fighting a losing battle with the Government-BDP machine and decided to eschew confrontation as a means of getting what he wanted. Linchwe thus withdrew his support from the BPP and placed it behind the party in power, with the result that the BDP won all but one of the Council seats in the 1974 elections in Kgatleng District and also took the Mochudi seat in the National Assembly from the BPP.[29]

The new period of cooperation was symbolized "by a photograph in the Botswana *Daily News* of Linchwe and President Seretse Khama walking hand in hand through Mochudi."[30]

Those chiefs who were loyal to the BDP could be mobilized to check opposition activity in the rural areas. The holding of public meetings required the permission of the local chief. In a number of cases in 1974, the opposition party failed to get permission to address the *kgotla*. For example, "The BPP opposition candidates [were often] not . . . allowed to address meetings in the Serowe *kgotla*."[31] Representatives of the government, however, were exempt from these restrictions. According to the Minister of Local Government and Lands, "It is inappropriate that Ministers should have to seek permission to hold a meeting. It is proposed therefore that Ministers should be exempted from this [procedure]."[32]

According to a study of the 1974 elections, there were a number of registration problems throughout the country.[33] To what extent those problems were caused deliberately, as opposed to resulting from sloppy administration, is unclear. One conscious decision, however, had been made to manage the nature of the electorate. Voters had to be registered to vote prior to the dissolution of Parliament, but Botswana has no provision for absentee voting. In addition to diplomats and students abroad, this effectively disenfranchises twenty to thirty thousand mine workers and others living and working in South Africa. This group could be expected to be highly politicized and possibly grist for the mill of the opposition parties.

The containment strategies of the BDP leadership should not be overstressed. Overall, the BDP has been much fairer to opposition parties than is common in LDCs. While the media are clearly government instruments, "they are not used as channels of ideological cant."[34] Nonetheless, as was the case in 1969 and 1974, the BDP "has not hesitated to use the legal powers at its disposal to maintain its position on the few occasions when it has been effectively challenged."[35]

Electoral Mobilization

In 1974 the BDP leadership made a conscious attempt to go beyond containment in order to stop any further erosion of support in the rural areas. The party approached the 1974 elections as "a well oiled and financed machine," having

> . . . hired fifty organizers, bought twenty-two bicycles and twelve new vehicles, purchased twenty-four loudspeaker systems, mounted a two week course on campaigning for twenty-four people, held regional seminars, produced material on campaigning, paid for the printing of 35,000 copies of [its] Manifesto, and thousands of copies of posters, and paid part of the expenses of candidates.[36]

As K. P. Morake, then minister of education, described it, the BDP "went to the election like a teacher who has thoroughly done his preparations."[37]

In order to solidify urban political support, the government targeted the rapidly growing civil service and local government services. In 1969 many civil servants had supported the BNF. The public sector grew rapidly between 1969 and 1974, from less than six thousand to more than ten thousand people. In April 1974, following an investigation by a salaries review commission, large wage increases were awarded to all sectors of the civil service. The minimum daily wage paid to unskilled workers in the civil service went up from Rand .80 to Rand 2.0 ($1.00 to $3.00). The increase ranged from over 150 percent at the lowest level to 17 percent at the top end of the scale. Occurring some five months before the elections, the salary increase may have contributed to a solidification of civil service support for the Khama government.

In the rural areas, the BDP mobilized government officials in an attempt to prevent further defections of rural voters. "Ministers, assistant ministers, senior (government) officials and district commissioners travelled throughout the country."[38] Some government resources were involved in BDP electioneering.

Beyond this, the cabinet, nervous about the 1974 elections becoming a repetition of the 1969 elections, "decided a year before [the election] that the party needed drastic action to show that it was serving the rural areas in a tangible way."[39] Little had been done to promote rural development since independence and the cabinet, buoyed by a healthy budget surplus and a stable of willing donors, concluded that the announcement of a program to provide activity on the ground before the 1974 elections would testify, at least symbolically, to the government's commitment to the rural areas. A number of existing projects were targeted, completion dates were put forward, and the projects were grouped together as a package under the label of the Accelerated Rural Development Programme (ARDP). The projects focused on infrastructure, schools, clinics, and water supplies and tended to satisfy basic needs rather than stimulate rural production directly. (The ARDP will be discussed more fully in Chapter 10.)

Apathy or Contentment

The BDP government was able "to spend its way out of political trouble in 1974."[40] The BDP emerged with an overwhelming majority of electoral support, up from a low of 68 percent of the total vote in 1969 to almost 78 percent in 1974. The party also recaptured three of the National Assembly seats held by the opposition and increased its number of District Council seats from 113 to 149.

The 1974 victory was a somewhat shallow one, however, given the severe decline in voter turnout, as illustrated in the National Assembly election results. (See Table 7.1.) Only 31.2 percent of the registered voters cast ballots for the contested National Assembly seats. Almost 17 percent fewer votes actually were cast in 1974 than in 1969. The twenty-seven National Assembly seats won by the BDP represented "at most the approval through the ballot of no more than 22.8% of those eligible to vote."[41]

Some BDP officials, making the best of bad situation, suggested that the results reflected a complacent electorate. Batswana did not vote because they were satisfied with the existing government, and, in any event, many voters failed to understand the need to renew the mandate. Politicians, as were traditional leaders, should be selected once, for life. It was difficult "to alter people's feelings that inheritance and status within an ethnic unit are more

Table 7.1   Botswana National Assembly Elections, 1969–1979

	BDP	BNF	1969 BPP	BIP	IND
Total vote	52,518	10,410	9,329	4,601	—
% of Total Vote	68.1	13.5	12.1	6.0	—
No. Seats Contested	31*	21	15	9	—
Returned Unopposed	3	0	0	0	—
Seats Won	24	3	3	1	—
	BDP	BNF	1974 BPP	BIP	IND
Total Vote	49,047	7,358	4,199	3,086	321
% of Total Vote	77.7	11.5	6.6	4.8	15.
No. Seats Contested	32	14	8	6	3
Returned Unopposed	4	0	0	0	0
Seats Won	27	2	2	1	0
	BDP	BNF	1979 BPP	BIP	IND
Total Vote	101,078	17,324	9,983	5,813	278
% of Total Vote	75.2	12.9	7.4	4.3	12.
No. Seats Contested	32	16	14	5	2
Returned Unopposed	2	0	0	0	0
Seats Won	29	2	1	1	0

Source: Data compiled from three reports on the general elections of 1969, 1974 and 1979, prepared by the supervisor of elections, publications, in March 1979, December 1974 and December 1979, by the Government Printer, Gaborone.

   Table compiled by E. Philip Morgan. "Botswana: Development, Democracy and Vulnerability," in Southern Africa: The Continuing Crisis, 2nd ed., Gwendolyn M. Carter and Patrick O'Maera, eds. (Bloomington: Indiana University Press, 1982), p. 238.

*One new constituency added in 1974.

legitimate as qualifications for leadership posts than party political contests."[42]

   Apathy may be a more appropriate description, however. Significant numbers of voters may have concluded that the voting exercise was not a significant activity. Beyond this, some of those who were apathetic also may have been alienated from the political process. If an individual believes that it is not possible to influence events and concludes that no benefits can be derived from participation, then there is no reason to participate.

   Some evidence suggests more than undifferentiated indifference. The electorate in 1974 may have been influenced by the dissatisfaction of the traditional leadership. In some areas, chiefs and subchiefs, angered by their sense of helplessness in the face of their loss of authority and by the heavy-handed nature of the district commissioner's administrative control, may have encouraged people to abstain from voting. The 1974 election may be significant in that it pinpoints both a growing alienation from Botswana's political leadership and a serious reduction in support for the BDP government by the population as a whole.

The 1979 Elections: A Combination of Strategies

While the BDP took some comfort in the reversals suffered by the opposition in 1974, there was considerable consternation over the extremely low level of voter turnout. The issue of voter turnout would be addressed in the preparations for the 1979 elections. As a result of those elections, two of the three opposition parties, the BIP and the BPP were effectively eliminated from electoral competition. The BDP doubled its total votes, from forty-nine thousand votes in 1974 to over one hundred thousand votes in 1979. (See Table 7.1.)

Of the opposition parties, only the BNF maintained its viability as an opposition movement. It retained two National Assembly seats from the Southern (Ngwaketse) District and garnered significant levels of support in several other areas. Most important, BNF President Kenneth Koma tripled his vote in Gaborone, the largest and one of the fastest growing urban areas in Botswana.

Coming into the 1979 elections, the ruling BDP had a threefold strategy: (1) The political leaders would continue to use the power of the state to curb opposition "excesses" during the course of the campaign; (2) As in 1974 the government's rural development efforts would be demonstrated visibly in districts with significant opposition strength; and (3) BDP leaders attempted to replenish the party by bringing in opposition, or potential opposition, activists.

The Threat of State Sanctions

There was a major change in the use of incumbents to manage events in the 1979 elections. BDP party leaders were much more open in their public statements about the potential harnessing of district and national administrative power to curb opposition political activities. Rather than the quiet use of the district-level bureaucracy to monitor and, occasionally, to intervene in political activities, national leaders openly articulated their perception that some opposition political activity might be subversive. Targeted for such accusations was the Botswana National Front. The president and his cabinet painted the opposition, especially the BNF, "as an insidious threat to democracy, intimating that they were plotting revolution."[43]

The escalation of hostilities between the BDP and the BNF was not a one-sided affair. As early as 1975 the BNF leadership had begun to flirt with a rhetoric of violence. The BDP leadership had responded by suggesting that as the BNF continued to lose elections it could be expected to resort increasingly to "seditious acts such as assassinations and sabotage."[44] In 1976 the president publicly linked "external threats" to a spillover from the Zimbabwe war and called for vigilance against "opportunists" within Botswana.

The rhetoric of threat and counterthreat between the ruling BDP and the BNF became more strident between 1976 and 1978. In 1977, for example, BNF President Koma claimed that the BDP would win in 1979 because of intimidation, but that it would be the last time. He alleged that his party was perceived as being illegal and that he was being followed by the special branch of the police. The president's reply to this was equally harsh. "For every bullet they throw at us, we shall shell them to counter that."[45]

Three incidents in 1977 and 1978 indicate the extent of the government's sensitivity to criticism. Patrick Van Rensburg, a well-known South African liberal, was active in rural development and community self-help during this period through his brigades movement. By 1977 he had become more critical of aspects of Botswana's rural development policy that, he said, were increasing inequity within the country. In November 1977 he made a speech at the University College of Botswana that was highly critical of the government. Ten days later Van Rensburg was attacked by name in the National Assembly for perverting Botswana's youth. He was alleged to be tied to, and a spokesman for, the BNF and to be undermining democracy in the country. Shortly thereafter, Van Rensburg temporarily left the country.

In 1978 a second incident occurred at the University College of Botswana when antigovernment demonstrations broke out over the prosecution of a Botswana soldier who had killed three Europeans near the Southern Rhodesian border. The BNF took an active role in the soldier's defense. As a result of the demonstration, the government closed down the university and deported two black South African university lecturers. Many of the students boycotted the graduation ceremonies and President Khama's inauguration as chancellor. In his inaugural speech, the president attacked the students who used the university to study "destructive revolutionary dogma with no relevance to our circumstances." The whole incident "dramatized the increase in student activism and government overreaction to political demonstrations."[46]

The third incident occurred in June 1978. BNF President Koma and sixteen other members of the party were preparing to attend a youth conference in Havana, Cuba. Just prior to their departure, the Ministry of Home Affairs withdrew the passports of all seventeen opposition politicians.

In explaining the action, the president declared that the BNF leaders were a subversive element in a country already threatened increasingly by an unstable, regional political situation.

The 1979 election year began with a rhetorical outburst from the BDP that set the tone for the campaign. In February Vice President Quett Masire warned the population against the activities of dissident elements. He spoke of "circumstances under which opposition parties might be banned; for instance if 'they endanger the lives of the people in one way or the other, it would be irresponsible to leave the parties in existence.'"[47] The president accused the opposition of indulging in disruptive, left-wing policies and said that the BNF was composed of "social malcontents" who had contributed nothing to the national welfare but "wanted political power at all costs."[48] In July the president described any support for the opposition as throwing

> the country to the wolves. The BNF in their desperate struggle for political power, would be only too happy to confirm that there is no democracy in this country and that the country is ripe for a bloody revolution, which is their aim, but an aim we must frustrate.[49]

Parliament was dissolved on 27 August 1979 with the polling date for the elections set for 20 October 1979. The BDP's rhetoric continued unabated during the two-month campaign. Despite the combined number of opposition candidates for parliamentary seats being one short of the 17 needed to form a government, "the BDP appeared to believe it necessary to persuade the majority population that any victory for opposition candidates at this stage in history would be a disaster for the country."[50]

On September 25th, the president stated that if anybody threatened Botswana's democratic structure, that person or persons would meet a strong reaction from the government. He also described the opposition as composed of "self-styled intellectuals who are busy brainwashing the people with conflicting attitudes borrowed from other countries."[51] In an October 12th speech in the western city of Maun, an anti-government stronghold, President Khama accused the opposition of going so far as to capitalize on the drought and the outbreak of hoof and mouth disease to unfairly attack the BDP. The president's speech was laden with scathing attacks on ethnic prejudices and what he said were revolutionary infiltrations into the country.

The tone of government rhetoric throughout the 1979 campaign was the most strident since independence, at a time when the opposition posed no threat to the BDP's dominance. At the heart of the government's campaign was the threat, no more than lightly veiled, that the BDP could and would use the power of the state to ban or restrict opposition parties or individuals considered to be a threat to the country's security. To what extent this was merely campaign rhetoric without substance is not clear, but it is significant that for the first time since independence, the idea of placing restrictions on individual or group activity was discussed seriously by top Botswana politicians, including President Khama himself.

Mobilization of BDP Support

The use of the district and national bureaucracies to mobilize support took two forms prior to the 1979 elections. The 1974 pattern of making rural development projects highly visible, particularly in borderline districts, was continued. In addition, the district administration and the government in general initiated a massive re-registration of voters because of the very low voter turnout in the 1974 elections.

Although there was not a nationwide project during the 1979 campaign on the order of the Accelerated Rural Development Programme during 1974, one of the cornerstones of the two-month pre-election period was the announcement by government ministers of new rural development projects in a number of key districts. For example, on September 8th, Vice-President Masire opened a number of completed development projects in Kgatleng District (an area of considerable opposition support) and announced that an additional 1,458,000 Pula had been allocated for extra educational facilities in Kgatleng. On October 4th and 5th, the minister of education opened completed development projects in the Northeast District and Kweneng District, respectively. In the Northeast, a BPP stronghold, the total worth of projects in the areas of health, education, water points, roads, and community development was more than a quarter million Pula. The Kweneng District expenditures were in the same infrastructure areas as in the Northeast and totaled 186,000 Pula. Finally, in Maun on October 12th, the president spoke of new developments in the long-postponed second abattoir, a major issue in that part of Botswana. In each district throughout the two-month period, smaller, but highly visible, infrastructure projects were opened by cabinet ministers and other BDP candidates for the National Assembly.

Because of their concern with the low voter turnout in 1974, the BDP leadership paid a great deal of attention to local-level political organization prior to the 1979 elections. In 1977 a party youth wing was established, and an effort was made to develop a more active membership in the party's district branches.

Perhaps more important in terms of the voter turnout, district officials throughout the country (as well as the national radio and print media) promoted re-registration during the three-year period leading up to the 1979 elections. The elections office in Gaborone and in the districts continued to issue election cards until the eve of the election. On election eve it was stated in the *Botswana Daily News* that

> . . . the polling percentage is . . . expected to be boosted by the massive enlightenment programme launched by the Government since three years back. The Department of Information and Broadcasting has run jingles and programmes on the radio, plus cartoons and columns in the *Daily News* emphasising the elections theme.[52]

As a result of the re-registration campaign and the "get-out-the-vote" effort, the turnout in 1979 was 58.4 percent.

Patterns of Co-optation

The third aspect of the BDP's overall electoral strategy for 1979 has implications for the future of politics in Botswana. A number of steps were taken to co-opt opposition sympathizers and bring them into the ranks of the BDP. At one level the BDP encouraged many former civil servants, who were "government wise," to enter active politics at both the local and national level. Large numbers of the first post-colonial generation of bureaucrats began to retire during this period, and unless brought into the BDP fold, they could form the nucleus of an opposition group.

At the national level, the BDP continued the pattern of co-optation begun in 1974 when Chief Linchwe II was wooed away from the BPP. Daniel Kwele, a former BNF president, had been neutralized by his appointment as Northeast District Council secretary. In 1978 it was announced that the president had appointed Kwele to be a special member of Parliament. Kwele was built up as a candidate for Parliament in the opposition Northeast District and, in fact, came within 143 votes of taking the BPP's last parliamentary seat in 1979. Perhaps because of Kwele's electoral success, and in order to enhance his prestige for the 1984 elections, Kwele was made assistant minister of local government and lands in the postelection cabinet.[53]

This pattern of co-optation is not without precedent in other African states, where able and ambitious opposition leaders, wearied by years in the political wilderness, succumb to the temptations of office and join the governing party. If such a pattern of co-optation becomes widespread in Botswana, it could mean the end of any hope that a viable opposition movement will be maintained, and one of the last African, multiparty political systems could move toward a de facto, one-party political system.

Politics in the Post-Khama Era

The elevation of Vice-President Masire to the presidency, following President Khama's death in 1980, scrupulously followed the letter of the Botswana constitution. Masire was nominated unanimously by the BDP and elected by a vote of 32 to 34 in the National Assembly (there were two abstentions). The public display of unanimity did not obscure completely the potential divisions within the ruling BDP, however. Early speculation centered on a number of potential rivals to Masire, including Daniel Kwelagobe (Ministry of Information and Broadcasting), Gaositwe Chiepe (Ministry of Mineral Resources and Water Affairs), Archie Mogwe (foreign minister), and Ian

Khama (the president's son, a brigadier in the Botswana army and chief of the Bamangwato).

Potential opposition to Masire is likely to come from two sources. The first is a growing radical group within the BDP, centered among the backbenchers, who would like to see a harder line taken against South Africa externally and a more socialist-oriented domestic policy that focuses on the problems of the rural and urban unemployed. A second group could coalesce around Ian Khama and restoration of Bamangwato dominance of the presidency (President Masire is from Ngwaketse in the south). As the late president's son, Ian Khama is a natural successor, and his position in the Botswana Defence Forces gives him both wider visibility and a second vector of support.

President Masire's first year in office did not dampen the muted criticism of his leadership that had begun with his struggle (within the BDP party caucus) to gain the nomination after President Khama's death. There was an underlying assumption within Botswana political circles that Masire had not yet solidified political control over the BDP machinery, and some grassroots opposition to Masire remains, particularly within the Central District.

The most telling evidence of Masire's lack of support surfaced in May 1982 when the government announced that Masire's portrait would replace that of the late President Khama on the nation's currency and that only the current president's picture could be displayed in public places. There were a number of angry protests in the Mahalapye area of the Central District. In one incident several hundred BDP supporters walked out of a meeting with the minister of education, K. P. Morake. Discontent continued over the currency issue throughout 1982.

Prior to the 1984 election, there was a perception among a number of Batswana, particularly in the Central District, that Masire was simply a "caretaker" president in that he had not been elected to office by the voters. This perception of Masire, based on a misunderstanding of the Constitutional provisions for succession, reinforced ethnic antagonism over national-level political control. This issue was only partly resolved by the BDP victory in the 1984 elections, and even now there continues to be speculation that Ian Khama or some other Central District candidate will challenge Masire in 1989.

The Botswana Democratic Party

Tensions over Masire remained within the ruling BDP two years prior to the 1984 elections. With the decline of opposition parties as a significant political force, an "unofficial" opposition developed within the BDP backbench. In a number of key votes, BDP backbenchers allied themselves with the opposition members of Parliament (MPs) against government policy. There were several very close divisions of the house, including a number of important votes on aspects of the 1982 budget. On several occasions, for example, the Livestock Control Regulations Bill in 1981, Parliament rejected government-sponsored legislation.

A number of BDP backbenchers are said to feel cut off from the party leadership and to believe that government ministers increasingly were unwilling to take political advice and instead listen only to their civil servants and their expatriate advisors. Masire himself has come under muted criticism, privately from the opposition and not so privately from Gaborone's attentive public.

The so-called young Turks criticized Masire for surrounding himself with nonpolitical administrators. Five of the eleven members of the pre-1984 cabinet were retired civil servants on government pension. Younger MPs and party leaders attack the BDP's "paternalism" and the party leadership's unwillingness to address the increasing inequities that have resulted from a decade of economic growth. They advocate less emphasis on growth and more attention to distribution and social equity. Among the contentious issues are the now visible dangers of Botswana's mineral mono-economy, what is seen as the government's excessive conservatism in its investment policy, and, prior to late 1981, the government's excess liquidity. Critics suggest that Botswana is too open to the established foreign companies, while there is not enough risk-taking among governmental and parastatal institutions in support of local Batswana entrepreneurs. Younger party cadres want the government to take a more active role in combating increasing underemployment in both the rural and urban areas and to act more assertively vis-à-vis South Africa. The BDP faces growing radicalism within the university and a generalized resentment over the continuing influence of expatriates.

President Masire and other leaders of the BDP counter by emphasizing the economic gains that Botswana has made in the twenty years since independence. The president also points to the dangers of instability that have plagued so many other African states, stressing the importance of political stability for Botswana's future economic development. Such stability, according to Masire, must be linked directly to, and be a part of, the concept of democracy.

Political uncertainties in Botswana were complicated by the death of Vice-President Lenyeletse Seretse on 4 January 1983 after a long illness. Lenyeletse Seretse, appointed vice-president after President Khama's death, was a cousin of the late president. When President Masire, to the surprise of some observers, appointed the minister of finance and development planning, Peter Mmusi, as the new vice-president, the traditional balance between president and vice-president ended. Mmusi is from the south, as is Masire, and the two leaders are long-time political allies. The president's critics in the Central District argue that he broke the pact, established at independence, that either the president or the vice-president must come from the Central District.

The Opposition Parties

After the 1979 elections, opposition politics revolved around the issue of a united opposition pact. In April 1980, BNF president, Kenneth Koma, called for a united front of opposition parties in the 1984 elections in order to avoid what he called the BDP's "widely touted one party state."[54] A meeting between the BNF and the BPP occurred in September of that year. The possibilities of a political alliance were discussed, but an agreement on a united front was not reached.

The threat of an opposition alliance caused some concern within the ruling BDP. Both President Khama, before his death, and President Masire, spoke out against the proposed merger. In August 1980 Masire talked of "enemies [some of them local] . . . looking for loopholes in our nationhood . . . to bring down those who have been brought to power."[55] The former executive secretary of the BDP, Patrick Balopi, MP for Francistown, said that an opposition merger would tamper with the popularity of the BDP, and he warned that the opposition should not seek power by violence or the barrel of the gun. He went on to say that if the opposition came to power "there will be much brutal killing of that party's opponents."[56]

Opposition parties in Botswana appear to be caught in the historical circumstances of their formation and are becoming irrelevant to Botswana's evolving political system. Much of their rhetoric reflects their origins as political movements and does not focus on contemporary political issues. The BPP, for example, at its twenty-first party convention, pledged to create a socialist and pan-Africanist Botswana. In June 1981 the BIP accused the BDP of "chieftainship politics" and of looking "back to the Bangamwato for another chief to lead it to yet another . . . chieftainship electoral victory."[57] The BNF leadership accused the BDP of exploitation and called for the creation of a classless society.

A new opposition party, the Botswana Progressive Union (BPU), was founded in June 1982 under the leadership of Daniel Kwele, the former specially elected MP and assistant minister of local government and lands. Kwele was dropped from the cabinet in March 1982 for his internal opposition to government policies and his championship of Kalanga nationalism. He had opposed openly a government motion on employment in 1980 that was considered anti-Kalanga. The BPU hoped to benefit from the disaffection felt by both Kalanga and the Bamangwato from the ruling BDP.

In spite of the powerlessness of the opposition parties, the debate between the BDP and opposition groups grew in stridency prior to the 1984 elections. Kwele, as head of the BPU, accused the BDP of "terror" tactics and of planning to rig the elections. If that happened, Kwele threatened, the BDP should be overthrown by the barrel of the gun.

Accusations and counter-accusations between the BNF and the BDP were acrimonious as well. Labeling the BNF a subversive element, BDP Party

Secretary Kwelagobe enjoined, "There is no assurance that [all] the political parties in Botswana seek the continuance of the prevailing democratic system."[58] According to BDP leaders, the BNF had tried to infiltrate both the police and the military forces in 1981 in order to foment revolution. The BDP also accused the BNF of penetrating the student council and other student bodies at the university. In April 1982 Minister of Education K. P. Morake labeled the University College of Botswana a hotbed of subversion and claimed that "sensitive political issues including coups" were discussed at clandestine meetings held on university grounds.[59]

The leadership of the BNF has consistently claimed that the BDP is paving the way for the establishment of a one-party state and an authoritarian system. Accusing the BDP of election fraud, the BNF called for United Nations supervision of the electoral process and threatened to boycott the 1984 elections.

The BDP won the August 1984 elections, although with a somewhat reduced electoral majority. The opposition garnered five National Assembly seats, four for the BNF and one for the BPP. Two cabinet ministers, Foreign Minister Mogwe and Home Affairs Minister K. L. Disele, were defeated by opposition candidates. In addition, Vice-President Peter Mmusi in a court-imposed by-election brought about by ballot irregularities, was defeated by the BNF opposition leader Kenneth Koma in a Gaborone constituency. The opposition also made significant gains in the local elections.

Conclusion

The 1984 election results suggest that opposition politics are not completely moribund in Botswana. It seems equally clear that the BNF is the only politically viable opposition movement in the country. With the rapid urbanization of Gaborone and, to a lesser extent, of the other towns in eastern Botswana, the BNF may pose a threat to BDP political control in the next decade. If this threat materializes, it will provide the acid test of the viability of Botswana's multiparty political system.

Much is made of the fact that Botswana is one of the few remaining multiparty states in Africa. Its formal pattern of political competition closely resembles that in North America and western Europe and suggests a uniqueness to political developments in this small southern African country that is only partially warranted. Some academics and journalists focus on Botswana's "democracy" to an extent that borders on "Botswanaphilia," a pattern of infatuation not dissimilar to the "Tanzaphilia" of a decade ago.

It has not been my purpose in this chapter to contradict the usual assumptions about multiparty politics in Botswana. It has, in fact, started with the observation that Botswana has open elections, freedom of speech and reasonable opposition access to the media. What I am suggesting is the need to go beyond the formal assumptions of a multiparty political system in order to understand how the ruling BDP uses the advantages of its incumbency and the administrative mechanisms of the state to maintain its predominant political position within the country.

Such an analysis of Botswana should be no different in its focus than are comparable analyses of Britain, France, Sweden, or the United States. To avoid such issues as the use of the bureaucracy as a mechanism of political mediation and control in the Botswana context, when this is a major theme in the analyses of bureaucratic politics and political-administrative relationships in many other environments, does little to protect Botswana's fledgling political institutions. Instead, this avoidance would place Botswana's politics in a special category in which critical analysis would be avoided because Botswana's political system is deemed more "civilized" or "western" than those systems accused of excesses in Uganda, Chad or Zaire.

Botswana's political elites see themselves as modernizers with a responsibility to develop the country commercially to the highest level possible given its economic resources. It is to the bureaucracy that political elites turn, both to stimulate economic growth and to curb the excesses of the ethnic right and the socialist left. From the perspective of the BDP, the extremes of the radical left, of African socialism, of the far right, and of ethnic conservatism are equally unacceptable.

David Apter suggested that "the most interesting possibility for stratification policies in the modernizing autocracy is the reliance on bureaucratic and military organizations to maintain the stratification system." He said that political elites have three options for controlling their political environment: (1) to increase political recruitment through the military and the bureaucracy; (2) to allocate resources and resource disposal to the military; and (3) to employ the military organization as a coercive instrument.[60] To these three options I would add a fourth: to employ the bureaucracy, or part of it, as an overt mechanism of political mediation and mobilization.

Responsibility for political mobilization and control has taken two forms in Botswana. During most of the first decade after independence, the government used district bureaucracy as a monitor of district political activity and, when necessary, as an agent of intervention to control potential political challenges to the ruling BDP. By 1974 a second pattern of political mediation had evolved. The district officer remained potentially an agent of political control, but the government's strategy for the districts broadened to include electoral mobilization and the co-optation of actual or potential political opponents to bring them into the ranks of the BDP.

Botswana's politics are characterized by a continuity of role relationships at the district and national levels that have been inherited, at least partially, from the colonial period. This continuity from the colonial period causes

Botswana's administrative system to be not as dissimilar from those of other African states as has sometimes been assumed.

The death of Botswana's first president, Seretse Khama, and the accession of Vice-President Masire, is a milestone in Botswana's political development. The transition to a second presidency has occurred and the political system survived. The antagonism between the ruling party and its frustrated, if largely impotent, opposition, however, as reflected in the debate leading up to the 1984 elections, is likely to continue unchanged. Furthermore, if it should come to pass that Botswana does move to a de facto or de jure one-party state under President Masire, the responsibility for such a change will not belong to the Masire administration alone. The seeds were planted prior to independence, as was the case in a number of other African countries, with patterns of mediation and control that gave opposition political parties little opportunity to develop viable alternatives to the party that happened to be in power when the mantle of state authority was transferred from the colonial power to the indigenous political elites.

Notes

1. Hoyt Alverson, *Mind in the Heart of Darkness: Value and Self-Identity and the Tswana of Southern Africa* (New Haven: Yale University Press, 1978), p. 72.

2. A new party, the Botswana Progressive Union, was formed in 1982.

3. The need to keep the district administration's responsibilities in perspective was expressed by Richard Weisfelder in a personal communication to the author.

4. John Holm, "Rural Development and Elections in Botswana," *How Botswana Votes*, Sam Decalo, ed. (forthcoming), p. 1 (in manuscript).

5. The district security team is composed of the DC, the district police commander, and the officers commanding the special branch and the criminal investigation division.

6. As indicated by the registrar of the High Court, 23 September 1974—L.G. 1/6/14, vol. 2.

7. Report of the District Commissioners' Conference held on 23-24 July 1974—L.G. 3/3, vol. 3.

8. See Richard Vengroff, *Local–Central Linkages and Political Development in Botswana* (Ph.D. diss., Syracuse University, 1972), p. 128.

9. *Ibid.*, pp. 216-217.

10. Matante to Gillett, D.C., Francistown, 19 July 1969, in L.G. 16/9/1, vol. 2.

11. Matante to Office of the President, 23 July 1969, in L.G. 16/9/1, vol. 2.

12. Permanent Secretary, Ministry of Local Government and Lands, to Office of the President, 12 September 1969, in L.G. 16/9/1, vol. 2.

13. Matante to D.C., Francistown, 13 October 1969, in L.G. 16/9/1, vol. 2.

14. D.C., Francistown, 13 October 1969, in L.G. 16/9/1, vol. 2.

15. Oral interview with Julian Tennant, Town Clerk, Francistown, 2 July 1975 and Oral interview with Daniel Kwele, Council Secretary, Northeast District Council, Francistown, 2 July 1975.

16. L.G. 16/9/1, vol. 2, District Administration.

17. P. G. Matante, K. M. Nkhwa, and T. W. Motlhagodi to Permanent Secretary, Ministry of Home Affairs, 3 April 1969—L.G. 16/9/1, vol. 2.

18. Permanent Secretary, Home Affairs, through P.S., L.G.L. to the DC, Ghanzi, 6 June 1969.

19. DC, Ghanzi, to Permanent Secretary, Ministry of Local Government and Lands, 1 July 1969—Ghanzi District Files, C.Z./3, this and subsequent quote.

20. Oral interview with Chief Linchwe II, 23 May 1975.

21. For example, Linchwe has reinstated male and female initiation rights that had fallen into disuse.

22. This account is based on interviews with the following people in Gaborone and Kanye: E. B. Egner, 30 March 1975; Julian Tennant, former DC, Kanye, 3 July 1975; Chief Seepapitso, 4 June 1975; R. Fitzherbert, former DC, Kanye, 17 July 1975; Philip Steenkamp, 20 August 1975; Emery Roe, then D.O. (D), Kanye, 6 June 1976; and B. R. Chibana, Council Chairman, Southern District Council, 6 June 1975.

23. Former Chief Bathoen to Sir Seretse Khama, 1 July 1969, in L.G. 16/9/1, vol. 2.

24. Oral interview with Julian Tennant, 3 July 1975.

25. Bathoen to Sir Seretse Khama, 1 July 1969, in L.G. 16/9/1, vol. 2.

26. Oral interview with R. Fitzherbert, 17 July 1975.

27. Oral interview with Emery Roe, 6 June 1976.

28. Tennant was replaced in 1973, but stayed on as Town Clerk, Francistown, from 1973 to 1976. Fitzherbert was relieved in 1974 but was appointed Resident Magistrate, Maun and Ghanzi Districts, 1975.

29. John A. Wiseman, "Conflict and Conflict Alliances in the Kgatleng District of Botswana," *Journal of Modern African Studies*, vol. 16, no. 3 (September 1978), p. 494.

30. *Botswana Daily News*, November 25, 1977, p. 1.

31. Donald K. Kowet, *Land, Labour Migration and Politics in Southern Africa: Botswana, Lesotho and Swaziland* (Uppsala, Sweden: Scandinavian Institute of African Studies, 1978), p. 207.

32. *Ibid.*, p. 204.

33. Jack Parson, "A Note on the 1974 General Election in Botswana and the U.B.L.S. Election Study" (Gaborone: unpublished manuscript, 1978), p. 12.

34. Morgan, "Botswana," p. 239.

35. Christopher Stevens and John Speed, "Multi-Partyism in Africa. The Case of Botswana Revisited," *African Affairs*, vol. 77, no. 304 (January 1978), p. 386.

36. Jack Parson, "Botswana," (book length manuscript), p. 73 in typescript.

37. *Ibid.*, p. 89.

38. Kowet, *Land, Labour Migration*, p. 206.

39. John D. Holm, "Liberal Democracy and Rural Development in Botswana," *African Studies Review*, vol. 25, no. 1 (March 1982), p. 95.

40. Stevens and Speed, "Multi-Partyism," p. 386.

41. Parson, "A Note on the 1974 General Election," p. 12.

42. *Ibid.*, p. 13.

43. E. Philip Morgan, "Section on 'Botswana' for the 1979/80 edition of *Africa Contemporary Record*, Colin Legum, ed., p. 1 (in typescript).

44. See E. Philip Morgan, "Botswana," *Africa Contemporary Record*, 1975/76, Colin Legum, ed. (London: Rex Collings, 1976), p. B526.

45. *Africa Contemporary Record, 1977/78*, Colin Legum, ed. (London: Rex Collings, 1978), p. B816.

46. *Africa Contemporary Record, 1978/79*, Colin Legum, ed. (London: Rex Collings, 1979), p. B801.

47. *Ibid.*, p. B802.

48. *Ibid.*

49. *Botswana Daily News*, July 11, 1979, p. 1.

50. E. Philip Morgan, "Section on 'Botswana,'" p. 2.

51. *Botswana Daily News*, September 26, 1979, p. 1.

52. *Botswana Daily News*, October 19, 1979, p. 2.

53. The limits of co-optation became apparent when Kwele, after being dropped from the cabinet in 1983, resigned from Parliament and the BDP to form yet another opposition party, the Botswana Progressive Union.

54. *Botswana Daily News*, April 9, 1980, p. 1.

55. *Botswana Daily News*, August 26, 1980, p. 1.

56. *Botswana Daily News*, June 3, 1980, p. 2.

57. *Botswana Daily News*, June 8, 1981, p. 1.

58. Both of the above quotes from "Botswana," *African Contemporary Record*, 1982/83 (NY: Holmes Mier, 1982), p. B603.

59. *Botswana Daily News*, December 8, 1982.

60. David E. Apter, *The Politics of Modernization* (Chicago: University of Chicago Press, 1965), p. 135.

8

Local Government Institutions: Patterns of Autonomy and Control

In 1974 William Tordoff noted, "The growth of strong district councils is being encouraged [by the Botswana government] and it is intended that they will increasingly become the focal point of rural administration, responsible for promoting the general well-being and economic development in the area."[1] What intrigued Tordoff was that eight years after the end of colonialism, local government in Botswana continued to show an independence almost unheard-of in Africa. Local politicians routinely criticized government policy, both within the districts and at the national level.

Most African countries began the post-colonial period with autonomous local governments. Within ten years of independence, however, local authorities throughout the continent were shorn of their autonomy, as nationalist leaders returned to a colonial style of administration. Botswana's district councils have suffered from most, if not all, of the ills that have befallen other local governments in Africa. This broad spectrum of problems includes inadequate staffing and finances, misuse of council funds, and attempts by opposition forces within councils to challenge the ruling Botswana Democratic party (BDP) government. Yet, twenty years after independence, Botswana's district councils continue to perform important political and administrative functions.

In this chapter I will be examining district councils as local-level political structures in Botswana, one of the few African states that continues to maintain elected, decentralized political institutions. The unique is often more interesting than the commonplace, and the question that leaps to mind is why have Botswana's district councils been able to maintain at least a modicum of autonomy.

Four political factors account for the resiliency of Botswana's district councils.

1. Before 1966 the chronological sequence of the local government's evolution in Botswana strengthened the autonomy of the district councils.
2. The development of a bureaucratic rivalry between two key ministries, Local Government and Lands (MLGL) and Finance and Development Planning (MFDP), preserved the autonomy of local government. Particularly during the crucial first decade after independence, the MLGL defended the autonomy of its district councils as part of a turf battle with the MFDP.
3. The district councils benefited from the openness of the functioning multiparty political system. Tolerance of council volatility was part of a general acceptance of political opposition as long as such opposition provided no serious threat to the dominant party's grip on the national political apparatus.
4. The district councils survived long enough to be perceived as useful mechanisms of service delivery and as local extensions of the national bureaucratic apparatus.

The Postindependence Crisis, 1966–1970

District councils were established by the Local Government Act of 1965. Their statutory responsibilities included the provision of primary education and basic health services and the development of rural roads and village water supplies. In 1968 the government created two local-level institutions structurally linked to the district councils: district land boards and village development committees. With the subsequent creation of district development committees in 1970, six institutions coexisted at the local level (the district and tribal administrations were colonial holdovers).

The creation of district councils did not meet with universal approval within Bechuanaland. Traditional authorities were particularly incensed at what they saw as a British government-BDP conspiracy to betray them. In spite of their support for the BDP in the 1965 elections, the chiefs had been relegated to a powerless upper house of Parliament (the House of Chiefs) and had seen almost all of their local powers and responsibilities transferred to district councils over which they had little control.

Two of the ablest chiefs, Bathoen II of the Ngwaketse and Linchwe II of the Bakgatla, strongly opposed the councils. Linchwe described the council system as alien to Botswana traditions and an example of "late colonialism."[2] Bathoen was so dissatisfied with the weakness of the traditional administration that he ultimately resigned (in 1969) as chief, after forty-two years in that position, and became active in politics as a leader of the opposition Botswana National Front (BNF). Other chiefs complained in

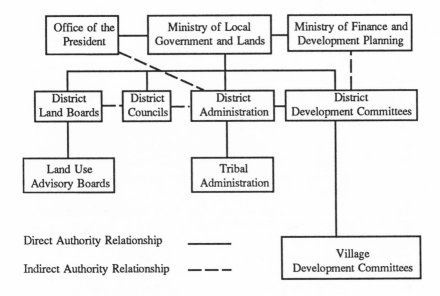

Figure 8.1 District Level Organizations in Botswana

varying degrees about their loss of authority, but they were either too weak politically or too poorly educated to oppose the BDP. They hoped they could preserve at least some residual authority over matters of traditional law and protocol.

Budgetary and Staffing Problems

The framers of the 1965 Local Government Act intended that councils be autonomous financially and derive their principal revenues from a local-government income tax. In terms of legislation, however, council bylaws were subject to ministerial approval. Central government grants were to be used for specific developmental purposes, and the MLGL was made responsible for council audits.

It became clear almost immediately that the councils were not viable institutions; they faced major personnel and budgetary problems. A 1967 memorandum by A. J. Dixon, drew attention to the major staffing problem faced by the councils. The 1965 Local Government Act had provided for the appointment of a council secretary, a treasurer, and other officials as deemed necessary. In practice, however, district councils absorbed all tribal administration staff who were "of a very low calibre."[3]

In his memorandum, Dixon called for changes in staffing procedures and, more specifically, for the use of defined patterns of recruitment for council administrative officers. Short of recommending a unified civil service with a common cadre of central and local government civil servants, Dixon suggested the creation of a unified, local-government service that would be part of a broader attack on inadequate working conditions and low wages for local employees. The Unified Local Government Service (ULGS) and the Unified Teaching Service were created in 1973 and 1975 respectively, effectively solidifying the central government's control over local personnel matters.

The personnel problem continued to plague local government and accounted for several manifestations of failure in the councils' daily operation. Council staff often did not act on council resolutions or implement projects. Routine office tasks were neglected and council secretaries found they had little control over their offices. Financial records were kept improperly and seldom audited. There were also cases of misuse of funds. In many cases, councilors were unable to deal with the workings of the council or handle the complexities of issues facing them. It soon became clear to planners that the demands for projects that were placed upon the councils "far exceeded the abilities . . . of councils to pay for them."[4] Far from being autonomous financial institutions, they increasingly became dependent upon central government grants.

The government envisioned that in the first years after independence there would be a mildly decentralized system of district administration in which councils would exercise "a considerable degree of self-determination in local affairs."[5] Dissatisfaction with the capacity of the councils set in quickly, however, and within five years of independence government had created new institutions, including central-government controlled, district development committees that would undercut the fledgling councils and raise questions about the future of local government. A number of central ministries, most particularly the MFDP, had become increasingly sceptical of the ability of councils to act. Central government, the planners concluded, would have to assume the major responsibility for local-level development projects.

By 1970 the Botswana government was turning again to a more centralized authority for the district officer to counteract the administrative and political vacuum that had appeared at the district level. Two qualifications should be made, however. Even after 1970, councils in Botswana continued to show a suprising amount of life as compared to their counterparts in other African states. Botswana planners were less dissatisfied with the council system as such than they were with council administrative weakness. Second, policy makers within the MLGL were determined to strengthen the councils, rather than abandon them. The relationship between the district administration and district councils became a hotly contested inter ministerial issue after 1970.

Faith in the Center, 1970–1975

Perceptions of the utility of the council system reached a low point in 1970 when the decision was made within the Office of the President to strengthen the role of the district administration, at the expense of the district councils, in the area of rural development. The future of the councils was in doubt between 1970 and 1971 as critics in the Office of the President and the MFDP began to discuss the total dismantling of the district council system. At that point, however, the MLGL concluded that attacks on the council system in reality were attacks on its turf, and administrators in that ministry became the primary defenders of the existing council system.

The opening salvo of criticism against the councils came in a report by two MFDP officials, C. Baur and J. Licke, both Peace Corps volunteers. Each had worked with district councils and had become thoroughly disenchanted with them. Their report reflected the view of MFDP planners. Criticizing both councilors and council staffs, the two officials "emphasized that a high proportion of the present staff were unsuited for council duties and are for practical purposes untrainable."[6] They concluded that as agents for development, the councils would fail.

Baur and Licke argued further that the councils were beyond repair. They were "inherently inefficient and expensive." The solution was not to strengthen the councils; this was impossible, given the country's labor shortages. District councils should be suspended and council functions should be transferred to an upgraded district administration advised by the chief and a small board of local notables. The district commissioner should be the primary coordinator of all development activities in the district, should coordinate all central government departments, and should act as a catalyst for social mobilization.

MFDP officials took the Baur and Licke report very seriously. Their conclusions became the dominant view within the MFDP, and increasingly within the Office of the President as well. Official policy, intended to upgrade the district administration at the expense of the councils, was reflected in a presidential circular in late 1970. In the circular the scant attention paid to councils clearly reflected Baur's and Licke's thinking about local administration.[7]

MLGL officials were slow to react to attacks on the council system. They were aware of the council's weaknesses and had established a commission of their own to examine ways of strengthening the local government system. Throughout most of 1970 and into 1971, the MFDP took the initiative on rural development. A number of MLGL officials believed that "what had happened in Kenya [loss of council authority to a strengthened district administration] would inevitably happen here."[8]

Resistance to MFDP incursions into district affairs was stimulated finally by the Tordoff Commission report on local government in late 1970. In the Tordoff report it was argued that local authorities should be developed into an effective instrument of administration and development within their areas, but the conclusion was that "the District Councils . . . are at present a long way from achieving this objective."[9] Council staffing and finance had to be strengthened considerably and, at least for the present, the "parochial outlooks" of many council members and staff required a temporary central structure that could achieve national unity and encourage the growth of strong local authorities The district administration should provide the structural framework. Thus, although the MLGL's ultimate goal was a strong council system, as the system was developed a "scaffold" would be required to keep the new institutions from collapsing. In effect, the district administrations would put themselves out of business with the growth of strong district councils acting as the focal point for the economic development of their area.

The Tordoff Commission report was followed by a presidential circular that set in motion a number of the report's reforms.[10] Once again the district administrations were the primary actors in the area of rural development, and the district development committee (DDC) was created as a district-level clearing house for rural development activities. The DDC's main functions were to supervise and coordinate the work of all central government departments, local authorities, and nongovernmental agencies. As a "team leader" the district commissioner would supervise the DDC's planning activities. The government created the positions of district officer (development) (DO[D]) and district officer (land) (DO[L]) to act as district planners. Throughout the 1970s and into the 1980s, both positions were filled by expatriate volunteers from the United States and Canada.

The Tordoff Commission's short-term recommendations were similar to those of Baur and Licke. The long-range goals of the former were quite different from those of Baur and Licke, however, and the differences reflected the growing bureaucratic rivalry between the MLGL and the MFDP. Debate focused on the relationship between the councils and the newly established DDCs. Throughout the period between 1971 and 1975, the two ministries were to see themselves as rivals in the initiation of policy and the allocation of resources. The MLGL increasingly found it necessary to defend the councils' autonomy from threats by other ministries, particulary by the MFDP.

District Councils vs. District Development Committees

Much of the sparring between the district councils and the district development committees occurred between their proxies at the center, the MLGL and the MFDP. Disputes developed over such things as patterns of recruitment for the district officers (development) who served as DDC secretaries, and patterns of communication between the DDCs and the center.

The recruitment issue concerned the loyalties of the DDCs and the expatriate DO(D)s. Although the DDCs were not tied to any particular ministry, legally the DO(D)s were responsible to the district commissioners and through them to the Ministry of Local Government and Lands. On the other hand, the DO(D)s dealt primarily with planning officers in the Ministry of Finance and Development Planning on proposals for new development projects. The three-way relationship among the DO(D)s, the MLGL, and the MFDP led to a number of instances of real or perceived insults on the part of one or more of the actors.

MFDP officials argued that the DDC and the DO(D) should be supervised by MFDP planning staff. By 1972 the MFDP had concluded that although the DO(D)s would be supervised nominally by the district commissioners, they should work independently on all economic and planning matters in their districts. MFDP officials were concerned that the new DO(D)s would become normal additions to district administration staff, rather than working solely on development projects. Therefore, primary communication and instructions on DDC matters would occur between the DO(D)s and MFDP planning officers. Ideally, DO(D)s would belong to the MFDP planning officer-economist cadre.

MLGL officials took a different position on communication with the DO(D)s. They objected particularly to two MFDP practices: (1) The MFDP was issuing verbal instructions or "guidance" to DDC members over the telephone and at DDC meetings; and (2) MFDP staff had been making "visits of inspection" to district administration offices and the district councils.[11] Both practices were "bound to confuse people and give the impression either of overall supervision of DDCs by Finance and Development Planning or of dual control at the ministerial level."[12] A Ministry of Local Government and Lands minute in 1972 indicated that:

> We have stressed that only this Ministry should issue instructions to DCs [and DO(D)'s]. If Finance and Development Planning wants to give instructions to DDCs, they should ask us to issue them. If they write directly to DCs . . . they will be administering the DDCs not "advising and assisting the responsible Ministry" [which I think is the way we review their role].[13]

Relations between the two ministries became tense during the period of 1971 to 1973.

After 1970 the relationship between district councils and the DDCs was the major administrative question facing the Ministry of Local Government and Lands. Councilors and council staff were unhappy about what they saw as a downgrading of councils in favor of a body dominated by the central government. At the first meeting of the Southern District Development Committee in July 1971 (the Southern District was an opposition stronghold), the District Council chair "argued strongly that the DDC was a duplication of existing agencies and would weaken the authority of the

Council."[14] He suggested that the District Council should become the focus of all development activities and that the central government's field officers, such as the district commissioner, should be made ex officio members of the council. Similar sentiments were expressed by members of other district councils.

However much the central government would disclaim in advance any DDC interference, district council staff and councilors continued to perceive a conflict, and council secretaries would claim that they were being kept in the dark on development matters. Several district council secretaries expressed concern that correspondence affecting their areas of responsibility was not being addressed to them, nor were copies being sent to district council offices. One council secretary claimed that he heard regularly about major policy issues from the district administration at DDC meetings.[15]

While the government's avowed aim was to make the council the focal point of development matters in the district, council members and staff felt that, under the DDC umbrella it was the central government ministries, rather than the district councils that were providing the largest component of the district's development plan.[16] Many district councilors complained that DDCs had become the senior district-level institution and that district councils had been reduced to the status of an advisory body with less influence than traditional authorities.

In 1972 and 1973 the MLGL took steps to address the staffing and budgetary problems of the councils. Ministry officials hoped that with the councils' position strengthened, there would be fewer misunderstandings by other ministries (especially the MFDP) over the role of local government. In order to strengthen council personnel, the MLGL announced that henceforth all council staff would come under the jurisdiction of the Unified Local Government Service. This would eliminate the "tribal" base of council staff selection, create a salary structure and conditions of service that would attract qualified staff into the local government and, through the merit system and an equitable pay scale, ensure that all councils, rich and poor, had equal levels of trained personnel.[17]

The planning capacity of the district council would be strengthened and the DO(D) would turn over many of the council's planning responsibilities to new council planning officers. DO(D)s would continue to be responsible for the coordination of district-level central government projects and to act as a channel of information between the central government and local authorities. The district commissioner would continue to support council structures and act as an impartial arbiter among the various interests within the district.

After 1973 the MLGL also tried to address the financing issue. Councils were hardly able to balance their budgets for statutory recurrent expenditures, two-thirds of which went for primary education. By 1972 every council except one had a deficit, and it was clear that local governments would need external funding for development projects. Central government grants were introduced in order to support council development activities. Between 1971/72 and 1975/76, the councils' dependence upon deficit grants grew (see Tables 8.1 and 8.2). That dependence changed the nature of local authorities. Increasingly the councils functioned as bureaucratic extensions of the central government. Now council development expenditures would have to be approved by both the DDC and the central government.

As the MLGL strengthened council administration, it defended any encroachment on council authority by other ministries. MLGL officials continually pointed to the fact that councils were statutory bodies with specific responsibilities, defined by law, whereas the DDCs were nonstatutory, planning and coordinating agencies that should not "normally initiate action except at the specific request of Councils."[18] Ministry officials warned against any tendency "to create an 'inner circle' of technocrats and planners from which [local] administrators who bear the real implementing responsibility are gradually excluded."[19]

The Search for Reform: 1973–1984

District land boards were created in 1970 as part of the larger process of transferring the functions of traditional authorities to "modern" local institutions. Previously, the chiefs had the ultimate authority over all land allocation. After 1970 land boards assumed all responsibility for land allocation. The new land boards consisted of the chief, the chief's representative, two members selected by the district council, and two members appointed by the Ministry of Local Government and Lands.

In 1975 the government announced changes in the country's land tenure. Under the new Tribal Grazing Land Policy the responsibilities of the land boards broadened to include the zoning and allocation of grazing land (both commercial and communal). Data for the allocation would be provided by new land-use policy advisory groups (a seventh local level structure) and appropriate departments of the central government.

The land boards were responsible for defining the criteria used to evaluate land applications, based upon conditions prevailing in the district. After the applications had passed a preliminary examination, the land board would send them on to the MLGL for final approval. Land boards also were mandated to receive advice from district conservation committees on good animal husbandry, to supervise the use of all commercial land, and to enforce the conditions of commercial land use in cooperation with the conservation committees.

The introduction of land boards established a new set of bureaucratic procedures over this vital aspect of rural development. If the land boards were to have new responsibilities regarding land classification, lease allocation, and the adjudication of land disputes, their administrative resources would have to be strengthened. Despite some sporadic efforts, however, both the

Table 8.1   Summary of Deficit Grants to District Councils, 1972–1976 (in pula)

Districts	1971/1972 Grants	Percent of Expenditures	1973/1974 Grants	Percent of Expenditures	1975/1976 Grants	Percent of Expenditures
Central	148,153	19	233,688	22	1,922,915	62
Kweneng	55,538	20	72,269	24	508,725	59
Southern	56,052	22	73,560	25	569,805	66
Northwest*	—	—	—	—	401,275	62
Kgatleng	38,596	23	48,196	27	372,350	69
Northeast	61,626	45	72,444	47	295,075	73
Southeast	37,073	31	44,223	37	152,750	56
Kgalagadi	30,518	34	44,734	44	269,240	75
Ghanzi	24,591	35	35,761	47	159,990	66
Total	452,147		624,875		4,652,125	

Sources: Botswana Government: 1971 Audit (Gaborone: Price, Waterhouse, 1974); *Town and District Councils: Estimates of Revenue and Expenditure, Recurrent Budget, 1973–76* (Gaborone: Government Printer, 1973–76).
*Includes Chobe and Ngamiland.

Table 8.2   Central District Income and Expenditures, 1972–1976 (in pula)

	1971/72	1973/74	1975/76
Income	748,005	806,801	1,098,865
Expenditures	770,563	1,040,489	3,098,865
Deficit Grants	148,153	233,688	1,922,915
Percentage deficit covers of actual expenditure	19%	22%	62%
Development grants	106,000	371,139	432,670[1]

Sources: Botswana Government Audit (Gaborone: Price, Waterhouse, 1974); *Town and District Councils: Estimates of Revenue and Expenditure, Recurrent Budget, 1973–76* (Gaborone: Government Printer, 1973–76); and Ministry of Local Government and Lands, Government File L.G. 3/c/2 XC.

*Covers only a 6-month period.

human and physical resource development of the land boards were slow and ad hoc.

Land board resources were insufficient to cope with the increasing demand for land-related services. Land-use planning and administration required additional technical and management capabilities and budgetary support. The land boards capacity was linked directly to district council capacity since they shared a common staff. Thus, problems of land board capacity became part of the basis for official intimations that local government might have to be restructured.

In August 1977 the minister of local government and lands appointed an interministerial committee to "review Land Board operations and submit . . . recommendations . . . as to how the[y] [could] better accomplish their work."[20] The terms of reference for the committee were: (1) the extent of defiance of land board decisions; (2) empowerment of customary courts to handle land cases; (3) a special court or tribunal to deal with land cases; (4) methods of enforcement and collection of fines; (5) additional funding requirements of the land boards and other aspects of their development; (6) the current relationship between district land boards and district councils; and (7) the feasibility of adjudicating disputes over traditional land. The objective of the committee's review was to point out in a white paper the alternative structures, functions, and procedures that would accommodate the imperatives of land policy.

The interministerial committee recommended that land board procedures, physical plant, and budgetary resources be strengthened. The committee strongly recommended that a crash training program for land board staff be developed and noted:

> The general condition of office procedures and record keeping leaves much to be desired, due to poor working conditions, lack of systems and equipment, and lack of direction from the Ministry of Local Government and Lands in resolving these problems.[21]

Despite the land boards' serious staffing problems, it was not until early 1981 that the MLGL made a serious attempt to establish a training program for land board administrators.

Although the interministerial committee's report was completed in November 1977, a white paper on land administration did not appear. The committee could not resolve the division of labor, responsibilities, and authority between land boards and district councils over land-use policy, planning, and allocation.

There were two interpretations as to why a white paper was not written. One view was that committee members could not agree on a formula for joining or separating land policy from land administration. The report does reveal consensus on one issue, however, namely, that "tribal land should be administered at the level of local government" whatever the division of authority between councils and land boards may be.[22] In short, the committee did *not* recommend a greater role in land policy for the district administration (i.e., the central government). The second interpretation was the official one; land board reform entailed far-reaching implications for other local government institutions that were beyond the committee's terms of reference. Therefore, a more broadly based assessment of local government was needed.

The interministerial committee's aborted review of land administration caused the government to abandon the committee and create a new body, the Presidential Commission on Local Government Structure (LGSC). The LGSC was created in September of 1978 with a broader, but much more ambiguous mandate. Its terms of reference were to review the structure of all institutions of local government including the district administration, district and town councils, the tribal administration and land boards, all existing land-use legislation, and current arrangements for promoting rural development. The LGSC was to recommend changes necessary "to establish a clear pattern of authority at district level, and effective channels of communication between districts and central government."[23] The government also asked the LGSC to consider the implications of its proposals for staffing, training, conditions of service, and financing.

The LGSC agreed with the major recommendations of the interministerial committee's report on the land boards and suggested that they be implemented at once, beginning with increased autonomy to allocate land to individuals. District councils should retain their political responsibility for land-use policy; two land board members should sit on council planning committees, however, in order to ensure coordination between land allocation policy and its administration.

After examining the district administration, the LGSC recommended that the residual aspects of the colonial system should be eliminated and that the role of the district commissioner should be changed. The district commissioner should be restyled as a district development director with purely development and planning responsibilities. The district development director would not perform magisterial or administrative duties formerly associated with the office of district commissioner, "which should now be abolished. The DC's non-development functions should be passed to other agencies."[24]

The Unified Local Government Service should be reorganized in order to place major control of council personnel in the hands of local authorities, rather than with the Ministry of Local Government and Lands. A new local government service commission should be established to handle personnel matters for "senior officers."[25] All officers serving within the district administration should be members of the ULGS instead of being considered central government civil servants.

The recommendations of the LGSC suggest that the commissioners believed the trend toward more central control over local authorities should be halted. Locally elected bodies and their administrative staff should have considerable autonomy, with the central government merely providing the overall coordination of development policy.

The LGSC report was completed by the end of 1979. It was not released until the beginning of 1981, however. In September 1981 the government published a brief, ten-page white paper that ignored all of the LGSC's major recommendations for strengthening local institutions. The cursory rejection of the LGSC recommendations was a major setback for those forces in Botswana committed to genuine (devolved) local government.

In 1982 the government announced the appointment of a presidential commission on land. The politics of presidential commissions had turned full circle. In large part, the land commission was to tackle the several unresolved questions left from the LGSC. The land commission began its work in mid-1983 and its report was published in 1984. The report was focused on the narrow question of land allocation, however, and the fundamental problems faced by local-level institutions were not addressed. The search for local government reform remained illusive, and local authorities today continue to face some of the severe staff and budgetary problems that have plagued local government in Botswana since 1966. Decentralization

> . . . in the sense of a substantial allocation of responsibility to the representatives of the people in the districts is hardly a reality. . . . The central government . . . has consistently failed to provide the necessary financial and human resources to enable them to improve their capacity.[26]

Why has the colonial system of district administration been left largely intact since independence? In the aggregate the recommendations of the Presidential Commission on Local Government Structure would have created the conditions that might have allowed local authorities a sense of efficacy, a prerequisite to the effective implementation of land and rural development policies. The stalled reforms reflect the ambivalence of central government policy makers toward effective local institutions. Central government policy makers often articulate a dissatisfaction with the competence of local institutions. Their dissatisfaction, in turn, justifies continued central control. Rejection of the restyled district development director would suggest that the position, shorn of the trappings and authority of the colonial district commissioner, would be too neutral for those people in the capital who want to maintain leverage over local affairs.

District Councils and the Political System

District council elections in Botswana have mirrored results at the national level. In the 1969 elections the Botswana Democratic party won 113 of the 165 elected district council seats. BDP figures were 149 out of 176 in 1974 and 147 out of 176 in 1979. Because of their geographical base, the opposition parties have been able to garner majorities in several district councils. When this occurs, however, the Ministry of Local Government and Land uses its statutory authority to appoint additional council members in order to create a government party majority.

✳ Local election results suggest, more than do the national results, that support for opposition parties is widespread. In the four elections held in Botswana since 1965, opposition parties have been able to elect councilors in all nine district councils and in three of the four town councils. (See Table 8.3 for local government election results from 1965 to 1974.)

Since Botswana's constitution has assured a government majority in all district and town councils, district councils are not a threat to the ruling BDP. As a result, criticism of district councils, when it occurs, often comes from the civil service, rather than from political sources. For example, political elites took little interest in the dialogue between the Ministry of Finance and the Ministry of Local Government regarding council authority over district planning activities.

Local-level politicians are different from national political leaders in a number of ways. They are less educated than the national leadership and are less likely to share a world view with the civil service than are the national leaders. Local politicians also are likely to enjoy traditional status within the district. Their concern with local economic issues sometimes brings them into conflict with the national political and economic elites represented by the BDP.

At the same time, although many local politicians have links with traditional leaders, their interests are not identical. After doing research in the Kweneng District, Richard Vengroff suggested that post-colonial local-level institutions were unable to replace traditional authorities as the channels of political communication.[27] In other words, councils and land boards do not serve as effective agents of political penetration to the village level. To many people in the rural areas,

> the District Councils must . . . seem almost as remote as the central Government in Gaborone. . . . In addition, councillors . . . are drawn from an elite group, wealthier and better educated than the populace as a whole.[28]

Ultimately, the nature of the political system must affect the status and future of local government in Botswana. The two possible explanations as to why active and vocal councils are tolerated by Botswana's political elites represent two different views of local government. They are related to how one interprets the nature of the political process in one of the few multiparty political systems extant on the African continent.

One interpretation suggests that decentralization of authority is likely to occur in a nation that most clearly fits a "pluralist" model of political participation. Botswana's political system is one of the few in the Third World in which, to use Herbert Werlin's term, political processes are "elastic." Political systems are defined as elastic when there are "easy and

Table 8.3   District and Town Council Election Results, 1966–1979

District and Town Councils	Seats Won in 1965 Elections					Seats Won in 1969 Elections						Seats Won in 1974 Elections					
	BDP	BPP	BIP	IND	Total Seats	BDP	BPP	BIP	BNF	IND	Total Seats	BDP	BP	BIP	BNF	IND	Total Seats
District Councils																	
Northwest	7	1	--	--	8	7	--	6	--	--	13	9	--	4	--	--	13
Ghanzi	10	--	--	--	10	9	--	1	--	--	10	10	--	--	--	--	10
Kgalagadi	11	--	--	--	11	10	--	--	--	1	11	11	--	--	--	--	11
Northeast	2	4	--	1	7	2	5	--	--	--	7	2	5	--	--	--	7
Central	31	1	--	--	32	31	1	--	--	--	32	32	--	--	--	--	32
Kgatleng	8	6	--	--	14	7	6	--	1	--	14	14	--	--	--	--	14
Kweneng[1]	17	--	--	--	17	16	--	--	1	--	17	21	--	--	--	--	21
Southeast	11	2	--	--	13	8	3	--	2	--	13	11	1	--	1	--	13
Southern	24	--	--	--	24	13	--	--	11	--	24	14	--	--	10	--	24
Town Councils																	
Gaborone	7	--	--	1	8	4	--	--	4	--	8	8	--	--	--	--	8
Francistown[1]	2	6	--	--	8	2	6	--	--	--	8	5	4	--	--	--	9
Lobatse	6	1	--	1	8	4	--	--	4	--	8	7	--	--	1	--	8
Selebi-Phikwe	--	--	--	--	--	--	--	--	--	--	--	6	--	--	--	--	6[2]

Sources: Richard Vengroff, *Botswana: Rural Development in the Shadow of Apartheid* (Rutherford, NJ: Fairleigh Dickinson University Press, 1977) and Government of Botswana, *Report of the Commissioner of Elections* (Gaborone: Government Printer, 1970 and 1974).

[1] Number of seats increased for 1974 elections.

[2] New council in 1974 elections.

spontaneous working relations . . . in which leaders usually get what they want by various forms of subtle persuasion."[29] Werlin argued that some degree of decentralization is related to "elasticity of control" within the political system. Elasticity of control exists when

> . . . the full authority of central governments is usually held in abeyance only to be released when absolutely necessary. . . . This means that interference of a disciplinary or compulsory sort on the part of the central government is potentially possible but actually rare, while varying forms and degrees of supervision and guidance are common.[30]

A second interpretation suggests that benefits accrue to political elites from the existence of a vocal and outspoken local government system. Thus, Botswana's political elites could be viewed as practicing a "style" of government that necessitates a plurality of political institutions. The political process in Botswana most closely approximates Murray Edelman's "symbolic politics." Politics are symbolic when "political forms . . . come to symbolize what large masses of men need to believe about the state in order to reassure themselves."[31] A distinction can be made between political activity as public drama and political activity directed by organized groups and individuals toward tangible economic benefits. In the former case, "the focusing of attention [is] on settings [and that is in] itself evidence either that there is a conscious effort to manipulate meanings and mass response or that the setting is inappropriate to the action."[32] In Botswana the local government system would be part of the country's symbolic political setting that contributes to what people need to believe about the state in order to reassure themselves; images largely devoid of reality.

Does elasticity of political control or symbolic political activity best describe local government in Botswana? Although councilors remain active and vocal participants in the political process and occasionally criticize the relatively light-handed central government, I would argue that this activity is largely symbolic. Councilors remain independent and critical, but in fact the council system is an administrative extension of the national government hierarchy. Thus, council challenges to central government policy have little, if any, impact upon political decisions at the national level and are largely an aspect of the "style" of politics practiced in Botswana.

The Nature of Local-Level Opposition

Opposition political leaders have found that district councils provide a forum for political criticism of the government and in rare cases local authorities can obstruct central government plans and projects. Challenges are often more effective at the local level because the opposition is so weak nationally. Generally, all of the opposition parties combined hold less than five of the thirty-five elected seats in the National Assembly.

Resolutions passed by district and town councils are a major source of political criticism of the national government and the ruling BDP. Councilors, and even council administrators, take public positions that are at variance with official government policy. Because of the looseness of the BDP as a political movement, there is significant criticism and opposition to government policy even from within the ranks of BDP councilors.

Events in Botswana's volatile Northeast District illustrate the nature of local-level politics. The opposition Botswana People's party has had an electoral majority in the district council since independence. From 1971 to 1979 the council secretary was a former leader of the Botswana National Front. The population of the Northeast District is largely non-Setswana-speaking; most of the district councilors speak Kalanga, a language linked with ethnic groups in neighboring Zimbabwe.

There is considerable political resentment of central government among councilors in the Northeast. A particular source of tension has been the role of the central government-dominated, district development committee that is seen by local politicians as infringing upon district council authority. In 1975, for example, the Northeast District Council voted to "censure" the DDC for "undermining the political authority of the district council."[33] According to the council secretary at the time, "We have a body which is neither elected nor appointed locally which is having a decisive influence over council decisions."[34]

By 1980 resolutions critical of the central government were routine in the Northeast District. At one point Northeast councilors debated whether or not council headquarters should be moved from Francistown to the countryside to "be closer to the people." In another session the council criticized the central government for its language policy.[35] The council continually scrutinizes the activity of the central government-appointed district commissioner for incursions into areas of self-defined local government responsibility.

Attitudes in the Northeast District are exaggerated by the strength of the opposition in that area but they are not unrepresentative of other councils in Botswana. A council chair in the southern part of the country noted that "District councils have come to see the central government as undemocratic. They [district councilors] feel that Councils should be the political authority in the district and they are very jealous of their position." Throughout Botswana there is evidence of tension between the central government and councils.

Councilors' challenges to central government are often visible at national development conferences, an annual event in Botswana. At a 1975 national development conference, a district representative complained that "the Central government has constantly tried to pull power away from District Councils and this plan [a new set of guidelines for District Development grants] is no exception."[36] Resentment over fiscal supervision is common. Also in 1975, one critic reflected a particular resentment over the role of the central government audit:

> The audit Department is out on a witch-hunt. Its solution to everything is to get us some better expatriates to help us in the Districts. Then, when they are too clever, you bring them back to the center.[37]

District councilors and their staffs perceive their relationship to the central government to be, at least partially, a hostile one. Their outspokenness and their challenges to government policy are indicative of their perception of independence from government authority. Challenges to the DDCs have been at the center of this hostility. Throughout the 1970s council administrators continued to challenge the legitimacy of the DDC. In 1975 council secretaries called upon the central government to dismantle all of its development operations at the district level and to turn over all responsibility for development to local authorities. Calling for the virtual abolition of the district administration, the council secretaries argued:

> It was *agreed* that in the interests of decentralization and efficiency the Conference of Council Secretaries felt that DDCs should be disbanded. District Officers of Development . . . would be assigned to Councils as Chief Planning Officers and their placement would become a [Council] responsibility.[38]

That these challenges from the periphery are routinely tolerated by central government politicians and administrators in an African state suggests a surprising degree of confidence in the stability of the political system. A degree of elasticity, as Werlin defines it, undoubtedly is a part of that tolerance. Nevertheless, much of the public and private criticism of councilors and council administrators focuses on their inability to act independently of central government authority. Councilors and local government bureaucrats are frustrated by a political and administrative system that allows them to say what they wish but prohibits independent action. One might suspect that the central government tolerates council dissent because local authorities are largely irrelevant to the decision-making process in the country.

The Limits of Council Autonomy

Local government in Botswana basically reflects the political system of which it is a part. Local politicians, whether representatives of the opposition or of the ruling BDP, are often frustrated in their relationship to the political system because they perceive themselves as being largely irrelevant to the decision-making process. Since Botswana is a one-party dominant state and that one party lacks an overriding ideology or mechanism to communicate within the country, the surface pluralism of an active, articulate local government masks an underlying administrative unity.

According to Edelman, political activity is rendered symbolic when public political activity is largely irrelevant to the understanding of the policy-making process. The distinction is between "politics as a spectator sport and political activity as utilized . . . to get . . . tangible benefits."[39] Comments by councilors and administrators indicate that their perception of political activity is of a decision-making process beyond their influence. Councils are tolerated in Botswana because they represent a decentralized style of government, an image that political elites would like to perpetuate in the minds of the citizenry or of foreign donors. Administratively, councilors are isolated from their own employees and from the lines of communication between the center and the periphery. Therefore, council political activism is largely irrelevant to the policy process.

Relations between council staffs and central government employees are not without tensions, yet local government employees are part of a de facto, unitary administrative system. Two characteristics of the district council-central government' relationship are indicative of that unity: (1) staffing procedures for local government; and (2) financial arrangements between the central government and district councils.

District council employees come under the jurisdiction of the Unified Local Government Service. The ULGS was created on 29 June 1973 as a division within the Ministry of Local Government and Lands. Prior to that time a pattern of recruitment and training did not exist. The majority of the local government staff had been incorporated into the councils from the old tribal administrations. Council employees are responsible to the Ministry of Local Government and Lands through the ULGS establishment secretary and the MLGL is responsible for the appointment, transfer, and discipline of each local government employee.

The unified staffing has limited the autonomy of the district councils, which is perceived clearly by district council politicians and their staffs. As one council chair stated, "We are very aware of the fact that District councillors are being excluded from the decision-making process. Councils are becoming Departments of Local Government with the ULGS simply giving instructions to council staffs to the exclusion of the elected councillors."[40]

Council administrative staff also perceive central government control over council employees. During an interview one council secretary charged that

> the central government isn't interested in decentralization of authority. The central government is trying to deconcentrate power rather than decentralize it. This is dangerous. We have become a part of the bureacracy. This gives all the power to the civil servants; none to the politicians.[41]

If appointment and staffing procedures are one method of maintaining central government control over the councils, local government's almost total dependence upon central government financing is a second method. Since 1970 councils have become dependent increasingly upon central government assistance for both recurrent expenditures and development projects. The Central District's pattern of financing illustrates this trend. Its dependence upon central government grants grew in the ten years between 1966 and 1976 to the point that by 1976, the central government was funding 62 percent of its recurrent costs. The Central District received close to one million pula in development grants for 1976 alone. By 1981 the district had become even more dependent on central government monies.

MLGL officials made it quite clear to the councils what the financial arrangements would entail. For example, in proposing district administration supervision over council finances, the MLGL argued that it had the primary responsibility for council budgets because "in effect . . . [the central] Government has approved, in general terms, roughly 70% of each Council's deficit of income in relationship to its expenditure."[42] The attitude of S. W. Fryer, then finance officer in the MLGL Common Service Division, was typical of the central government's position. In a 1975 speech to local government staff at the Institute of Development Management, Fryer took note of complaints about the central government's incursions into local government autonomy. These incursions, he argued, were related directly to the district council deficit of 4,652,125 pula in 1975/76. He pointed out that "no government will just hand over rand [pula] 4.6 million without knowing what it is all in aid of and whether it is justified. . . . Thus . . . the Botswana Government . . . has to exercise considerable control over District Council budgets . . . [and] a considerable degree of central government . . . control of local authorities."[43]

Beyond the personnel and financial links that limit local government autonomy in Botswana, the country's evolving socio-economic system provides another kind of administrative unity. Political elites are content to leave the major portion of the decision-making process in the hands of an administrative elite (still heavily expatriate in its composition) with which it shares a number of socio-economic characteristics. Politicians and administrators are members of a small, well-educated group that controls most of the cattle industry, as well as related sectors in the domestic economy (within the framework of a largely free enterprise system). This administrative state system is reflected in the relationships between central government bureaucrats and local government staff.

The ULGS, which staffs the councils, currently [1986] has 3,300 employees. That figure represents close to 20 percent of all public service employees and about 13 percent of all those employed in the formal sector. Individuals employed by local political authorities represent a significant segment of the socio-economic elite. According to Wyn Reilly,

> Most of those who wield power in the districts belong to the same politico-bureaucratic elite group sharing similar values, interests, and objectives. Whether they are civil servants of the district administration, or either elected or appointed members of the local authorities—the councils, the land boards, or the tribal administration—while a relevant question, is less important than their association with a powerful socio-economic elite.[44]

Without doubt, the formation of the ULGS was a critical variable in ensuring the survival of the councils as mechanisms of government service delivery. The rapid increase in ULGS jobs meant the buildup of vested economic interests that were separate from, yet linked to, the national public service.

The combination of administrative unity and financial dependence separates local government politicians from their own staff and the policy-making process. To a great extent, the councilors' independent attitudes reflect their resentment of central government dominance over district council administrative staff. The central government tolerates a good deal of political autonomy in the councils because it is aware of the separation between politicians and administrators at the local level and that council assertiveness is largely symbolic, contributing to an evolving myth of political participation in Botswana.

Wherever challenges to the political system are potentially threatening to the stability of the current political elite, controls will be introduced to defuse opposition to the regime. Nonetheless, political elites value the "open" political system in which outspoken district councils play a part. The district councils are tolerated because they reflect this openness and their presence contributes symbolically to the legitimacy of the existing political system and the socio-economic conditions that go with it. Should the district councils cease to contribute "symbolically" to the legitimacy of the existing BDP-dominated regime, undoubtedly they would become as expendable as they have been in most other African countries.

Conclusion

A fairly standard sequence of events occurred in the newly independent African states' flirtation with the district council form of local government. Usually councils were instituted hastily during the last stages of colonial rule. After independence came a period of great faith in the ability of councils to act as an autonomous link between the center and the periphery, and important functions would be transferred to the local authorities. This initial period of optimism, however, dissipated quickly and was replaced by a growing disappointment with the councils' ability to handle problems. A recentralization of authority in the capital city then became almost inevitable.

Generally, four reasons are given for the decline of local government autonomy in African states.

1. Local councils suffer from severe financial constraints and become dependent increasingly upon central government handouts for their continued existence.
2. Local council administrative personnel are inadequately trained and able personnel are often drawn to the more prestigious central government positions.
3. Local councils often are plagued with corruption and inefficiency to an even greater extent than occurs at the national level.
4. Local councils often are perceived by national political elites as reflective of ethnic or regional political activity and thus are a source of divisiveness, rather than of integration. National elites fear the councils becoming a platform for countervailing sources of power.

National governments often feel compelled to neutralize local councils by abolishing them, by integrating them into a national administrative apparatus, or by "packing" them with loyal supporters through either an appointive clause in the constitution or the legislation that established local government in the first place.

As a result of some combination of the above, within ten years of independence, district councils throughout Africa were shorn of much of their autonomy, and the central governments returned to a dependence on some variance of the colonial prefectoral system of government. What is surprising to see in an African state such as Botswana is the continuance of a relatively autonomous council system some twenty years after independence. Only a handful of such autonomous systems exist in Africa.

Botswana's district councils have enjoyed a number of advantages over their counterparts in other African states. The council system, as it evolved in Botswana, was a product of the post-colonial period and did not suffer from the identification with colonial resistance to independence that occurred elsewhere in Africa. The system was imposed upon the districts by Botswana's political elites in order to break the political power of the traditional authorities and to provide an alternative mechanism for political communication.

As was the case in many other countries in Africa, a certain amount of disenchantment with the councils set in at the national level as council weaknesses became apparent. Botswana's councils suffered from many of the political, administrative, and economic problems that were endemic to other councils in Africa. There was a concerted effort by some central government officials to dismantle the councils and turn many of their functions over to the district administration and other central government ministries.

The future of the district councils, however, became entangled in an interbureaucratic rivalry between the Ministry of Local Government and Lands, and the Ministry of Finance and Development Planning. Officials in the Ministry of Local Government saw challenges to district councils as a threat to their administrative authority. Thus, the Ministry of Local Government came to the defense of the councils as an organization whenever attempts were made to encroach on the council's autonomy.

Botswana's district councils continue to be active, often vocal organs of local government and a major source of criticism of central government activities. The political activism of the district councils in Botswana is in stark contrast to council behavior in most other African states. The political effectiveness of councils and councilors must be evaluated in the context of an interpretation of the Botswana political system. Without doubt Botswana politics show a degree of elasticity and openness. There is little overt coercion in either national or local politics, with argument and persuasion being the primary mechanisms of political conversion. It would be premature, however, to suggest that Botswana's council system represents a decentralization of decision making. Instead, the council system appears to be part of a "style" of symbolic politics that is practiced in Botswana.

Decentralization of political criticism should be contrasted with an administrative unity that encompasses both national and local government civil servants. Thus, administrative unity and the inclination of the political elite to abrogate a considerable amount of authority to the administrative system have effectively isolated local councils and councilors from most of the decision-making process. The result is that council political rhetoric functions primarily as "pictures of the mind," to use Edelman's words, while the policy-making process occurs elsewhere, often far away from the district, in the offices and corridors of central government ministries.[45]

Notes

1. William Tordoff, "Local Administration in Botswana, Part II," *Journal of Administration Overseas*, vol. 13, no. 1 (1974), p. 302.

2. Quoted in Naomi Mitchison, *Return to the Fairy Hill* (London: Heineman, 1966), p. 257.

3. Memorandum, A. J. Dixon, 23 October 1967, L.G. 1/6/14, vol. 1. Dixon was a lecturer in Public Administration, University of Botswana, Lesotho and Swaziland, Gaborone Campus.

4. C. Baur and J. Licke, "District Councils: Their Problems, the Present Situation, Ministry of Finance and Development Planning," F.D.P. 90/9/2, n.d. (mimeographed). Over 70% of council expenditure went to education in 1969.

5. Ministry of Local Government and Lands, *Annual Report, 1967* (Gaberones, 1968), p. 23.

6. Baur and Licke, "District Councils," F.D.P. 90/9/2.

7. Presidential Circular, 1970, "District Commissioners, District Councils and Ministerial Staff at District Level Coordinating Work," L.G. 19/3, vol. 3.

8. Oral interview with E. B. Egner, Assistant Secretary, Ministry of Local Government and Lands, 5 May 1975.

9. William Tordoff, M. A. B. Sarpong, and D. L. Pilane, "Report of the Local Government Study Group" (Gaborone: mimeographed, 1970), Botswana National Archives File S.M.193C1. The Ministry of Local Government and Lands had brought in, as a consultant on local government, William Tordoff, a political scientist who was then professor of government at Manchester University. Tordoff, along with M. A. Sarpong (a Ghanaian with many years of government service in Ghana) and D. L. Pilane (at that time director of personnel) spent a number of weeks interviewing council and district administration personnel prior to issuing their report.

10. Presidential Circular of 1970, "District Commissioners, District Councils and Ministerial Staff at Coordinating Work," L.G. 19/3, vol.1.

11. E. B. Egner, Assistant Secretary, Ministry of Local Government and Lands, Minute M.2, L.G. 19/3, vol.1.

12. This was expressed by one official in the Ministry of Local Government and Lands, L.G. 19/3.

13. E. B. Egner, Minute M.2 L.G. 19/3, vol. 1.

14. Minutes, Southern District Development Committee, 26 July 1971, L.G. 3/3/6, vol. 1.

15. On this point see C. P. Sekga, Council Secretary, Kweneng, 12 October 1973, L.G. 3/3, vol. 3.

16. "Memorandum on District Development Committees, 1971," L.G. 19/3, vol. 1.

17. L.G. 1/5/15, vol. 1. Much of this information is based on an oral interview with W. K. F. Boakgomo, Establishment Secretary, Unified Local Government Service, 22 March 1975.

18. P.S. Ministry of Local Government and Lands to P.S. Ministry of Mineral Resources and Water Affairs, 18 November 1973, L.G. 3/3, vol. 3.

19. P.S. Ministry of Local Government and Lands, Circular Letter to all Ministries and the District Administration, 2 November 1973, L.G. 3/3, vol. 3.

20. *Interministerial Committee Report on Land Board Operations*, February 1978 (Gaborone: Government Printer, 1978).

21. Tribal Grazing Land Programme, Review No. 1 of 1978, Rural Development Unit, Ministry of Finance and Development Planning, p. 28. See also Louis A. Picard with Klaus Endresen, *A Study of the Manpower and Training Needs of the Unified Local Government Service, 1982–1992*, 2 vols. (Gaborone: Government Printer, 1981).

22. *Interministerial Committee Report on Land Board Operations*, p. 42.

23. *Botswana Daily News*, September 4, 1978, p. 1.

24. *Report of the Presidential Commission on Local Government Structure*, vol. 1 (Gaborone: Government Printer, 1979), p. 5.

25. *Ibid.*, p. 8. "Junior" equals LGA 4-6 and equivalent. "Senior" equals LGA 1-3 and equivalent.

26. Wyn Reilly, "Decentralization in Botswana—Myth or Reality?" *Local Government in the Third World: The Experience of Tropical Africa*, Philip Mawhood, ed. (Chichester, U.K.: John Wiley and Sons, 1983), pp. 171-172.

27. Richard Vengroff, *Botswana: Rural Development in the Shadow of Apartheid* (Rutherford, N.J.: Fairleigh Dickinson University Press, 1977), pp. 69-72.

28. Christopher Colclough and Stephen McCarthy, *The Political Economy of Botswana: A Study of Growth and Distribution* (London: Oxford University Press, 1980), p.41.

29. Herbert H. Werlin, "Elasticity of Control: An Analysis of Decentralization," *Journal of Comparative Administration*, vol. 2, no. 2 (1970), p. 192.

30. *Ibid.*, p. 4.

31. Murray Edelman, *The Symbolic Uses of Politics* (Urbana: University of Illinois, 1970), p. 2.

32. *Ibid.*, p. 4.

33. Minutes of the Third General Meeting of 1975 of the Northeast District Development Committee, 22 July 1975, D.D.C./4 IV (60).

34. Oral interview with Daniel Kwele, Council Secretary, Northeast District, 2 July 1975, 47; *Botswana Daily News*, 14 August 1975.

35. Government requires that the language at council meetings be either English or Setswana rather than the indigenous language of the area, Kalanga, which most of the councillors speak.

36. This information is based on notes made while attending the Third National Conference of District Development Committees, 14–17 April 1975. All quotes from this conference are kept anonymous, as they were generated in the course of nonpublic discussion. This writer served as evaluator for the Eighth National Development Conference in December 1980. A similar diversity of views existed there.

37. Briefing session on local government and finances, National District Development Council, 17 April 1975. Notes taken by the author.

38. National Conference of District Council Secretaries, 11 May 1975, Conference Minutes, C.D.C./A/1/1.

39. Edelman, *Symbolic Uses of Politics*, p. 5.

40. Oral interview with B. R. Chibana, Council Chairman, Southern District, 6 June 1975.

41. Oral interview with Daniel Kwele, Council Secretary, Northeast District, 2 July 1975.

42. Discussion of Council Finances, Third National Conference of District Development Committees, 14-17 April 1975.

43. Speech by S. W. Fryer, Finance Officer, Ministry of Local Government and Lands at the Institute of Development Management, University of Botswana, Lesotho and Swaziland, 6 June 1975.

44. Reilly, "Decentralization in Botswana," p. 41.

45. Edelman, *Symbolic Uses of Politics*, p. 5.

9

The Politics of
Human Resource Constraints

There were about sixty women scrambling to get into the back of the
Bedford truck parked in front of the District Council offices in Kanye
in southern Botswana. It was a sultry January day and the occupants
of the Bedford had only a hot and dusty ride to look forward to.
Luggage was scattered around them, some tied to the top of the
vehicle, the rest squeezed in among the riders. By 11:30 in the
morning, the last bundle had been tied to the roof of the cab, the last
passenger squeezed into the back of the lorry, and the driver pulled
away. It was the beginning of the school term and these primary
school teachers were returning to their "bush" schools in the western
part of the country.

School teachers in Botswana are, in effect, extension workers. They live in
the towns and major villages in the east and return to their western postings
at the last moment prior to the beginning of the term. They are, both
figuratively and literally, at the frontier of human resource development in
Botswana.

Decisions made about human resource development can tell us much
about a country's priorities. Education and training are very expensive and in
a country such as Botswana, which has a human resource shortage, choices
have to be made about the allocation of a small labor force. By examining
these choices in Botswana, we will gain a broader understanding of the policy
preferences of its political elites.

In this chapter I will focus on two aspects of human resource
development and allocation in Botswana. First, I will examine the policy of
public sector localization since independence and, in particular, human
resource allocation to the rural areas. Second, I will examine the role of the
civil servant in the political and policy process and as a member of the
country's evolving socio-economic elite.

Localization Policy after Independence

Administrative and political elites in Botswana did not face the issue of localization of the civil service directly during the first decade after independence. Throughout this period the upper and middle levels of the civil service continued to be dominated by expatriates. Indeed, to date (1987) expatriate administrators play a greater role in Botswana than they do in any other country in southern Africa. In general, this preponderance of expatriates is a result of the paucity of educational development in Bechuanaland during the colonial period when, to a greater extent than occurred in other British colonies, Africans were employed exclusively at the unskilled or semiskilled levels in the civil service.

A second factor has influenced this phenomenon, however. The political leadership of the Botswana Democratic party, perhaps because of the dyarchy which had developed between 1962 and 1965, did not see expatriate administrators as a threat, but more as collaborators in the establishment of "the administrative state."[1]

At independence in 1966, the government was heavily dependent upon European administrators. (See Table 9.1.) Out of a total civil service establishment of 3,054, 17 percent were Europeans. During the first two years of independence, this pattern did not change significantly. Between May 1966 and April 1967, an additional 152 expatriates were appointed. (See Table 9.2.) By the beginning of 1968, there were over 700 expatriates in the public service.

Over the next two years, the government expanded the civil service considerably in order to provide for the increasing responsibilities of government in the post-colonial period. In 1969 a United Nations economic consultant pinpointed the problem. Noting a 50 percent increase in established posts between 1967 and 1969, he remarked that "too many posts [were] established; that promotions had been far too fast . . . [and] training had been inadequate."[2] He noted that out of a total civil service establishment of 4,265 in 1969, there were 656 vacancies and 684 posts filled by expatriates.

The Luke Commission Report

The government's response to the 1966 Luke Commission report on localization marked a major turning point in the evolution of Botswana's public sector human resource policy.[3] Luke had recommended a vigorous approach to localization, noting that some lowering of standards would be an acceptable price to pay for the creation of a national civil service. He recommended long-term changes in education to meet the country's future needs and stressed the short-term importance, both politically and symbolically, of placing Africans in key, highly visible administrative posts.

Table 9.1   Staffing Patterns in the Bechuanaland Civil Service,
1964

Position Category	African	European-Designated [1]	European Non-Designated [2]
Superscale	0	28	1
Administrative	9	27	5
Professional and			
Scientific	4	32	21
Technical	38	19	143
Executive	51	6	61
Clerical	260	0	25
Jr. Technical	119	0	17
Secretarial	15	3	37
Industrial Staff	253	0	2
Police	610	55	3
Prisons	70	1	1
Nursing	124	2	9
Teaching	9	4	29
Substaff	961	0	0
Total	2,523	177	354
Total European Establishment: 531			

Source: Gilfred Gunderson, "Nation-Building and the Administrative State: The Case of Botswana" (Ph.D. diss., University of California, Berkeley, 1970), p. 230.

[1]Colonial Overseas Services
[2]Locally employed Europeans

Luke stressed that for localization to be successful, the "transformation" process within the civil service would have to be given the highest priority.

Luke recommended a rapid expansion of the country's educational and training capacity, without which the civil service would remain caught in a cycle of human resource shortage for some time to come. Above all, Luke argued, localization was important because of the psychological motives of self-worth and national pride behind African demands.

No immediate action was taken on the Luke Commission recommendations because of the imminence of independence. In 1967 a white paper on the Luke Commission report was released and debated in the National Assembly. Although the Commission's recommendations were discussed, most of the report's substance was ignored, neither accepted nor rejected. In a 1973 report on localization, it was noted in passing that, "few of the transformation recommendations put forward by Luke were implemented."[4] Senior administrators, mostly former colonial officials, felt that the Luke Commission report recommended excessive localization.

Table 9.2 Appointments and Promotions in the Botswana Civil Service, May 1966 to April 1967

| | Appointments by Salary Scale | | | |
	Superscale	A Scale	B Scale	C Scale
Citizens or local candidates first appointed on permanent and pensionable terms[1]	0	9	23	342
Appointments on contract or non-pensionable terms, including appointments of noncitizens[2]	4	17	57	73

| | Promotions by Salary Scale | | | |
	Superscale	A Scale	B Scale	C Scale
Citizens or local officers promoted or upgraded[1]	9[3]	3	64	228
Noncitizen pensionable officers promoted or upgraded to[2]	23[4]	3	53[5]	0

Source: Gilfred Gunderson, "Nation-Building and the Administrative State: The Case of Botswana" (Ph.D. diss., University of California, Berkeley, 1970), p. 248.

[1]Africans.
[2]Europeans.
[3]Includes two acting appointments.
[4]Includes thirteen acting appointments.
[5]Includes seven acting appointments.

The Botswana government countered with the argument that for years to come there would not be sufficient personnel to staff all cadres of the civil service with Batswana. The government's inability to localize was linked to the failure to develop a sound educational system during the colonial period. In the 1967 white paper it was stressed that standards should not be lowered as a result of localization. President Khama stated forcefully in 1967, "We would never sacrifice efficiency on the altar of localization," and he merely noted the dissatisfaction within the civil service over localization and what he called "an aggressive mood towards the expatriates."[5]

Luke had recommended that certain senior, politically sensitive positions be localized immediately in order to ensure loyalty to the current government and to demonstrate symbolically the creation of a "national" service. The Office of the President ignored this recommendation, noting that sufficient safeguards already in the system would ensure that all senior positions would be localized as soon as personnel were available.

Independence, rather than bringing in a flood of local officers, brought a large number of colonial administrators from other former British territories. The continuing expatriate presence in the Botswana civil service (as well as in the private sector) practically resulted from the fact that for many of the Europeans, Botswana was the last stop in their movement south, following localization in west and east Africa.   In 1969 opposition candidates complained that Botswana had become "the 'graveyard of the East African Elephants,' white former East African civil servants who had come to Botswana after losing their jobs further North."[6]

Localization figures in January 1968 indicate that 24 percent of all senior and middle-level civil service posts were held by expatriates. Most of the expatriates were on two- or three-year contracts. In total expatriates filled 80 percent of the technical posts and 92 percent of the professional and scientific posts.

The influx of expatriates was linked directly to the Botswana government's strategy for economic change, which stressed mining and urban and infrastructure development, rather than rural agricultural production and social services. The former activities required large numbers of technical and professional officers. Since there were no local people who could be trained for these positions, the importation of expatriates was deemed the price to be paid for rapid economic growth.

The government's intention to continue to recruit and retain expatriates and, most likely, to increase their numbers in absolute terms as the level of development activities grew, was stated forcefully in the 1967 white paper on localization. For years to come, expatriates would be the primary source of technological and specialized staff in the professional field.

Decisions on localization in the late 1960s were taken by the BDP leadership in collaboration with a small cadre of former colonial officials. The two groups had worked together between 1962 and 1965, during the "minister-trainee" period prior to internal self-government. Several members of this small cadre of expatriates later became citizens of Botswana and continued to occupy key positions in the public service until well into the 1970s (when several retired to positions in the private sector).

The 1969 Election and its Aftermath

The BDP losses in the 1969 elections, limited though they were, disturbed senior officials in the government and within the BDP's ruling circles. In part, disaffection from the BDP, particularly in the urban areas, was linked to dissatisfaction among civil servants with the progress of localization.

Opposition parties had made localization an issue in the campaign and the leadership of the Botswana Civil Servants Association (BCSA) complained bitterly about the influx of civil servants from other countries.

Localization was particularly slow within the senior levels of the administrative service.

After the shock of the 1969 elections, the BDP leadership saw the need to broaden its political alliance, particularly in the urban areas. This entailed a more aggressive, though controlled, localization policy that would result in an Africanized bureaucracy with vested interests in a BDP-controlled state in which "the political structures of rule . . . are mere window dressing to expedite continued . . . rule by [the] administrative hierarchy."[7]

Dissatisfaction with the pace of localization continued after the elections with the BCSA acting as the focal point for criticism of the government's human resource policy. In 1970 a Ford Foundation localization adviser complained that there was no effective plan for localization.[8] For the next fifteen years, government officials would continue to take a rather ad hoc view of supporting the localization of all posts as rapidly as possible, "consistent with the maintenance of reasonably acceptable standards of efficiency."[9] By 1986 localization remained far from complete; the absolute number of expatriates in Botswana had increased, rather than decreased.

Yet after 1970 there is some evidence that the BDP took a more serious view of the problem. In that year the government scrapped the executive public service commission system, which had not been under the civil service establishment secretary and created a unified personnel management unit, the Directorate of Personnel, located within the Office of the President.

After the elections President Khama had indicated a willingness to listen to the BCSA's complaints. In a speech to the BCSA in 1970, the president acknowledged the criticism that had been leveled at the government by civil servants and the "bone of contention" that had developed over localization, and he assured his listeners that the government was making a "radical reappraisal . . . [and adopted a] more vigorous and systematic approach to the problems of localization and training."[10]

In 1971 the government announced the appointment of a presidential commission on localization with a mandate to examine progress and to design an overall strategy for the development of "a completely national Public Service."[11] Furthermore, the commission's terms of reference established it as a permanent body responsible for monitoring localization policy. The commission's findings were published in 1973. Recognizing "a substantial localization problem," the commission recommended an expansion of the country's educational and training institutions and "the optimum utilization of the students emerging at the secondary and post-secondary level."[12]

A summary of the civil service establishment as of 1972/73 is presented in Table 9.3. Although the number of expatriates had declined slightly since 1968, the number of vacancies had increased dramatically to almost four hundred. The majority of these vacancies were filled by expatriates in 1974 and 1975 because of the rapid expansion of the economy.

Table 9.3   Localization in the Botswana Public Service,
1972–1973.   (Excludes Industrial Class Position.)

Ministry	Establishment	Citizens	Expatriates	Vacant
Office of the President	226	158	32	36
Ministry of Finance and Development Planning	191	94	36	61
Ministry of Health, Labour and Home Affairs	190	114	30	46
Ministry of Agriculture	208	78	81	49
Ministry of Education	279	77	156	46
Ministry of Commerce, Industry and Water Affairs	164	32	76	56
Ministry of Local Government and Lands	92	48	18	26
Ministry of Works and Communications	210	53	88	69
Independent Posts:				
Administration of Justice	14	4	8	2
Attorney-General	21	8	9	4
National Assembly	3	2	—	1
	1,598	668	534	396

Source: Government of Botswana, Report of the Presidential Commission on Localization and Training in the Botswana Civil Service and the Government Statement on the Report of the Commission (Gaborone: Government Printer, 1973), p. 23.

Government policy focused on absorbing new university graduates and secondary-school leavers into the administrative cadres. The government's premise was that although localization in technical and professional areas was not possible, because of institutional incapacity and the unavailability of qualified Cambridge certificate-holders, administrative positions could be filled by new university graduates or, more commonly, through promotion from the clerical and executive levels. The latter pattern was followed throughout the 1970s, leaving large numbers of civil servants with only a secondary education in senior positions by 1980.

Localization policy remained cautious (perhaps overly) in the 1970s. The Ministry of Finance and Development Planning's severe underestimate of the level of economic growth that was occurring had a major impact on projections of staffing needs. Until 1975 estimates of staffing needs were based on the assumption that the major localization effort would be to localize existing posts. There was no assumption of growth of the establishment nor calculations of resignations or retirements.[13]

Botswana's first attempt at a human resource survey confirmed much of the BCSA's criticism. According to the manpower survey, the government had not been able to localize even the government sector, although that sector was better off than the private or parastatal sectors. Most important, the conductors of the survey found rapid government expansion combined with an increasing localization effort, in comparison to the other sectors of the economy that were being starved of human resources.

Civil service growth rates for the period 1972 to 1978 averaged 13 percent per year, with growth rates after 1978 almost as high (over 7 percent). Growth rates were particularly high in the technical, professional, and senior administrative posts. The actual human resource shortage can be measured by the vacancy rates in 1978-1979. These ran at approximately 20 percent for the senior-level administrative, technical, and professional (A-level) posts. This fact, plus an expatriate presence accounting for 9 percent of the establishment, suggests a staffing shortage of almost one-third of the 1978 civil service establishment.

After 1975 the civil service began to receive a small, but steadily growing number of university graduates each year. By the mid-1980s university graduates were a significant core of the civil service. Some of these early graduates, with close to ten years of service, moved into more senior administrative positions and, although more rarely, into professional positions. The rapid expansion of the civil service in the decade between 1975 and 1985 absorbed this pool of graduates, however, leaving severe staff shortages at the middle and senior level as reflected in the extremely high vacancy rates throughout most of the decade. (See Table 9.4.)

During the 1970s and into the 1980s, the number of expatriates in the civil service continued to expand. As late as 1984 the civil service employed 950 expatriates. Although as a percentage of the establishment, expatriates declined from 42 percent to 13 percent, the absolute number of expatriates almost twenty years after independence is staggering.

Between 1974 and 1977 the number of expatriates grew from 950 to 1,770 in the parastatal sector and from 2,250 to 2,460 in the private sector. By 1978, a highwater point, there were more expatriates in the country than ever before. Although the number of expatriates in the public and parastatal sectors began to decline slowly after 1978, the absolute growth of expatriates, including those in the private sector, is likely to continue throughout the 1980s. Estimates in 1984 suggest that even in the public sector the gap will not be closed before the late 1980s or early 1990s. Ultimately, localization is linked to the capacity of the country to manage development activities, and political elites in Botswana have continued to place localization second to economic expansion and development.

Nonetheless, the presence of expatriates with very conspicuous patterns of consumption has widespread ramifications for Botswana society, particularly, but not exclusively, in the capital city. The expatriate presence

Table 9.4   Expansion of the Botswana Civil Service, 1964 to
1984

	Established Posts	Strength (Position Filled)	Citizens	Expatriates	Vacancies	Citizens as % Est.	Citizens as % Strength
1964a	2,575	2,175	1,492	683	400	57.9	68.5
1972b	6,150	5,153	4,484	669	997	72.9	87.0
1977	8,683	6,495	5,695	800	2,188	65.5	87.7
1979	10,083	7,105	6,294	811	2,978	62.4	88.5
1984	15,347	14,297	13,347	950	1,050	86.9	98.3

Sources: Rough calculations based on Government of Botswana, National
Manpower Development Report (Gaborone: Government Printer, 1983);
Government of Botswana, National Development Plans, 1979–1985 (Gaborone:
Government Printer, 1979); Government of Botswana, Establishment Register,
1984–85 (Gaborone: Government Printer, 1984); Government of Botswana,
Interim Report on NDP V (Gaborone: Government Printer, 1983). 1984 figures
prone to some error but suggest direction.

aSenior and middle-level positions only: 762/607/105/502/155 for first five
columns.

bAll levels except industrial class, drivers, and specialized cadres; e.g.,
nurses and teachers.

puts a strain on housing and primary- and secondary-level educational
facilities. In addition, the presence of expatriates has an impact on the "style
of government," the patterns of governmental decision making and the
planning and policy choices that are made at the macrolevel. "The short
period many . . . [expatriates] served limited their contribution and made the
job of training and localization more difficult. There was less time to find
the best mode of operation and understand the wider setting into which their
activities fitted."[14]

A second presidential commission on localization was appointed in 1976
and published its findings in 1977. This commission's recommendations
were "disappointing" because "no attempt was made to undertake any
manpower planning."[15] The commission noted the failure of the standing
committee on localization to monitor localization efforts and provide annual
reports on the status of human resource development. The committee was
not being used as an instrument of government to enforce government's
personnel policy.

The 1977 commission report was largely a statistical exercise,
containing a numerical examination of existing establishments, ministry by
ministry. It assumed that localization could be completed by filling existing
vacancies and replacing expatriates. No attempt was made to measure

progress by making comparisons with the 1972 report although it was noted that localization was 64.5 percent completed at the senior administrative and professional level with 1,356 out of 2,102 senior positions localized by 1977.[16] Little reference was made in the commission report, except by inference, to growth in the civil service or to the number of expatriates still filling established posts.

Localization Policy After 1977

Botswana's personnel policy has continued to take a minimalist approach since the 1977 commission on localization, with continued dependence upon expatriates for the critical technical-professional and planning positions. This excessive caution with regard to localization is often criticized but, "outside commentators have generally failed to grasp the depth of feeling Botswana policy makers had about the lack of progress during the colonial period."[17] The late 1970s and early 1980s were years of rapid economic growth, particularly in the mining sector, and government commitment to localization remained secondary to its strategy of economic development.

Civil servants, as represented by the Botswana Civil Servants Association, remained dissatisfied with the pace of localization. A series of salary commission reports did placate them somewhat. Salaries increased significantly between 1975 and 1985 and the decade saw significant personal advancement in the civil service hierarchy, advancement based primarily on seniority, however, rather than on skill acquisition or institutionalized training. Prior to 1980, there was not even a search for information on private sector and parastatal localization.

As the administrative cadre became localized after 1980, the pattern of job responsibility shifted in a number of ministries from the expatriate generalist administrators to the technical and professional officers (still largely expatriate). The administrative cadre's area of responsibility contracted as a result of localization.

The growth rate in the civil service continued at about 7 percent through the mid-1980s, and the absolute number of expatriates increased. The level of vacancies remained very high as well, peaking at about 30 percent at the end of the 1970s. The continued growth in the number of expatriates means that "the localization problem is now more difficult to solve—in both proportional and absolute terms—than it was at independence."[18]

A number of proposals have been made for an accelerated program of training that would provide additional personnel for both central and local government as well as the parastatal and private sectors. The Luke Commission report had recommended a vigorous approach to training as "a continuous and a continuing process; it must be viewed as an instrument for creating efficiency and as planned investment by Government and staff alike which would yield rich dividends."[19]

The Botswana Civil Servants Association also demanded an accelerated training program as a means of localizing the civil service. The BCSA particularly recommended the development of an institutional capacity for training within Botswana in order to develop human resource skills at home.

The government's view of the importance of training was more cautious. In the white paper written in response to the Luke Commission Report, it was suggested that training efforts would be limited for some time. In-service training would be very difficult because of the already heavy workloads of senior administrators. For the same reason it would not be possible to have a full-time training officer within government departments and ministries.

Institutional training, whether in Botswana or overseas, would be very difficult to develop because of the shortage of officers who had the necessary prerequisites, that is, Cambridge "O" levels. Furthermore, the government would find it difficult to release senior staff for long overseas courses without disrupting the work of the ministries.

The government's attitude toward training is reflected in its rationale for rejecting the idea of a separate recruitment and training branch within the Office of the President. This would not be feasible because of "the small size of the Public Service and the absence of funds."[20] The small size of the country, the government concluded, made it difficult to develop a capacity for planning, staffing, and staff development.

The government's response to the Luke Commission report was symptomatic of an attitude within policy circles that training was not an integral part of personnel management and that scarce resources were not available for such a peripheral activity. It would be more than a decade before government policy would begin to address the issue of training seriously.

After 1975 some minimal reference was given to the idea of in-service training for civil servants being promoted on the basis of long years of service. The government supported the creation of an Institute of Development Management that was linked to this mid-level upgrading as a stopgap strategy for promoting administrative officers without a university education.

One of the recommendations of the 1977 presidential commission on localization was that the government should appeal to donors for support for the institutional development of local training institutions (such as the Botswana Training Centre and the Institute of Development Management). The 1972 commission had recommended that the government should accept overseas scholarships only as a last resort, because reliance on scholarships would retard the institutional development of educational and training facilities within Botswana.

Through the mid-1980s, however, there was little donor support for improving institutional training capacity within Botswana. The government continued to depend upon overseas donors for most of the higher education and post-graduate specialized training, all of which took place overseas. Virtually no money was allocated for in-country training in the U.S. Agency for International Development's Southern African Manpower Development Assistance Program (SAMDAP) that ran from 1979 to 1983.[21] Its successor, the Botswana Workforce and Skills Training (BWAST) program, provided only about $350,000 for in-country training during the five years (1983-1988) of the project.[22]

The layering process of developing an in-country training capacity has exacerbated the problem. Building up courses step by step, from the certificate level to the diploma level to the professional has meant that training in local institutions, such as the Botswana Polytechnic, the Botswana Institute of Administration and Commerce, and the Institute of Development Management, has been very low level.

As of 1985 the government had not addressed the problem of the training backlog within the civil service. In 1977, 47 percent of the civil service had only a junior secondary school certificate or a general certificate of education and a third of those who entered the administrative cadre (which requires a first degree) did not have a university education. This backlog of training that built up throughout the decade of the 1970s meant that promotions to very senior positions without the prerequisite training or skills development would occur until the end of the 1980s. There continue to be significant numbers of secondary-school leavers and even junior certificate-holders in very senior positions.

Human Resource Allocation at the Local Level

District councils and district land boards collectively employed 3,400 persons in 1985. This compares with approximately 21,000 positions in the central government. Land board staff are considered to be members of the district council staff. In 1978 the education of two-thirds of the council staff was still below the minimum required (junior certificate) for entry into the civil service, and "the average age of those without secondary certificates . . . [was] 32."[23]

Throughout the 1970s administrative capacity was a major problem for both the district administration and the district councils. In a 1973 report on rural development in Botswana, it was stated, "Administrative capacity is, and is likely for some time to remain, a serious constraint on development." Administrative capacity, not finance, must be "regarded as the key scarce resource to be used sparingly."[24] This assessment was as true for the Ministry of Local Government and Lands (and the entire government) as it was for the district-level administration.

In one sense the district-level administration faced an even greater problem than did the rest of the government.

> It seems to be an unwritten law that any officers who prove to be good in the field must immediately be posted to Gaborone . . . . Perhaps it is high time thought was given seriously to the creation of equivalent posts in the district so that officers in the district . . . who perform well can be made to aspire to a higher position in the district and so become an asset to rural development.[25]

It was unlikely, of course, that such a development would occur until the central government offices had been localized. As an official in the Ministry of Local Government and Lands noted in 1969, "When the government lion has eaten its fill of manpower then Councils will get better people."[26] The 1973 localization report barely mentions district administration or local government, noting only the departure of remaining expatriate district commissioners. Nor was there any discussion of the presence of volunteer expatriates who were increasing at that time.

Localization Studies

Neither the 1973 nor the 1977 localization report addressed the problems of local government administrators. They had inherited staff from the tribal councils that preceded them. In 1973 a number of steps were taken to strengthen the district councils both financially and in terms of human resources. Henceforth all council staff would come under the jurisdiction of the new Unified Local Government Service.[27] Three major goals were announced: (1) elimination of the "tribal" base of council staff; (2) creation of a salary structure and conditions of service that would attract quality staff; and (3) equality of access to staffs regardless of the councils' resource base.

In its approach to local government, the Ministry of Local Government and Lands recognized that local staffing could not upgrade councils quickly enough, and it was decided that each council should have an expatriate planning officer who would act as a counterpart to the district officer (development) in the district administration and that technical jobs would be filled by volunteer officers.[28] By 1975, the volunteer component at the district level had grown considerably.

In August 1975 a total of 103 volunteers were serving in the Ministry of Local Government and Lands or in district councils. In the councils, out of a total A-level establishment of 650 (including some 150 administrative-class officers), there were 80 volunteers. Of the total of 92 administrative-class officers in the MLGL, including the district administration, 23 were volunteer officers. (See Table 9.5.)

In 1978 a number of studies were commissioned to examine various aspects of district council operations. Collectively, these reports provide a picture of the structural limitations that plagued the district councils and land boards after 1975.

Table 9.5   Volunteer Officers in District Councils, the District Administration, and the Ministry of Local Government and Lands in August 1975.[1]

Position	Origin of Volunteers								Total
	U.S. Peace Corps Service	Canadian Volunteer Service	British Volunteer Service	Swedish Volunteer Service	Danish Volunteer Service	Norwegian Volunteer Service	German Volunteer Service	Other	
Council Administrators and Planning Officers	17	3	1	1	--	--	1	--	23
Council Works Supervisors, Construction Supervisors, and Technical	23	--	1	--	7	6	4	--	41
Social Workers and Nurses	7	1	--	--	4	1	2	1	16
Ministry Headquarters	5	--	2	--	--	--	--	1	8
District Officers (Development)	7	7	1	--	--	--	--	--	15
Total	59	11	5	1	11	7	7	2	103

Sources: Government of Botswana, Establishment Register: Republic of Botswana, 1975–76 (Gaborone: Government Printer, 1975); "Establishment Register: Ministry of Local Government and Lands," 1975 (mimeographed); "Establishment Register: Unified Local Government Service," 1975 (mimeographed); and L. Gronkvist, "Report on Staff Inspection of Local Government Offices," Gaborone, 1975 (mimeographed).
[1]Includes volunteers requested by April 1975.

In April 1978 a Swedish architecture firm conducted a study of the rural building development program in Botswana as it related to the district councils. Building construction and maintenance is one of the responsibilities of district councils and their staffs, one that councils would feel increasingly in coming years.

In the past the councils had encountered severe difficulties in supervising building construction and maintenance. A major problem was proper supervision of contractors, especially small contractors. The councils were unable to handle the complex responsibilities that are inherent in the management of infrastructure. At the heart of the problem, according to the architects' report, was the fact that Batswana working in council building and maintenance projects were faced with "legal and technical jargon written in English."[29] Many administrators simply could not communicate with the contractors in their own language.

The Ministry of Local Government and Lands also commissioned an investigation of the "human resource requirements; formal and informal training; and staff development of personnel from both Central and Local Government who are directly concerned with the process of district and urban development plan formulation, implementation and administration."[30] In the resultant report the author concluded that the formation of the Unified Local Government Service had not improved the local government personnel system and that the councils' staffing needs continued to be serious impediments to their efficient operation. The author also concluded that the differences in quality of staff between central and local government were severe and likely to persist. As long as they did, council operations would be adversely affected.

A third study was commissioned by the Swedish government to help the MLGL formulate an assistance program to upgrade local government. In addition to recognizing the staffing shortages facing the councils, structural problems in the councils and in the ULGS were also cited in the study's report. Although salaries for ULGS staff gradually had been paired with counterpart ranks and grades in the national civil service, discrepancies between the two services still remained. The range of incentives and organizational mobility were more restricted in the ULGS than in the civil service.[31]

The central government continued to give a lower priority to upgrading local government personnel than to upgrading central government personnel. Training opportunities, both at home and abroad, went disproportionately to central government civil servants. The first in-country training course for senior ULGS council staff lasting longer than a few days occurred in 1975, ten years after the district councils were established.

Until the early 1980s, training for the ULGS staff remained perfunctory and ad hoc. In the late 1970s the Institute of Development Management

(IDM) offered general administration and management courses to council secretaries and secretaries of the major committees, including the land boards. The councils' junior staff, however, remained in great need of training and have had to compete with others in the civil service for places in courses at the Botswana Institute of Administration and Commerce (BIAC). Often minimum educational qualifications have kept ULGS staff out of BIAC and IDM courses that were relevant to their needs. In general, the central government received the best educated graduates from the country's educational institutions and the local government received the rest. In the 1982 *Report of the Presidential Commission on Economic Opportunities* , it was stated:

> In the years since Independence Central Government has taken the lion's share of available qualified Batswana. Localization of key decision-making posts within Government itself was naturally a high priority, and much of the country's development effort consisted of expanding imperfect government services.[32]

All land board staff have been localized. Enormous technical requirements, however, are involved in the land reform and district development plans, as well as in the related services, such as water and rural roads, that councils must manage. Yet, highly qualified technicians were kept in the central government ministries. Despite the need for technical capacity, the 1977 localization commission pointed out that the ULGS could not compete with the central government for scarce technical personnel:

> There can be no point in the Local Government Service attempting to compete with Central Government for the service of such rare citizens as qualified engineers, architects, water technologists and the like. When the needs of Central Government have been met there will be a spill-over into the Local Government Service, and meantime the Councils will have to depend upon the services of expatriates, local retired officers, volunteers and the few who have a personal preference for local government service.[33]

In light of the various reports that surfaced in the late 1970s, the government of Botswana requested that Sweden provide financial support

> . . . to district councils through the financing of specific projects related to their implementation and maintenance capacity, including projects for strengthening other agencies such as the district administrations and district development committees which already provide considerable direct and indirect assistance to councils.[34]

Because of the congruence among the various reports, "the top priority in terms of improving council capacity is the training of existing council staff.[35] The first component of Swedish assistance included support for both formal training of local government staff in courses outside of Botswana, as well as in-service training. In-service training would take place in the established institutions in Botswana and through a mobile government training team for nonformal, on-the-job training in the districts.

As a result of the Swedish support, a staff development and training officer was appointed to the Ministry of Local Government and Lands, and a mobile training unit was set up to run short courses for council staff in "circuit" fashion throughout each of Botswana's ten districts. In late 1980 the Institute of Development Management established a certificate program in local administration to help upgrade council staff. Yet, what was needed was local government training that was relevant and practical and carried out within the country; this was not really understood at the senior levels of government.[36]

Human Resource Limitations

The capacity of the ULGS staff failed to improve. In a 1981 investigation into the staffing and training needs of the ULGS, it was found that the majority of those holding positions at all levels of service (75 percent of the middle senior posts and 67 percent of the junior posts) were unqualified to perform their jobs.[37] The report concluded that "the manpower situation within the Unified Local Government Service is so serious that it verges on being catastrophic in the next few years."[38]

The dramatic shortage of qualified personnel meant "that the best staff were overworked and too frequently transferred from post to post as fresh crises arose; morale was generally low; poor standards became the norm; and local government was regarded as a second-class service which in turn discouraged the best graduates from making a career in ULGS."[39] Numerous reports from 1970 onward had emphasized the importance of ULGS staff training, but by the middle of 1981 very little training had occurred and few detailed training plans had been chosen, even though donor financing was available.

The 1981 ULGS human resource and training needs study may have been a turning point in the central government's attitude toward local government training. In the 1982 *Report of the Presidential Commission on Economic Opportunities*, it was argued:

> Since 1978 eight Reports have compiled roughly 1,000 pages on this issue. The latest [by Picard] described the situation as verging on the catastrophic . . . . The allocation to ULGS of more newly qualified manpower is important, but it is much more important to give local government more of the more able experienced Batswana public officers . . . even if it involves the "delocalization" of some central government posts.[40]

In 1982 the ULGS training report was accepted by the cabinet, and the Ministry of Local Government and Lands prepared an implementation document. Among the actions taken since 1982 are:

1. The appointment of council personnel and training officers and the appointment of ULGS training officers.
2. The appointment of a staff development and training officer.
3. The development of a technical training program for ULGS at the Botswana Polytechnic.
4. The development of in-service training modules by the Swedish Institute of Public Administration.
5. The allocation of more graduates to the ULGS.

Only after 1982 (sixteen years after independence) was there some evidence that the government of Botswana had become committed to a more systematic approach to human resource development for the district councils and land boards. The basis of the ULGS training program would be donor support, however. Although Botswana officials have argued since the mid-1960s for the need to develop an in-country training capacity, most donors (with the exception of Sweden) have resisted this strategy, opting for the more traditional allocation of overseas scholarships at the first and advanced degree level. Without this training institution development, it will be very difficult to provide a relevant, locally based training that is linked directly to work experience in the rural area.

The Bureaucracy as a Political Interest Group

Although legally Botswana has a multiparty political system, in fact the country is dominated by the Botswana Democratic party founded by Seretse Khama and currently led by President Masire. The BDP lacks any overriding ideology or mechanism to communicate politically within the country, and the surface pluralism masks an underlying administrative unity.

Botswana's political elites are content to leave decision making mainly to administrators with whom they share a number of socio-economic characteristics. There is little sign in Botswana

> of political initiative, of that spirit of political competition that leads ambitious Ministers to build up whatever ministry they happen to be in—a spirit that can make for vigorous and inventive government as well as strong decision. Consequently much of the initiative continued to rest with . . . local upper and middle level civil servants.[41]

Members of the BDP and senior level administrators are representative of an educated, cattle-owning elite that controls most of the cattle industry and related sectors in the domestic economy. Outside Parliament and the electoral process, party elites do not represent a separate set of actors in the policy-making process.

The Administrative State

A small political establishment and the state civil service constitute Botswana's "administrative state." The small political elite consists of members of the cabinet (less than fifteen including the president and vice-president), other members of the National Assembly (twenty three members including six special members), fifteen members of the House of Chiefs (representing the country's traditional leadership) and the 176 members of the district councils. The entire political stratum probably includes less than three hundred individuals.

By 1984 cabinet ministers were receiving an average of slightly over P 25,000 per year in salary and expenses. The president's salary was approximately P 30,000 per year. In salary and expenses noncabinet members of Parliament earned approximately P 18,000 per year, and members of the House of Chiefs (who served on a part-time basis) earned approximately P 5,000 per year. Local government councilors, who except for council chairs, are only marginally members of the political establishment, drew slightly more than P 3,000 per year in responsibility allowance and travel and subsistence allowances. (It should be remembered that government salaries probably account for only a small portion of the income of councilors, traditional administrators, and members of parliaments.)

In 1984 six grades in the Botswana civil service had starting salaries of more than P 2,000 per year. The highest civil service grades are superscale positions with a basic salary (to which allowances and perks are added) of between P 15,828 and P 23,952. Thus, the top salary for a civil servant was over $20,000 per year plus allowances. In a country such as Botswana, however, where the per capita income is around $900 per year, all employees above the industrial class must be considered a marginal part of an economic elite. The lowest clerical salaries, for example, start at P 1,608 per year.[42]

Of crucial importance is that salaries in the public sector remain very high in relation to the rest of the economy. After a dip below colonial expatriate levels in the 1970s, salaries for superscale (senior) employees have increased to nearly their 1967 (European) levels in actual purchasing power. In addition to the higher salaries are fringe benefits such as car loans, cheap housing, and opportunities for training, travel abroad, and making money outside the civil service in cattle ownership, retail trade investment, or early retirement into the private sector.

At the bottom end, industrial-class wages have more than doubled in actual terms since independence. Middle-level wages also have risen significantly, especially since the wage increases of the mid-1970s. The only pressure to keep salaries down has come in the form of guidelines for the private sector, which regularly had been going against the policy. The guidelines are largely symbolic, however, not given teeth by legislative sanctions, and in any case not applicable to the public sector that has received salary increases timed strategically to coincide with general elections.

The Botswana *Establishment Register* lists 21,663 positions for 1984-85. This register includes all civil servants above the industrial level, except political appointees. It excludes local government employees (including teachers) and traditional administrators, a total of around nine thousand persons in the ten districts. By contrast to the public sector only twelve thousand persons in the private sector were making over P 2,000 per year. Thus, no other group in the country approaches the economic power of the thirty thousand central and local government civil servants. As noncitizens the small European farming community and the European- and Asian-dominated trading community at best can have only an indirect influence over the policy process. No other groups in the country approach the upper-middle class status of the bureaucracy.

Modern sector development in Botswana is creating a salaried elite in terms of consumption patterns. The income disparity between the rural and urban sectors was sixfold in 1970 and increasing. Public sector employment in the government is responsible generally for the high level of wages in the urban areas.

Nowhere is the growing inequity between urban and rural income levels illustrated more clearly than in the area of cattle ownership.[43] With the exception of the mining industry (which employs only a few thousand Botswana citizens), cattle is the major income earner in the country. After independence accumulated capital was invested in substantial rural properties, primarily cattle.[44] In 1970, 29 percent of the rural population owned no cattle whatsoever, while another 21% had less than ten head each. Thus, half the population possessed only 5 percent of the national herd. On the other side of the coin, 6 percent of the cattle-owners possessed 40 percent of the national herd of one and a half million cattle.[45] Investment in large cattle herds is an ongoing process in Botswana.

> Management of the cattle post was less a family affair than an economic enterprise. Local people were hired to take charge of the cattle while regular supervision was possible during weekend visits. The government salary provided [civil servants] with the means to sustain their active and extensive rural interests while at the same time allowing them to take advantage of the superior facilities in town.[46]

Not only is the national level in Botswana dominated by an economic elite of large cattleowners, but local political structures also are controlled by a fairly tightly knit elite based on economic characteristics. In a survey of three southern districts, it was found that 29 percent of all families had twenty-five cattle or more but only 12 percent had over fifty head. Among the district councilors surveyed, however, 62 percent had more than twenty-five cattle, while 42 percent had more than fifty head.[47] Clearly, the economic advantages for political and administrative elites extend beyond the capital city to regional centers throughout the country.

Preliminary evidence on the effects of the land tenure changes announced in 1975 indicated that this differential at the local level was widening as a result of the commercialization of land. The new land policy failed to attack the root of the problem, namely that of inequality of access. Commercialization had a strong, built-in bias in favor of those who are better off, while neglecting or impeding others. In a government-sponsored evaluation of the new grazing land policy published in late 1977, it was argued that its introduction was having an enormous effect upon Botswana's economic stratification. "There is no doubt that the T.G.L.P. [Tribal Grazing Land Policy] will affect the already highly skewed income distribution more negatively."[48] According to 1976 government income distribution survey, "the implications for the Government's new Tribal Grazing Land Policy are that it is going to be difficult to spread the benefits of the new policy."[49] As a result, "the effect of the policy will be to make the distribution among cattle owning households even more unequal than it is already, since it is the bigger farmers who already have assets . . . which are . . . preconditions for the policy to function."[50]

The "Tribal Grazing Land Policy" (TGLP), designed to create a new category of commercial land, ultimately had to be "sold" to, and implemented by, district-level politicians and administrators. Thus, it was essential that the policy makers build a coalition of support for the new policy. Surveying administrative attitudes toward the TGLP would indicate the extent to which such a coalition had been created successfully, as well as illustrate the nature of the interaction between public policy and the interests of bureaucratic groups. From the results of a study in 1975 of the attitudes of civil servants toward the proposed new land policy, it was clear that bureaucrats understood their socio-economic status and the extent to which they would or would not benefit from policy positions.[51]

In order to test administrative attitudes toward the TGLP, interviews were conducted with over 150 district-level officials between April and August of 1975. The period was suitable for a survey of administrative attitudes because it began with the late March presidential announcement, at the annual conference of the Botswana Democratic party, that presentation of a new grazing land policy was imminent and ended with the August national conference on that new policy. The interview sample included district administrators, technical field staff, local government officials, and a selection of officials from key ministries in the central government. During the course of the two-hour open-ended interview, primarily concerned with matters unrelated to land reform, respondents were asked what they knew about, and how they felt about, the TGLP then being discussed in the National Assembly. An overall view of administrative attitudes toward the proposed changes in land tenure is presented in Table 9.6. A plurality of all

Table 9.6   Administrative Attitudes Toward New Land Policy, by Administrative Type

Type of Response	District Administrators (% respondents)	All Other Administrators (% respondents)
Good idea—land should be personal property	40	32
Will hurt small cattle owners—need to equalize access to land	25	22
Changes will be a political bombshell	20	3
There will be resistance from traditional authority	5	7
There has been no consultation	5	3
Don't understand it—don't know about it	5	32
Total %	100	99
n =	20	126

Source: Louis A. Picard, "Bureaucrats, Cattle and Public Policy: Land Tenure Changes in Botswana," *Comparative Political Studies*, Vol. 13, No. 3 (October 1980); from interview data used in this article.

those interviewed believed that the TGLP was a good idea and that some land should be available for private ownership.

Not all field administrators were happy about the new policy, however. Approximately a quarter believed the new policy was wrong because it would hurt the small farmer. A planning officer in the Ministry of Local Government and Lands put it this way:

> The utility of the policy on land depends on who gets it. Ultimately it depends upon the sincerity of the political leaders and many are very cynical. There will be an extent to which the rich get richer and the successful cattlemen will completely control the grazing.[52]

A district officer stated the case more strongly: "The effects of the new policy will be disastrous. The monopolists will end up with all the land."[53]

If we break down the interview respondents by areas of responsibility and approximate salary level (Table 9.7), we see that within the Botswana field administration all groups held generally positive attitudes toward the new land policy, except one: the expatriate. In Botswana expatriates can be found at all levels of the civil service, including local government. Close to a third of those interviewed were expatriates on either volunteer or "expert" contracts. The volunteer expatriate district officers (development) were suspicious of the new policy, two-thirds of them concluding that the policy would be counterproductive. According to one British volunteer, "It seems to be a way of putting off the problem and making it worse. It's a way of making the rich richer. There's not much on the social justice side here."[54]

The expatriates' concern for the small farmer was expressed by one respondent who explained, "It isn't that we don't need a new land policy here in the district but I just don't think that this is the policy we need. I'm very apprehensive because we are a small district with very little extra land. There will be a lot of in-fighting over land use and some people are bound to lose out in the end."[55]

The responsibility and salary-level breakdown (Table 9.7) also illustrated another pattern. The enthusiasm for the policy expressed by central government officials diminished from level to level, i.e., from the latter group to the elite district administration and technical professional staff to local government employees. It might be argued that this relative lack of enthusiasm is related to the fact that local government employees and junior technical staff are less highly educated and less likely to know much about the policy. Close to a third of the technical field staff and local government employees interviewed stated that they did not know much about the policy nor did they really understand it.

Another factor must be kept in mind, however. Bureaucrats at the lower end of the salary scale (Table 9.7) might be expected to perceive that they are less likely than their better-paid colleagues to benefit from the new land policy. By factoring out local government employees according to administrative type and salary (Table 9.8), we see considerable difference between higher- and lower-level officials in attitudes about the new land policy. Whereas half of the senior officials (council secretaries and their assistants) thought that the land policy was a good one, their middle- and lower-level employees were much less enthusiastic. Junior administrators and clerical employees expressed this largely in terms of a lack of understanding of the policy, but close to 40 percent of the technical professional employees actually were suspicious of the policy and perceived it as being potentially harmful for the small farmer. Undoubtedly, most junior-level employees on a 1975 salary of P 500-1,600 per year perceived a wide gap between themselves and the senior political and administrative leaders, who had salaries of P 7,000-10,000 per year. Many individuals in local government thought of the latter as being "big men" and the major beneficiaries of the new land policy. As one district council treasurer said, "I don't know how the policy will work and perhaps it will improve things, but people will be afraid of it; there is this problem with the rich people you know."[56]

Of all the administrators interviewed, the older ones, administrators in their forties and fifties, were much more likely to feel that the new grazing land policy was a good one. Of course, older administrators also were more likely to have a considerable investment in the cattle industry and enough business experience to see the benefits that they would reap as a result of the changes in land policy. Younger administrators, in their twenties and

Table 9.7 Administrative Attitudes Toward New Land Policy, by Salary and Administrative Responsibility Levels

| Type of Response | Central Government Administration R4860-7284 (%) | District Administration R2412-4860 (%) | Administrative Responsibility and Related Salary Range | | | |
			Technical/ Specialist in the Field R1894-4572 (%)	Local Government Employees R1560-3840 (%)	Traditional/ Political R750-1000 (%)	District Officers Development (Expatriate) app. R500[1] (%)
Good idea—land should be personal property	61	40	36	33	54	--
Will hurt small cattle owners—need to equalize access to land	17	25	4	27	6	67
Changes will be political bombshell	4	20	12	--	--	17
There will be resistance from traditional authority	--	5	12	6	13	8
There has been no consultation	--	5	4	6	--	--
Don't understand it/ don't know about it	18	5	32	28	27	8
Total %	100	100	100	100	100	100
n =	23	20	25	51	15	12

Source: Louis A. Picard, "Bureaucrats, Cattle and Public Policy: Land Tenure Changes in Botswana," *Comparaive Political Studies,* Vol. 13, No. 3 (October 1980); from interview data used in this article.

[1]Volunteer wage scale on expatriate contract most of which is paid externally.

Table 9.8   Local Administrative Attitudes Toward New Land Policy, by Administrative Type and Related Salary Range

| Type of Response | Administrative Type and Related Salary Range | | | |
	Senior Administrators R2880–3840 (%)	Technical/ Professional R1920–2640 (%)	Junior Administrators/ Clerical R576–1680 (%)	Expatriate App. 500[1] (%)
Good idea—land should be personal property	50	38	34	25
Will hurt small cattle owners—need to equalize access to land	16	31	8	50
Changes will be a political bombshell	—	—	—	—
There will be resistance from traditional authority	8	—	—	16
There has been no consultation	8	—	8	8
Don't understand it/ don't know about it	16	30	50	—
Total %	98	99	100	99
n =	12	13	12	12

Source: Louis A. Picard, "Bureaucrats, Cattle and Public Policy: Land Tenure Changes in Botswana," *Comparative Political Studies*, Vol. 13, No. 3 (October 1980); from interview data used in this article.

[1]Volunteer wage scale

thirties, with less experience and a smaller investment in cattle, were less likely to be supportive of the policy.

Information on the respondents' educational level supported this contention. In general, the older administrators did not have a post-secondary education, whereas younger administrators usually did. In fact, the higher the level of education, the more likely was the administrator to be suspicious of the grazing land policy. (See Table 9.9.)

During the interviews it became clear that ideology influenced attitudes toward the new grazing land policy and that ideology had a high correlation with age and education. Presumably the respondents' ideological positions will change over time as younger and better educated administrators move up the salary scale and have more money available to invest in cattle. The patterns of administrative attitudes that emerged from the 1975 study

Table 9.9   A Sample of Administrative Attitudes Toward New
Land Policy, by Level of Education

Type of Response	Respondents' Educational Level	
	Primary and Secondary (%)	Post-Secondary (%)
New Land Policy is a good idea	44	24
New Land Policy will hurt the small farmer	9	32

Source: Louis A. Picard, "Bureaucrats, Cattle and Public Policy: Land Tenure
Changes in Botswana," *Comparative Political Studies*, Vol. 13, No. 3 (October
1980); from interview data used in this article.

suggested that the basis of a coalition in support of the new land policy did
exist among district-level administrators.

Conclusion

Political elites have taken a very cautious approach to localization in
Botswana. Human resource policy since 1966 "essentially protected rather
than challenged the status quo—both in education and in the market for
skilled labour."[57]

Human resource policy in the 1960s was made by a coalition of BDP
political elites and largely expatriate senior officials. After the 1969
elections political elites saw the need to expand access carefully to the
administrative sectors of government in a manner that broadened the socio-
economic elite as a byproduct of localization. At the same time the country
continued to rely on expatriate personnel primarily in the technical,
professional, and economic planning fields.

In the development of human resources in the rural areas, a degree of
asymmetry exists between the government's stated policy to promote rural
development and the rural bureaucracy's organizational capacity to implement
that policy. Local government institutions in Botswana do not have the
capacity to fulfill their responsibilities. At least until 1982, central
government policy makers were not willing to increase the capacity of the
local-level institutions. Bureaucrats in Botswana clearly perceive their own
socio-economic interests. This fact suggests that the cautious view of
political elites toward localization policy and their unwillingness to allocate
human resources to the rural areas must be linked to the political and socio-
economic context of rural development policy.

Local-central relationships have changed very little since the colonial
period. The nature of the state in Botswana contains much that was inherited

from colonial Bechuanaland. The needs of the state require that central authority be maintained over local-level political activity, and the confluence of administrative and political interests would be toward a rural development policy that is conducive to existing political interests, a policy that stresses economic growth and the expansion of existing areas of economic activity, generally limited to the mining and cattle industries. That this policy has had short-term payoffs for Botswana is without question. An examination of Botswana's rural development strategy (or its neglect) since 1966 suggests that there may be problems in the 1980s and 1990s as rapid population growth and high levels of urbanization threaten to eliminate these short-term gains.[58]

Notes

1. Gilfred Gunderson, "Nation-Building and the Administrative State: The Case of Botswana" (Ph.D. diss., University of California, Berkeley, 1971).

2. C. S. Magat, "A Review of the Machinery of Government of Botswana," Report on a Mission to Botswana of the Regional Advisor in OPM, United Nations Economic Commission for Africa," (October 29, 1969), p. 10.

3. T. C. Luke, *Report on Localization and Training* (Gaborone: Bechuanaland Government Printer, 1966).

4. J. C. N. Mentz, "Localization and Training in the Botswana Public Service, 1966-1976" (Ph.D. diss., University of South Africa, 1981), p. 74.

5. "His Excellency, Sir Seretse Khama, K.B.E., Speaks to the Botswana Civil Service," supplement to the *Botswana Daily News*, BNB 702 (1) ARC 37.14.2., both quotes, p. 2.

6. W. J. A. McCartney, "Botswana Goes to the Polls: Khama Government Retains Power in the Face of Lively Opposition and Paves Road to Economic Take-Off," *Africa Report*, vol. 14, no. 8 (December 1969), pp. 28-32.

7. Gunderson, "Nation Building," p. 245.

8. Cabinet Memorandum, No. 38/71 on file DP 27/24/(4) RCN, dd 22 July 1971 as cited by Mentz, "Localization and Training," p. 194.

9. Government of Botswana, "Statement on Government Policy in Relation to the Elimination of Racial Discrimination and the Furtherance of Localization in Statutory Corporations and Private Enterprise," presented to the National Assembly, August 1967 (Gaborone: Government Printer, 1967), p. 1.

10. Sir Seretse Khama, "Statement to the Executives of the Botswana Civil Servants Association in Gaborone on Monday, February 23, 1970, on Recruitment, Localization and Training in the Civil Service" (Gaborone: Government Printer, 1970), p. 2.

11. Government of Botswana, *Report of the Presidential Commission on Localization and Training in the Botswana Civil Service and the Government*

Statement on the Report of the Commission (Gaborone: Government Printer, 1973), p. 2.

12. *Ibid.*, pp. 23 and 16.

13. Christopher Colclough, "Some Lessons from Botswana's Experience With Manpower Planning," *Botswana Notes and Records*, vol. 8 (1976), p. 136.

14. Michael Stevens, "Aid Management in Botswana: From One to Many Donors," *Papers on the Economy of Botswana* , Charles Harvey, ed. (London: Heinemann, 1981), pp. 173-174 for first quote, and p. 174 for second quote.

15. J.C.N. Mentz, "Localization and Training," p. 175.

16. Government of Botswana, *Report of the Presidential Commission on Localization and Training in the Botswana Public Service, 1977* (Gaborone: Government Printer, 1977), p. 115.

17. Stephens, "Aid Management," pp. 173-174.

18. Colclough, "Some Lessons," p. 131.

19. Luke, *Report on Localization*, p. 204.

20. "Statement on the Luke Report," p. 19.

21. *Southern African Manpower Development Project* (Washington, D.C.: U.S. Agency for International Development, 1978).

22. *Botswana Workforce and Skills Training* (BWAST) (Washington, D.C.: U.S. Agency for International Development, 1982).

23. E. B. Egner, *District Development in Botswana*, a report to the Swedish International Development Agency, September 1978, p. 7.

24. Robert Chambers and David Feldman, *Report on Rural Development* (Gaborone: Government Printer, 1973), p. 2.

25. N. E. K. Sebele, District Commissioner, Serowe, Annual Report, 1973, 28 December 1973, in L.G. 1/6/10 vol. 3.

26. In G. O. Orewa, "Report on the Public Administration Mission at Botswana," United Nations Economic Commission for Africa, M69-2208, November 1969, p. 7.

27. Unified Local Government Service Act No. 13 of 1983. LG 1/5/15, vol. 1.

28. L.G. 1/6/10, vol. 3.

29. *Study of Rural Building Development in Botswana: Interim Report*, Consultancy report to the Ministry of Local Government and Lands by White Architects (Stockholm, Sweden, April 2, 1978), pp. 29, 34.

30. "Terms of Reference of the Local Government and District Administration Training Study," in David A. Watson, *Report on a Study of Local Government and District Administration Training* (Gaborone: Government Printer, June 1978), pp. 87-88.

31. Egner, *District Development*, pp. 10-22 and *passim*.

32. Government of Botswana, *Report of the Presidential Commission on Economic Opportunities* (Gaborone: Government Printer, May 1982), p. 37.

33. *Presidential Commission on Localization*, 1977, p. 57.

34. Republic of Botswana, "Project Memorandum for Submission to SIDA District Development Support Sector, 1978/79–1982/3" (Gaborone: mimeographed, 1978).

35. *Ibid.*, p. 10.

36. Wyn Reilly, "District Development Planning in Botswana," *Manchester Papers on Development*, no. 3 (December 1981), p. 54.

37. Louis A. Picard with Klaus Endresen, *A Study of the Manpower and Training Needs of the Unified Local Government Service, 1982-1992* , 2 vols. (Gaborone: Government Printer, 1981). See also Louis A. Picard, *District Administration Training in Botswana* (Gaborone: Ministry of Local Government and Lands, 1984).

38. Picard with Endresen, p. iv.

39. Wyn Reilly, "Decentralization in Botswana—Myth or Reality?" *Local Government in the Third World: The Experience of Tropical Africa*, Philip Mawhood, ed. (Chichester, U.K.: John Wiley and Sons, 1983), p. 158.

40. *Report of the Presidential Commission on Economic Opportunities*, p. 82.

41. David Jones, *Aid and Development in Southern Africa: British Aid to Botswana, Lesotho and Swaziland* (London: Croom Helm, 1977), p. 114.

42. Salary and Establishment Figures from Government of Botswana, Establishment Register, 1984–85 (Gaborone: Government Printer, 1984), pp. 154-155.

43. See Louis A. Picard, "Bureaucrats, Cattle and Public Policy: Land Tenure Changes in Botswana," *Comparative Political Studies*, vol. 13, no. 3 (October, 1980), pp. 313-317 for an elaboration of this.

44. Morag Bell, "Modern Sector Employment and Urban Social Change: A Case Study from Gaborone, Botswana," *Canadian Journal of African Studies* , vol. 15, no. 2 (1981), p. 275.

45. H. A. Fosbrooke, "Land and Population," *Botswana Notes and Records*, vol. 3 (1971), pp. 174-176.

46. Bell, "Modern Sector Employment," p. 275.

47. John Holm, "Rural Development in Botswana: Three Basic Political Trends," *Rural Africana*, no. 18 (Fall 1972), p. 87.

48. Bernhard Weimer, "The Tribal Grazing Land Policy—Some Critical Aspects in a Policy for Rural Development," *The Case of Botswana National Policy on Tribal Grazing Land* (Gaborone: National Institute for Research in Development and African Studies, 1977), p. 46.

49. Government of Botswana, The Rural Income Distribution Survey in Botswana (Gaborone: Government Central Statistics Office, 1976), p. 112.

50. Weimer, "The Tribal Grazing Land Policy," p. 46.

51. Picard, "Bureaucrats, Cattle and Public Policy."

52. Oral interview, June 1975.

53. Oral interview, June 1975.

54. Oral interview, July 1975.

55. Oral interview, May 1975.

56. Oral interview, June 1975.

57. Colclough, "Some Lessons," p. 149.

58. See John D. Holm, "Liberal Democracy and Rural Development in Botswana," *African Studies Review*, vol. 25, no. 1 (March 1982), pp. 83-102.

10

Changing
Rural Development Priorities
in a Growth Economy

> Government is committed to actively interventionist economic and
> social policies. . . . The Government will . . . address itself to
> employment creation . . . [and] programmes that directly support
> production. . . . Especially relevant to rural employment creation are
> the increasing concern of District Councils (and other district level
> officials) with promoting productive activities and the rural
> employment efforts of the Ministry of Commerce and Industry.[1]

As do most five-year development plans, Botswana's Fifth National
Development Plan (1979–1985) implied a rational approach to development
management. The above quote portrays an interventionist administration
mobilizing an underdeveloped rural population to increased levels of
agricultural and industrial productivity. An examination of Botswana's rural
development policy provides a dose of realism and a sense of the limits of
development administration in an African state.

In this chapter I will be addressing a number of interrelated themes
related to the evolution of rural development policy in Botswana between
1966 and 1985. A continuity exists between the origins and growth of
Botswana's labor export economy during the colonial period and the
commodity export patterns that have developed after independence. Although
workers continue to move to South Africa in significant numbers, an
increasing portion is being siphoned off to provide support for domestic
economic activities.

The Botswana example suggests that in order to understand rural
development needs, we must examine the policy's intended goal and the
impact of rural economic activity on different populations. The purpose of
rural development policy has shifted over the years since 1966, and policy
goals often have been ad hoc and incremental. Two general concerns have
predominated, however: (1) the development of a growth economy based on

mining and large-scale cattle exportation; and (2) political acquiescence, particularly in the rural areas.

The policy-making process is not value free. It represents the priorities of an interlocking set of elites within Botswana, and it is tempered by the nature of the international economic system. This interlocking and overlapping set of elites encompasses both political leaders, the senior levels of the bureaucracy, a small commercial and agricultural elite, and traditional leaders. The resource allocation process increasingly threatens to breach this alliance apart, and since independence the role of the bureaucracy has been the penultimate influence over the policy process.

National Economic Policy

Botswana has had an enviable record of economic growth in the twenty years since independence. In 1966 the country was classified as one of the least developed countries in the world. By 1981, Botswana had been included as one of the World Bank's group of success stories. The gross domestic product increased from pula 345 million in 1978/79 (1 1978 pula = 1.4 U.S. dollars) to pula 500 million in 1979/80, an increase of 27 percent in real terms. World Bank statistics pointed to Botswana as the best economic performer in Africa between 1970 and 1978, with a 16.1 percent growth rate for the period. The per capita gross national product stood at Pula 450 a year in 1980.

The primary thrust behind this economic growth has been the development of the mineral sector. After independence a major copper-nickel mining complex opened at Selebi-Phikwe that, despite some economic problems, has had a major economic impact on the country. A large coal mine also has begun operation at Morupule, with a proven and estimated reserve of seventeen billion tons. Some estimates put the reserves as high as 100 billion tons, and plans are underway to export ten to fifteen million tons a year overseas, primarily to Europe.

Diamonds have had the most dramatic impact upon the country, however. Mineral production has increased every year since independence, and at the end of calendar year 1979 the value of mining production was up 85 percent. Diamonds contribute 96 percent of Botswana's mineral revenue and the country is now (1987) the world's third largest producer of diamonds. When the new mining complex at Jwaneng began operation in 1982, diamond production more than doubled, and in 1983 Botswana's diamond production surpassed that of South Africa.[2]

Mineral exploitation was not without its costs. The opening of the country's mines required an enormous investment in infrastructure for mines located in areas with little or no population. The diamond mines at Selebi-Phikwe have been plagued by technical and marketing problems from the beginning. Critics suggest that Botswana is held hostage to unproductive copper-nickel mines because of the large up-front infrastructure investment and the five thousand jobs that the Selebi-Phikwe mines generate.

Overdependence upon mining can distort the economy. The increased salary differential that developed in Botswana after 1972 was a direct result of the emerging mining sector, an example of an unbalanced economic strategy that does not stimulate the entire country.[3] At the same time, infrastructure requirements for mining have caused scarce resources to be diverted from other sectors of the economy, sectors that could have a more direct impact on the majority of the population.

Problems of Diversification

Mineral development is the source of most of Botswana's wealth, but the cattle industry is the preferred investment for the majority of Botswana's citizenry. With a national herd of over three million head, the cattle industry is the most important economic activity in the country in terms of its impact on the population, and it accounts for 20 percent of the nation's gross domestic product. The ownership of cattle is very uneven, with 45 percent of the population not owning cattle and 5 percent owning half the national herd.

Arable agriculture is a very risky affair for Botswana's small farmers. Farming activity is largely subsistence and totally dependent upon the vicissitudes of the country's unpredictable rainfall patterns. For the foreseeable future, the country is likely to remain dependent upon food imports, especially from South Africa, and particularly in years of poor rain.

The manufacturing sector, apart from the meat processing industry, is negligible. The little primary activity that does exist occurs in Botswana's three main towns, the capital Gaborone, Francistown, and Lobatse. The country can be characterized as having an underdeveloped open economy, in which primary products are exported and manufactured items are imported. As do many developing countries, Botswana suffers from a chronic trade deficit, although the effects of the deficit are mitigated by the country's strong mining sector.

At issue is the extent to which any kind of income redistribution is possible. Little of the economic revenue generated from the mining industry goes to the average citizen. Rural incomes have not risen very much, increasing only 5.6 percent between 1966 and 1973. Unemployment and underemployment are the weak points of an otherwise active economy, and the spector of uncontrolled unemployment has begun to haunt policy makers. A report in the *South Africa Labour Bulletin* painted a grim future for Botswana's employment prospects. The report's author argued that Botswana could provide work for only 200,000 of the 365,000 people in the work force and that 45 percent of the work force was underutilized.[4] Of those employed only sixty thousand had paid employment in the private sector.

At the same time, the availability of jobs in South Africa has decreased dramatically and will continue to do so over the next several years. The number of Botswana citizens employed in South African mines dropped from thirty-one thousand in 1977 to nineteen thousand in 1981. The drop in available jobs has been four thousand per year through the decade of the 1980s. South Africa's deliberate policy of shifting labor migration patterns toward its own "homelands" has long-term significance for Botswana. Only 9 percent of the population currently is employed in the urban sector, and urban underemployment is a growing problem. At the same time, urban migration is expected to reach serious proportions, with an estimated 27 percent of the population (260,000 persons) living in towns by 1987.

In spite of the low level of employment opportunity in the urban areas, urban investment garnered the lion's share of development money throughout the 1970s. Beginning with the overwhelming cost of establishing a new national capital in Gaborone between 1963 and 1966 and extending to the establishment of new mining towns at Selebi-Phikwe, Orapa, and Jwaneng, urban investment has continued to be very high in relationship to the predominantly rural nature of Botswana. As late as 1984 urban development continued to amount to more than 50 percent of the Ministry of Local Government and Lands' development budget.

The government is Botswana's single most important employer, with central and local government agencies producing more than 50 percent of all jobs by 1985. The government's policy on wages has implications for the economy as a whole. A 1980 government report on salaries in the civil service provided for close to a 30 percent increase in the salaries of civil servants at all levels of government.[5]

There have been many notable achievements in Botswana since independence. Economic growth has been phenomenal in the period since 1966. Aggregate increases in output, in and of themselves, however, are less important than the structural composition of such growth. The concentration on growth in the mining and cattle industries has had a number of consequences for society as a whole.

> Many people, having neither cattle nor wage employment, have been largely excluded from the effects of economic growth. Their productive potential has not been enhanced in any fundamental way. ... [In addition], the growth is fragile: the livestock sector is vulnerable to changes in the weather cycle, and has caused major conservation problems; the mining sector is externally oriented, and the main factors which affect its sources of capital and technology, and its markets, are beyond Botswana's sphere of influence.[6]

Botswana continues to be dependent upon the revenues generated from the southern African Customs Union that includes South Africa and Botswana's former High Commission partners, Lesotho and Swaziland. Until 1979 Customs Union revenues accounted for the single largest segment of Botswana's revenue. This type of revenue has negative implications in that it is not related to the stimulation of economic activity within the country, and it is a major factor in the dependency relationship between Botswana and South Africa.

At issue for Botswana is how much economic independence is possible in terms of economic diversification, agricultural self-sufficiency, and lessening its ties to South Africa's economy. Rural development strategies are a possible mechanism for diversification and self-sufficiency, but they require a commitment by political elites to economic strategies that may conflict with the maximization of growth indicators. Such a commitment impies a "revolution in political, bureaucratic and rural attitudes."[7] Given the economic needs of existing socio-political elites this commitment is not likely. An examination of Botswana's rural development strategies since independence clearly indicates the current priorities of the country's political leadership.

Early Rural Development Efforts

At independence Botswana was haunted by the specter of starvation and severe economic dislocation. Several years of poor rain, beginning just prior to independence and continuing until the late 1960s, resulted in one of the periodic spells of extended drought that have been the bane of Botswana's agricultural and livestock development since the beginning of the twentieth century. Experts predicted that it would take more than five years to recover from the effects of the 1960s' drought.

Food-For-Work Programs

Rural development activities dovetailed with colonial and post-colonial efforts at food supply through "food-for-work" programs throughout the 1960s. These programs, supervised by district officers, represented the first concerted effort by the Bechuanaland and Botswana governments to engage district-level officials in activities designed to ameliorate economic conditions in the rural areas.

By the end of 1965 it was necessary to provide food for 360,000 persons, 65 percent of the population. The efforts to feed that number of people strained government finances to the limits, and it was only external assistance provided by the Oxford Committee for Famine Relief and the United Nations World Food Program, as well as the Colonial Development and Welfare Fund and private contributions, that prevented mass starvation.[8]

Early food distribution was of an emergency nature, but as the worst effects of the drought were halted, it became government policy to link food supplement programs with village self-help projects, working through newly established village development committees. Some rural development efforts, underlying the expansion of agricultural extension services, were funded from the government's development budget. The food-for-work programs encouraged several small-scale, rural development projects and an increased emphasis on agricultural extension services that involved "pupil farmer" and "pupil stockmen" schemes.

During the colonial period, rural development efforts had been linked to building construction activities in the "tribal" areas. Much of the construction was to fill the government's requirements for offices, court rooms, police stations, government houses, and graded roads to the district headquarters. Independence did little to change this pattern, and development expenditure in the rural areas continued to be small and directed generally to the government's own needs. Meager attempts at providing social services, schools, health clinics, and hospitals resulted from tribal administration initiative and missionary activity.[9] The promotion of the cattle industry beginning with the construction of the Botswana Meat Commission abattoir in Lobatse in the early 1950s, was the one rural sector-economic activity promoted by both the colonial and post-colonial governments.

In the 1968 to 1973 National Development Plan little is said about rural development beyond the notation that Botswana would look to agriculture and livestock production for short-term increases in the national income. A limited amount of money was made available during the 1968–1973 plan for expanding the agricultural extension system. Emphasis was on economic growth indicators projecting an annual growth rate of between 6 percent and 10 percent, and "fundamental to the plans and policies of the Government is a determination to make the country a financially viable entity in the shortest possible time."[10]

Major economic investment during the first five-year plan was committed to the mining sector and supporting infrastructure. During the first four years of the 1970-75 National Development Plan, 42 percent of the total development budget was allocated to the infrastructure for the Selebi-Phikwe mining complex, whereas only 8 percent went into rural development. The disparity between urban and rural income per capita was already sixfold in 1965, and the gap widened during the 1960s.

Rural Development Priorities

A conscious decision had been made at independence to postpone rural development activities in order to obtain an internal source of government income by developing the country's mining industry. Politicians promised that revenues from diamond and copper and nickel exploitation would then be invested in rural development activities. "Mining for rural development" became a popular phrase in the late 1960s.[11] Beyond this, emphasis was on self-help. Rural dwellers would have to take the initiative to improve their condition.

Local initiative was the crucial ingredient in the government's strategy. The government's contribution would be limited to the payment of salaries for community development extension staff who would be "catalysts" for self-help projects. It was hoped that some development would occur in the rural areas as a result of international donors and that this would lead to a general rural development program when monies from the mining sector became available.

Cynics viewed Botswana's strategy as rural development on the cheap. Holm found the severe neglect of rural development particularly striking in a country where over 80 percent of the population lived in the rural areas. What puzzled him was the fact that throughout the 1970s,

> Botswana's rural development program [was] minimally funded, relatively unconcerned with the mass of the population, controlled by national rather than local officials, heavily foreign funded and controlled, and yielded few results which benefit the living conditions of the average voter.[12]

An examination of Botswana's rural development policy in the decade between 1973 and 1983 allows one to trace the continuities in Botswana's rural sector strategy over time that provide at least a partial answer to Holm's puzzle.

As Botswana's rural development policy has unfolded since 1970, conflicts of interest between large cattle-owners and the majority of the rural population have been increasing. A rural income distribution survey taken in 1974-75 showed that the non-cattle owning households comprised about 45 percent of all the rural households, or just over one-third actually were engaged in agriculture. Forty percent of the rural households owned up to 50 head each, accounting for one-fourth of the national herd, and the remaining 15 percent of the population, the large cattle-owners, owned 75 percent of the national herd.

The 1969 elections indicated to the BDP government for the first time that it did not have full contol over the rural areas. While confirming the BDP's authority, the elections also marked a partial breakdown in the alliance between traditional authorities and the BDP ruling elites.

The threat of a conservative, rural-based party manifested itself when Bathoen II resigned his chieftainship and joined the newly formed opposition party, the Botswana National Front. The BNF captured three seats from the BDP in the Southern District (Kanye, north; Kanye, south; and Ngwaketse/Kgalagadi) and Bathoen himself defeated then vice-president, Quett Masire.

After 1969 it was clear that political threats to the government would come from disenchantment in the rural areas and among traditional elites, rather than from urban left-wing movements. An articulated policy of rural development was one way to ensure at least some degree of political quiescence in the rural areas. In the 1970-1975 National Development Plan, published just after the elections, considerably more space was devoted to rural development than in the previous five-year plan.[13] Nevertheless, the government's strategy remained dependent on the spinoff effects of mineral production and urban economic activity.

Operationally, officials saw rural development as an ad hoc district-level activity linked to the preparation of the district development plan.[14] Rural development, according to the newly appointed assistant minister of local government and lands, required better coordination, increased levels of communication and the creation of a strong cooperative team within the district.[15] Rural development was seen as a district-level activity, one that was divorced from what central government did.

By the beginning of 1972 politicians were paying more attention to the question of rural development. President Khama made a number of speeches on the subject and there were several regional meetings and a national rural development conference. Donor funding was solicited for a wide range of rural development projects. Yet, the government still had not issued a statement as to what rural development meant.

In 1971 a committee had been appointed to draft a rural development policy for the government's consideration and adoption. That report, *Rural Development in Botswana*, was made public in March 1972. It was less a strategy of development than a statement of goals and a checklist of departmental activities in the rural areas.[16] Government policy revolved around three major goals: (1) to increase basic social services; (2) to halt the deterioration of the land through overgrazing; and (3) to promote of "social justice."

Returns to the nation from intensive capital investment in mining would be reinvested, and the proceeds would be used to promote labor-intensive activities and improve services in the rural areas. Rural development at the local level remained undefined, with the emphasis on the "responsibility for the preparation and coordination of district development plans."[17] There was much discussion of social justice; it was a qualified social justice, however, that "must not lead us into assuming that the living standards of all the population can be raised by redistributing the assets of the few people who are relatively well off." Although noting the uneven distribution of cattle within the country, the government cautioned "we should, of course, do nothing which will make our cattle industry less productive, or which would reduce its income earning capacity."[18] Whereas occasional reference had been made to the need for job creation, in practice rural development activity came to be defined as infrastructure projects, schools, health posts, roads and water reticulation.

Much energy was expended, both nationally and at the district level, on the preparation of district-level plans. The massive 1,500-page third volume of the *National Development Plan 1973-1978*, entitled *Development Plans for Local Authorities*, contains the results of these efforts.[19] The plans, uneven in both length and quality, are summaries of existing or proposed projects rather than a strategy for development, but they do provide a useful, district-by-district survey of the infrastructure and physical development throughout the country in the early 1970s.

Physical Infrastructure

The emphasis on infrastructure was inevitable given Botswana's paucity of infrastructure at independence. Nevertheless, the physical project emphasis would influence rural development planning until the mid-1980s. The rural development coordinator in the Ministry of Local Government and Lands stated in 1972,

> My own view is that we need a "project-oriented" approach to DDCs, i.e., we start with the projects and build them into a plan, not a "programme oriented" approach where DDCs spend the next 3-6 months gathering "planning data" which may never be used.[20]

By 1973 Botswana policy makers were coming under the influence of a number of planners who had garnered most of their experience in east Africa, most often in Kenya. The rural development program in Kenya contributed a number of expatriate staff who, on completion of their contracts in east Africa, came to Botswana to work in the Ministry of Finance and Development Planning and the Ministry of Agriculture. Not surprisingly, the Kenya experience provided a model for rural development activity in Botswana, a model with which the political elites were comfortable.

In March 1972 two Kenya planners, Robert Chambers and David Feldman, arrived in Botswana to study rural development under the sponsorship of the Ford Foundation.[21] The two consultants spent three months in Botswana before returning to the Institute for Development Studies in Nairobi to write their findings. The Chambers and Feldman *Report on Rural Development* was released by the Ministry of Finance and Development Planning in February 1973.[22] In a white paper published in May of the same year, the government responded to the massive (281 pages) Chambers and Feldman report.[23] Chambers and Feldman aside from providing a sector-by-sector analysis of government policy, made a number of general comments and recommendations on development strategy. In the white paper, much briefer (17 pages) than the consultants' report, a clear picture emerges of official thinking on development in the early 1970s. Between them, the two documents established the guidelines for rural development through the end of the decade.

Chambers and Feldman warned of the inherent contradictions between unconstrained economic growth and social justice. The key to rural development was to find a balance between the two. Rapid capital accumulation of the kind that was occuring in Botswana would result in deepening patterns of social cleavage between owners of capital and wage earners. The government's desire to maximize revenue was at variance with the reallocation of that revenue from mining to the rural sector.

The two consultants recommended a greater degree of economic self-sufficiency through an aggressive policy of import substitution. They warned against unconstrained movement away from a subsistence economy to a cash economy. In order to maximize the impact of the spread of development in the rural areas, there would have to be restraints on economic growth.

In the white paper, on the other hand, the government committed Botswana to a rapid return on mineral exploitation and other viable modern industries continue to be based primarily on the "spin off" principle, by which revenues from the mining sector (as well as from technical assistance programs) would be used to develop physical infrastructure at the district level.

Revenue generated from mining also would be used to promote new secondary industries and properly planned urban development. Job opportunities in the urban areas would create employment for the rural unemployed and an increased demand for agricultural products. The government was less than sanguine about the prospects for import substitution and decreased economic dependence upon South Africa.

Botswana elites accepted the specifics of the Chambers and Feldman report without addressing the substantive issues relating to equity, social justice, and job opportunities raised in the course of the investigation. The elites managed to avoid the hard questions raised by many outside studies of Botswana's rural development program. Rural development policy was based on the assumption that inequities between the urban and rural areas would continue and even increase. Rather than being based on the mobilization of the rural population for social and economic change, rural development policy was designed primarily to ensure political quiescence. Armed with the white paper recommendations, districts were ready in late 1973 "to move towards planning of district physical infrastructure and services."[24]

The Accelerated Rural Development Programme (ARDP)

Setbacks in the 1969 elections, limited though they were, weighed heavily on Botswana political elites as the 1974 elections approached. BDP leaders were determined to stop any further erosion of support in the rural areas and to try to regain some of the support that had been lost. In order to do this, the BDP would have to find a way to convince rural voters that the government was making economic development in the rural areas a priority in the 1973-1978 development period.

The idea that politicians finally hit upon was the Accelerated Rural Development Programme (ARDP). Using development grants from Germany, Norway, Sweden, and other donors, the government would implement a highly visible, physical infrastructure spending program in all ten of Botswana's districts during the twelve months prior to the election.[25] The ARDP, announced in November 1973, was to be particularly visible on 26 October 1974, when Botswana's citizens would go to the polls.

Under the ARDP rural development indeed did become openly identified with government spending projects, visible symbols of the BDP's concern for progress in the rural areas. The ARDP was designed to ensure political loyalty within the districts, rather than to stimulate social change or economic development. The program would mobilize voters in the 1974 elections to support the BDP and entailed "the expansion of state structure in the rural areas."[26]

At a cabinet meeting on 23 November 1973, the president ordered the Ministry of Finance and Development Planning to produce proposals for an accelerated program of rural development to be presented at the next cabinet meeting on 30 November.[27] According to the presidential directive, "The primary objective is for projects to be visible, on the ground, by September 30th, 1974."[28] That was twenty-six days before the general election.

The cabinet concentrated on four key infrastructure areas: water reticulation, primary schools, rural health buildings, and road improvement. Responsibilities were parceled out within each ministry involved. Within the Ministry of Local Government and Lands, responsibility was divided. The central government would implement large or major village projects under the direction of the chief architect and the MLGL, while the small village projects would be carried out by direct contract labor under the supervision of district councils and MLGL officials.[29] Large village contracts came to 6 million pula, while small village projects totalled 2 million pula.

Theoretically, the district development committees had planning responsibilities for large as well as small village projects. In fact, however, DDC/Council activity revolved around the 2 million pula provided for small village projects. Councils and the district administration were very much agents of the MLGL and the Ministry of Finance and Development Planning. Indeed, even the MLGL was a somewhat passive actor. Funds for the implementation of major village projects were coordinated by the rural development unit of the MFDP, political supervision was in the hands of the vice-president (and Minister of Finance and Development Planning), and project reports went directly to the cabinet.[30] In a circular memorandum to all ministries in late December 1973, the permanent secretary to the President reiterated the importance that the government placed on the ARDP:

> Subject to the exigencies of the fuel situation, it is the President's wish that this accelerated programme should take precedence at whatever level may be required over other matters in order that its objectives may be attained by 30th September, 1974.[31]

Implementation of small village projects depended upon the district administration and district councils. The three people most involved were the district officer (development), the council planning officer, and the council works superintendent. All three positions were filled almost always by expatriates from volunteer agencies. Politically the small village project was the most important aspect of the ARDP. It was designed to ensure some government physical impact on the smallest villages during the election year and the political mobilization of rural voters in support of the BDP in the general elections. A significant portion of the small village project was carried out by the handful of expatriate volunteers in the district administration and the district councils.

Roughly 11 million pula were spent on rural development under the Accelerated Rural Development Programme. Although not completed until the end of 1975 (over a year after the election), most, if not all, of the ARDP projects were in progress by the cabinet's 30 September 1974 deadline. The BDP was successful in the 1974 elections, gaining three seats in the National Assembly and increasing its overall percentage of the votes from 69.6 to 77.7 percent. BDP gains in the district councils were even more impressive. The party increased its total share of elected seats by 31.8 percent (from 113 in 1969 to 149 in 1974). Only one district council (Northeast) returned an elected majority for the opposition.

Policy makers equated rural transformation under the ARDP with concentrated infrastructure development. The program was aimed at pump priming through a trickle-down strategy, from salaries paid by contractors (some of whom were located in South Africa or Rhodesia), and at the political symbolism inherent in the presence of the roads and buildings in the rural areas. Nor was self-help a major component of the ARDP. Although village development committees were formed in the late 1960s, in many districts they quickly became moribund. Some small village projects required the villages to provide bricks through the food-for-work program but generally self-help probably contributed less than 2 percent under the ARDP.

After 1973 rural development efforts tended to steer clear of projects that might involve, and perhaps politicize, rural dwellers. In a 1977 evaluation of the ARDP, which was more favorable than many government officials expected, the author cautioned,

> . . . development is not bricks and mortar. It is one thing . . . to get schools, health posts and roads built and water supplies installed. It is quite another, and more difficult to ensure that they operate, are well staffed, and are accessible to all. It is yet harder to achieve the national aim of an equitable distribution of incomes, when so many of the poorest people are precisely those who are furthest away, least

well educated, worst informed, least in contact with government and least able to help themselves.[32]

The ARDP "was not designed to confront, and did not confront, the central issue of the poorer people in the rural areas."[33] It represented one prong of a two-edged strategy of rural activity in the 1970s, the other being the "Tribal Grazing Land Policy." If the ARDP represented symbolism and political quiescence, the TGLP represented substance and economic transformation. The nature of that economic transformation tells us much about the political allocation process in Botswana.

The Tribal Grazing Land Policy (TGLP)

On 14 July 1975 President Khama launched the government's new grazing land policy in a speech to the Botswana National Assembly. The crux of the new policy was contained in the president's statement that:

> In Commercial Farming Areas groups and individuals will be given exclusive rights to specific areas of grazing land. These areas include much of the existing sand veld cattle post areas where bore hole owners at present pay nothing for the land they use. Ranches will be encouraged, including fencing and piping of water. The land will cease to be held in the traditional way. A lease will be given and rent will be payable to the local authorities in return for the exclusive rights given in the lease.[34]

As discussed earlier, Botswana's cattle industry has an economic impact on the majority of its citizens. Close to 50 percent of the population have an investment in Botswana's 3.5 million head of cattle, ranging from the ownership of fewer than a dozen head, up to huge "Texas style" ranches with herds numbering in the tens of thousands. Grazing land historically has been communal.

With a rapidly increasing national herd in a fragile physical environment, Botswana's land had become drastically overgrazed. Particularly within the vicinity of the country's major villages, but increasingly throughout the eastern part of the country,

> uncontrolled grazing has led to serious range degeneration particularly within villages and near water sources. Denudation, sheet erosion and bush encroachment have become increasingly obvious.[35]

The TGLP was designed to alleviate this problem.

Origins of the TGLP

Ecologically, Botswana's problems have many analogies to the Sahel region of west Africa and the dry lands areas of northern Kenya and Uganda. Periodic droughts that brought loss of animals and even human starvation had led the colonial government to establish communal water points in the tribal reserves.

In the twenty years since independence, uncontrolled grazing around communal bore holes has led to serious range deterioration within the villages and near water sources. The characteristics of this deterioration are denudation of the land, sheet erosion, and brush encroachment. The effects of the deterioration are particularly devastating on small cattleowners, most of whom keep and graze their herds near their villages because they cannot afford the high cost of drilling a bore hole.

Between 1966 and 1970, there was a sudden jump in the number of wealthy stock owners drilling bore holes for cattle posts in the remote, formerly empty areas of western Botswana. Over time, control of these bore holes effectively took the place of collective land rights in the remote areas of the country. Although existing statistics are not very reliable, data from the 1973-1978 National Development Plan suggest that there were 3,740 private bore holes in Botswana, generally located in the western two-thirds of the country. Small farmers were being left behind on increasingly degraded range, their way toward expansion in the west blocked by rings of privately financed bore holes controlled by Botswana's small socio-economic elite.

The spark that set off the search for a new land policy was the Conference on Sustained Production from Semi-Arid Areas, held in October 1971 under the sponsorship of the United Nations Conference on the Human Environment. Conference participants, many of whom were expatriates, concluded that there had to be a "radical reform of current land use and animal husbandry practices to ensure proper management of grazing." Some form of land commercialization was inevitable, particularly in the western regions. As one commentator stated, "The present form of land use is not necessarily the future form of land use, and as the country develops socially and economically, patterns of land use are apt to be more varied and intricate."[36]

Two major elements of what ultimately became the government's new land use policy orignated with the 1971 conference: (1) commercialization of land in the western part of the country; and (2) formation of syndicates in the east that would be allowed to fence portions of the tribal communal land.

Between 1971 and 1974, hints of a policy change began to appear in official documents and official statements on land use. Although many in Botswana were not aware of it, the main lines of the government's new policy were made public in a government white paper in March 1972, a full three years before the 1975 announcement of the TGLP. The policy that would best solve the ecological problems and was most acceptable to socio-economic elites was the large-scale demarcation of fenced and watered ranches, coupled with control over land acquisition and some control over herd size. In the white paper the government was quite specific with regard to overgrazing: "Large herds require extensive grazing areas. The larger cattle owners will . . . be encouraged to acquire land grants . . . for which economic rental will be charged."[37]   At the heart of the government's new grazing land policy would be the creation of commercial land.

By 1973 policy directions had been set, although the nuances remained to be fleshed out and the political elites needed a rhetoric of policy making to initiate the public to the forthcoming changes.   The rhetoric was developed by the expatriate advisors who wrote the various policy studies that preceeded the 1975 TGLP.   The most important of these studies was the 1973 Chambers and Feldman report.

Although the authors manifested genuine concern in their report for the poor subsistence-level rural dweller, the report's specifics reflect previous government thinking.   Chambers and Feldman advocated a firm movement toward commercialization of land in the communal areas. Individual tenure was both inevitable and necessary, and "a basic principle of any effective land and livestock policy must . . . be the identification of individual stockholders or of groups of stockowners with exclusive rights to particular land surfaces."[38]   At the crux of the report was a recommendation that a category of land be created that would be available for rent on a fifty-year lease.   Leases for this commercial land should be issued to individuals, syndicates, cooperatives, companies, and any other legal entities.

Chambers and Feldman stressed the need to protect the small stockholder, but they also recognized the "political realities" of the situation and noted, "It will be a matter for the conscience and magnanimity of the large cattle owners to what extent and in what ways they can make settlements of livestock and watering facilities [available] for those who have been dependent on them."[39]   To put it simply, the welfare of the majority of subsistence-level Batswana inevitably would be in the hands of a few wealthy farmers.

In response to Chambers and Feldman, the government issued a white paper in May 1973 accepting the principles of commercial land and of fencing "by individuals or groups provided nobody else has valid claim over the areas they want to fence and can support their claim with evidence they have used the land in recent years, or have the capacity to use the land in the future."[40]   In addition, the government made two other provisions. First, some fencing was also to be allowed in the communal areas (near the major villages) by syndicates as well as by other groups and organizations. Second, in a departure from the Chambers and Feldman recommendations, those who leased commercial land still would be allowed to keep a certain number of cattle in the communal areas.   In effect, the government gave the best of both grazing systems to the wealthy cattle owners.

The TGLP was not announced until six months after the 1974 elections. Politically, the land issue was an unsettling one, and the political elites saw the need for a quiet period during the electoral campaign.   Prior to the announcement of the TGLP there were several months of bureaucratic bargaining and coalition building in order to create a political environment conducive to acceptance of the new policy.

Policy making prior to the announcement of the new plan occurred at three levels. At the policy decision level fewer than thirty political leaders (in and around the cabinet level) and a similar number of senior bureaucrats were involved in drafting the TGLP. At the second level, and prior to the public announcement of the new plan, policy makers attempted to create a coalition of support for the policy within the bureaucracy, fending off critics of the proposed changes who challenged the orientation toward commercial ownership. Finally, the government followed the publication of the principal policy documents with a phased, public "consultation" process.

The decision to make a public announcement of the new land policy was made at the cabinet level in late 1974. Overall political responsibility for the project was given to then Vice-President Quett Masire and his Ministry of Finance and Development Planning. Bureaucratic responsibility for writing the policy was placed with the rural development unit of that ministry, the division of land utilization in the Ministry of Agriculture, and the lands division of the Ministry of Local Government and Lands. Planning officers in each of the ministries, most of whom were expatriates, were central to the policy's preparation.

Resistance to the New Land Policy

Bureaucratic resistance to the TGLP did not become widespread until after the 1974 elections. In December of that year, a Presidential Directive was sent to all ministries ordering the preparation of a TGLP policy document.[41] From this point on, policy makers were divided into two camps: those who saw commercialization as inevitable and, in fact, desirable and those who felt that the TGLP would leave large numbers of rural dwellers, particularly in the semiarid territories, landless and without a livelihood. Many who saw the new land policy as inevitable worked in the Ministry of Finance and Development Planning and its rural development unit. Opponents, both expatriates as well as some Batswana, usually were found in the Ministry of Local Government and Lands and, to some extent, in the district administration.

During this period middle-level policy makers in Botswana often were young idealistic expatriates, many of them volunteers or former volunteers. It was among this group that opposition to the TGLP developed. Several became concerned with what they saw as a potential "land grab," in which they were being asked to take part. As evidence for this, some pointed to a "quick and dirty" land resource survey of eastern Botswana conducted in 1973.[42] Others pointed to the danger of allowing syndicates to fence, particularly in the land-scarce eastern districts of the country, arguing that all land in the communal areas should remain under district council and land board control and open to all members of the community.

Opposition to the TGLP started very late, and the policy's critics developed a two-pronged strategy. First, they began to criticize openly aspects of the land policy within meetings of the district level bureaucracy in order to draw attention to the policy's controversial nature and stimulate pressure to modify it. At the same time, through intrabureaucratic negotiations, the critics hoped to modify the language of the government white paper on TGLP.

Debate opened in April of 1975 at the third national conference of district development committees. The minister of local government and lands gave a strong speech calling for critical discussion of land policy. During the speech, actually written by an expatriate in the ministry who opposed the policy, the minister said, "The implementation programme being prepared is designed so that most of the vital, practical decisions will be decentralized and taken at the District level. The Government will lay down policy and guidelines but these must be interpreted and implemented locally to suit local conditions."[43] Many at the conference saw the speech as an invitation to take a critical look at the policy and adjust it to local conditions within the districts.

Advocates of the TGLP had two concerns: (1) that people would identify the land policy with the rich, based "on the assumption that the rich tend to have a more powerful voice in *kgotla* . . . [tribal meetings]"; and (2) that public discussion would shift from implementation of the TGLP to a discussion of the policy itself. Although the policy had not yet been made public, in a Ministry of Finance and Development Planning memorandum in April 1975, it was noted that "it should be made clear that the public discussion is not being undertaken in order to debate the land development policy per se. Rather, the position is that we have the policy and a proposition for implementing it."[44] The goal would be to sell the policy and dispel criticism of it.

Critics of the policy at the April DDC conference pointed to its capital-intensive nature. The TGLP would create few rural jobs and would increase the inequities among cattle-owning households. Not only would commercial land go to large cattleowners almost exclusively, but syndicates in the communal areas would be dominated by relatively well-off cattle holders. The author of one of the conference papers noted that syndicates in the Kgatleng District were monopolized by "the wealthier Bakgatla [who] gained the early watering rights and the best grazing, as the poor man was unable to take advantage of the scheme."[45]

In May 1975 opponents of the land policy appealed to senior district-level staff at a meeting of district officials at the Institute of Development Management (IDM). In an impromptu debate with representatives of the rural development unit of the Ministry of Finance and Development Planning, TGLP opponents told district officials:

> You should feel free to criticize the policy if you feel that it is dangerous. There has been no consultation so far. There are dangers in the plan. Stand on your own feet now or you will be blamed later. Government is nervous about this policy. If they get a hostile reaction when they go public they may abandon it. If they get an apathetic response they will go through with it. You must keep in mind that the people writing the land policy are not unaware of the mystique of land and tribe.

There was a sharp response from Ministry officials. Pointing to the TGLP critics, one member of the rural development unit responded,

> You should not persist in discussing a policy which has already been decided. These decisions were made two years ago. . . . Whatever we may talk about here, these things should not be discussed at the district level. These are very ticklish subjects and they must await cabinet and Presidential clearance. All discussion of land development policy has been concluded. We have the green light to go ahead with the land policy as it is presented. We must give this land to the people who can afford to develop it and get on with it.[46]

Local government officials at the IDM were surprised at the hardening of the issues and at the extent to which the policy decisions had already been finalized. As one council secretary put it, "We at the local level are at a disadvantage. We had hoped that this was a first step at local level consultation. Now we find that policy is coming straight from the top. Now we are left holding the bag." In fact, what the council secretaries were witnessing was a rear guard action against the TGLP with little hope of success.

TGLP opponents gained access to the drafts of the White Paper relatively late, less than six weeks before the new policy was to be made public. A number of versions had been prepared, all by expatriates. The initial version was written in the Ministry of Agriculture and the Ministry of Finance and Development Planning and reflected the thinking of the rural development unit and then Vice-President Masire. The draft was focused on the need to create commercial ranching areas. Better opportunities should be provided for large and small farmers to increase their family income. Range destruction could be avoided through range management and limitations on the number of cattle per acre. According to the draft's authors, the new land tenure system was a prerequisite for these improved management techniques because "the new management systems must involve fencing areas over which exclusive rights are recognized."[47] The goal of TGLP was to create conditions under which groups and individuals would be granted occupancy rights.

Critics of that first draft, based in the Ministry of Local Government and Lands, set out to revise it prior to cabinet approval. The strategy was simple. Because they had little hope of making major revisions to the document, they would introduce nuances of change. Thus, throughout the document the critics put greater emphasis on the need to promote social development and stressed the need for land use planning for the whole country.[48]

In the revised version the authors focused on the need for social justice in the communal areas. At one point the wording of the text was changed from "Determine areas available for commercial development taking into account communal and national needs" to "Work out how much land is left for commercial development after taking into account communal and national needs." The term "social justice" became prominent in the text. Priority should be given to small stockholders and those without cattle. Only if there were land left after the formation of group ranches and syndicates should it be made available for individual commercial use.

In fact, a number of major changes were introduced subtly throughout the document. A maximum land-holding clause was added; no individual was to own more than two areas or a maximum of sixty thousand acres. The revised draft contained several new provisions to protect the reserved areas from land use and guidelines relating to ownership and rent. Rents should be designed so that "local authorities obtain a great deal more revenue than in the past from their main asset which is the land. Unless this policy is met, the policy will fail to meet the requirements of social justice."

The first draft had not contained a discussion of the problem of absentee ownership. In the revised version the authors included penalties for absentee owners who did not provide competent resident managers or ensure that labor resources were not exploited ruthlessly. (The use and exploitation of the Basarwa ("bushmen") are no doubt alluded to here.) They also included shorter leases, fifteen years to fifty years, as opposed to the flat fifty-year lease written into the original draft, and restrictions on lease transfers.

The two documents differed most in their conclusions. The authors of the revised document included a discussion of "moral issues," in which they argued that

> considerably more work will need to be done to ensure that our concern for the conservation of land resources is not an end in itself. . . . [It will] be meaningless, in fact abhorrent, if the way in which it is done is to make the rich richer while the poor stay as they are. The policy will be a success only if it succeeds in both short and long terms in reducing the gap between the rich and poor.

Finally, the authors of the revised version had a very different view of public consultation. The authors of the original draft had stated that "the purpose of the public consultation must be made quite clear. It is not land development policy that is being discussed. The policy has been decided, as long ago as 1973. What is to be discussed is how to implement that policy." Whereas in the revised version the authors declared,

> It is not intended to steamroller public opinion. Most members know nothing about the land development policy, although the policy was decided as long ago as 1973. . . . The program of action which we are embarked upon does not yet have anywhere near the required degree of public support and approval.

The authors of the revised document concluded by arguing that parts of the policy would have to be revised by Parliament in light of public opinion prior to final implementation. They viewed the public announcement of the new policy as little more than the opening of a genuine public debate.

A third version of the White Paper, written by the Ministry of Agriculture in simple English for purposes of translation into Setswana, became available within the government about 1 July 1975.[49] Inadvertently, it is a much more honest document than either of the two earlier drafts. The authors of this third version stressed the technical issues of land misuse, rather than economic or social issues. They emphasized better cattle and stated three major principles: (1) the need for fences, management and breeding; (2) the ability of larger cattleowners to fill those needs; and (3) the inability of smaller cattleowners to fill those needs unless they banded together.

The justification was simple. Commercial land was a necessity for owners and groups to be able to "fence their land, control grazing and keep more cattle." When that happens, "everyone benefits. We can keep more cattle and have better cattle." The new land policy would provide relief for the communal areas and would rid the communal areas of the "big men" who would have to move to the commercial areas. This was stated in the third version despite the fact that the TGLP would allow large owners to continue to keep a portion of their cattle in the communal areas.

The implication was that local people would control the communal lands, but the government would "check to see if [local boards write] a fair and good plan" for land use in the districts. In discussing commercial land, however, the document is painfully honest. The authors of this draft frankly stated that in the commercial areas, "owners will have exclusive rights to the land and water there" and pointed out that under the new land policy "if you have enough cattle, the Government will help you get a loan. Then you will be able to fence your land and keep more cattle." The authors are discretely silent as to what would happen to an individual who does not have enough cattle. A clearer portrayal of the potential results of the TGLP could not have been provided.

Government White Paper No. 2 of 1975 (TGLP) was made public after the presidential announcement of the TGLP on 14 July 1975. The bulk of it was written by officials from the Ministry of Agriculture and the rural development unit of the Ministry of Finance and Development Planning. These officials assumed that there was sufficient good, unused grazing land to allow:

1. the "big men" to leave overgrazed communal areas to establish their own commercial area cattle post and thereby significantly relieve grazing pressure in communal areas;
2. the "small men" from communal areas to join together and establish shared, commercial-area cattle posts, further relieving grazing pressure and expanding the number of commercial-area beneficiaries;
3. sizeable areas to be set aside for future use by those having few or no cattle, or for future generations of livestock owners;
4. an expansion of grazing land immediately available to overstocked or growing communal areas; and
5. the setting aside of reserves for wildlife, mining, and other nonagricultural purposes.

To be fair to the officials who wrote the fourth and final document, it should be noted that their version did indicate that the revision written by "dissidents" in the Ministry of Local Government and Lands had some effect. The final document's authors made a general reference to the need for open debate about the policy. As did the authors of the revised version, they stated, "It is not intended to steamroller public opinion. . . . Government wants to encourage wide public discussion of the policy."[50] They even inferred that the policy might be revised if that should prove necessary, and they referred to the social justice issue to a greater extent than did the authors of the original draft.

If the authors of the final document ultimately accepted some of the generalizations in the MLGL revised version, opponents of the TGLP had little effect on the specifics of the plan. The rural population would have to rely on the fairness of the government to look after their interests and to protect them against the rich farmers. That many of the changes introduced in the revised versions were dropped brings this assumption about the government's protection at least somewhat into question. For example the authors of the white paper omitted any reference to the "income distribution problem" raised in the revised version. Instead, they argue that the traditional system of land tenure should be blamed for poverty. The TGLP would "ensure that the available grazing is properly used and distributed . . . and every tribesman [will] have as much land as he needs to sustain himself and his family."

The idea of an economic rent was also not included in the final version. In the earlier drafts it had been stated that those allocated commercial land under the new policy should pay an economic rent to the district councils. No reference was made to this in the final document. Furthermore, the final draft did not contain any provisions for penalizing absentee landlords who misused their position or exploited their labor. In addition, lessees of commercial land would be allowed to sublease all or parts of their land.

Authors of the earlier versions had argued the need to phase out private bore holes in the communal areas in order to preserve the communal rights of small stockholders. In the final version some exceptions to this were provided, where some farming and cattle keeping are mixed, and the requirements were considerably weaker for land acquisition. Other arguments omitted from the final document concerned the need to "discourage the acquisition of large tracts of land by absentee land owners"; the upper limits requirements, that is, the provision for giving preference to those without existing leases; and the need for constitutional protection of reserve land.

The net effect of the struggle between the opponents and the advocates of the TGLP had a negligible influence on the content of the final policy document. With the public announcement of the TGLP, government officials shifted to a new phase of the policy process, the publicity campaign. In August 1975 district officials met in a special TGLP session of the National District Development Conference, during which they were briefed on the "consultation process."

The Effects of the TGLP

In 1976 the government of Botswana began a campaign to inform the public about the new land tenure policy. Radio "listening groups" were formed throughout the country and a series of programs was broadcast on all aspects of the policy and the assumptions behind it. Cabinet ministers and senior bureaucrats traveled around the country and spoke in *kgotla* meetings to explain the policy. In spite of this public relations campaign, which was unusual for Africa, there is evidence "that a large proportion of the population does not understand the TGLP."[51] The public remained sceptical. Questionnaire returns indicated that "there was genuine concern over how the declaration of leasehold ranches would benefit the majority of people who did not have sufficient resources to begin commercial farming."[52]

The move to commercial ranches occurred in a number of stages between 1976 and 1981. Just prior to the TGLP's announcement in July 1975, the Botswana government began a land-use planning exercise throughout the country. The exercise had two purposes: to determine land characteristics in grazing land areas and to determine the capacity of district-level institutions to manage the TGLP program. Between 1975 and 1976, district officials traveled throughout the rural areas to document water source distribution, grazing conditions, and population patterns.

As part of the land-use planning exercise, zoning surveys were made of the entire country in order to divide land into the three TGLP categories of commercial, communal, and state (reserve) land. Once land was zoned as commercial, the district land boards would assign a team to carry out a demarcation exercise that would involve public consultation. The survey team was to hear individual claims prior to the allocation of ranches. The final stage of the process was to be the formal signing of leases by the individuals or groups allocated commercial land.

Approximately 12 percent of Botswana's land was designated commercial, 30 percent communal, and 25 percent was left uncommitted. Conspicuously absent was any land designated for future reserves, a key component of the TGLP. The remainder of the land (33 percent) fell out of the scope of the TGLP exercise.

Between 1976 and 1978, the land boards drew up leases and set rental conditions. Because of the discovery of significant numbers of stockless people, a supplementary population survey was held in 1978 to determine the extent to which the TGLP would dislocate residents in commercial areas. After 1978 the government's attention turned to the allocation process.

Initially, the allocation of land was very slow; between 700-1,000 ranches had been demarcated, but only 25 ranches were allocated, and no leases had been signed formally. The allocation process accelerated in the 1980s, however, and by the end of 1981, 302 ranches had been demarcated, 119 allocated, and 19 leases signed. (See Table 10.1.) Officials expected to demarcate and allocate between 50 and 70 ranches a year throughout the 1980s.

As early as 1977 it had become clear to observers on the scene that the TGLP would not work as intended. Originally, commercial land was to be allocated after the needs of the rural areas were met. In practice, however, commercial areas were designated first and "it turned out that designating commercial zones was a major target of the zoning exercise."[53] Both the planning exercise and the implementation process revealed intractable problems unanticipated by the authors of the TGLP document or the policy makers who developed the policy itself. The fact that the land-use planning exercise was undertaken *after* the policy had been promulgated called into question the entire set of assumptions upon which the written policy was based. In a 1980 Ministry of Agriculture evaluation of the TGLP, the author concluded

> that the TGLP land use planning exercise found that most of the assumptions made by planners of the policy were incorrect. There were *no* large areas of empty land in Botswana into which large herdowners could move. There were large numbers of people in the areas zoned commercial, particularly hunters and gatherers in the Western Sandveld. As yet no policy decisions have been made as to what will happen to those people who were forced to leave.[54]

Most large cattle owners have been unwilling to move to the commercial sites. The start-up costs for the TGLP ranches, as envisioned in the White Paper, were extremely high. Only the largest cattle owners decided that the investment required to establish a TGLP ranch was worthwhile. The authors of the TGLP evaluation concluded that there would be little, if any, movement of cattle out of the crowded communal areas.

Table 10.1   Status of TGLP Ranch Allocation, 1981

District & Area	Ranches Demarcated	Ranches Advertised	Ranches Allocated	Leases Signed
Ngwaketse				
Samane	15	15	15	10
2nd Allocation Area	22	22	—	—
CDC Group Ranches	6	3	3	3
Central				
Lepasha	12	12	7	6
Western Sandveld	—	—	—	—
Kgalagadi				
Tshane	10	10	8	—
Makopong	13	—	—	—
Werda	10	—	—	—
Middlepits	10	—	—	—
Kweneng				
Western	63	17	14	—
Northeast	59	14	—	—
Ngamiland				
Hainveld	72	72	66	—
Southwest Ngami	—	—	—	—
Ghanzi				
Makunda	10	6	6	—
Kgatleng				
Northwest	—	—	—	—
Totals	302	171	119	19

Source: Government File A34/14 II.

The new policy required district land boards to set limits on the number of stock in the communal areas, with the excess to go to the commercial areas. Following the radio campaign, however, "No administratively feasible and democratically acceptable means could be found to create such limits in the commonage and the idea was dropped."[55] As a result, very little unused land has been left for small holders that is close enough to settlements, and overcrowding in the communal areas continues.   The Presidential Commission on Land Tenure concluded in 1983 that

> . . . communal grazing areas do not appear to be enjoying the relief anticipated by the TGLP White Paper . . . through the removal of large herds to TGLP ranches. . . . [S]ome TGLP ranch holders have not, as expected, confined their herds to their ranches but continue to use communal grazing areas.[56]

From the beginning there was significant resistance to the stock limitation requirement, one of the key ecological provisions in the TGLP

White Paper and a major justification for the shift to a new land tenure system. In the radio consultation campaign, "stock limitations were universally criticised."[57] As a result, the TGLP's stock limitations were dropped.

Two other aspects of the new policy were unacceptable to cattle owners. The TGLP required fencing of commercial lands. Given the up-front investment costs, fencing was extremely unpopular and was quietly scrapped. Rent was the other area of controversy. Economic rents were to be used to help develop communal land areas. Cattle owners with aspirations for the TGLP land were less than enthusiastic about the payment of an economic rate for land. As a result of their opposition, rents were set at a subeconomic level of 4 thebe (3 cents) per hectare, or P 256 ($240) per year for a 6,400-hectare (24-square-mile) ranch. In addition, no rent would be collected for the first three years so that cattle owners could develop their ranches.

Policy makers originally assumed that there was sufficient land in the larger districts of the west and northwest to create commercial ranches. Ungrazed land in these areas, however, is remote from the population and the rail system, has a doubtful water supply, is infested with poisonous plants, and generally is less healthy for livestock than are presently grazed areas. Thus, progressive cattle posts in these areas will be expensive to develop and run; only a few very large ranchers are in a position to venture development in such areas. Although these areas could stand as reserves for the future, they are not attractive now to small cattle owners and therefore cannot serve as expanded grazing for overstocked communal areas. Thus, "the assumption of plenty of land can be seen as too optimistic."[58]

More generally, Botswana has much less capacity for new bore holes than was originally estimated. A major investigation of Botswana's water resources indicated that the country was rapidly approaching the point of no return for bore hole drilling and its effect upon the country's water table. Without increased access to water, Botswana's cattle industry had reached its upper limits by the mid-1980s.

The land-use planning exercises also revealed that policy makers had not really addressed the problem of the rights of either the hunting and gathering Basarwa groups or the resident populations of workers in most cattle post areas. The "failure to consider the position of those without stock who already inhabit and use the areas now zoned as commercial" was one of the major omissions of the 1975 TGLP document.

There is a danger that land tenure changes (as of 1986) in the western Kalahari sandveld will severely restrict the mobility of hunter-gatherer groups, force them out of their present areas and transform people who are self-sufficient in food production into economic dependence. In the mid-1970s Hitchcock found that of all those with economic interests in the commercial zone of the western sandveld, only 12 percent controlled a water point, 8 percent owned cattle but did not have a water point, 16 percent had only small stock (goats and donkeys), and close to 70 percent did not own livestock of any kind. Many of the TGLP's basic assumptions were incorrect and "if the policy is implemented without specific measures being instituted to insure that people are not deprived of their rights, then serious social repercussions could result."[59] In other words, if nothing were done to modify the TGLP in the western sandveld, then the traditional users simply would have to move.

During the TGLP's early implementation period, the question of compensation for residents who had to be moved became a major issue. Under Tswana traditional law each individual should have access to sufficient land to support his or her family. This suggests that compensation for land should be in kind. In some cases, however, the land boards decided to compensate the dispossessed with cash, the average payment ranging between P 40 and P 370. In at least one case, a lessee was relieved of any financial responsibility for compensation.

Throughout the first five years that the TGLP was in effect, a noticeable lack of attention was paid to the communal areas. This ran contrary to the avowed purpose of the TGLP in which the creation of commercial lands was advocated in order to relieve pressure on, and promote the development of, land used by small cattle owners. In the TGLP White Paper little was said about the communal areas. Policy makers were "of the view that little more than veterinary care was possible."[60]

Group ranching was deemed the only way to increase the efficiency of communal lands. This idea never caught on among Botswana's rural dwellers, however. With the failure of the group ranching strategy, the "TGLP itself was suddenly left without an official, credible development program for small holders, that could provide at least political counterbalance to the policy's central focus on commercial interests."[61]

The major criticism of the new system of land tenure was that it would intensify the development of a property-owning elite in the country. According to one critic, the TGLP "emerged primarily as a mechanism for a variety of medium and large-scale cattle owners to enhance their position through exclusive land rights which amount to a form of private ownership."[62] Following this argument, the technical basis of the policy (land preservation and ecological balance) and its social equity provisions were neither dominant nor central to the probable results of the policy's implementation. The policy did not reduce the number of cattle in the country. By 1982, as stated earlier, that number had increased to three and a half million head.

Inequalities increased as a result of the TGLP. In a 1979 official evaluation of the new policy, it was alleged that the policy was having an enormous effect upon Botswana's economic stratification. "There is no doubt that the TGLP will affect the already skewed income distribution more negatively."[63] According to the authors of *The Rural Income Distribution*

Survey in Botswana, "the implications for the Government's new Tribal Grazing Land Policy are that it is going to be difficult to spread the benefits of the new policy."[64] As a result, "the effect of the policy will be to make the distribution among cattle owning households even more unequal than it is already, since it is the bigger farmers who already have assets . . . which are . . . preconditions for the policy to function."[65]

A 1980 examination of the TGLP by the United Nations Food and Agriculture Organization (FAO) confirmed earlier scepticism. In the report on its study, the FAO warned of the danger that under the TGLP "development of the poor [could be] made more difficult as they are progressively impoverished; income disparities grow; and dependency increases."[66] The report of the Presidential Commission on Land, released in early 1984, reflected the main lines of concern expressed by critics of the program.

> It is apparent . . . from [the significant] criticism of TGLP that the initial zoning of grazing land as commercial and communal overestimated the amount of unused land which could be zoned commercial. . . . Overstocking continues to be a problem. . . . The Commission was struck by the general misuse of grazing land by cattle owners.[67]

Lacking in the commission's report, however, were any detailed recommendations for correcting the problem.

Arable Agriculture

Communal First Development Areas

The development of agriculture, other than livestock, received little attention before 1978. In the Fourth National Development Plan (1975-1980), 73 percent of the capital allocation for agriculture was budgeted for livestock development. As a policy, however, the TGLP increasingly became a political liability after 1979. A variety of factors made communal and arable lands more attractive as alternative rural development priorities in the 1980s.

The continuing success of diamond production (Botswana became the world's third largest producer in 1984, outstripping South Africa) meant a growing accumulation of capital within state coffers and, to a lesser extent, within the bank accounts of Botswana's socio-economic elites. Increased access to donor aid, because of Botswana's strategic importance, buttressed this domestic capital and required an outlet in the rural areas to meet the "basic needs" criteria that was becoming the clarion cry of many foreign aid agencies.

Domestic policy makers became concerned about rural pressures and spiraling population growth figures (well over 3 percent per annum).

Structural unemployment in the rural areas, combined with a devastating drought after 1981, caused large numbers of rural dwellers to migrate to the already overpopulated urban areas. The cutback on labor migration to South Africa threatened additional unemployment among rural Batswana.

Three alternative development strategies evolved after 1979 to absorb excess domestic capital and donor funds: (1) the Communal First Development Areas plan (CFDAs); (2) the Arable Lands Development Programme (ALDEP); and (3) the Financial Assistance Policy (FAP). All three, despite rhetoric to the contrary, were designed to meet the growing demands of Botswana's small but influential middle class to increase rural productivity and stimulate rural industrialization and job creation.

The Village Area Development Programme and the CFDAs

Under the TGLP most government attention and support went to the development of commercial land. The Communal First Development Areas were designed to shift priorities to the unrezoned communal lands, both agricultural and grazing, that would have to support the bulk of Botswana's rural population.[68] The strategy behind the CFDA was avowedly that of integrated rural development. CFDAs would be declared in several of Botswana's districts. Extension services and infrastructure and agricultural development activities would be clustered initially in areas most conducive to boosting agricultural and rural industrial production.

The initial embodiment of integrated rural development was the Village Area Development Programme (VADP). The VADP was launched in April 1975 with the goal of fostering social justice and ecological balance in the western Kalahari area. As a model of integrated rural development, the VADP was "built upon a decentralized, means-oriented, bottoms-up approach, rather than the sectoral, ends-oriented, top-down approach."[69] The integrated rural development approach was seen by many to be the key to stemming the movement of rural dwellers to the urban areas. The basis of the VADP strategy was an extensive land-use planning exercise in the Matsheng area of the Kgalagadi District and the development of appropriate, local-level implementation structures. The land-use planning exercise would explore the possibilities of developing group ranching projects while ensuring wildlife preservation and the economic utilization of wildlife resources.

Problems with the VADP, that would later plague the CFDAs and the ALDEPs, were the overemphasis on infrastructure development and the expansion of social delivery services and institutional structures. Little was done to develop group ranching activities or to rationalize wildlife exploitation or preservation. According to the author of a 1978 evaluation of the VADP, "the project has done nothing to generate incomes or improve their distribution."[70]

The CFDA's approach followed directly from the VADP's land-use planning component. The Matsheng land-use planning exercise was considered to be the most impressive activity of the VADP. As such it became the prototype for the CFDAs' approach throughout Botswana. In 1979 according to a consultant on communal area development, "The Matsheng Plan . . . represents an early attempt in Botswana to design a comprehensive development programme for improving the local management of communal grazing areas. It was felt that the experience gained in the Matsheng area could be of value to similar undertakings elsewhere . . ." under the CFDA's plan.[71]

On 13 November 1980 at the seventeenth meeting of the Rural Development Council, the council chair, Vice-President Lenyeletse Seretse noted that relatively little progress had been made on communal area development. The Rural Development Council recommended that "Communal TGLP should be 'tried and tested' in Communal First Development Areas selected by each district."[72]

The CFDAs would provide a nationwide platform for the land-use planning approach developed in the VADP and other pilot programs. Initially there would be no new projects in the CFDAs; instead, existing projects would be speeded up to increase their impact. More generally, the CFDAs would provide a "Test Bed for employment generating activities."[73] The focus of CFDA's activity would be "on increasing production and employment in rural areas."[74] Additional activities would involve the improvement of land use and natural resource use and the strengthening of local land-management institutions.

Several specific actions were earmarked for the CFDA's experiment:

1. linking of livestock and arable agricultural activities;
2. strengthening the connection between agricultural activities and rural industrial activity;
3. improving planning and administrative capacity at the local level; and
4. continuing the infrastructure improvements, especially where related to productive activities.

In broad strokes, at least, the CFDA's plan was a direct descendent of the Village Area Development Programme.

The Arable Lands Development Programme and
The Financial Assistance Policy

Based on the proposition that "it takes five to seven times as much land to produce calorific value obtainable from meat than can be provided by one unit of land under cereals," the Arable Lands Development Programme was to be the centerpiece of CFDA's activity.[75] ALDP's purpose was "to develop an improved technology 'package' and then disseminate this package at a

subsidized cost to farmers."[76] The ALDEP had three overall goals: (1)
increase food crop production to the point of self-sufficiency, thereby
reducing dependence upon foreign food imports; (2) raise incomes from crop
production, particularly those of poor farm households; and (3) generate
agricultural employment to curb urban migration. The ALDEP target group
was to be the sixty thousand small farmers in Botswana who plough less
than ten hectares of land. Important target subgroups included the thirty-five
thousand households without direct access to animal power and the 30 percent
of rural households headed by women.

The ALDEP originated from a 1978 study of employment in Botswana
that recommended a new rural development strategy based on the creation of a
self-sufficient peasantry with an income sufficient to eliminate the pull of
high urban wages.[77] By 1979 an ALDEP pilot project was in place in
Kgatleng and Tutume Subdistrict that involved twenty-five farmers in each
area at a cost of P 956,000. The second year of the project saw the ALDEP
expanded to five hundred farmers throughout the country. The ALDEP was to
generate ten thousand to twelve thousand new jobs in the rural areas by 1985.
The key was to make agricultural returns more attractive.

> Most of Botswana's workers are self-employed farmers. They do not
> work more because it is not worth it. . . . A quantum jump in . . .
> traditional (agricultural) returns is vital if the hard work of farming is
> to attract young Batswana; and nothing else can provide work for
> most of them.[78]

The Ministry of Agriculture's estimates on the ALDEP's employment
generation potential were somewhat more modest. The ministry projected
that the ALDEP, if successful, could generate only five thousand new jobs
during the life of the Fifth National Development Plan (1979-1985).

The ALDEP had five major components:

1. The government would provide credit and subsidies to enable farmers
   to purchase farm implements.
2. The government would develop a system to provide draft power in the
   form of cattle or, more controversially, donkeys for those farmers
   without access to animals.
3. Appropriate Ministries would undertake capital-intensive projects
   including water development and fencing projects.
4. Under the Botswana Agricultural Marketing Board (BAMB),
   marketing facilities would be provided as close to farming areas as
   possible.
5. Output prices would be increased to encourage farmers to invest more
   time, energy, and capital, particularly in "risky enterprises."

The government would also provide other social and infrastructure services,
including roads, health posts, and schools, to encourage continued settlement
in the rural areas, and particularly in the farming areas.

The Financial Assistance Policy, approved by the National Assembly in April 1982, would complement the ALDEP program, although it was targeted at both urban and rural areas. The FAP would provide direct grants to support new, productive employment for what the government called "new and expanding productive ventures" that create new exports or substitute for imports. Three levels of project grants would be available: large-scale projects of more than P 750,000, medium-scale projects between P 10,000 and P 750,000 and small-scale projects of less than P 10,000. The small-scale grants, administered by rural industrial officers and district and town Councils would provide additional support for small-scale agriculture and rural industrialization.

Postscript to the ALDEP

The ALDEP, FAP and CFDAs were ongoing projects in late 1985 when this was being written. Nonetheless, enough evidence is in to raise at least some questions about the nature of Botswana's rural development strategy in the 1980s. At a most basic level is the extent to which a semiarid country such as Botswana should increase its resource investment in high risk arable agricultural activities. Food self-sufficiency is the ultimate goal of the Botswana government, particularly in the area of cereal production. Yet, drought and the scarcity of underground water make the country a highly unlikely candidate for significant arable agricultural production.

Donors have been very cool toward the ALDEP. During the program's first two years, government officials had great difficulty in finding bilateral or multilateral support for ALDEP projects. The third year of the ALDEP coincided with the first year of the 1982-1985 drought that devastated all of southern Africa, Botswana included.

The ALDEP has been plagued with problems since its inception. By the early 1980s the program was "strictly limited in scope and still lacked a research basis and concrete guidelines."[79] Farmers in Botswana have shown little enthusiasm for it. During its first four years the ALDEP was unable to stop the movement away from arable agriculture. Between 1966 and 1982, the percentage of households engaged in crop production declined from 87 percent to 70 percent. At the same time a "near-stagnant productivity has led to a dramatic decline in crops from 90% before independence to an average of 50%. . . . Some households even appear to prefer non-employment to arable agriculture."[80]

As planning developed for the ALDEP, there was very little political input in the process. As has been so often the case in Botswana, the ALDEP was the product of a largely expatriate team of experts in the Ministries of Agriculture and Finance and Development Planning. Politicians have come into the picture after the fact to use ALDEP as a catchall strategy for resolving the problems of structural unemployment and rural underdevelopment. Thus, according to the author of a 1979 evaluation of the ALDEP, although the most optimistic job creation figures under the program represent only 3.3 percent of the 1978-1988 full-employment target of 360,000 jobs, "the ALDEP is . . . being canvassed as crucial to the prospects for narrowing the gap between the rich and poor in this century."[81]

The program's critics claim that the development of the ALDEP made a number of fundamental miscalculations about Botswana society. One potential problem area is in treating the family as an individual unit. The ALDEP provides draft power on this basis, which, according to Alverson, is incorrect in Botswana.

> The traditional Setswana institutions most important to production in contemporary arable agriculture center on the distribution of rights and privileges of access to draft power and the contractual or other regularized means for exchanging labor for labor or for other factors of production. . . . Any arable policy which would unwittingly disrupt the bases of reciprocity upon which borrowing is based will have the effect of depriving the poorest farmers of significant draft power.[82]

Another issue of contention focuses on changing assumptions about residence patterns under the ALDEP. There is a trend in Botswana to assume that rural dwellers increasingly will take up permanent residence in the land areas well away from the major villages. In the past decade (1976-1986), the government has gone a long way toward providing basic social services, water, health, education, and roads for Botswana's major villages. Thus, "introduction of the ALDEP programme for arable agriculture implies that the majority of poor people will be called upon to move out of the villages and settle at arable lands which presently have no roads, water supplies, schools, health facilities or food relief distribution points."[83]

Ultimately, what is in question is the combination of regional and international economic restraints and political will. Egner believes that the Botswana political elites lack the political will to reorder their priorities in terms of rural development. In 1979 he argued, "Botswana is unable to muster the capacity to implement rural capital development projects, other than mining projects at . . . [a] rate which economic growth requires."[84]

Rural development can, and often does, disturb the social fabric of a society. Since independence Botswana has been concerned with political stability despite the relative weakness of the political opposition. Many in the political elite fear even a partial mobilization of the rural population, perceiving that Botswana's political stability requires the political inertia of the rural poor.

Ultimately, however, rural development policy allocates scarce resources. A fundamental shift in rural development policy would disturb the vested interests that currently exist in the rural areas. Crop production, similar to livestock production, is dominated by the few. Only 20 percent of the farmers account for over 60 percent of the output. At the other extreme, 50 percent of the poorest farmers produce only 10 percent of the cereal output of the country. Furthermore, there is a direct correlation between the ownership of cattle, which are used for draft power, and success in arable agriculture. The accumulation of land under the TGLP is only one aspect of the changing patterns of access to land. In 1978 a concerned official noted that "there is an incipient *land grab* which gets worse if arable agriculture becomes more profitable."[85]

The rhetoric behind the ALDEP suggested a bias toward the small subsistence farmer that was attacked broadly by many within Parliament and throughout the country. As a result a gradual shift has occurred to provide more support for middle-level and larger farming units, and "the ALDEP Programme is likely to not really reach its target groups: the poor and very poor."[86] Instead, it is more likely that the ALDEP will benefit the middle-level and wealthier farmers. The distribution of subsidies granted thus far reinforces this suggestion. Donor financing priorities and the needs of local elites reinforce each other. Instead of eliminating "the underlying bias toward the large scale cattleowner/arable farmer," the ALDEP will exacerbate the differences within rural society. Agricultural production will become less of a marginal activity in the future than it has been in the past. Market-oriented commercial sectors will increase productivity but at the expense of the entrenchment of the wealthier classes of farmers. At the same time, the migration of rural dwellers to the urban areas will continue.

Conclusion

Botswana, with its growth economy and its access to donor funds, has been able to achieve levels of social service delivery denied many LDCs, particularly in Africa. Since 1966, "stringent efforts have been made to see to it that everyone, however poor and wherever he lives can have his health looked after, see his children going to school, drink clean water and, in extremity, obtain relief from actual starvation."[87]

Little has been done, however, to increase the level of rural productivity, create new sources of wealth in the rural areas, or induce cattle owners to move into other areas of economic activity. Beginning in the early 1960s, from the Accelerated Rural Development Programme to the Tribal Grazing Land Policy to the Arable Lands Development Programme and the Communal First Development Areas plan, we have seen remarkable continuity in rural development policies. Focus has been, and most likely will continue to be, on infrastructure projects and social delivery services, rather than on agricultural productivity and rural industrialization. Mineral and urban development will continue to receive the lion's share of the development funds until well into the 1990s.

Botswana's rural development policy continues to reflect a pattern of technocratic solutions for political problems. The country could serve as a "textbook" for the types of development policy recommended by the World Bank. Expatriates continue to play a major role in what has been a bureaucratically dominated state since 1966. Ultimately, policy makers in Botswana continue to perceive rural development as linked to a more fundamental "modernization" process that assumes a dichotomy between the traditional and the modern economies. This assumption ignores the structural links between rural agricultural underemployment and the labor reserve system that operates throughout the southern African region.

Inevitably, the primary beneficiaries of government policy in the areas of economic and rural development have been the organizational elites, bureaucratic, professional, and political, who dominate the system. Nowhere is this more clearly demonstrated than in the nature of the agricultural (and livestock) policy in which

> environmental constraints . . . do not seem to systematically be biased against particular groups or classes. However, to a large extent the means to partly or wholly overcome these constraints, are unequally distributed. In some cases economic constraints aggravate the effects of environmental ones. Generally, economic constraints on crop production affect the poor and the very poor more than the rich or even the middle group.[88]

Access to state assistance to solve the problem of environmental constraints may be the key to understanding rural development strategies in Botswana. Civil servants, who collectively both determine and carry out rural development policy, also have a major stake in the rural sector, particularly in the ownership of cattle. Ultimately, politics in Botswana are linked directly to the changing nature of the bureaucratic elites and their ties to the ruling party.

Notes

1. Government of Botswana, *National Development Plan, 1979–1985* (NDP V) (Gaborone: Government Printer, 1979), p. 76.

2. Department of Mines, *Annual Reports*, 1979, 1980, 1981 and *Financial Times* (London) October 21, 1983. Botswana, with a production of 10m carats, is the third-largest producer in the world, preceded only by Zaire and the Soviet Union.

3. Dudley Jackson, "Income Differentials and Unbalanced Planning—the Case of Botswana," *Journal of Modern African Studies*, vol. 8, no. 4 (December 1970), pp. 553-562.

4. See "Botswana," *Africa Contemporary Record, 1980–1981*, Colin Legum, ed. (New York: Africana Publisher, 1981), p. B663.

5. W. R. Meswele, *Report of the Salaries Review Committee* (Gaborone: Government Printer, 1980).

6. Christopher Colclough and Stephen McCarthy, *The Political Economy of Botswana: A Study of Growth and Distribution* (Oxford: Oxford University Press, 1980), pp. 242-243.

7. E. B. Egner, "Review of Socio-Economic Development in Botswana, 1966–1979 (Gaborone: Swedish Agency for International Development, 1979), p. 2.

8. "Handing Over Notes," A. N. Baillie, D.C., Gaborone, September 1970—L.G. 19/9/1, vol. 2. See also Bechuanaland Protectorate, *Annual Report, 1966* (London: Her Majesty's Stationery Office, 1967).

9. See the Government of Botswana, *Transitional Plan of Social and Economic Development* (Gaberones: Government Printer, 1966).

10. Government of Botswana, *National Development Plan, 1968–1973* (Gaborone: Government Printer, 1978), p. 8.

11. Government of Botswana, *Rural Development in Botswana* (Gaborone: Government Printer, 1972), p. 2.

12. John Holm, "Rural Development and Elections in Botswana," (unpublished essay, 1981), pp. 4-5.

13. Government of Botswana, *National Development Plan, 1970–1975* (NDP II) (Gaborone: Government Printer, 1970), p. 13.

14. L.G. 19/3, vol. 1.

15. Interview on Radio Botswana with K. P. Morake, Assistant Minister, Ministry of Local Government and Lands, 2 June 1972.

16. Government of Botswana, *Rural Development in Botswana: Government Paper*, no. 1 (Gaborone: Government Printer, 1972), p. 3.

17. *Ibid.*, p. 21.

18. *Ibid.*, quotes, pp. 4, 6.

19. *Government of Botswana, National Development Plan, 1973–1978, Part II: Development Plans for Local Authorities* (Gaborone: Government Printer, 1973.

20. E. B. Egner, Minute 1, 1 December 1971—L.B. 19/3, vol. 1.

21. Robert Chambers was very heavily involved in the planning of Kenya's Special Rural Development Program. See Robert Chambers, *Managing Rural Development* (Uppsala, Sweden: Scandinavian Institute of African Studies, 1974).

22. Robert Chambers and David Feldman, *Report on Rural Development* (Gaborone: Government Printer, 1973).

23. Government of Botswana, *National Policy for Rural Development, Government Paper No. 2 of 1973* (Gaborone: Government Printer, 1973).

24. Savinggram to all DCs and Council Secretaries, 19 November 1973—L.G. 3/3, vol. 3.

25. The requests for the grants were submitted in 1972. "Request by the Government of the Republic of Botswana to the Swedish International Development Association for Financial Assistance for the Implementation of a Village and Rural Water Development Programme," Ministry of Finance and Development Planning, October 1972.

26. Savinggram, from P.S. Ministry of Local Government and Lands to all DCs and Council Secretaries, 22 November 1973. See P.U. 13/9/1.

27. Cabinet Memorandum, Q. K. J. Masire, Vice-President and Minister of Finance and Development Planning—F.D.P. 13/5/1.

28. Memorandum, James W. Leach, 26 November 1973—F.D.P. 13/1/1.

29. Minute, J. W. Leach, Rural Development Coordinator, 28 February 1974—L.G. 19/1, vol. 6.

30. Minute, 27 November—L.G. 32/11, vol. 2. A.R.D.P.—Physical Planning, and Memorandum, James W. Leach, Coordinator for Rural Development, 28 December 1973—F.D.P. 13/1/1.

31. Permanent Secretary to the President to All Permanent Secretaries, 27 December 1973—O.P. 10/5 (file 14).

32. Robert Chambers, *Botswana's Accelerated Rural Development Programme, 1973–1976: Experience and Lessons* (Gaborone: Government Printer, 1977), p. 36.

33. *Ibid.*, p. 38.

34. Sir Seretse Khama, *Speech Launching the Grazing Land Policy*, 14 July 1975 (Gaborone: Government Printer, 1975).

35. B. K. Temane, "Agrarian Reform, Institutional Innovation, and Rural Development: Major Issues in Perspective," paper presented to seminar on land tenure, Madison, Wisconsin, July 1977, p. 2.

36. T. M. Barrett, S. Colclough and D. Crowley, eds., *Proceedings on the Conference on Sustained Production From Semi-Arid Areas*, October 11–15, *Botswana Notes and Records*, Special issue no. 1 (Gaborone, 1971), first quote, p. 27 and second quote, p. 255.

37. Government of Botswana, *Government paper no. 1* (Gaborone, 1972), p. 6.

38. Chambers and Feldman, *Report on Rural Development*, p. 124.

39. *Ibid.*, p. 120.

40. Government of Botswana, *National Policy for Rural Development, 1973*, p. 6.

41. Presidential Directive on Land Development Policy: Eastern Tribal Land, 17 December 1974, CAB 44/74.

42. Record and Minutes of the 2nd National Conference of District Development Committees 3–7 December 1973, Ministry of Local Government and Lands, L.G. 19/1/3. Material that is uncited below comes either from participant observation (and recorded in a research diary) or from confidential interviews conducted with Botswana administrators.

43. Records and Minutes of the 3rd National Conference of District Development Committees 14–18 April 1975, Ministry of Local Government and Lands, L.G. 3/7/2.

44. Both quotes from Tribal Land Development: Report of the Consultation Committee, Ministry of Finance and Development Planning, MFDP 55/2/11.

45. Minutes of the 3rd National Conference of District Development Committees, L.G. 3/7/2.

46. Both quotes and one in succeeding paragraph from author's research diary.

47. Government of Botswana, Draft Government paper no. 2, Proposals for Implementing Government Policy on Grazing Land Development (Gaborone: May 1975).

48. Government of Botswana, Edited Draft: Government paper no. 2, Proposal for Implementing Government Policy on Grazing Land Development (Gaborone: June 1975). All following quotes from above.

49. Government of Botswana, *Tribal Grazing Land: Government's Policy:* Third Draft (Gaborone: Botswana Extension College, June 1975).

50. Government of Botswana, *National Policy on Tribal Grazing Land* (Gaborone: Government Printer, July 1975), p. 18.

51. Stephen Sanford, "Keeping an Eye on TGLP," National Institute of Development and Cultural Research, Working Paper No. 31 (Gaborone: University College of Botswana, July 1980), p. 4.

52. Ambrose Masalila, "Botswana's National Policy on Tribal Grazing Land: Towards a Strategy for Rural Development," *Botswana's Economy Since Independence*, M. A. Oommen, F. K. Inganji, and L. D. Ngcongco, eds. (New Delhi: Tata McGraw-Hill, 1983), p. 154.

53. Robert K. Hitchcock, *Kalahari Cattle Posts: A Regional Study of Hunter-Gatherers, Pastoralists, and Agriculturalists in the Western Sandveld Region, Central District, Botswana* (Gaborone: Government Printer, 1978), p. 59.

54. Sanford, "Keeping an Eye on TGLP," pp. 8-9.

55. "Botswana: Project Findings and Recommendations," Report prepared for the Government of Botswana by the FAO (Rome, 1980), p. 16-17.

56. Government of Botswana, *Report of the Presidential Commission on Land Tenure* (Gaborone: Government Printer, December 1973), p. 13.

57. Government of Botswana, *Tribal Grazing Land Programme Review No. 1 of 1978* (Gaborone: Rural Development Unit, Ministry of Finance and Development Planning, 1978), p. 14.

58. *Ibid.*

59. Hitchcock, *Kalahari Cattle Posts*, p. 390.

60. "Botswana" FAO Report, p. 25.

61. Steve Lawry, "Land Tenure and Land Policy in Botswana: The Case of the Tribal Grazing Lands Policy" (Land Tenure Center, Madison, Wisc., unpublished paper, June 1982).

62. Colclough and McCarthy, *Political Economy of Botswana*, p. 119.

63. Jack Parson, "The State, Class and Land Tenure in Rural Botswana" (December 1979), pp. 36-37 (in typescript).

64. Government of Botswana, *The Rural Income Distribution Survey in Botswana* (Gaborone: Central Statistics Office, 1976), p. 112.

65. Bernhard Weimer, "The Tribal Grazing Land Policy—Some Critical Aspects in a Policy for Rural Development," *The Case of Botswana: National Policy on Tribal Grazing Land*, Bernhard Weimer, ed. (Gaborone: National Institute of Research in Development and African Studies, 1977), p. 47.

66. "Botswana," FAO Report, p. 17.

67. Government of Botswana, *Report of the Presidential Commission on Land.*

68. Masalila, "Botswana's National Policy," p. 158.

69. Marcia L. Odell, *Village Area Development Programme: A Review and Evaluation of an Experiment in Integrated Rural Development* (Gaborone: Government Printer, 1978), p. 4.

70. *Ibid.*

71. Steve Lawry, *Communal Area Planning and Development*   (Gaborone: Ministry of Local Government and Lands, n.d.), p. 3.

72. P.S., Ministry of Agriculture to Ad Hoc Research Coordinator Committee and NIR, Communal Areas Research, A 34/14 II (6).

73. Jeremy A. Peat, "Employment Creation: Problems and Policies," *Botswana's Economy Since Independence*, p. 210.

74. Senior Rural Sociologist, (TGLP), "The Role of the Districts in Communal Areas Research and Development," Paper presented to the Ad Hoc Coordinating Committee Special Meeting on Communal Areas Research, National Institute of Research, Gaborone, 25 February 1981 in A34/14 II, (6).

75. Zbigniew A. Kkonczacki, "Botswana's Development Program: A Critique of Strategy"   (Dalhousie University, unpublished paper, October 1975),   p. 14.

76. Government of Botswana, *The Midterm Review of NDP V* (Gaborone: Government Printer, August 1983), p. 14.

77. Michael Lipton, *Botswana: Employment and Labour Use in Botswana*, 2 vols. (Gaborone: Government Printer, 1978), pp. 20-22.

78. *Ibid.*, p. viii.

79. Neva Seidman Makgetla, "Finance and Development: The Case of Botswana," *Journal of Modern African Studies*, vol. 20, no. 1 (March 1982), p. 83.

80. R. M. K. Silitshena, "Rural Development and Social Justice—The Case of Botswana," Paper prepared at the Commonwealth Geographical Bureau Conference (Lusaka, Zambia, 9-15 June 1982), p. 12.

81. E. B. Egner, "Review of Socio-Economic Development in Botswana, *1966–1979*," Prepared for the Swedish International Development Agency, Gaborone, Botswana, October 1979, p. 13.

82. Hoyt Alverson, "Arable Agriculture in Botswana: Some Contributions of the Traditional Social Formation" (Gaborone: Institute of Development Management, n.d.), pp. 14, 12.

83. Egner, "Review," p. 15.

84. *Ibid.*, p. 10.

85. Quoted by Jack Parson, "Rural Botswana," 1979, p. 108 and 117 (in typescript).

86. Johannese B. Opschoor, "Crops, Class and Climate," *Botswana's Economy Since Independence*, p. 174.

87. Egner, "Review," p. 14.

88. Opschoor, "Crops, Class and Climate," p. 174.

11

Conclusion

In recent years there has been a resurgence of interest in the evolution of the capitalist state. In his discussion of what he called "the productive state," Carnoy pointed out that, increasingly, the evolution of modern capitalism in Europe is linked to the evolution of the state system. Thus, the nation-state system accounted for the series of factors that allowed advanced capitalism to develop.[1] This view of the productive state is not new. In the ninteeenth century, Max Weber stressed the importance of the legal-rational administrative system as a prerequisite to capitalist formation.[2]

For students of African development theory, the failure of socialist experiments, such as in Ghana, Guinea, Tanzania, and Mozambique, has led to the conclusion that "African countries, irrespective of current political ideology, cannot really expect to jump the capitalist phase."[3] Because of both the importance that the state has played in the development of European capitalism and the resurgence of interest in capitalist development in the Third World (as expressed in "privatization" reforms called for by bilateral and multilateral donors), the historical context of the evolution of capitalist Botswana is of critical importance to students and practitioners of development management.

Although Botswana is a small country with a fairly recent history as an integrated polity, I have stressed in this book the importance of a broad approach to the study of state formation and the evolution of state structures. I have focused on the richness of historical experience and on the need to examine a number of sectoral areas within the historical reality of the state. Approaching state formation with broad strokes, both over time and across a number of issue areas, allows the researcher to use theoretical insights in order to ask appropriate questions without permitting the theory to put limits on the analysis. As Crawford Young suggested, interest is increasing in the remarkable range of ideological orientations and patterns that has come to characterize African states in the 1970s and 1980s.[4]

A replication of the Botswana experience is not possible, given the historical uniqueness of each nation-state. Nonetheless, as a broad view of one model of African capitalism, the Botswana experience is of critical importance. Jackson and Rosberg stated that

> the rationalist-planning state model of government has been found wanting in many parts of the world besides Africa, but African governments are less likely than almost any others to be reliable instruments of socioeconomic progress.[5]

Despite its dependence on South Africa and the west, Botswana can be seen, in comparison to other African countries, as an example of state-planned economic growth.

Throughout this book I have focused on four issue areas—mechanisms of state control, local-level political institutions, human resource policy, and rural development policy—that served as analytical constructs to illustrate the nature of state formation and the dynamics of the political process over time. The form for this book has been comparative with the measure of comparison being the colonial and post-colonial states.

A long-term view of political development in Botswana beginning with patterns of pre-colonial mediation and control confirms a continuity of patterns of our time. Colonialism froze traditional institutions in the 1880s. One can see in Botswana, as in many African states, a continuity of elites that transcends the colonial period even into republic status. These elites, fearing the kind of fragmentation that was common within the Tswana state systems prior to 1880, have found comfort in the centralizing tendencies of colonial administrative structures.

One of my primary concerns in this study has been to provide the historical and societal context for the relative autonomy of Botswana and of its dominant socio-economic elites. I have been guided by the principle that

> first there is the need theoretically to posit the possibility of some relative autonomy of the African state, not to deny its possibility. Then it is necessary to investigate the degree to which it exists in each case, especially since the degree of autonomy will vary over time as a result of a complex interplay of internal and external socio-economic and politico-strategic forces.[6]

Of critical importance in understanding the nature of the Botswana state is to examine the extent to which the state has acquired "relative autonomy" from a dominant class, domestic or international.[7] In comparison to the advanced industrial societies of Europe and North America, Botswana would not appear to have acquired much autonomy. The comparison, however, is made more aptly with other African states. The evidence presented in this book suggests that in certain sectors pockets of autonomy are developing in Botswana.

The colonial administrative state is the source of most administrative practices in Botswana today. The nature of the state is bureaucratic rather than political, with an administrative hierarchy that is authoritarian in its approach to the policy process. Patterns of political mediation and control, and the critical role of the district commissioner with those patterns, have been inherited from the colonial period. The goals of the center have changed over time, however. Before World War II, the colonial administration in Mafeking was concerned with the maintenance of political control and softening up the territory for the transfer to South Africa. By the late 1950s the central concern had shifted to the nature of the regime that would come to power after the formal granting of independence. Colonial authorities had treated the Bechuanaland (Botswana) Democratic party, with its contained nationalism, as an incumbent party as early as 1962. Since independence in 1966, the concern has been to maintain the status of the dominant socio-economic elite, and there is a clear link between state action and class formation in Botswana throughout the post-colonial period.

Botswana is a de facto one-party state with an electoral process that is symbolic of a style of political rule rather than a source of alternative political leadership. The purported uniqueness of the Botswana political system is somewhat superficial. The government is led by a cohesive group of elites who see themselves as modernizing agents, content to leave responsibility for political mediation and the management of a top-down strategy of economic growth to the bureaucracy. The relative openness of the Botswana state and its stability over two decades suggest that it has met the goals of post-colonial "statesmanship" in two ways. First, state doctrine in Botswana has gone a long way toward constituting a civil society, and Botswana has begun to construct an organic relationship between civil society and the state. Second, the Botswana state has maintained a credibility for "developmentalism," the state management of economic development, that is unusual in Africa.[8] This is in contrast to the "state welfarism" that has been followed by "state decline" throughout much of Africa.[9]

It is the relative success of this state-managed, top-down strategy of economic growth in Botswana that is critical. Botswana should not be seen in comparison to advanced industrial states but with other and larger African states that have not been able to use state structures to plan and implement socio-economic change. From that perspective, the Botswana model suggests that at least a modest form of development management is feasible. This factor is worth consideration within the context of calls for "privatization" and the increasing emphasis on nongovernmental voluntary organizations in much of the development literature.

Local-level governmental institutions have been the end point of this political analysis. Modern institutions date back to the shift from parallel rule to indirect rule in the 1930s. From that time we can see the beginnings of externally imposed bureaucratic structures at the district level throughout Botswana. Under colonialism autonomous monarchs were transformed gradually into bureaucratic appendages. Local political institutions were late in coming to Botswana as the result of two factors: (1) the ambivalence of colonial elites about the ultimate status of the territory vis-à-vis South Africa; and (2) the potential for resistance from traditional authorities who feared that the loss of their bureaucratic function would leave them as functionless appendages. And yet once established, local-level institutions have continued to exist at least in form, if not in substance, on a continent where autonomous local-level structures virtually have disappeared.

After 1966 bureaucratic structures at the district level were transferred from the traditional administration to district and town councils. Despite this change, however, there remain common patterns in the relationship between the center and periphery that are a continuation from colonial Bechuanaland. Central government views local institutions as bureaucratic extensions, rather than as autonomous political institutions. Local politicians, although often vocal and critical, reflect a style of politics rather than a decentralization of authority, and their presence masks an administrative unity that encompasses both national and local-level bureaucrats.

A major constraint upon the use of the state as an instrument of development in Botswana has been the extreme shortage of human resources in the public, parastatal, and private sectors.[10] Few states in Africa faced the paucity of trained managers and technicians that Botswana faced at independence in 1966. The response of Botswana elites to this severe human resource shortage was the forthright and long-term dependence upon expatriate managerial talent, a dependence that continued well into the 1980s.

Bechuanaland shifted recruitment patterns within the civil service twice in the twentieth century. In 1933 Bechuanaland stopped hiring South Africans and moved to the Colonial Administrative Service, thus placing the territory more firmly within the British imperial system. In the late 1950s the territory moved haltingly toward a localization policy. Throughout the colonial period and into the first years after independence, the localization policy was gradualist and based upon an assumption that localization should not compromise administrative standards.

The move to the Colonial Administrative Service solidified the elitist status of the civil service. Localization policy was set in the late 1960s by a coalition of European administrators and BDP leadership. It was only after 1969 that the BDP government committed itself to a more vigorous policy of localization and expanded its own coalition as it created a national bureaucracy. This bureaucracy has become a key component of the socio-economic elite and probably the most important, numerically. Human resource allocation reflects policy choice, and the absence of trained personnel in the rural areas is a clear indication of the low level of emphasis put on rural development before 1980. Post-1981 developments suggest a possible change in policy priorities for the decade of the 1980s and beyond, as the focus moves to rural industrialization and arable agricultural development.

An examination of the content of Botswana's rural development policy confirms its low level of priority. The twin vectors of influence, South

Africa and Britain, ensured that Botswana would have a pattern of economic development that was uneven and linked to the much stronger South African economy. During the colonial period a policy of fiscal neglect, unparalleled in its parsimony even in colonial terms, was combined with a regulatory policy that would lock Botswana into the South African labor reserve and a dependency relationship with the Republic. At the same time, policy makers placed a high priority on one aspect of rural development, the cattle industry. Colonial policy, reinforced in the post-colonial period, committed the country to cattle production partially at the expense of agricultural productivity, while trade regulations were structured to exclude African participation in the commercial sector.

A policy of rural development that provides for both economic growth and more equitable access to economic resources has been particularly elusive in African states. The problems caused by colonial fiscal parsimony in Bechuanaland could have been resolved easily with the expansion of Botswana's mineral-based economy after independence. The structural problems caused by the labor reserve and agricultural underdevelopment were more difficult to tackle, however. Thus, policy makers focused on economic growth measures, primarily mining and cattle, and on an expansion of the infrastructure that had been neglected badly during the colonial period. Little was done to create new sources of wealth or to increase the level of rural production (excluding livestock development).

An examination of rural development policy suggests continuity from pre- to postindependence, rather than change. Policy choices do illustrate areas of autonomy in the Botswana economy, however, primarily in the cattle industry where the interests of local socio-economic elites, including civil servants, are reflected. Rural development policy is a public policy area that is less prone to international dislocation than mining is and can be influenced by indigenous decision makers. Although mining may play a more important role in the economy, policy makers view cattle production as politically more significant because the indigenous elites have a stake in it.

Botswana's bureaucracy, as a policy dominant socio-economic group, approaches economic development sectorally. An examination of the decision-making process in the rural development area suggests that the corporatist literature does make a contribution to an understanding of the policy process in African states. As part of an elite social system, the bureaucracy has been able to use the state structure to preserve areas of autonomy from the dictates of the international economy and the demands of rural dwellers. Evolving interest groups in Botswana are conservationist, rather than expansionist, in their approach to development activities, which suggests that short-term achievements of rapid growth may be cancelled by long-term structural constraints in what remains a very dependent economy.

Less-developed states today are characterized often as weak and soft and penetratable by foreign governments and nongovernmental organizations.

Dependency theorists see states as nonautonomous entities dependent upon the international economic order. Development management, however, requires strong state structures that can define choice. Without strong national structures, development efforts are not likely to be successful. Yet, as Robert Bates pointed out, although major forces affecting the prosperity of Africa originate in the northern tier states, "African states stongly influence the specific ways in which these forces affect them."[11]

A common criticism of African states is "the prevailing tendency of dealing with the peasant economy through inert state bureaucracies."[12] The failure to improve rural production and the development of what Hyden called the "predatory" state are the principal causes of economic stagnation throughout the African continent.[13] The Botswana example suggests that "collectivities of officials may be able to formulate and implement distinctive strategies or policies."[14] Furthermore, the fact that the country has maintained its political and administrative institutions for two decades now suggests that there is likely to be continued systems maintenance in the future. According to Stephen Krasner, "Once institutions are in place they will perpetuate themselves."[15] Socioeconomic elites with access to the public policy process can have a major impact on the allocation of resources.

Given the foregoing examination of state structures and processes in Botswana, I would suggest that policy elites are more autonomous than they are often portrayed in studies of other LDCs. Public policy in Botswana, at least in certain sectors, is made by a national elite of development managers operating within institutional forms. At the same time I believe this study confirms the "need to analyze states in relation to sociocultural contexts."[16] Furthermore, as Skocpol noted, "Exactly how— even whether—order may be maintained and economic accumulation continued depends in significant part on existing state structures and the dominant-class political capacities that those structures help to shape."[17] Evidence of this autonomy, assuming a shift in the priorities of Botswana's dominant elites (unlikely though that might be), offers what little hope exists for successful national-level development management efforts.

Notes

1. Martin Carnoy, *The State and Political Theory* (Princeton: Princeton University Press, 1984), pp. 137-140.

2. See Max Weber, *General Economic History* (New Brunswick: Transaction Books, 1981) and comments by Randell Collins, "Weber's Last Theory of Capitalism: A Systemization," *American Sociological Review*, vol. 4, no. 45 (December 1980), pp. 925-942.

3. Goran Hyden, *No Shortcuts to Progress: African Development Management in Perspective* (Berkeley: University of California Press, 1983).

4. Crawford Young, "Class, Ethnicity, and Nationalism" (unpublished paper, n.d.), p. 75.

5. Robert H. Jackson and Carl G. Rosberg, "The Marginality of African States," *African Independence: The First Twenty-Five Years* (Bloomington: Indiana University Press, 1985), p. 56.

6. Thomas M. Callaghy, "External Actors and the Relative Autonomy of the Political Aristocracy in Zaire," *State and Class in Africa*, Nelson Kasfir, ed. (London: Frank Cass, 1984), p. 62.

7. See Crawford Young and Thomas Turner, *The Rise and Decline of the Zairian State* (Madison: University of Wisconsin Press, 1985), p.11 for a discussion of this issue.

8. Young and Turner suggest these two prerequisites for state formation. See *Ibid.*, pp. 28-29.

9. *Ibid.*, p. 44.

10. The NASPAA study of human resources in Southern Africa makes this point. See *Improving Management in Southern Africa* (Washington: National Association of Schools of Public Affairs and Administration, July 1, 1985).

11. Robert H. Bates, *Markets and States in Tropical Africa: The Political Basis of Agricultural Politics* (Berkeley: University of California Press, 1981), p. 8.

12. Goran Hyden, "Urban Growth and Rural Development," *African Independence: The First Twenty-Five Years*, Gwendolen M. Carter and Patrick O'Meara, eds. (Bloomington: Indiana University Press, 1985), p. 197.

13. *Ibid.*, p. 199.

14. *Ibid.*, pp. 20-21.

15. Stephen D. Krasner, "Approaches to the State: Alternative Conceptions and Historical Dynamics," *Comparative Politics*, vol. 16, no. 2 (January 1984), p. 240.

16. Theda Skocpol, "Bringing the State Back In: Strategies of Analysis in Current Research," *Bringing the State Back In*, Peter B. Evans, Dietrick Rneschmeyer, and Theda Skocpol, eds. (Cambridge: Cambridge University Press, 1985), pp. 20.

17. *Ibid.*, p. 26.

Selected Glossary

Africanization The replacement of European colonial administrators with citizens of the newly independent state who are of African origin. In Botswana, the term was contrasted with localization which implied the replacement of Europeans with local citizens regardless of race.

African Advisory Council A council established in 1921 and called the "Native Advisory Council" until 1940. The council was made up of the major Bechuanaland chiefs and their advisors. The role of the council was to discuss with the resident commissioner matters affecting African interests and the administration of tribal monies. There were 38 members of the council in 1951. The African Advisory Council held its last meeting in 1964 and was superceded by the movement to internal self government in that year.

Assistant Commissioner Term used prior to 1895, to describe the deputy to the resident commissioner who lived in and administered the Bechuanaland Protectorate.

British Bechuanaland The five districts in an area south of the Molopo River and the Ramathlabama Spruit that was inhabited by Batswana but that was transferred to the Cape Colony in 1895 and separated from the Bechuanaland Protectorate. It is today a part of the Republic of South Africa and forms the core of the "homeland" of Bophuthatswana.

Bechuanaland Protectorate The area north of the Molopo River that remained under British imperial rule after 1895 and became the Republic of Botswana in 1966.

Colonial Administrative Service Colonial civil servants, recruited from London, who served throughout the British empire, except for the Indian subcontinent and Sudan. These administrators could be transferred from one colony to another. However, in practice only the highest level of administrators were transferred. In addition to the colonial administrative service, there were nineteen other empire-wide services. Only four percent of

276

the administrators who governed Britain's empire were members of unified services, however. The rest were recruited locally and were not transferable.

District Administration The basic unit of administration in a British African colony. The district administration was headed by a district commissioner who was the direct representative of the governor (or the resident commissioner in the case of the High Commission Territories). In one form or another the district administration continues to be the basic unit of government in most former British colonies.

District Administrators The collective term used to refer to the district commissioner and the other district officers (sometimes called assistant district commissioners) who governed British colonies at the primary level.

District Commissioner The head of the district and legal representative of the crown within a British colony. There are ten district commissioners in Botswana today.

Divisional Commissioner In 1951, the British administration divided Bechuanaland into two parts, North and South, for administrative purposes. Each part of the country was headed by a divisional commissioner, situated at Francistown and Lobatse respectively. The divisional commissioner was in an intermediary position between the resident commissioner and the district administration. The position was abolished in 1964.

District Officer The general term used to describe the members of the district administration including both the district commissioner and his assistants.

European Advisory Council An advisory body created in 1921 in Bechuanaland to provide European residents with representation in the affairs of colonial administration. There were eight members of the council in 1951. It was superceded in 1961 with the establishment of the legislative council.

European Blocks Areas of Bechuanaland where land could be alienated (sold) to Europeans. These included the Tuli, Lobatsi, Ghanzi, and Gaberones blocks and the Tati in Francistown (now Northeast District).

Executive Council A cabinet-like administrative body made up of eight members (including four unofficial or "political" members) who headed the embryo departments which would later become Botswana's ministries.

Government Secretary The deputy to the resident commissioner who functioned as the head of the secretariat in Mafeking and as the officer in charge of the administration of the colony. The official title of the person holding this office for most of the colonial period was "Deputy Resident Commissioner and Government Secretary."

High Commissioner Chief representative of the United Kingdom directly responsible for the High Commission Territories of Basutoland, Bechuanaland and Swaziland. Laws promulgated for the High Commission

Territories were officially done in his name. The position was created in 1910 and lapsed in 1964. Until 1931, the position was combined with that of the Governor-General of the Union of South Africa. From 1931 to 1964, the position was combined with that of the British High Commissioner (Ambassador) to South Africa.

Hut Tax Tax, originally ten shillings, placed upon the "hut" or residence of adult male Africans, in order to generate revenue to make the colonial administration in Bechuanaland fiscally self-sufficient and to sti - mulate African movement into the labor market. The tax was introduced in 1899 and is also referred to at various times as a poll tax and a "native tax."

Imperial Administration A term used to refer to the rules and regulations enforced in a colony or a protectorate which were imposed from London rather than developed locally within a colonial territory or region.

Imperial Reserve An area near Mafeking that housed the offices and residences of the Bechuanaland Protectorate administration. As the administrative capital of the Protectorate, the area remained under British rather than South African administration until 1966. It was later used as the administrative headquarters of the Bophuthatswana "homeland."

Joint Advisory Council A council appointed in 1951 to advise the Bechuanaland government on the social and economic needs of the territory. It consisted of eight members appointed from the European Advisory Council and eight members from the African Advisory Council. It was superceded in 1961 by the creation of a legislative council.

Legislative Council A council established in 1961 that consisted of twenty-one elected members, (ten European, ten African and one Asian) and fourteen appointed official and unofficial members. In 1964, all thirty-two members of the legislative council were elected on the basis of universal franchise and at independence in 1966, it became the national assembly of the Republic of Botswana.

Localization The replacement of colonial administrators with citizens of the newly independent country. Unlike the term "Africanization," localization does not imply racial exclusiveness.

Minutes Notes made in government files by administrators describing or mandating action. For example, minutes written by the resident commissioner, in red ink, were considered directives for administrative action.

Native Advisory Council Name given to the African Advisory Council between 1921 and 1940.

Native Authority The legally designated title for chiefs recognized by the British colonial administration as the heads of "Tribal Administration" in African reserve areas or African authorities appointed by the British administration in the non-reserve areas.

Official Members Members appointed to Bechuanaland councils who were officials of the colonial government.

Poll Tax Tax on the residence of adult male Africans. Also called a "Hut Tax" in Southern Africa.

Pula The Botswana unit of currency introduced in 1976. In 1979, it was worth about 1.40 in U.S. dollars.

Rand The South African unit of currency after 1961. The rand was used in Botswana until the introduction of the Pula in 1976. In 1975, the rand was worth about 1.60 in U.S. dollars. The rand has been worth 20% less than the Pula since the late 1970s. Prior to 1961, the South African Pound (£) was used in South Africa and the BLS countries.

Reserve Area An area designated by the colonial administration as legally reserved for the permanent residence of Africans. In Bechuanaland, the terms "reserve areas" and "tribal areas" were used interchangeably. In Bechuanaland the non-European districts were coterminous with the reserve areas.

Resident Commissioner The title given to the principal British administrative official in Bechuanaland. The resident commissioner as the chief executive of the Protectorate was mandated to carry out the proclamations issued by the High Commissioner and to ensure the maintenance and order of the territory. The name of the chief executive was changed to "Queen's Commissioner" in 1964 with the abolition of the High Commission.

Resident Magistrate The term used to designate the head of the district administration in Bechuanaland and the other High Commission Territories prior to 1936. Resident Magistrates were aided by assistant resident magistrates and Grade I and Grade II clerks. The nomenclature was changed to district commissioner and district officer in 1936.

Secretariat The term used to refer to the collective offices of the resident commissioner (and government secretary). The secretariat was the administrative entity which supervised the general administration of the territory in contradistinction to government departments such as agriculture, livestock, and public works. The Bechuanaland secretariat was located in the imperial reserve in Mafeking, twelve miles south of the Bechuanaland Protectorate border.

Tribal Administration The term used to describe the traditional administration headed by a chief (native or tribal authority). After 1933, the chief was assisted administratively by a tribal secretary, tribal clerks, and a tribal treasurer. After 1954, the chief was advised by an appointed tribal council.

Tribal Council A council, which was established after 1954, that was appointed by a chief to advise the tribal authority on the social and economic needs of the district. Tribal councils were superceded by elected district councils in 1966.

Unofficial Members Members appointed to Bechuanaland Councils who were not representatives of the colonial administration, but who were representative of various private interests in the Protectorate.

Selected Bibliography

Aguda, Akintola, "Legal Development in Botswana from 1885 to 1966," *Botswana Notes and Records*, vol. 5 (1973), pp. 52–63.

Alverson, Hoyt, *Mind in the Heart of Darkness: Value and Self-Identity and the Tswana of Southern Africa* (New Haven: Yale University Press, 1978).

Ashton, E. H., "Democracy and Indirect Rule," *Africa*, vol. 27, no. 4 (October 1947), pp. 235–251.

————, "The High Commission Territories," in *The Handbook on Race Relations in South Africa*, edited by Ellen Hellmann and Lech Abrahams (London: Oxford University Press, 1949).

Baring, Sir Evelyn, "Economic Developments Under the High Commission in South Africa," *African Affairs*, vol. 51, no. 204 (July 1952), pp. 222–230.

Barnes, Leonard, *The New Boer War* (London, Hogarth Press, 1932).

————, *Soviet Light on the Colonies* (Middlesex: Penguin, 1944).

Barrett, T. M., S. Colclough, and D. Crowley, eds., *Special Issue No. 1, Botswana Notes and Records: Proceedings on the Conference on Sustained Production From Semi-Arid Areas, October 11–15* (Gaborone, 1971).

Basutoland, Bechuanaland and Swaziland: Report of an Economic Survey Mission (London: Her Majesty's Stationery Office, 1960).

Bechuanaland Protectorate Report, 1959 (London: Her Majesty's Stationery Office, 1959).

Bell, Morag, "Modern Sector Employment and Urban Social Change: A Case Study from Gaborone, Botswana," *Canadian Journal of African Studies*, vol. 15, no. 2 (1981).

Benson, Mary, *Tshekedi Khama* (London: Faber and Faber, 1965).

Bent, R. A. R., *Ten Thousand Men of Africa* (London: His Majesty's Stationery Office, 1952).

Best, Alan G., "Gaborone: Problems and Prospects of a New Capital," *The Geographical Review*, vol. 60, no. 1 (January 1970), pp. 1–14.

————, "General Trading in Botswana, 1890–1968," *Economic Geography*, vol. 46, no. 4 (October 1970), pp. 598–611.

Bodenmuller, Rolf, *Botswana, Lesotho and Swaziland: Their External Relations and Policy Towards South Africa* (Pretoria: Africa Institute of South Africa, 1973).

Bourke-White, Margaret, "The White Queen," Photo essay, *Life*, vol. 28, no. 10 (March 1950), pp. 95–97.

Chambers, Robert, *Botswana's Accelerated Rural Development Programme, 1973–1976: Experience and Lessons* (Gaborone: Government Printer, 1977).

Chambers, Robert, and David Feldman, *Report on Rural Development* (Gaborone: Government Printer, 1973).

Chirenje, J. Mutero, *A History of Northern Botswana, 1850–1910* (Rutherford, N.J.: Fairleigh Dickinson University Press, 1977).

Cohen, Denis L., "The Botswana Political Elite: Evidence from the 1974 General Election," *Journal of Southern African Affairs*, vol. 4, no. 3 (July 1979), pp. 347–371.

Cohen, Denis L., and J. D. Parson, eds., *Politics and Society in Botswana* (Gaborone: University of Botswana, Lesotho and Swaziland, 1974).

Colclough, Christopher, "Some Lessons from Botswana's Experience with Manpower Planning," *Botswana Notes and Records*, vol. 8 (1976).

Colclough, Christopher, and Stephen McCarthy, *The Political Economy of Botswana: A Study of Growth and Distribution* (London: Oxford University Press, 1980).

Comaroff, John C., "Rules and Rulers: Political Processes in a Tswana Chiefdom," *Man*, vol. 13, no. 1 (March 1978), pp. 1–20.

Cownie, David S., "Comments on the Application of Evaluation Research Methodology on Botswana," *Journal of Contemporary African Studies*, vol. 3, no. 1/2 (1983–84), pp. 129–152.

Dachs, Anthony J., "Missionary Imperialism—The Case of Bechuanaland," *Journal of African History*, vol. 13, no. 4 (December 1972), pp. 647–658.

Dale, Richard, "Botswana," in *Southern Africa in Perspective*, edited by Christian P. Potholm and Richard Dale (New York: Free Press, 1972), pp. 110–124.

Douglas-Home, Charles, *Evelyn Baring: The Last Proconsul* (London: William Collins, 1978).

Doxey, G. V., *The High Commission Territories and the Republic of South Africa* (London: Royal Institute of International Affairs, 1963).

Duggan, William, *A History of Agricultural Development in Southern Africa* (New York: Sage, 1985).

———, "The Kweneng in the Colonial Era: A Brief Economic History," *Botswana Notes and Records*, vol. 9 (1977).

Dundas, Sir Charles, and Hugh Ashton, *Problem Territories of Southern Africa* (Johannesburg: South African Institute for International Affairs, 1952).

Edwards, Isobel, *Protectorates or Native Reserves?* (London, Africa Bureau, 1956).

Edwards, Robert H., "Political and Constitutional Changes in the Bechuanaland Protectorate," in *Boston University Papers on Africa: Transition in*

African Politics, edited by J. A. Butler and A. A. Castagno (New York: Praeger, 1967), pp. 135–165.

Egner, E. B., *District Development in Botswana*, a report to the Swedish International Development Agency, September, 1978.

————, "Review of Socio-Economic Development in Botswana, 1966–1979" (Gaborone, Swedish Agency for International Development, 1979).

Ettinger, Stephen, "South Africa's Weight Restrictions on Cattle Exports from Bechuanaland, 1924–1941," *Botswana Notes and Records* , vol. 4 (1972), pp. 21–29.

Falconer, J., "History of the Botswana Veterinary Services, 1905–1966," *Botswana Notes and Records*, vol. 3 (1971), pp. 74–79.

Fitzgerald, T., *Report on the Salaries and Conditions of Service in the Public Services of the South African High Commission Territories, 1947–1948* (Maseru, Basutoland: Government Printer, 1948).

Fosbrooke, H. A., "An Assessment of the Importance of Institutions and Institutional Framework in Development," *Botswana Notes and Records*, vol. 5 (1973), pp. 26–36.

————, "Land and Population," *Botswana Notes and Records*, vol. 3 (1971), pp. 172–187.

————, "The Role of Tradition in Rural Development," *Botswana Notes and Records*, vol. 3 (1971), pp. 188–191.

Furse, Sir Ralph, *Aucuparius, Recollection of a Recruiting Officer* (London: Oxford University Press, 1962).

Gabatshwane, S. M., *Introduction to the Bechuanaland Protectorate History and Administration* (Kayne, Bechuanaland: Privately published, 1957).

————, *Seretse Khama and Botswana* (Gaborones: Bechuanaland Press, 1966).

————, *Tshekedi Khama of Bechuanaland: Great Statesman and Politician* (London: Oxford University Press, 1961).

Gillett, Simon, "Notes on the Settlement in the Ghanzi District," *Botswana Notes and Records*, vol. 2 (1970), pp. 52–55.

————, "Survival of Chieftancy in Botswana," *African Affairs*, vol. 72, no. 287 (April 1973), pp. 179–185.

Goldsworthy, David, *Colonial Issues in British Politics, 1945–1971* (Oxford: Clarendon Press, 1971).

Government of Botswana, *The Development of the Public Service* , Legislative Colonial Paper No. a20 of 1964–65 (Gaberones: Government Printer, 1964).

————,"Bechuanaland Protectorate Motion: That This House Supports the Views and Proposals Set Out in the Government White Paper Entitled 'The Development of the Public Service'" (extract) (Gaborones: Government Printer, 1964).

————, *Interministerial Committee Report on Land Board Operations*, February, 1978 (Gaborone: Government Printer, 1978).

————, *The Midterm Review of NDP V* (Gaborone: Government Printer, August 1983).

————, *National Development Plan, 1968–1973*(Gaborone: Government Printer, 1968).

————, *National Development Plan 1970–1975*, (NDP II) (Gaborone: Government Printer, 1970).

————, *National Development Plan, 1973–1978, Part II: Development Plans for Local Authorities* (Gaborone: Government Printer, 1973).

————, *National Development Plan, 1979–1985*, (NDP V) (Gaborone: Government Printer, 1979).

————, *National Policy for Rural Development, Government Paper No. 2 of 1973* (Gaborone: Government Printer, 1973).

————, *National Policy on Tribal Grazing Land* (Gaborone: Government Printer, July 1975).

————, *Report of the Presidential Commission on Economic Opportunities* (Gaborone: Government Printer, May 1982).

————, *Report of the Presidential Commission on Land Tenure* (Gaborone: Government Printer, December 1983).

————, *Report of the Presidential Commission on Local Government Structure*, vol. 1 (Gaborone: Government Printer, 1979).

————, *Report of the Presidential Commission on Localization and Training in the Botswana Civil Service and the Government Statement on the Report of the Commission* (Gaborone: Government Printer, 1972).

————, *Report of the Presidential Commission on Localization and Training in the Botswana Public Service, 1977* (Gaborone: Government Printer, 1977).

————, *Rural Development in Botswana: Government Paper No. 1 of 1972* (Gaborone: Government Printer, 1972).

————, *The Rural Income Distribution Survey in Botswana* (Gaborone Government Central Statistics Office, 1976).

————, *Transitional Plan of Social and Economic Development* (Gaberones: Government Printer, 1966).

————, *Tribal Grazing Land Programme Review No. 1 of 1978* (Gaborone: Rural Development Unit, Ministry of Finance and Development Planning, 1978).

Grant, Sandy, "Church and Chief in the Colonial Era," *Botswana Notes and Records*, vol. 3 (1971), pp. 59–63.

Greaves, Lionel B., *The High Commission Territories: Basutoland, Bechuanaland Protectorate and Swaziland* (London: Edinburgh House Press, 1954).

Griffiths, J. E. S., "Notes on the History and Functions of Local Government in Botswana," *Journal of Administration Overseas*, vol. 10, no. 2 (April 1971), pp. 127–133.

Hailey, Lord William M., *An African Survey* (London: Oxford University Press, 1938).

————, *An African Survey, Revised 1956* (London: Oxford University Press, 1956).

————, *Native Administration in the British African Territories, Part V, The High Commission Territories: Basutoland, the Bechuanaland Protectorate, and Swaziland* (London: Her Majesty's Stationery Office, 1953).

————, *The Republic of South Africa and the High Commission Territories* (London: Oxford University Press, 1963).

Halpern, Jack, *South Africa's Hostages: Basutoland, Bechuanaland and Swaziland* (Harmondsworth: Penguin, 1965).

Hartland-Thunberg, Penelope, *Botswana: An African Growth Economy* (Boulder, Colorado: Westview Press, 1978).

Harvey, Charles, ed., *Papers on the Economy of Botswana* (London: Heinemann, 1981).

Harvey, Charles, *The Use of Monetary Policy in Botswana, in Good Times and Bad* (Sussex, U.K.: Discussion Paper, May 1985).

Hepburn, J. D., *Twenty Years in Khama's Country* (London: Hodder & Stoughton, 1895).

Hermans, Quill, "Towards Budgetary Independence: A Review of Botswana's Financial History, 1900 to 1973," *Botswana Notes and Records*, vol. 6 (1974).

Hill, Christopher R., *Bantustans: The Fragmentation of South Africa* (London: Oxford University Press, 1964).

Hinchey, M., *Symposium on Drought in Botswana* (Gaborone: Botswana Society, 1978).

Hitchcock, Robert K., "Tradition, Social Justice and Land Reform in Central Botswana," *Journal of African Law*, vol. 24, no. 1 (Spring 1980), pp. 1–34.

———, *Kalahari Cattle Posts: A Regional Study of Hunter-Gatherers, Pastoralists, and Agriculturalists in the Western Sandveld Region, Central District, Botswana* (Gaborone, Government Printer, 1978).

Hitchcock, R., and M. Smith, *Proceedings of the Symposium on Settlement in Botswana* (Gaborone: Botswana Society, 1982).

Hodgson, Margaret L., and W. G. Ballinger, *Britain in Southern Africa, No. 2, Bechuanaland Protectorate* (Alice, South Africa: Lovedale Press, 1933).

Holm, John D., *Dimensions of Mass Involvement in Botswana Politics: A Test of Alternative Theories*, Sage Professional Papers in Comparative Politics, vol. 5, series no. 01-052 (Beverley Hills, Calif.: Sage Publications, 1974).

———, "Elections in Botswana: Institutionalization of a New System of Legitimacy," *Elections in Africa*, edited by Fred Hayward (Boulder: Westview Press, 1986).

———, "Rural Development in Botswana: Three Basic Political Trends," *Rural Africana*, no. 18 (Fall 1972), pp. 80–92.

———, "Liberal Democracy and Rural Development in Botswana," *African Studies Review*, vol. 25, no. 1 (March 1982).

Holm, John D., and Richard Morgan, "Coping with Drought in Botswana: An African Success," *Journal of Modern African Studies*, vol. 23, no. 3 (September 1986).

Hubbard, Michael, *Agricultural Exports and Economic Growth: A Study of Botswana's Growth Industry* (London: Routledge and Kegan Paul, 1986).

Huxley, Elspeth, "The Rise of the African Zealot," *Corona*, vol. 2, no. 5 (May 1950), pp. 163–166.

Hyam, Ronald, *The Failure of South African Expansion, 1908–1948* (London: MacMillan, 1972).

Jackson, Dudley, "Income Differentials and Unbalanced Planning—The Case of Botswana," *Journal of Modern African Studies*, vol. 8, no. 4 (December 1970), pp. 553–562.

Jones, David, *Aid and Development in Southern Africa: British Aid to Botswana, Lesotho and Swaziland* (London: Croom Helm, 1977).

Khama, Sir Seretse, *From the Frontline: Speeches of Sir Seretse Khama*, Gwendolyn M. Carter and E. Philip Morgan, eds. (London: Rex Collings Ltd., 1980).

Khama, Tshekedi, *Bechuanaland, A General Survey* (Johannesburg: Institute of Race Relations, 1957).

———, *Bechuanaland and South Africa* (London: African Bureau, 1955).

———, *Political Change in African Society* (London: African Bureau, 1956).

Knight, David B., "Botswana at the Development Threshold," *Focus*, vol. 26, no. 2 (November–December 1975), pp. 9–13.

Kowet, Donald, *Land, Labour Migration and Politics in Southern Africa: Botswana, Lesotho and Swaziland* (Uppsala, Sweden: Scandinavian Institute of African Studies, 1978).

Kuper, Adam, *Kalahari Village Politics* (Cambridge: The University Press, 1970).

Lawry, Steve, *Communal Area Planning and Development* (Gaborone: Ministry of Local Government and Lands, n.d.).

Leggasick, Martin, "The Sotho-Tswana Peoples Before 1800," in *African Societies in Southern Africa*, edited by Leonard Thompson (London: Heinemann, 1969), pp. 86–125.

Lewis, Stephen, "Botswana: Diamonds, Drought, Development, and Democracy" *CSIS African Notes*, no. 47 (September 11, 1985), pp. 1–7.

Lipton, Michael, *Botswana: Employment and Labour Use in Botswana*, two volumes (Gaborone: Government Printer, 1978).

Luke, T. C., *Report on Localization and Training* (Gaborones: Bechuanaland Government Printer, March 1966).

Makgetla, Neva Seidman, "Finance and Development: The Case of Botswana," *Journal of Modern African Studies*, vol. 20, no. 1 (January 1982), pp. 69–86.

Maylam, Paul, *Rhodes, the Tswana, and the British: Colonialism, Collaboration and Conflict in the Bechuanaland Protectorate, 1885–1899* (Westport, Conn.: Greenwood Press, 1980).

McCartney, W. J. A., "Botswana Goes to the Polls: Khama Government Retains Power in the Face of Lively Opposition and Paves Road to Economic Take-Off," *Africa Report*, vol. 14, no. 8 (December 1969), pp. 28–32.

Mitchson, Naomi, *Return to the Fairy Hill* (London: Heinemann, 1966).

Mockford, Julian, *Seretse Khama and the Bamangwato* (London: Staples, 1950).

Moorson, Richard, and Lionel Cliffe, "Rural Class Formation and Ecological Collapse in Botswana," *Review of African Political Economy*, no. 15/16 (1980), pp. 35–52.

Munger, Edwin S., *Bechuanaland: Pan-African Outpost or Bantu Homeland?* (London: Oxford University Press, 1965).

Nengwekhulu, R., "Some Findings on the Origins of Political Parties in Botswana," *Pula: Botswana Journal of African Studies*, vol. 1, no. 2 (June 1979), pp. 47–76.

Odell, Marcia L., *Village Area Development Programme: A Review and Evaluation of an Experiment in Integrated Rural Development* (Gaborone: Government Printer, 1978).

Oommen, M. A., F. K. Inganji, and L. D. Ngcongco, eds., *Botswana's Economy Since Independence* (New Delhi: Tata McGraw-Hill, 1983).

Parson, Jack D., *Botswana: Liberal Democracy and the Labor Reserve in Botswana* (Boulder: Westview Press, 1984).

———, "Cattle, Class and the State in Rural Botswana," in *Journal of Southern African Studies*, vol. 7, no. 2 (April 1981), pp. 236–255.

———, "Political Culture in Botswana: A Survey Result," in *Journal of Modern African Studies*, vol. 15, no. 4 (December 1977), pp. 639–650.

———, "The Trajectory of Class and State in Dependent Development: The Consequences of New Wealth for Botswana," *Journal of Commonwealth and Comparative Politics*, vol. 21, no. 3 (November 1983), pp. 38–60.

Parsons, Neil (Q.N.), "The Economic History of Khama's Country in Botswana, 1844–1930," in *The Roots of Rural Poverty in Central and Southern Africa*, edited by Robin Palmer and Neil Parsons (Berkeley: University of California Press, 1977), pp. 113–143.

———, "'Khama & Co.' and the Jousse Trouble, 1910–1916," *Journal of African History*, vol. 16, no. 3 (1975), pp. 383–408.

———, *A New History of Southern Africa* (London: MacMillan, 1982).

———, "On the Origins of the BamaNgwato," *Botswana Notes and Records*, vol. 5 (1973), pp. 82–103.

———, "Shots for a Black Republic? Simon Ratshosa and Botswana Nationalism," *African Affairs*, vol. 73, no. 293 (October 1974), pp. 449–458.

Perham, Margery, and Lionel Curtis, *The Protectorates of South Africa: The Question of Their Transfer to the Union* (London: Oxford University Press, 1935).

Picard, Louis A., "Administrative Attitudes and Time in Bechuanaland and Botswana," *SICA Occasional Papers Series*, American Society of Public Administration (Fall 1984).

———, "Administrative Reorganization—A Substitute for Policy? The District Administration and Local Government in the Bechuanaland Protectorate, 1949–1966," *Botswana Notes and Records*, vol. 12 (1984), pp. 85–96.

———, "Bureaucrats, Cattle, and Public Policy: Land Tenure Changes in Botswana," *Comparative Political Studies*, vol. 13, no. 3 (October 1980), pp. 313–356.

———, "Bureaucrats, Elections and Political Control: National Politics, the District Administration and the Multi-Party System in Botswana," in *Politics and Rural Development in Southern Africa: The Evolution of Modern Botswana*, edited by Louis A. Picard (London: Rex Collings, 1985), pp. 176–208.

————, "Development Administration Revisited: Administrative Attitudes in Tanzania and Botswana," *Journal of Contemporary African Studies*, vol. 2, no. 1 (October 1982), pp. 31–58.

————, *District Administration Training in Botswana* (Gaborone: Ministry of Local Government and Lands, Government Printer, 1984).

————, "District Councils in Botswana—A Remnant of Local Autonomy," *Journal of Modern African Studies*, vol. 17, no. 2 (October 1979), pp. 285–308.

————, "From Bechuanaland to Botswana: An Overview," in *Politics and Rural Development in Southern Africa: The Evolution of Modern Botswana*, edited by Louis A. Picard (London: Rex Collings, 1985), pp. 3–25.

————, "Independent Botswana: The District Administration and Political Control, *Journal of African Studies*, vol. 8, no. 3 (Fall 1981), pp. 98–110.

————, "Rural Development in Botswana: Administrative Structures and Public Policy," *Journal of Developing Areas*, vol. 13, no. 3 (April 1979), pp. 283–300.

————, "Self-Sufficiency, Delinkage and Food Production: Limits on Agricultural Development in Africa," *Policy Studies Review*, vol. 4, no. 2 (November 1984), pp. 311–319.

Picard, Louis A., ed., *Politics and Rural Development in Southern Africa: The Evolution of Modern Botswana* (London: Rex Collings, 1985).

Picard, Louis A., with Klaus Endresen, *A Study of the Manpower and Training Needs of the Unified Local Government Service, 1982–1992*, two vols. (Gaborone: Government Printer, 1981).

Picard, Louis A., and E. Philip Morgan, "Policy, Implementation and Local Institutions in Botswana," in *Politics and Rural Development in Southern Africa: The Evolution of Modern Botswana*, edited by Louis A. Picard (London: Rex Collings, 1985), pp. 125–156.

Pim, Sir Alan, *Financial and Economic Position of the Bechuanaland Protectorate, Report of the Commission Appointed by the Secretary of State for Dominion Affairs, March, 1932*, Parliamentary Report, Cmd. 4368 (London: His Majesty's Stationery Office, 1933).

Polhemus, James H., "Botswana Votes: Parties and Elections in an African Democracy," *Journal of Modern African Studies*, vol. 21, no. 3 (September 1983), pp. 397–430.

Potholm, Christian P., and Richard Dale, eds., *Southern Africa in Perspective: Essays in Regional Politics* (New York: The Free Press, 1972).

Ramage, Sir Richard, *Report on the Structure of the Public Services in Basutoland, Bechuanaland and Swaziland, 1961* (Capetown: Cape Times, Ltd, 1962).

Raphaeli, Nimrod, Jacques Roumani, and A. C. MacKellar, *Public Sector Management in Botswana* (Washington, D.C.: World Bank, 1984).

Redfern, John, *Ruth and Seretse, 'A Very Disreputable Transaction'* (London: Victor Gollancz, 1955).

Reilly, Wyn, "District Development Planning in Botswana," *Manchester Papers on Development*, no. 3 (December 1981).

————, "Local Government in Botswana," in *Local Government in the Third World: The Experience of Tropical Africa*, edited by Philip Mawhood (Chichester, U.K.: John Wiley and Sons, 1983).

Robins, Eric, *White Queen in Africa* (London: Robert Hale, 1967).

Robson, Peter, "Economic Integration in Southern Africa," *Journal of Modern African Studies*, vol. 5, no. 4 (December 1967), pp. 469–490.

Sanford, Stephen, "Keeping an Eye on TGLP," National Institute of Development and Cultural Research, Working Paper No. 31 (Gaborone: University College of Botswana, July 1980).

————, *Management of Pastoral Development in the Third World* (London: John Wiley, 1983).

Schapera, Isaac, *The Bantu Speaking Tribes of South Africa* (Cape Town: Maskew Miller, 1937).

————, *The Ethnic Composition of Tswana Tribes* (London: London School of Economics Monographs, 1952).

————, *Government and Politics in Tribal Societies* (New York: Schocken Books, 1967).

————, *A Handbook of Tswana Law and Custom* (London: Frank Cass, 1970).

————, *Married Life in an African Tribe* (Harmondsworth: Penguin, 1971).

————, *Migrant Labour and Tribal Life: A Study of Conditions in the Bechuanaland Protectorate* (London: Oxford University Press, 1947).

————, *Native Land Tenure in the Bechuanaland Protectorate* (Alice, South Africa: Lovedale Press, 1943).

————, "Notes on the Early History of the Kwena," *Botswana Notes and Records*, vol. 12 (1980).

————, *The Political Annals of a Tswana Tribe* (Cape Town: Cape Town University Press, 1947).

————, *Tribal Innovators: Tswana Chiefs and Social Change, 1795–1940* (London: The Anthone Press, 1970).

————, *Tribal Legislation Among the Tswana of the Bechuanaland Protectorate* (London: London School of Economics and Political Science, 1943).

————, *The Tswana* (London: International African Institute, 1968).

————, *The Tswana: Ethnographic Survey of Africa, South Africa, Part III* (London: London School of Economics Monographs, 1952).

Selwyn, Percy, *Industries in the Southern African Periphery* (Boulder: Westview Press, 1975).

Shaw, Timothy, M., and Kenneth Heard, eds., *Cooperation and Conflict in Southern Africa: Papers on a Regional Subsystem* (Washington, D.C.: University Press of America, 1976).

Sillery, Anthony, *The Bechuanaland Protectorate* (London: Oxford University Press, 1952).

————, *Botswana: A Short Political History* (London: Methuen & Co., 1974).

————, *Founding A Protectorate: History of Bechuanaland, 1885–1895* (The Hague: Moulton & Co., 1965).

————, *John MacKenzie of Bechuanaland* (Cape Town: Balkema, 1971).

————, *Sechele: The Story of an African Chief* (Oxford: George Ronald, 1954).

Skinner, T. F., *Review of Emoluments of the Public Service of the Bechuanaland Protectorate* (Gaborones: Government Printer, 1964).

Smit, P., *Botswana: Resources and Development* (Pretoria: Institute of South Africa, 1970).

Spence, J. E., *The Politics of Dependence* (London: Oxford University Press, 1968).

Stevens, Christopher, and John Speed, "Multi-Partyism in Africa. The Case of Botswana Revisited," *African Affairs*, vol. 77, no. 304 (January 1978), pp. 381–387.

Stevens, Richard P., *Historical Dictionary of the Republic of Botswana* (Metuchen, N. J.: The Scarecrow Press, 1975).

————, *Lesotho, Botswana and Swaziland: The Former High Commission Territories of Southern Africa* (New York: Praeger, 1967).

Succession to the Chieftainship of the Bamangwato Tribe, Cmd. 7913 (London: His Majesty's Stationery Office, 1950).

Surridge, Sir Rex, *Report of the Commission Appointed to Examine the Salary Structure and Conditions of Service of the Civil Service of Basutoland, Bechuanaland and Swaziland, 1958–1959* (Parrow, Cape: Cape Times, 1959).

Tagart, E. S. B., *Report on the Conditions Existing Among the Bamangwato Reserve of the Bechuanaland Protectorate and Certain Other Matters Appertaining to the Natives Living Therein* (Pretoria: Government Printer, 1933).

Tlou, T., "The Nature of Batswana States: Towards a Theory of Batswana Traditional Government—The Batswana Case," *Botswana Notes and Records*, vol. 6 (1974).

Tordoff, William, "Local Administration in Botswana, Part I," *Journal of Administration Overseas*, vol. 12, no. 4 (October 1973), pp. 172–183.

————, "Local Administration in Botswana, Part II," *Journal of Administration Overseas*, vol. 13, no. 1 (1974), pp. 293–304.

Turner, Biff, "A Fresh Start for the Southern African Customs Union," *African Affairs*, vol. 70, no. 280 (July 1971), pp. 269–276.

van Rensberg, Patrick, *Report from Swaneng Hill: Education and Employment in an African Country* (Stockholm: Africa Institute, 1974).

Vengroff, Richard, *Botswana: Rural Development in the Shadow of Apartheid* (Rutherford, N.J.: Fairleigh Dickenson University Press, 1977).

Watson, David A., *Report on a Study of Local Government and District Administration Training* (Gaborone: Government Printer, June 1978).

Weimer, Bernhard, ed., *The Case of Botswana: National Policy on Tribal Grazing Land* (Gaborone: National Institute of Research in Development and African Studies, 1977).

White Architects, *Study of Rural Building Development in Botswana: Interim Report* (Consultancy Report to the Ministry of Local Government and Lands by White Architects, Stockholm, Sweden, April 2, 1978).

Weiseman, John A., "Conflict and Conflict Alliances in the Kgatleng District of Botswana," *Journal of Modern African Studies*, vol. 16, no. 3 (September 1978).

————, "Multi-Partyism in Africa: The Case of Botswana," *African Affairs*, vol. 76, no. 302 (1977), pp. 70–79.

Young, B. A., *Bechuanaland* (London: Her Majesty's Stationery Office, 1966).

Index

AAC. *See* African Advisory Council
Accelerated Rural Development
    Programme (ARDP), 162, 240–243
Act of Union (1910), 39–40
Africa. *See* individual countries
African Advisory Council (AAC), 62,
    83, 135
African Civil Service Association,
    71, 83, 86, 87, 123. *See also*
    Bechuanaland Civil Service
    Association
Africanization. *See* localization
African National Congress (ANC),
    123, 132, 134, 137
Afrikaans, 42
Agency for International
    Development, 214
Agency on the Rand, 112
Agriculture, 233; colonial policy,
    114–115; rural development,
    257–263. *See also* Rural
    development
ALDEP. *See* Arable Lands
    Development Programme
Alverson, Hoyt, 145
Amery, L. S., 40, 43, 46, 74
ANC. *See* African National Congress
Apartheid, 41
Arable Lands Development
    Programme, 259–263
Arden-Clarke, Charles, 52, 55

ARDP. *See* Accelerated Rural
    Development Programme
Arrowsmith, E. P., 77, 78, 80
Asbestos, 116, 117
Ashton, E. H., 80
Ashton, Hugh, 41

Bakhalaghadi, 154
Ballinger, William, 49, 99
Balopi, Patrick, 171
Baring, Sir Evelyn, 56, 57, 121
Barnes, Leonard, 38, 49, 99
Basarwa, 48, 154
Basters, 7
Bathoen II, Chief, 50–52, 54, 56;
    1969 election, 157–159
Baur, C., 181, 182
Baxter, Mr., 133
BDP. *See* Botswana Democratic Party
Bechuanaland, Administration,
    31–42; British, 28–29;
    Protectorate, 29–31
Bechuanaland Civil Service
    Association, 88. *See also* African
    Civil Service Association
Bechuanaland People's Party (BPP),
    137, 140
Bechuanaland Protectorate Federal
    Party (BPFP), 136, 137
Bilingualism, 42
BIP. *See* Botswana Independence